Brilliant
Mac® OS X
Lion

Steve Johnson

Perspection, Inc.

Prentice Hall
is an imprint of

Harlow, England • London • New York • Boston • San Francisco • Toronto
Sydney • Tokyo • Singapore • Hong Kong • Seoul • Taipei • New Delhi
Cape Town • Madrid • Mexico City • Amsterdam • Munich • Paris • Milan

Pearson Education Limited

Edinburgh Gate

Harlow

Essex CM20 2JE

England

and Associated Companies throughout the world

Visit us on the World Wide Web at:

www.pearson.com/uk

Original edition, entitled MAC OS® X LION™ ON DEMAND 1st edition, 0789748193 by JOHNSON, STEVE; PERSPECTION, INC., published by Pearson Education, Inc., publishing as Que/Sams, Copyright © 2012 Perspection, Inc.

ISBN: 978-0-273-76473-1

British Library Cataloguing-in-Publication Data

A catalogue record for this book is available from the British Library

10 9 8 7 6 5 4 3 2 1

15 14 13 12 11

Printed and bound in the United States of America

Brilliant Guides

What you need to know and how to do it

When you're working on your computer and come up against a problem that you're unsure how to solve, or want to accomplish something in an application that you aren't sure how to do, where do you look?? Manuals and traditional training guides are usually too big and unwieldy and are intended to be used as an end-to-end training resource, making it hard to get to the info you need right away without having to wade through pages of background information that you just don't need at that moment – and helplines are rarely that helpful!

Brilliant guides have been developed to allow you to find the info you need easily and without fuss and guide you through the task using a highly visual, step-by-step approach – providing exactly what you need to know when you need it!!

Brilliant guides provide the quick easy-to-access information that you need, using a detailed index and troubleshooting guide to help you find exactly what you need to know, and then presenting each task on one or two pages. Numbered steps then guide you through each task or problem, using numerous screenshots to illustrate each step. Added features include "See Also…" boxes that point you to related tasks and information in the book, whilst "Did you know?…" sections alert you to relevant expert tips, tricks and advice to further expand your skills and knowledge.

In addition to covering all major office applications, and related computing subjects, the *Brilliant* series also contains titles that will help you in every aspect of your working life, such as writing the perfect CV, answering the toughest interview questions and moving on in your career.

Brilliant guides are the light at the end of the tunnel when you are faced with any minor or major task!

Acknowledgements

Perspection, Inc.

Brilliant Mac OS X Lion has been created by the professional trainers and writers at Perspection, Inc. to the standards you've come to expect from Que publishing. Together, we are pleased to present this training book.

Perspection, Inc. is a software training company committed to providing information and training to help people use software more effectively in order to communicate, make decisions, and solve problems. Perspection writes and produces software training books, and develops multimedia and Web-based training. Since 1991, we have written more than 100 computer books, with several bestsellers to our credit, and sold over 5 million books.

This book incorporates Perspection's training expertise to ensure that you'll receive the maximum return on your time. You'll focus on the tasks and skills that increase productivity while working at your own pace and convenience.

We invite you to visit the Perspection Web site at:

www.perspection.com

Acknowledgements

The task of creating any book requires the talents of many hard-working people pulling together to meet impossible deadlines and untold stresses. We'd like to thank the outstanding team responsible for making this book possible: the writer, Steve Johnson; the technical editor, Beth Teyler; the production editor, James Teyler; proofer reader, Beth Teyler; and the indexer, Katherine Stimson. We'd also like to thank Alan Greth for his contributions to the book.

At Que publishing, we'd like to thank Greg Wiegand and Laura Norman for the opportunity to undertake this project, Cindy Teeters for administrative support, and Sandra Schroeder for your production expertise and support.

Perspection

About The Author

Steve Johnson has written more than 60 books on a variety of computer software, including Adobe Photoshop CS5, Adobe Flash CS5, Adobe Dreamweaver CS5, Adobe InDesign CS5, Adobe Illustrator CS5, Microsoft Windows 7, Microsoft Office 2010 and 2007, Microsoft Office 2008 for the Macintosh, and Apple Mac OS X Snow Leopard. In 1991, after working for Apple Computer and Microsoft, Steve founded Perspection, Inc., which writes and produces software training. When he is not staying up late writing, he enjoys playing golf, gardening, and spending time with his wife, Holly, and three children, JP, Brett, and Hannah. Steve and his family live in Pleasanton, California, but can also be found visiting family all over the western United States.

Contents

Introduction xvii

1 Getting Started with Mac OS X Lion 1

Starting Mac OS X 2
Exploring the Finder and Desktop 4
Using the Mouse or Multi-Touch Gestures 6 **New!**
Working with Menus, Toolbars, and Panes 7
Using Menus for Quick Results 8
Choosing Dialog Options 9
Working with Icons 10
Viewing Windows 12 **New!**
Managing Windows 14 **New!**
Using the Sidebar 16 **New!**
Using Toolbars 17 **New!**
Displaying and Using the Dock 18 **New!**
Displaying and Using Stacks on the Dock 19 **New!**
Exposing Windows in Mission Control 20 **New!**
Grouping Windows in Mission Control 21 **New!**
Switching Users 22 **New!**
Sleeping, Restarting, and Shutting Down 24 **New!**

2 Managing Files and Folders 25

Opening and Viewing Disks 26
Viewing and Opening Documents 28 **New!**
Changing the Window View 30
Arranging Files and Folders in Icons View 32 **New!**
Working with Files and Folders in List View 34
Viewing Files with Cover Flow View 36
Working with Files and Folders in Columns View 37
Viewing Files Using Quick Look 38 **New!**
Going to Common or Recent Places 39 **New!**
Organizing Files and Folders by Color 40
Creating and Renaming Files and Folders 42 **New!**

Copying and Moving Files and Folders 44 **New!**

Using Spring-Loaded Folders 46

Sharing Files or Folders with Others 47

Deleting and Restoring Files and Folders 48

Getting and Setting File Information 50

Creating a CD or DVD Using the Finder 52

Mounting and Ejecting Disks 54

3 Finding What You Want with Spotlight 55

Finding Information Using Spotlight 56 **New!**

Finding Information in the Spotlight Window 58 **New!**

Filtering Spotlight Results 60

Grouping and Sorting Spotlight Results 62

Working with Spotlight Results 63

Setting Spotlight Preferences 64

Searching for Files Using the Find Window 66 **New!**

Searching for Hard to Find Information 68

Working with Find Window Results 69

Creating and Using Smart Folders 70

Getting Help While You Work 72

Getting Help Using Spotlight 74

4 Customizing the Finder 75

Understanding Finder Preferences 76

Showing Icons on the Desktop 77

Customizing the Way Windows Open 78

Showing or Hiding File Extensions 79

Customizing Finder Window Views 80 **New!**

Customizing the Toolbar 82

Customizing the Sidebar 84 **New!**

Customizing the Dock 86 **New!**

Creating Aliases 88

Customizing Mission Control 90 **New!**

Using Simple Finder 92 **New!**

5 Setting System Preferences 93

Understanding System Preferences 94

Viewing System Preferences 96

Locking and Unlocking Preference Settings 97

Changing Appearance Options 98 **New!**

Setting Up the Desktop 100 **New!**

Setting Up Screen Savers 101 **New!**
Setting the Date and Time 102
Changing Language Options 104
Changing Text Substitution Options 106 **New!**
Saving Energy and Managing Power 108
Selecting a Startup Disk 110
Changing the Way a CD or DVD Starts 111
Controlling Sound 112
Recognizing Your Speech 114
Letting Mac Do the Talking 116
Setting Universal Access Options 118 **New!**
Having VoiceOver Read from the Screen 120 **New!**
Setting VoiceOver Preferences 122 **New!**
Using VoiceOver Commands 124
Setting Ink Preferences 126

6 Using Mac OS X Applications 127

Getting Apps from the App Store 128 **New!**
Downloading and Installing Apps 130 **New!**
Using Mac OS X Apps 131 **New!**
Launching Apps 132 **New!**
Opening Apps and Files 134
Viewing Full Screen Apps 135 **New!**
Switching Between Apps 136
Quitting Apps 138
Playing Chess 139 **New!**
Creating an Address Book 140 **New!**
Editing an Address Book 142 **New!**
Managing and Sharing an Address Book 144 **New!**
Performing Calculations and Conversions 146
Capturing Images with a Digital Camera 148 **New!**
Capturing Screen Shots with Grab 149
Previewing Images and PDF's 150 **New!**
Using Apps with Auto Save 152 **New!**
Creating Sticky Notes 153
Managing Fonts with Font Book 154 **New!**
Activating, Deactivating, and Customizing Fonts 155
Working with Dashboard 156 **New!**
Using Dashboard Widgets 158
Adding and Removing Dashboard Widgets 160
Creating a Web Clip Dashboard Widget 162

7 Working with Documents **163**

Creating and Opening a Document	164	**New!**
Editing Text	166	**New!**
Recognizing Handwriting Ink	168	
Making Corrections	170	
Making Text Substitutions	171	**New!**
Checking Spelling and Grammar	172	
Looking Up Words with Dictionary	174	**New!**
Finding and Replacing Text	176	**New!**
Formatting Text	178	**New!**
Displaying Rulers	179	
Setting Paragraph Tabs	180	**New!**
Setting Paragraph Indents	181	
Changing Character Spacing	182	
Changing Line Spacing	183	
Adding Lists and Tables	184	
Applying and Creating a Style	186	
Inserting Special Characters	188	**New!**
Adding Pictures, Movies, or Files to a Document	189	
Saving and Closing a Document	190	**New!**
Using TextEdit for Web Design	192	
Setting TextEdit Preferences	194	

8 Printing and Faxing **195**

Understanding Printers	196	
Understanding Printer Drivers	197	
Adding or Removing a Printer	198	
Setting Print Settings	200	
Sharing a Printer	202	
Setting Up Page Options	204	
Setting Basic Print Options	206	**New!**
Previewing Documents	208	**New!**
Saving Documents as PDF Documents	209	
Managing Print Queues	210	
Creating a Cover Page	211	
Scanning Documents	212	
Sending Fax Documents	214	
Receiving Faxes Automatically	216	

9　Exploring the Internet　217

Connecting to the Internet　218
Setting Up a Modem Connection　220
Setting Up an Ethernet Connection　221
Setting Up a Wireless Connection　222
Setting Up Multiple Connections　223
Making an Internet Connection　224
Understanding Web Sites and Browsers　225
Starting and Customizing Safari　226　**New!**
Viewing the Safari Window　227　**New!**
Browsing the Web　228
Browsing the Web Using Tabs　230　**New!**
Using the Reader and Reading List　232　**New!**
Viewing Top Sites　234　**New!**
Changing the Home Page　235
Viewing a History List　236
Bookmarking a Web Page　237
Working with Bookmarks　238
Viewing and Bookmarking RSS Feeds　240
Filling Out Forms on the Web　242　**New!**
Searching the Web　244　**New!**
Printing a Web Page　246
Viewing PDF Files　247
Saving a Web Page　248
Saving Pictures or Text from a Web Page　249
Downloading Files Safely from the Web　250　**New!**
Setting Safari Preferences　252　**New!**
Setting Security Preferences　254　**New!**
Blocking Pop-Up Windows　255
Selecting a Default Browser and Engine　256　**New!**

10　Exchanging Messages Using Mail　257

Setting Up Accounts in One Place　258　**New!**
Starting Mail　259
Setting Up an Account　260　**New!**
Managing Accounts　262
Viewing the Mail Window　264　**New!**
Composing and Sending an E-Mail　265
Addressing an E-Mail　266
Adding Stationery to E-Mail　268
Formatting Message Text　269　**New!**

Adding an E-Mail Signature 270
Customizing the Mail Window 271 **New!**
Receiving and Reading E-Mail 272
Responding to E-Mail 274
Sending and Retrieving a File 276 **New!**
Managing E-Mail 278 **New!**
Deleting E-Mail 280 **New!**
Saving E-Mail 282
Searching E-Mail for Text 283 **New!**
Blocking and Flagging E-Mail 284 **New!**
Diverting Incoming E-Mail to Mailboxes 286
Creating a Smart Mailbox 287
Getting RSS Feeds in E-Mail 288

11 Conducting Live Chats and Video Conversations 289

Creating an Instant Message Account 290 **New!**
Starting iChat 292 **New!**
Viewing iChat 293 **New!**
Changing My Status 294 **New!**
Using the iChat Status Menu 295 **New!**
Adding a Buddy 296 **New!**
Changing a Buddy Picture 297 **New!**
Creating and Managing Buddy Groups 298 **New!**
Sending and Receiving Instant Messages 300 **New!**
Blocking a Buddy 302
Sending a File During an Instant Message 303
Having an Audio and Video Chat 304
Enhancing a Video Chat 306
Chatting on a Local Network 308
Changing the Appearance of a Chat 310
Getting Notification Alerts 312
Getting Started with FaceTime 313 **New!**
Making a Video Call with FaceTime 314 **New!**

12 Working with Music and Media 315

Starting and Setting Up iTunes 316
Viewing the iTunes Window 317
Setting Up iTunes to Automatically Play CDs 318
Getting and Playing Music from CDs 319 **New!**
Getting Media from the iTunes Music Store 320 **New!**
Using and Creating Playlists 322
Adding Media to a Playlist 324

Socializing with Ping 325 **New!**
Subscribing and Playing Podcasts 326
Using iPod or iPhone with iTunes 327 **New!**
Listening to Internet Radio 328
Erasing a CD or DVD 329
Burning CDs and Exporting to MP3 Players 330
Setting iTunes Preferences 332
Capturing Photos in Photo Booth 333 **New!**
Recording Movies in Photo Booth 334 **New!**
Adding Photo Booth Effects 335 **New!**
Playing and Browsing DVD Movies 336
Customizing the DVD Player 337
Playing QuickTime Movies 338 **New!**
Creating QuickTime Movies 340 **New!**
Exploring iMovie, iDVD, and iPhoto 342

13 Sharing Information in the Cloud 343

Joining the iCloud Community 344 **New!**
Getting Started with CloudApp 346 **New!**
Working with CloudApp Raindrops 348 **New!**
Setting CloudApp Preferences 349 **New!**
Using CloudApp on the Web 350 **New!**
Changing MobileMe Account Preferences 352
Managing MobileMe Mail 354
Creating a MobileMe Address Book 355
Working with MobileMe Calendar 356
Creating a MobileMe Gallery 358
Viewing and Sharing a MobileMe Gallery 360
Managing Files with iDisk 362
Setting iDisk Preferences 364
Sharing Files with MobileMe iDisk 366

14 Tracking and Synchronizing Information 367

Viewing the iCal Window 368 **New!**
Changing Calendar Views 369 **New!**
Creating and Working with Calendars 370 **New!**
Adding and Editing Calendar Events 372 **New!**
Publishing and Subscribing to a Calendar 374
Working with Reminders 376 **New!**
Printing Calendars and Reminders 377
Setting Up Synchronization 378
Resetting Synchronization 379

Keeping Track of Passwords with Keychain 380
Working with Keychains 381
Modifying Keychains 382
Adding Keychains 384

15 Setting Up Accounts and Maintaining Security 385

Understanding User Accounts 386
Activating the Login Window 387
Adding a User Account 388
Deleting a User Account 389
Setting File Access Permissions 390
Setting Account Access Privileges 391 **New!**
Setting Parental Controls 392
Specifying Log In and Start Up Items 394
Setting Fast User Switching 396
Setting Security & Privacy Preferences 397 **New!**
Restoring Password Access 398 **New!**
Protecting Your Computer with FileVault 400 **New!**
Managing Files with the Home Folder 401
Sharing Files with Other Users 402

16 Managing Files Using a Network 403

Using Network Sharing Services 404
Setting Up File Sharing 406
Sharing an Internet Connection 408
Configuring an Internet Firewall 409
Setting Up a Local Area Network 410
Setting Up a Network Connection 411
Setting Up for Different Network Connections 412
Setting Up a Bluetooth Wireless Network 413
Moving Items with Bluetooth 414
Setting Bluetooth Preferences 415
Browsing the Network with the Finder 416
Connecting to Another Computer 418
Connecting Your Mac Using a MobileMe Account 420
Sending Files Wirelessly with AirDrop 421 **New!**
Controlling a Computer with Screen Sharing 422 **New!**
Setting Up Mac and Windows to Share Files 424
Connecting from a Windows 7 or Vista Computer 425
Connecting from a Windows XP Computer 426
Connecting to a Network Over the Internet 428
Exploring Additional Utility Applications 430

17 **Maintaining Your Computer** **431**

Downloading and Installing Software 432
Automating Software Updates 433
Opening Compressed Files 434
Compressing and Uncompressing Files and Folders 435
Using Application Services 436
Understanding Disk File Systems 437
Formatting and Copying a Disk 438
Fixing Disk Problems 440
Optimizing a Disk 441
Starting Your Computer from a Mac OS Disk 442
Migrating Information Between Macs 443 **New!**
Monitoring System Activities 444
Viewing System Messages with the Console 446
Viewing System Information 447
Forcing a Restart 448

18 **Managing Hardware** **449**

Installing Hardware Devices 450
Removing Hardware Devices 451
Viewing Hardware Settings 452
Changing Keyboard Settings 453
Changing Mouse Settings 454 **New!**
Changing Trackpad Settings 455 **New!**
Changing Monitor Display Settings 456
Measuring Display Colors with the Digital Color Meter 458
Selecting Colors with the Color Picker 459
Matching Colors to Devices with ColorSync 460
Configuring Audio MIDI Devices 462
Preventing Hardware Problems 464

19 **Working with Mac OS X Along with Windows** **465**

Preparing a Mac for Windows 466
Installing Windows on a Mac 468
Starting Up with Mac OS X or Windows 470
Using Windows on a Mac 472
Removing Windows 474

20 **Backing Up Everything with Time Machine** **477**

Setting Up Time Machine for Backups 478 **New!**
Performing a Backup 479

Excluding Items from a Backup — 480 — **New!**
Working with a Backup — 481 — **New!**
Recovering Backed Up Items — 482 — **New!**
Recovering an Entire Computer System — 484 — **New!**
Creating a Disk Image to Backup Files — 486
Burning a CD or DVD from a Disk Image — 488
Restoring a Disk Image — 489
Backing Up Files onto a CD or DVD — 490

21 Automating Your Work — **491**

Introducing Automator — 492
Viewing the Automator Window — 494
Getting Started with Automator — 495
Opening an Existing Workflow — 496
Opening an Example Workflow — 497
Working with an Example Workflow — 498
Adding Actions to a Workflow — 500 — **New!**
Adding Variables to an Action — 501
Recording an Action — 502
Working with Workflows — 503
Running and Stopping a Workflow — 504
Saving a Workflow — 505 — **New!**
Using a Workflow as Plug-ins — 506 — **New!**
Understanding AppleScript Basics — 507
Using Ready-Made AppleScripts — 508
Writing and Recording AppleScripts — 510 — **New!**
Using AppleScript with Automator — 512

A Appendix: Installing Mac OS X Lion — **513**

Preparing to Install Mac OS X Lion — 514
Determining the Current Mac OS Version — 515
Getting Mac Information — 516 — **New!**
Getting Mac OS X Lion from the App Store — 517 — **New!**
Installing Mac OS X Lion — 518 — **New!**
Reinstalling Mac OS X Lion — 520 — **New!**

New Features — 521 — **New!**
Index — 527
Workshops — Online

Introduction

Welcome to *Brilliant Mac OS X Lion*, a visual quick reference book that shows you how to work efficiently with Apple Mac OS X Lion. This book provides complete coverage of basic to advanced Mac OS X skills.

How This Book Works

You don't have to read this book in any particular order. We've designed the book so that you can jump in, get the information you need, and jump out. However, the book does follow a logical progression from simple tasks to more complex ones. Each task is presented on no more than two facing pages, which lets you focus on a single task without having to turn the page. To find the information that you need, just look up the task in the table of contents or index, and turn to the page listed. Read the task introduction, follow the step-by-step instructions in the left column along with screen illustrations in the right column, and you're done.

What's New

If you're searching for what's new in Mac OS X Lion, just look for the icon: **New!**. The new icon appears in the table of contents and throughout this book so you can quickly and easily identify a new or improved feature in Lion. A complete description of each new feature appears in the New Features guide in the back of this book.

Keyboard Shortcuts

Most menu commands have a keyboard equivalent, such as ⌘+P, as a quicker alternative to using the mouse. A complete list of keyboard shortcuts is available on the Web at *www.perspection.com*.

How You'll Learn

How This Book Works

What's New

Keyboard Shortcuts

Step-by-Step Instructions

Real World Examples

Workshop

Get More on the Web

Step-by-Step Instructions

This book provides concise step-by-step instructions that show you "how" to accomplish a task. Each set of instructions includes illustrations that directly correspond to the easy-to-read steps. Also included in the text are time-savers, tables, and sidebars to help you work more efficiently or to teach you more in-depth information. A "Did You Know?" provides tips and techniques to help you work smarter, while a "See Also" leads you to other parts of the book containing related information about the task.

Easy-to-follow introductions focus on a single concept.

Illustrations match the numbered steps.

Numbered steps guide you through each task.

See Also points you to related information in the book.

Did You Know? alerts you to tips, techniques and related information.

Real World Examples

This book uses real world examples files to give you a context in which to use the task. By using the example files, you won't waste time looking for or creating sample files. You get a start file and a result file, so you can compare your work. Not every topic needs an example file, such as changing options, so we provide a complete list of the example files used through out the book. The example files that you need for project tasks along with a complete file list are available on the Web at *www.perspection.com*.

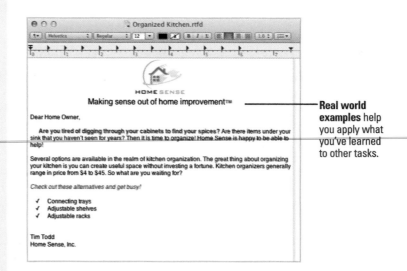

Real world examples help you apply what you've learned to other tasks.

Workshops

This book shows you how to put together the individual step-by-step tasks into in-depth projects with the Workshop. You start each project with a sample file, work through the steps, and then compare your results with project results file at the end. The Workshop projects and associated files are available on the Web at *www.perspection.com.*

Workshops

Introduction

The Workshops are all about being creative and thinking outside of the box. These workshops will help your right-brain soar, while making your left-brain happy; by explaining why things work the way they do. Exploring Mac OS X Lion's possibilities is great fun; however, always stay grounded with knowledge of how things work. Knowledge is power.

Getting and Using the Project Files

Some projects in the Workshops may include a start file to help you get started with the project, and a final file to provide you with the results so you can see how well you accomplished the task. The first step in a project specifies whether you need a project file to complete it.

Before you can use the project files, you need to download them from the Web. You can access the files at *www.perspection.com.* After you download the files from the Web, uncompress the files into a folder on your hard drive to which you have easy access from Mac OS X Lion.

Project 1: Customizing the Desktop

Skills and Tools: Desktop, Finder, Stacks, Mission Control, and Misc.

If your desktop gets cluttered, you can change view options or use stacks of folders with documents or applications to access material you're currently working on. If your dock starts to get cluttered, you can minimize windows to the associated application icon on the left-side of the dock instead of minimizing windows to the right-side of the dock. With Mission Control, you can display and switch between windows in an easy to view grid with window titles.

The Project

In this project, you'll display and customize the desktop and Finder to meet your workspace needs. You'll change view options for the desktop, create stacks,and use Mission Control to switch windows, minimize windows to the dock into an application icon. In addition, you'll show the date in the menu bar, show more commands in the menu bar, zoom desktop icons using the trackpad, and learn how to quickly get your Mac's serial number for support purposes.

The **Workshops** walks you through in-depth projects to help you put the Mac OS X Lion to work.

Get More on the Web

In addition to the information in this book, you can also get more information on the Web to help you get up to speed faster with Mac OS X. Some of the information includes:

Transition Helpers

◆ **Only New Features.**
Download and print the new feature tasks as a quick and easy guide.

Productivity Tools

◆ **Keyboard Shortcuts.**
Download a list of keyboard shortcuts to learn faster ways to get the job done.

Keyboard Shortcuts

If a command on a menu includes a keyboard reference, known as a keyboard shortcut, to the right of the command name, you can perform the action by pressing and holding the first key, and then pressing the second key to perform the command quickly. In some cases, a keyboard shortcut uses one key or three keys. For three keys, simply press and hold the first two keys, and then press the third key. Keyboard shortcuts provide an alternative to using the mouse and make it easy to perform repetitive commands. If you don't like a global shortcut key combination, you can change it. See "Changing Keyboard Settings," on page 453 for details.

Finding a Keyboard Shortcut

The Mac OS X Lion contains keyboard shortcuts for many commands and tasks in the different applications and utility programs. To find a keyboard shortcut for a menu command, click the menu with the command to display the keyboard shortcut keys. See the illustration below for key symbols on menus. To find a keyboard shortcut for a common task, use the list provided here. If you're searching for new keyboard shortcuts in Lion, just look for the letter: **N**. The **N** appears in the Keyboard Shortcuts table so you can quickly and easily identify new shortcuts.

Additional content is available on the Web.

More Content

◆ **Photographs.** Download photographs and other graphics to use in your documents.

◆ **More Content.** Download new content developed after publication.

You can access these additional resources on the Web at *www.perspection.com.*

Download and use **Photographs** to help you add impact to your documents.

Getting Started with Mac OS X Lion

1

Introduction

Mac OS X Lion is an **operating system (OS)**, a computer program that controls the basic operation of your Macintosh computer and the programs you run. A **program**, also known as an application, is task-oriented software you use to accomplish a specific task, such as word processing, managing files on your computer, or performing calculations.

The **Finder** is part of the Mac OS and starts when you turn on your computer. The Finder displays a menu bar and desktop on your screen that you can use to work with windows, icons, and files. A **window** can contain the contents of a file and the application in which it was created, icons (picture representations of an application or a file), or other usable data. This use of windows and icons is called a **graphical user interface** (GUI, pronounced "gooey"), meaning that you ("user") interact ("interface") with the computer through the use of graphics: icons and other meaningful words, symbols, and windows. A **file** is a collection of information (such as a letter or list of addresses) that has a unique name, distinguishing it from other files. You can use the Finder to open, copy, delete, list, and organize your computer files.

When you turn on your Macintosh computer, the Finder might ask you to log in. Your Macintosh is built to share with other people and work with other computers. If you are sharing your computer with others or accessing other computers over a network, you need to log in (type a user name and password) and log out to switch users or access information. When you're done working on your computer, you should put it to sleep for short periods or shut it down for longer stints.

What You'll Do

Start Mac OS X

Explore the Finder and Desktop

Use the Mouse or Multi-Touch Gestures

Work with Menus, Toolbars, and Panes

Use Menus for Quick Results

Choose Dialog Options

Work with Icons

View Windows

Manage Windows

Use the Sidebar

Use Toolbars

Display and Use the Dock

Display and Use Stacks on the Dock

Exposé Windows

Group Windows into Spaces

Switch Users

Sleep, Restart, and Shut Down

Starting Mac OS X

Mac OS X automatically starts when you turn on your computer. When you first start Mac OS X, you see the desktop screen, or a Login window depending on your installation. The Mac OS X desktop screen indicates you are using a stand-alone computer (you're the only person using the computer), while the Login window identifies you're on a shared computer. After you click or type your user name in the Login window, and then possibly type a password, you'll see the Mac OS X desktop.

Start Mac OS X Using a Stand Alone Computer

1. Turn on your computer, and then wait while Mac OS X loads.

 The Mac OS X Lion desktop screen appears.

Menu bar Desktop

Dock

Did You Know?

The Login window doesn't always appear. If Mac OS X is set up to log in automatically, you don't normally see the Login window. However, if you select the Log Out command from the Apple menu, you do see the Login window. If you see the Login window, click Restart to log in again automatically.

See Also

See "Adding a User Account" on page 388 for information on creating a user account.

See "Activating the Login Window" on page 387 for information on changing log in options.

For Your Information

Creating a Shared Computer

During the Mac OS X Lion installation process, you create a user account for the computer administrator and possibility other accounts for each person who uses your computer. An administrator account can create other user accounts, install software, and change computer settings. When you create accounts for more than one account, your computer changes from a stand-alone computer to a shared computer. Each user maintains separate files, a home folder, and preferences without affecting other users.

Start Mac OS X Using a Shared Computer

1 Turn on your computer and wait while Mac OS X loads.

The Login window opens.

2 Click or type your user name.

3 Type your password. Be sure to use the correct capitalization.

4 Press Return.

TROUBLE? *If you forget your password, your third attempt to type the password correctly displays your password hint, and a Reset button, where you can use the administrator's master password to create a new password.*

Did You Know?

The password is case-sensitive. Macintosh makes a distinction between uppercase and lowercase letters. Your password should be at least seven characters long, the optimal length for encryption, which is the process of logically scrambling data to keep a password secure.

You can set up your computer to automatically log in (by pass the Login window). Click the Apple menu, click System Preferences, click Users & Groups, and then select the administrator account. Next, click Login Options, select the Automatically Login pop-up, and then click an account. Type a password, and then click OK.

You can sleep, restart, and shut down from the Login window. In the Login window, click Sleep, Restart, or Shut Down, and then click the appropriate button or wait 60 seconds.

Login window

Exploring the Finder and Desktop

When you first start Mac OS X Lion, you see the Finder desktop with a transparent look and feel, or a log in screen (a way to identify yourself on the computer), depending on your installation. The desktop is an on-screen version of an actual desk, containing windows, icons, files, and applications. You can use the desktop to access, store, organize, modify, share, and explore information (such as a letter or a list of addresses), whether it resides on your computer, a network, or the Internet.

The desktop contains icons that represent volumes (such as your Hard Disk to store data), applications, documents, folders, and the Trash. If you upgraded your computer to Mac OS X from a previous version, your desktop might contain many different icons. These icons can also appear a number of different ways depending on your view. When you open an icon, a window or application appears, displaying its contents or an application work environment. The bar at the bottom

Menu bar

Menu status area

Finder window

Background picture on the desktop

Dock

of the desktop is called the **Dock** (if it's hidden, point to the bottom of the screen to display it); it allows you to start applications and switch among currently running ones. At the top of the screen is a **menu bar**, which contain commands you use to perform tasks and customize your environment. At the right end of the menu bar is the **menu status area**, which displays the time, date, current user, and application related icons—including Spotlight, AirPort, Volume, Eject, and Bluetooth to name a few. Your list of icons may differ depending on the applications you have installed. The Mac OS X Lion dynamic user interface includes a transparent look and feel with design themes and a reflective floor for the Dock. A **design theme** is a professionally designed look and feel that coordinates all aspects of the user interface, including the desktop, menus, and windows.

Fast user switching

Desktop icons

Open application window

Recent documents

Open application windows

Application commands

Open Application icon in the Dock

Using the Mouse or Multi-Touch Gestures

Macintosh desktop computers typically come with a mouse that contains a single button, while Macintosh portable computers come with a Multi-Touch trackpad. A **mouse** is a handheld input device you roll across a flat surface (such as a desk or a mouse pad) while a **trackpad** is a small pad device you tap or slide your fingers across, which is known as a **gesture**. You use a mouse or trackpad to position the **mouse pointer**, the small symbol that indicates the pointer's relative position on the screen. When you move the mouse or drag the trackpad, the mouse pointer on the screen moves in the same direction. The shape of the mouse pointer changes to indicate different activities. However, the pointer usually looks like an arrow pointer. Once you move the mouse pointer (the arrow's tip) to a desired position on the screen (known as pointing), you use the mouse button or trackpad as a button to tell your computer what you want it to do by either clicking (press and release), double-clicking (press and release twice quickly), dragging (press and hold, then move and release), or pressing (press and hold).

With the Multi-Touch trackpad, you can use gestures to naturally interact with your computer. You can click anywhere on the trackpad as a button, pinch two fingers to zoom in and out, swipe a finger to flip through photos or rotate images, or brush two fingers to scroll. To see how to perform gestures, customize how gestures work, and set options from your trackpad or mouse, open Trackpad or Mouse preferences.

With Lion, you can perform even more gestures (**New!**):

◆ **Rubber-band scrolling.** Swipe to the top or bottom of a list or a web page to scroll and it springs back.

◆ **Swipe forward and back.** Swipe left or right in apps, like Safari and Preview, to move between pages.

◆ **Tap to zoom.** Double-tap to zoom in on text or images in Safari and Preview.

◆ **Pinch to zoom.** Pinch using two fingers to precise zoom in or out of apps, like Safari, Preview, and iPhoto.

◆ **Swipe between full-screen apps.** Swipe to move from one full-screen apps to another.

◆ **Show Mission Control.** Swipe to open Mission Control.

◆ **Show Launchpad.** Pinch three fingers and your thumb to open Launchpad.

◆ **Show desktop.** Spread three fingers and your thumb to move all open windows off the screen, revealing the desktop.

In addition to the traditional mouse and trackpad, you can use other input devices, such as a mouse with two buttons (left and right), the Magic Mouse (a mouse device with a Multi-touch trackpad surface), the Magic Trackpad (a Multi-Touch trackpad device for a desktop computer), or writing tablet.

Dragging

Mouse pointer

Clicking

Pinching gesture

Multi-Touch trackpad

Working with Menus, Toolbars, and Panes

A **menu** is a list of commands that you use to accomplish certain tasks, such as when you use the View menu to open the Customize Toolbar dialog. A **command** is a directive that provides access to an application's features. Each application has its own set of menus, which are on the menu bar along the top of the application window. The menu bar organizes commands into groups of related operations. Each group is listed under the name of the menu, such as File or Help. To access the commands in a menu, you click the name of the menu, and then click the command name. If a menu command is gray, the option is not available at this time; availability depends on what is selected. If a command on a menu includes a keyboard reference, known as a **keyboard shortcut**, such as ⌘+1 for the As Icons command, you can perform the action by pressing and holding the first key, and then pressing the second key to perform the command quickly. When a menu command is followed by an ellipse (...), a dialog appears when you select it. On a menu, a **check mark** identifies a currently selected feature, meaning that the feature is enabled, or turned on. To disable, or turn off the feature, you click the command again to remove the check mark, or you can select another command (within the menu section, separated by gray lines) in its place. You can also carry out some of the most frequently used commands on a menu by clicking a button on a toolbar. A **toolbar** contains buttons that are convenient shortcuts for menu commands and navigation. A **pane** is a frame within a window, such as a Sidebar, where you can quickly access navigation controls. You can use menus, toolbar buttons, and commands in a pane to change how a window's contents appear.

Pane (Sidebar) Toolbar

Check mark Keyboard shortcut

Menu Submenu

Using Menus for Quick Results

The Finder uses several different types of menus to help you use the commands you need to get the results you want. The Finder uses four types of menus: pull-down, submenu, pop-up, and contextual. The **pull down** menu appears on the menu bar when you click a menu name or status icon in the menu status area. A **submenu** appears when you point to a menu with a triangle. A **pop-up** menu appears in a window or dialog when you click the double arrow. A **contextual** menu appears when you hold down the Control key while you click an item, such as an icon, text, or graphic or right-click an item. A contextual menu displays a list of commands related to the selected item. When you click a menu name, the menu stays open. If you don't want to select a menu command, you can click outside the menu or press the Esc key to close it.

Use a Pull Down Menu

1. Point to the name or menu status icon on the menu bar, and then click to open the menu.

2. Point to the menu option you want.

3. If a submenu opens, point to the menu option you want.

4. Click to select the command.

Did You Know?

You can rearrange menu status icons on the menu bar. Press and hold ⌘, and then drag the icon to reposition it.

Use a Contextual Menu

1. Point to the item on which you want to act upon.

2. Press and hold down the Control key, and then click to display a contextual menu.

 If you are using a mouse with two buttons, right-click the item.

3. Select the command you want.

Pull down menu Menu status icons

Submenu 3

Choosing Dialog Options

The Finder and Mac OS X applications use dialogs to carry out options, provide alert messages, and gather information. A **dialog** is a window that opens when the Finder or an application wants to alert you of an event, or you select a menu command or button followed by an ellipsis. In a dialog, you acknowledge an alert message or select various options, and then provide information for completing the command.

Choose Dialog Options

All dialogs contain the same types of options, including the following:

- **Tabs.** Click a tab to display its options. Each tab groups a related set of options.

- **Option buttons.** Click an option button to select it. You can usually select only one in a group.

- **Check box.** Click the box to turn on or off the option. A checked box means the option is selected; a cleared box means it's not.

- **Pop-up menu.** Click the arrow to display a list of commands or options, and then click the one you want.

- **Entry field.** Click in the field, and then type the requested information.

- **Up and down arrows.** Click the up or down arrow to increase or decrease the number, or type a number in the field.

- **Scroll bar.** Drag a slider control to change screen position.

- **Preview area.** Many dialogs show an image that reflects the options you select.

- **Slider.** Drag a slider control to change a screen position.

- **Push button.** Click a button to perform an action or command. A button name followed by an ellipsis (...) opens another dialog.

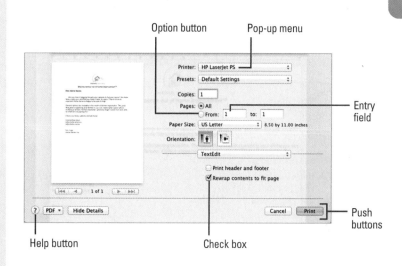

Option button Pop-up menu

Entry field

Help button Check box

Push buttons

Working with Icons

Mac OS X uses various icons to graphically represent different items on the desktop, in the Dock, or in a window. The icons represent applications, documents, folders, volumes, and the Trash. **Application icons** are programs you use to create documents. **Document icons** are files you create with applications. **Folder icons** are a storage area for files. **Volume icons** are storage devices, such as hard disks, removable disks, network disks, Internet computers, CDs, DVDs, and iPods. The **Trash icon** (located in the Dock) appears in three different ways: empty, full, and ejecting removable media. On the desktop or within a window, you can select and deselect one or more icons to perform tasks, such as opening, launching, copying, and moving. When you select an icon, the icon graphic and its name become highlighted. Within a Finder window, icons appear in different ways, depending on the window view you select.

Select Icons

◆ **Select an icon.** Click the icon you want to select.

◆ **Select multiple icons by clicking.** Click the first icon you want to select, hold down ⌘, and then click the other icons you want to select within the same window.

 TIMESAVER *Click the first icon, press the Shift key, and then click the last one to select every icon in between.*

◆ **Select multiple icons by dragging.** Position the mouse pointer to the left of the first icon you want to select, drag diagonally across the adjacent icons you want to select, and then release the mouse button.

 A shaded box appears as you drag to indicate the selection area.

◆ **Select all icons.** Click the Edit menu, and then click Select All.

 TIMESAVER *Press ⌘+A to select all icons.*

Start dragging here

Selection rectangle

Select multiple icons by dragging

Select multiple icons by clicking

Deselect Icons

◆ **Deselect all icons.** Click a blank area in the window or on the desktop.

◆ **Deselect an icon in a multiple selection.** Press and hold down ⌘, and then click the icon you want to deselect, while keeping the others selected.

Deselect all icons

Move or Copy Icons

① To move multiple icons, select the ones you want to move; to copy an icon, hold down the Option key.

② Point to the icons, and then drag them to the new location.

As you drag, a shaded image of the icon moves along with the mouse pointer.

TROUBLE? *Press the Esc key to cancel the move or copy.*

③ Release the mouse button and the Option key, if necessary.

TIMESAVER *Press ⌘+X to move or press ⌘+C to copy selected icons; and then press ⌘+V to paste them.*

Did You Know?

You can change the icon view size. In as Icons view, drag the Zoom control on the Status bar.

Viewing Windows

A window displays icons and other information in the Finder, and documents in an application. One of the powerful things about the Mac OS X is that you can open more than one window or application at once. You can identify a window by its name on the title bar at the top of the window. Before you can work with a window, you need to activate it first. The active window is the one in front with the available buttons (red, yellow, and green) in the upper-left corner. When you're done using a window, you can quickly close it to reduce the clutter on the desktop.

Parts of a Window

Windows in Mac OS X consist of the following parts:

- **Close button.** Closes the window.

- **Minimize button.** Shrinks the window to an icon in the Dock.

- **Zoom button.** Toggles the window size between full and a custom size.

- **Title bar.** Displays the name of the window.

- **Toolbar.** Displays buttons and controls for commonly used window commands.

- **Size control.** Allows you to set a custom window size.

- **Zoom control.** Allows you to set a view percentage in as Icons view.

- **Status bar.** Displays information about selected items.

- **Path bar.** Displays path information from the hard drive to the current folder (**New!**).

- **Sidebar.** Displays commonly used volumes and folders.

- **Column heading.** Displays the names of columns and sorts them (in list view only).

- **Search box.** Allows you to find files based on the name.

- **Scroll bar.** Displays the content of the window.

Open and Close a Window

◆ **Open a Finder window.** Double-click a volume or folder icon.

◆ **Open a new Finder window.** Click the File menu, and then click New Finder Window.

◆ **Close a window.** Click the red button to close the window, or hold down the Option key, and then click the red button to close all windows.

> **TIMESAVER** *If you see a dot in the center of the Close button, you need to save your changes.*

Click to close window Double-click to open Finder window

New Finder window

Activate a Window

◆ **Activate a window.** Click anywhere on the window, or click the Window menu, and then click the window name.

◆ **Activate and bring all Finder windows to front.** Click the Window menu, and then click Bring All To Front. All open Finder windows that are not minimized are moved in front of application windows.

◆ **Activate and bring a specific application window to the front.** Display the Dock, press (click and hold) an application icon to display a menu, and then select the window you want to make active.

◆ **Activate a window by cycling through them.** Click the Window menu, and then click Cycle Through Window.

> **TIMESAVER** *Press ⌘+` (accent) to cycle through open windows.*

Active window

Managing Windows

When you open multiple windows, your desktop can get cluttered with many open windows for the various applications you are using. To organize your desktop, you may need to move it to a different location or change the size of a window. Each window has resize buttons in the upper-left corner to minimize or zoom a window, and a size control in the lower right-corner that you can use to resize the window to a custom size. An icon appears in the Dock for each minimized window, which you can use to quickly switch between windows or redisplay it. You can Control-click the Finder or application icon to switch between open windows or press F9 to activate Exposé in Mission Control.

Switch Among Open Windows

1. If windows are visible, click in the window to make it active.

2. If the windows are not visible, Control-click the Finder or an application icon, and then click a window or press F9 to activate Exposé in Mission Control, and then click a window you want.

See Also

See "Exposing Windows in Mission Control" on page 20 for information on temporarily showing and hiding all windows.

Move a Window

1. Point to the window's title bar.

2. Drag the window to a new location, and then release the mouse button.

 TIMESAVER *Hold down the A key while you drag the title bar of an inactive window to move it without making it active.*

Use Buttons to Resize a Window

All windows contain the same sizing buttons:

◆ **Minimize button (active window).** Click the yellow button to shrink a window as an icon in the Dock, or double-click the title bar.

 TIMESAVER *Press ⌘+M to minimize the active window.*

◆ **Minimize button (all windows).** Hold down the Option key, and then click the yellow button or double-click the title bar to minimize all windows.

◆ **Redisplay minimized window.** Click the window's icon in the Dock or click the Window menu, and then click the window's name.

◆ **Zoom button.** Click the green button to toggle between the smallest possible size that fits on your screen, and the size you set with the size control.

Use the Mouse to Resize a Window

1. Move the mouse over the edge or corner of the window (cursor changes to a double arrow) (**New!**).

 An edge resizes up/down or left/right and a corner resizes up/down and left/right.

2. Drag the size control until the window is the size you want.

Minimize button
Zoom button

Minimized window

Using the Sidebar

The Sidebar is a panel which appears in the left column of Finder windows, that you can use to quickly access commonly used locations on your computer. The panel appears with multiple areas or sections, including Favorites (**New!**), Devices, and Shared. The Favorites section contains for folders, including your All My Files (**New!**), Applications, Desktop, Documents, Downloads (**New!**), Movies, Music, Pictures, and any Smart Folders. The Devices section contains items for volumes attached to your computer. To show or hide items in a section, point to the section name, and then click Show or Hide (**New!**). The Shared section contains shared and networked computers. You can use the Sidebar to move and copy documents to disks and folders on or connected to your computer, eject removable disks, and burn a CD or DVD.

Use the Sidebar

◆ **Display icons.** Click icons in the Sidebar to display contents.

◆ **Move or copy icons.** Drag the folder or document icons from the Contents pane to the Sidebar icon in order to move or copy them.

◆ **Add a file, folder or application.** Drag its icon to Favorites (display line) or select it, click the **File** menu, and then click **Add to Sidebar**.

◆ **Remove icon.** Control-click its icon, and then click **Remove from Sidebar**.

◆ **Change column width.** Position the mouse pointer over the divider, and then drag to change the width.

◆ **Hide or show sidebar.** Click the **View** menu, then click **Hide Sidebar** or **Show Sidebar**.

◆ **Eject a disk.** Click the **Eject** button next to any removable disk.

◆ **Burn a CD.** Insert a blank CD or DVD, drag files and folders to it, and then click the **Burn** button.

Sidebar

Eject button Drag here to change width.

See Also

See "Customizing the Sidebar" on page 84 for information on using Finder preferences to customize the Sidebar.

Using Toolbars

The toolbar, in a Finder window, provides easy access to commonly used window commands. You can use commands on the View menu to hide the toolbar and sidebar, to display more information in the window, or to show the toolbar to display tools and navigational controls. The Toolbar Control button is no longer available on the toolbar. When you hide the toolbar, the Finder also hides the Sidebar panel and window borders, and moves the status bar to display under the title bar.

Parts of a Toolbar

Toolbars in the Finder consist of the following parts:

◆ **Back and Forward buttons.** Displays the content from the previous or next window.

◆ **View buttons.** Displays the window in different views.

◆ **Action pop-up menu.** Displays commands for working with a window or selected items.

◆ **Arrange by button.** Displays the window contents by different attributes (**New!**), such as Date.

◆ **Search box.** Allows you to search for a file by name.

Show or Hide the Toolbar and Sidebar

① Click the **View** menu, and then click **Hide Toolbar** or **Show Toolbar**.

TIMESAVER Press ⌘+⇧+T to hide/show the toolbar.

If a double arrow appears at the right side of the toolbar, the window is too small to show all the icons. You can either resize the window, or click the double arrow, and then select a toolbar item.

To customize the toolbar, click the **View** menu, and then click **Customize Toolbar**.

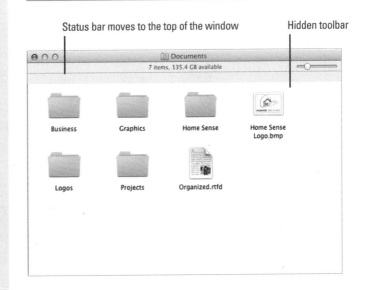

Displaying and Using the Dock

The Dock is a bar at the bottom of the screen that you can use to open frequently used applications and utilities, system preferences, Web sites and the Trash, as well as redisplay minimized applications and Finder windows. If you don't see the Dock at the bottom of your screen, then its automatically hidden. You can change an option in the Dock pane of System Preferences to always display the Dock. The Dock has two sides with a divider line separating the two. The left side is for applications and the right side is for everything else: stacks, files, documents, folders, and disks. When you point to an icon, its name appears above it. Document and folder icons in the Dock actually display an image of the contents to make it a little easier to distinguish between them. When you click an icon, it launches or opens it. When you launch an application, it's icon appears in the Dock with a shinny image below it; when an option is set in preferences (**New!**). When you press and hold an icon, a list of commands appears on a menu. When you quit an application or window not permanently placed in the Dock, its icon is removed from the Dock. In addition to the predefined icons in the Dock, you can also quickly and permanently add your own icons in the Dock.

Display and Use the Dock

- **Display a hidden Dock.** Move the mouse pointer to the bottom or side of the screen.

- **Open, launch or redisplay a minimized item.** Click its icon.

- **Choose commands for an item.** Press and hold or Control-click the icon in the Dock, and then click a command.

- **Choose commands for an open item.** Press and hold or Control-click the open icon in the Dock, and then click a command.

Open item Stacks Minimized item

Applications Divider All others

Press and hold or Control-click an icon in the Dock

Displaying and Using Stacks on the Dock

Folders in the Dock are called **stacks**. You can use stacks to reduce clutter and quickly access folders of documents, applications, downloads, and other folders. When you click a stack in the Dock, it springs open to display an arc or a grid of icons for the items in the stack. You can scroll through stacks, open folders, and navigate back. The Dock comes with two stacks, the Documents (**New!**) and Downloads folders, which stores your documents and downloaded items from the Internet. You can create more stacks by dragging the folder you want to the Dock and modify stacks by Control-clicking it in the Dock.

Work with Stacks on the Dock

◆ **Display a stack.** Click a folder in the Dock.

◆ **Open the stack folder.** Control-click the folder in the Dock, and then click **Open "name"** or point to **Options**, and click **Show in Finder**.

◆ **Open an item in a stack folder.** Click the folder in the Dock, and then click the item. If you click a folder in Grid view, you can click the return path icon in the upper left of the stack to return.

◆ **Add a stack to the Dock.** Drag the folder to the Dock.

◆ **Remove a stack from the Dock.** Control-click the folder in the Dock, point to **Options**, and then click **Remove from Dock**.

◆ **Change the stack display.** Control-click the folder in the Dock, and then click **Automatic**, **List**, **Grid**, or **Fan**. Automatic displays in a fan or grid depending on available space.

◆ **Change stack icon in the Dock.** Control-click the folder or stack in the Dock, and then click **Folder** or **Stack**.

◆ **Sort items in a stack.** Control-click the folder in the Dock, and then select the sort type (under Sort by) you want.

Fan stack for Documents folder

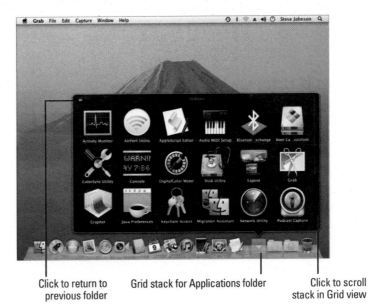

Click to return to previous folder Grid stack for Applications folder Click to scroll stack in Grid view

Exposing Windows in Mission Control

When you have multiple windows and applications open at the same time, the screen can get cluttered and make it difficult to work. Mission Control with Exposé let you quickly view all your open windows to make it easier to locate and work with them. Mission Control (F9 or portable Fn-F9) (**New!**) expands to make it quick and easy to determine what's running on your computer. It displays the Dashboard, desktop workspaces, and all open windows (grouped by application), even ones in full-screen view (as separate thumbnails). In Mission Control, you can click the Dashboard, a desktop ,or a window to bring it to the front. With Exposé, you can also quickly show all open windows in the current application at the same time (F10 or portable Fn-F10) or hide all the open windows to see your desktop (F11 or portable Fn-F11).

Use Exposé in Mission Control

◆ **Show all open windows at once with Mission Control.** Press the F9 or Mission Control (F3, if available) key or three finger swipe on a trackpad to start or exit.

For temporary use, hold down the F9 or Mission Control key, and then release.

◆ **Show all open windows in the current application.** Press the F10 key to start or exit. Press Arrow key to scroll to cycle through open and recent documents; press Tab to cycle through open and recent documents.

For temporary use, hold down the F10 key, and then release.

◆ **Hide all open windows (show desktop).** Press the F11 key to start or exit.

For temporary use, hold down the F11 key, and then release.

◆ **Activate a window.** Press F9 all open windows, point to a window to highlight it, and then click to activate and display the window.

◆ **Activate an application window.** Press and hold the ⌘ key, and then press Tab. Continue to press Tab, and then release to activate the one you want.

Mission Control screens

Shows all open windows at once

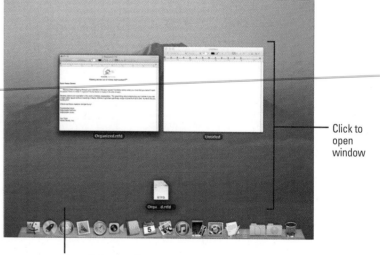

Click to open window

Exposé: Shows all open windows in current application

Grouping Windows in Mission Control

Spaces works in Mission Control (**New!**) to make working with different projects easier. With Spaces, you can group windows to reduce desktop clutter and organize materials into unique spaces, named Desktop 1, Desktop 2, etc. You can organize home, work, or other projects into different spaces. You can quickly view and select the space you want or switch between them. Each space displays only the windows for that space. You can spread out your work in different spaces by assigning an application to a space from its icon in the Dock. To work with Spaces, you open Mission Control using the F9 (portable Fn-F9) or Mission Control key or the Mission Control button in the Launchpad.

Use Spaces in Mission Control

◆ **View a space.** Press the Control key and the number key (1 for Desktop 1, etc.) for the space you want, or press the arrow keys to scroll the spaces.

◆ **View all windows in all spaces.** Press the F9 or Mission Control key (**New!**) to see all your windows within each space.

◆ **Add a space.** Press the F9 or Mission Control key (**New!**), point to right corner or press Option key to display **Add** (+) button, and then click it.

◆ **Delete a space.** Press the F9 or Mission Control key (**New!**), point a space or press Option key to display **Delete** (x) button, and then click it. You can't delete the Dashboard or Desktop 1.

◆ **Move a window between spaces.** Press the F9 or Mission Control key (**New!**) to view all your spaces, and then drag the window to an existing space or the **Add** (+) button to create a new space.

◆ **Options for spaces.** Click the **System Preferences** icon in the Dock, click the **Mission Control** icon, and then select the options and keyboard shortcuts you want (**New!**).

See "Customizing Mission Control" on page 90 for details.

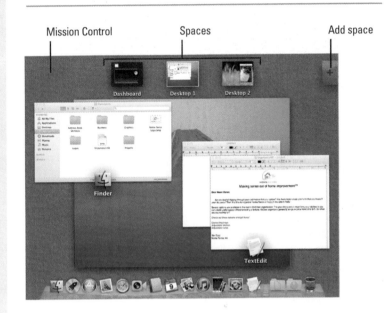

Mission Control Spaces Add space

Selected space Delete space

Switching Users

Many users can use the same computer. Individual Mac OS X accounts allow users to keep their files private and to customize the operating system with their own preferences. Mac OS X manages these separate accounts by giving each user a unique user name and password. When a user selects an account and types a password (if necessary), Mac OS X starts with that user's configuration settings and network permissions. When you want to change users, you can logout, which lets you either restore your workspace—known as Resume (**New!**)—or save and close all files and running applications before it signs you off the computer. Or, switch users, which quickly switches between users without having to logout, close applications, and save your current settings. With fast user switching, the name of the current user appears (by default, which you can customize (**New!**) in Users & Groups preferences) in the status menu area, where you can quickly switch to a new user. If you leave your computer unattended for any period of time, you can set additional security logout options to protect your information.

Fast User Switching

1. Click the *user name* in the upper-right corner of the menu bar.

2. Click the user account to which you want to switch.

 The name grayed out is the current user, and a check mark next to a name indicates that the user is logged in.

 If required, a Login window opens, requesting a password.

3. If necessary, type your password.

4. Click **Log In**.

 The computer switches to the new user's desktop (like a box switching sides), which includes the user's home folder, mail, and personal settings.

See Also

See "Setting Fast User Switching" on page 396 for information on enabling Fast User Switching.

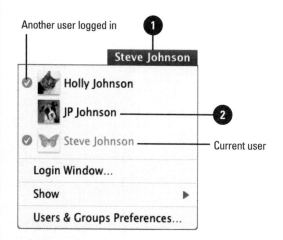

Another user logged in

Current user

Logout of Your Computer

1. Click the **Apple** menu, and then click **Log Out** *user name*.

 TIMESAVER *Press Shift+⌘+Q to log off. If you press the Option key while you select the Log Out menu command, Mac OS X skips the confirmation dialog.*

2. Select the **Reopen windows when logging back in** check box to use Resume (**New!**).

3. Click **Log Out** or wait 60 seconds to close all your applications, save your settings, and sign yourself off the computer.

 A Login window appears.

4. Click your name.

5. If required, type your password, and then click **Log In**.

Set Logout Security Options

1. Click the **System Preferences** icon in the Dock, and then click the **Security & Privacy** icon.

2. Click the **General** tab.

3. Select or clear the **Require password *X* after sleep or screen saver begins** check box, and then specify a time delay before the password is required.

4. Select or clear the **Log out after *X* minutes of inactivity** check box, and then enter the number of minutes you want.

 IMPORTANT *If any dialogs for unsaved documents or open applications appear, your computer will not log you out.*

5. Click the **Close** button.

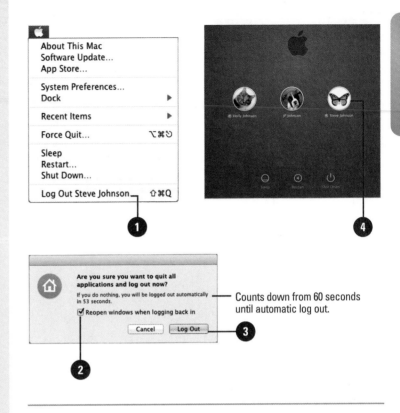

Counts down from 60 seconds until automatic log out.

Sleeping, Restarting, and Shutting Down

When you finish working on your computer, you can put it to sleep for a little while or shut it down for longer periods. If you install a software update or have a problem, you can restart—shutdown and start—your computer. Sleeping causes your computer screen to go blank and halt the spinning of your hard disk. Restarting or shutting down your computer allows you to restore—known as Resume (**New!**)—your workspace including applications to the exact place you left it or return to a clean desktop, which closes all open files and windows, and quits all open applications, before it turns off. Avoid pushing the power switch to shutdown, so you don't lose important data and cause system problems.

Sleep, Restart, or Shut Down

When you're done working on your computer, do one of the following:

◆ Sleep. Click the **Apple** menu, and then click **Sleep**.

> **IMPORTANT** *When your computer is inactive for a time set in Energy Saver preferences, Mac OS X puts your computer to sleep.*

> To wake up your computer, click the mouse button or press any keyboard key.

◆ Restart or Shutdown. Click the **Apple** menu, and then click **Restart** or **Shut Down**.

 ◆ Select the **Reopen windows when logging back in** check box to use Resume (**New!**).

 ◆ If other users are logged in, type the administrator name and password, and then click **Restart** or **Shut Down**.

 ◆ Click the **Restart** or **Shut Down** button or wait 60 seconds.

> **IMPORTANT** *If you press the Option key while you select the Restart or Shut Down command, Mac OS X skips the dialog.*

> **IMPORTANT** *If your computer has a power key, you can press it to display a dialog with Sleep, Restart, and Shut Down buttons.*

Sleep, Restart, and Shut Down commands

Resume setting duing a restart

Understanding Your Options

Option	When to use it
Sleep	When you want to stop working for a little while, save computer memory, and conserve power (ideal for saving battery life in a Mac portable computer).
Shut Down	When you finish working on your Macintosh and you want to turn off the power to the computer.
Restart	When you have problems and want to reset your computer (clear computer memory and reload system files).

Managing Files and Folders

2

Introduction

File management involves organizing and keeping track of files and folders. It helps you stay organized so information is easy to locate and use. A **folder** is a container for storing applications and files, similar to a folder in a file cabinet. As with a file cabinet, working with poorly managed files is like looking for a needle in a haystack—it's frustrating and time-consuming to search through irrelevant, misnamed, and out-of-date files to find the one you want.

Finder allows you to organize folders and files in a file hierarchy, imitating the way you store paper documents in real folders. Just as a file cabinet contains several folders, each containing related documents with dividers grouping related folders together, so the Finder file hierarchy allows you to organize your files in folders, and then place folders in other folders. At the top of each hierarchy is the name of the hard drive or main folder. This drive or folder contains several files and folders, and each folder contains related files and folders.

Using the file management tools, you save files in folders with appropriate names for easy identification, quickly and easily create new folders so you can reorganize information, delete files and folders that you no longer need, search for a file when you cannot remember where you stored it, create shortcuts to files and folders for quick and easy access, and compress files and folders to save space.

What You'll Do

Open and View Disks

View and Open Documents

Change the Window View

Arrange Files and Folders in Icons View

Work with Files and Folders in List View and Columns View

View Files with Cover Flow view

View Files Using Quick Look

Go to Common or Recent Places

Organize Files and Folders by Color

Create and Rename Files and Folders

Copy and Move Files and Folders

Use Spring-Loaded Folders

Share Files or Folders with Others

Delete and Restore Files and Folders

Get and Set File Information

Create a CD or DVD Using the Finder

Mount and Eject Disks

Opening and Viewing Disks

The desktop is the starting point to access every disk, folder, and file on your computer. When Finder Preferences are appropriately set to display desktop icons, the desktop displays several types of local, removable, and network drives. Drives and folders are represented by icons on the desktop. Each icon graphic represents a different type of disk. Disks are devices that store information used by the computer. The disk with the Mac OS X installed on it is called the **startup disk**, which is typically the hard disk inside your computer. The files related to Mac OS X are stored in the **System folder** on your startup disk. You should not move this folder or make any changes to its contents. Additional Mac OS X related files are stored in the **Library folder**, which stores system and application preference settings and files. Also on your startup disk is an **Applications folder** that contains the complete collection of Mac OS X programs on your computer. Lastly, the **Users folder** stores contents for individual user accounts on a shared computer. You double-click a disk icon, such as your hard disk or a removable disk, on the desktop to open a Finder window, displaying the contents of the disk. Once you open more than one drive or folder, you can use buttons on the toolbar to help you move quickly between folders.

Open and View Disks

1. If you want to view a disk, insert it in your drive.

 The removable disk appears on the desktop (if set in Finder Preferences) along with your other drivers, such as your hard disk or a network disk.

2. Double-click the drive icon on the desktop to open it.

 TIMESAVER *Press Shift+⌘+C or click the Go menu, and then click Computer to display disks.*

3. Double-click a folder icon in the Finder window to open it.

4. Click the **Back** or **Forward** buttons on the toolbar to return or move to a previously visited window.

 TIMESAVER *Hold down A and click a window's title bar to display a folder hierarchy menu.*

5. When you're done, click the **Close** button.

Drives on Computer

Did You Know?

You can display disk icons on the desktop. Click the Finder menu, click Preferences, click General, select the check boxes for the disk icons you want to show, and then click the Close button.

You can display icons in the Sidebar. Click the Finder menu, click Preferences, click Sidebar, select the check boxes for the icons you want to show, and then click the Close button.

You can open a disk or folder in a separate window. Click the Finder menu, click Preferences, click General, select the Always Open New Folders In A New Window check box, and then click the Close button.

An uneven CD or DVD may have trouble loading. If your CD or DVD drive seems to make vibrating noises, the disc's weight might be uneven. Sometimes with older drives, the CD or DVD won't load. If it does load, you're fine.

See Also

See "Changing the Window View" on page 30 for information on changing the display of a folder's contents.

See "Mounting and Ejecting Disks" on page 54 for information on using disks, CDs, and DVDs.

Typical Disks on a Computer

Icon	Type Description
	Local A hard magnetic disk (or hard disk) located inside your computer on which you can store large amounts of data. The disk stores all the files on your computer.
	External A hard magnetic disk (or hard disk) connected to your computer using a FireWire or USB plug. The disk provides extra storage.
	Network A hard magnetic disk (or hard disk) connected to your computer over a network. The disk provides extra storage and file sharing.
	iPod A portable hard magnetic disk that plays MP3 music and works with iTunes, which you can also use as a hard disk. The disk provides a compact, bootable hard drive.
	Removable A soft removable magnetic disk on which you can store 1 GB or more of computer data. USB drives are standard on all computers.
	Compact Disc-Read-Only Memory (CD-ROM) An optical disk on which you can read or copy up to 1 GB (typical size is 650, 700, or 740 MB) of data. The disc cannot be erased or burned with new data.
	Compact Disc-Recordable (CD-R) A non-reusable disc on which you can burn up to 1 GB (typical size is 650, 700, or 740 MB) of data in multiple sessions. The disc can be burned again with new data until full, but cannot be erased.
	Compact Disc-Rewritable (CD-RW) A reusable disc on which you can read, write, and erase data. Discs come in normal and high-speed formats (typical size is 650, 700, or 740 MB).
	Digital Video Disc (DVD) A disc that holds a minimum of 4.7 GB, enough for a full-length movie. The disc cannot be erased or burned with additional data.
	Digital Video Disc-Recordable (DVD-R) A non-reusable disc on which you can burn up to 4.7 GB of data in multiple sessions. The disc can be burned again with new data until full, but cannot be erased.
	Digital Video Disc-Rewritable (DVD-RW) A reusable disc on which you can read, write, and erase data. The disc holds up to 4.7 GB on each side.
	Flash A memory card the size of a large stamp that holds 128, 256, 512 MB, or greater. Flash drives connect directly into a USB plug and work on any Mac or Windows PC (no software required).

Viewing and Opening Documents

When you open a disk, the Finder window displays the contents of the disk, which includes files and folders containing information and software on your computer. Mac OS X creates a **Users folder** that contains a set of personal folders, known as the **Home folder**, for each user on a shared computer. The Home folder makes it easy to manage the personal and business files and folders you work with every day. The Home folder contains these folders: Desktop, Documents, Downloads, Library, Movies, Music, Pictures, Public, and Sites. Depending on your previous installation, devices installed, or other users, your personal folders might differ. You can quickly access your personal folders from the Favorites section (**New!**) of the Sidebar, including all files on your hard disk with the All My Files (**New!**) option. You can view file information, organize files and folders, and open files and folders. Once you open more than one folder, you can use buttons on the toolbar to help you move quickly between folders.

View and Open Documents

1. Double-click the Hard Disk icon on the desktop or in the Computer window.

 TIMESAVER *Press Shift+⇧⌘+C or click the Go menu, and then click Computer to display disks.*

2. In the Favorites section of the Sidebar, select from the following:
 - All My Files (**New!**)
 - Applications
 - Desktop
 - Documents
 - Downloads (**New!**)
 - Movies (**New!**)
 - Music (**New!**)
 - Pictures (**New!**)

3. To open a folder, double-click it.

4. If available, drag the scroll box, or click the scroll arrows to view additional documents.

5. To open a document, double-click the file to open its associated application and the document.

6. When you're done, click the **Close** button.

Did You Know?

You can quickly open the Home folder from the desktop. Press Shift+⌘+H. You can also click the desktop background, and then press ⌘+Up Arrow, which is the Enclosing Folder command on the Go menu. Since your Desktop folder is actually in your Home folder, using the command takes you back one folder level.

Your Favorites folder still exists. The Favorites folder from previous versions of the Mac OS is located in the Library folder of your Home folder. The Favorites folder contained links to your favorites files, folders, and Web sites in Microsoft Internet Explorer. If you want to use it, drag the Favorites folder to the Sidebar for quick and easy access.

See Also

See *"Changing the Window View"* on page 30 for information on changing the display of a folder's contents.

Folders in the Home Folder

Folder	Type Description
Desktop	Each users desktop is mirrored in this folder to keep one separate and maintain the unique custom look and feel.
Documents	A folder designated to store your personal documents and folders.
Downloads	A folder designated to store your items downloaded from the Internet.
Library	Each user maintains a personal Library folder, like the main Library folder for Mac OS X, to store your preferences, which includes fonts, e-mail, Internet bookmarks, keyboard layouts, and so on.
Movies	A folder designated to store your movie files; programs, iMovie, use this folder.
Music	A folder designated to store your music files; programs, iTunes, use this folder.
Pictures	A folder designated to store your picture files; programs, iPhoto, use this folder.
Public	A folder where you can place documents and folders that you can share with other users on your computer or a network.
Sites	A folder (if available with installation) where you can place Web pages that you can make available on the Internet, known as a **Web server.**

For Your Information

Opening a Document with a Different Program

Most documents on your computer are associated with a specific application. For example, if you double-click a document whose file name ends with the three-letter extension ".txt," Mac OS X automatically opens the document with TextEdit, a word processing application. There are situations, though, when you need to open a document with a program other than the one Mac OS X chooses, or when you want to choose a different default program. For example, you might want to open a text document in Microsoft Word rather than TextEdit so that you can take advantage of advanced features. To do this, Control-click the document icon you want to open, point to Open With, and then click the application you want to use to open the document, or drag the file onto the application icon in the Dock.

Changing the Window View

Mac OS X displays the contents of a drive or folder in different ways to help you find the information you're looking for about a file or folder. The available views include Icons, List, Columns, and Cover Flow. You can change the window view from the View menu, or you can click the View buttons on the Finder window toolbar.

Icons view displays icons, sorted alphabetically in horizontal rows, with the name of the file or folder below each icon. You can also customize the display to include information about the file next to each icon, or a miniature representation of the file or folder. A picture file displays a thumbnail preview of the image. A multi-page document or a QuickTime movie file allows you to thumb through the document or watch the movie. When you point to a multi-page document, such as a PDF, or a QuickTime move (.MOV), the thumbnail displays Previous and Next buttons or Play/Pause button, which you can click to view or play it as a thumbnail preview. The icon preview is also available in the Preview pane in Column and Cover Flow views. In

Icons view, you can drag the Zoom control slider on the Status bar to adjust the view percentage.

List view displays small icons, sorted alphabetically in a single vertical column with the name of the file or folder and additional information, such as date and size, in columns to the right.

Columns view displays icons, sorted alphabetically into vertical panes, or frames, which allows you to view information from two different locations. This arrangement enables you to view the file hierarchy of your computer and the contents of a folder simultaneously, making it easy to copy, move, delete, and rename files and folders.

Cover Flow view displays a flip through screen with a large preview of a documents first page at the top and displays list view at the bottom. This enables you to page through multipage documents or play movies. You can also display search results in an easy-to-read format.

Icons View

Point to icon to display buttons

Multi-page document QuickTime movie

30

Customize Views

Every window remembers its view settings independently. You might prefer to look at your Documents folder in List view, but your Applications folder in Columns view.

However, you can set view specific options to permanently customize the way you view icons in each view. In Icons view, you can change icon size, show item informa-tion or icon preview, label position, arrange-ment, and background. In List and Cover Flow views, you can change file size, date, and sta-tus related information. In Columns view, you can show icons and the preview column (summary information in the right column). See "Customizing Finder Window Views" on page 80 for more information about the spe-cific options.

List View

Columns View

Cover Flow View

Arranging Files and Folders in Icons View

When you select a folder view to display your files and folders, you can change the way individual files and folders are sorted by using the Arrange By button (**New!**) on the toolbar (all views) or Arrange By menu options on the View menu (Icons view only). You can sort the files by name, kind, application, date (several ways), size, or color label. In Icons view, you can have Mac OS X help you clean up your windows by automatically aligning icons to an invisible grid in rows and columns—which icons snap to when called to line up—by using Clean Up menu options (**New!**) on the View menu. The Arrange By button and menu options and the Clean Up commands are only temporary until you make changes to the window. If you want Mac OS X to automatically keep icons arranged or cleaned up, you need to select appropriate options using the Show View Options command on the View menu or use the Keep Arranged By menu options on the Action button (**New!**).

Arrange or Clean Up Items in Icons View

1 Display the desktop or open the folder you want to arrange.

2 To arrange icons, click a view icon, click the **Arrange By** button (**New!**) on the toolbar, and then click the view you want to use:

- ◆ **Name**
- ◆ **Kind**
- ◆ **Application** (**New!**)
- ◆ **Date Last Opened** (**New!**)
- ◆ **Date Added** (**New!**)
- ◆ **Date Last Modified**
- ◆ **Date Created**
- ◆ **Size**
- ◆ **Label**
- ◆ **None** (**New!**)

TIMESAVER *Press Control+⌘+1 (Name) thru 9 (Label) and Control+⌘+0 (None).*

3 Click the **Icons View** button on the toolbar.

4 To clean up icons, select the icons you want or deselect all, click the **View** menu, and then click **Clean Up** or **Clean Up Selection**.

Icons cleaned up by name

Did You Know?

You can override the grid settings as you drag. When the Snap To Grid setting is turned on (in Show View Options), pressing ⌘ lets you drag the icon freely; when the Snap To Grid setting is turned Off, pressing ⌘ snaps the icon to the grid. When you perform this operation, begin the drag before you press the ⌘ key.

You can use gestures in Icons view. In Icons view, you can swipe through rows of icons quickly (**New!**) using your Multi-Touch trackpad or Magic Mouse.

You can keep a folder arranged by a specified attribute. Open the folder in the Finder, click the Icons View button on the toolbar, click the Action button on the toolbar, point to Keep Arranged By (**New!**), and then click the view you want: Name, Date Modified, Date Created, Last Opened, Date Added, Size, Kind, and Label.

You can clean up folder icons by a specified attribute. Open the folder in the Finder, click the Icons View button on the toolbar, select icons as desired, click the View menu, point to Clean Up By (**New!**), and then click the view you want: Name, Date Modified, Date Created, Last Opened, Date Added, Size, Kind, and Label. You can also use shortcut keys: Option+⌘+1 (Name) thru 8 (Label).

See Also

See "Customizing Finder Window Views" on page 80 for information on setting options in Show View Options.

Options for Arranging Files and Folders

Option	Arranges Files and Folders
Name	Alphabetically
Kind	By type, such as all documents created using the TextEdit program.
Application (**New!**)	Chronologically by application type.
Date Last Opened (**New!**)	Chronologically by their last opened date.
Date Added (**New!**)	Chronologically by their last added to folder date.
Date Last Modified (**New!**)	Chronologically by their last modification date, with the latest modification date listed last.
Date Created	Chronologically by their creation date.
Size	By size, with the largest folder or file listed first.
Label	By color label
None (**New!**)	Not arranged by attribute.

For Your Information

Compressing Files and Folders to Save Space

You can compress files and folders into a single file using Stuffit compression software to decrease their size. Compressed folders are useful for reducing the file size of one or more large files, thus freeing disk space and reducing the time it takes to transfer files to another computer over the Internet or network. When a file is compressed, a copy is used in the compression, and the original remains intact. You can uncompress, or extract, a file from the compressed file and open it as you normally would. See "Compressing and Uncompressing Files and Folders" on page 435, and "Opening Compressed Files" on page 434 for more information about compressing and uncompressing files and folders.

Working with Files and Folders in List View

You can display files and folders in a variety of different ways, depending on what you want to see and do. When you view files and folders in List view, a default list of file and folder information appears, which consists of Name, Date Modified, Size, and Kind. If the default list of file and folder details doesn't provide you with the information you need, you can add and remove any file and folder information using Show View Options. If you need to change the way Mac OS X sorts your files and folders, you can use the column header buttons. Clicking on one of the column header buttons (such as Name, Date Modified, Size, or Kind) in List view, sorts the files and folders by the type of information listed in the column. If the columns are not organized in the order you want, you can use the mouse to quickly rearrange columns. If you see an ellipsis in a column, it is too small to display all the information in it. You can drag the column divider to change column sizes all at once or individually.

Show and Hide Folders in List View

1. Open the folder you want to view.

2. Click the **List View** button on the toolbar.

3. Click the triangle (pointing right) next to a folder in the list.

 TIMESAVER *Select the folder, and then press* ⌘*+Right Arrow.*

 The folder expands to display an indented list of folders and files from within the folder.

4. Click the triangle (pointing down) next to a folder in the list.

 TIMESAVER *Select the folder, and then press* ⌘*+Left Arrow.*

 The folder collapses.

Drag to change column width

Did You Know?

You can quickly show the full text with ellipsis. Point to the icon's name without clicking for a moment to display a balloon. Hold down the Option key to display it immediately.

Sort Files and Folders by Column in List View

1. Open the folder you want to view.

2. Click the **List View** button on the toolbar.

3. Click the column header name to sort the file and folder in ascending or descending order.

4. To reverse the column sort, click the column header name again.

Rearrange and Widen Columns

1. Open the folder you want to view.

2. Click the **List View** or **Cover Flow View** button on the toolbar.

3. To rearrange columns, drag the column header to a new position.

4. To change the width of columns, drag the column divider.

The width of the column changes and all the columns to the right shift based on the change.

Viewing Files with Cover Flow

Just as you use Cover Flow to flip through album art in iTunes, now you can use it to flip through your files. Cover Flow view displays a flip through screen with a large preview of a documents first page at the top and displays List view at the bottom. Cover Flow enables you to page through multipage documents or play movies. You can also display search results in an easy-to-read format. List view at the bottom of Cover Flow displays a default list of file and folder information, which consists of Name, Date Modified, Size, and Kind.

View Files with Cover Flow

① Open the folder you want to view.

② Click the **Cover Flow View** button on the toolbar.

③ Use either one of the following methods to display a file in Cover Flow.

◆ **Top pane.** Click the item, either slide of slider, or drag the slider to display the file you want.

◆ **Bottom pane.** Click the triangle (pointing right) next to a folder in the list to display an indented list of folders and files from within the folder, and then select the file you want to display.

Top pane

Drag to collapse/expand top pane

Drag to scroll through cover flow

Bottom pane

See Also

See "Working with Files and Folders in List View" on page 34 for information on using List view.

Working with Files and Folders in Columns View

Columns view makes is easy to display several levels of folders in alphabetical order at the same time within the same window. Column view displays the window in panes, which allows you to view information from different locations making it easy to copy, move, delete, and rename files and folders. When you click a disk or folder in the first pane, the second pane shows a list of all the folders in it. Each time you click a folder in one pane, the pane to its right shows its contents. The other panes slide to the left, in some cases, out of view, which you can scroll back to display them. When you find and click the file you want, the next pane to the right, the **Preview column**, shows a file icon and information about it. If the file is a picture or PDF, the Finder displays the picture or PDF miniature. If the file is a sound or movie, you can play it in the Finder window.

View Folders in Column View

1. Open the folder you want to view.

2. Click the **Columns View** button on the toolbar.

3. Double-click the folder you want to open in a pane.

 The contents of the folder appears in the next pane to the right.

4. To resize a column, drag its right-side handle.

5. Click the file you want to view in the Preview column.

Preview column

Keyboard Options for Columns View

Option	Description
Left or Right Arrow	Jumps one pane to the left or right
Up or Down Arrow	Within a pane, moves up or down to select an item

Viewing Files Using Quick Look

Quick Look allows you to view the contents of a file or folder without opening it or starting an application. Quick Looks works almost every where from files in iChat to files in Open dialogs (**New!**), not to mention get info on folders and hard disks. Content types (**New!**) include web pages in e-mail, addresses as Google Maps, Address Book contacts, and Spotlight results. If you select a single or multipage text document, you can read the text and scroll through it; if you select a video, you can play it. When you select more than one image or item, you can display a slide show and use arrow buttons to move from slide to slide. If you like to use gestures (**New!**) on a Multi-Touch trackpad, you can swipe to navigate between images and pages in a PDF or iWork document.

View Files Using Quick Look

1. Open the folder you want to view.

2. Select the one or more files or folder you want to view.

3. Press the Spacebar.

 ◆ You can also click the **Action** button on the toolbar, and then click **Quick Look** (if you select items, a number appears), or click the **Quick Look** button on a customized toolbar.

 TIMESAVER *Press* ⌘*+Y to display and exit Quick Look.*

4. If you selected more than one item or image, use the follow buttons to navigate through the items.

 ◆ **Previous and Next.** Navigate from slide to slide.

 ◆ **Index.** Display a pictorial index of the selected images or items. Click an index item to display it.

 ◆ **Plus.** Open the file in a matching application (**New!**).

5. To open the selected item, click the **Open with Preview** button.

6. To view the selected item in full screen, click the **Full Screen** button. To exit back, click the **Exit Full Screen** button.

7. When you're done, click the **Close** button or press the Spacebar.

Quick Look button

Use a swipe gesture to navigate between images, and pages in a PDF or iWork document.

Going to Common or Recent Places

Mac OS X keeps a list of your most recently used files, folders, and network computers. Instead of navigating through a long list of folders to open a recently used file, you can use the Recent Folders list to find it quickly. If you want to go to a common location, such as your computer, network connections, iDisk, Home folder, Desktop folder, Applications folder, Documents folder, Downloads folder (**New!**), Utilities folder, All My Files folder (**New!**), or one you specify, the Go menu makes it quick and easy. After you have opened several folders, you can use the secret folder hierarchy menu in a window's title bar to quickly go backwards through the chain of folders.

Go Places

1. Click the **Go** menu.

2. Select any of the following:

 ◆ **Common locations.** Click the name of the place.

 ◆ **Recent folders.** Point to **Recent Folders**, and then click the name of the folder.

 ◆ **Specific folder.** Click **Go to Folder**, type a path location, and then click **Go**. You can use the tilde (~) to indicate the Home folder, "~/Documents/".

3. To go backwards through the folders, hold down ⌘, click the window's title bar, and then click a location from the folder hierarchy menu.

 TIMESAVER *Press ⌘+[to go Back a folder; press ⌘+] to go Forward a folder.*

4. When you're done, click the **Close** button.

Did You Know?

You can quickly open recent applications and documents. Click the Apple menu, point to Recent Items, and then click the recently used application or document you want to open.

Organizing Files and Folders by Color

Giving an icon or folder a distinctive color can help you organize and find them later. Mac OS X provides seven different colors labels from which to select. The default color label names appear as Red, Orange, Yellow, Green Blue, Purple, and Gray, but you can customize them to suit your own needs and preferences, such as "Final," "In Progress," "Work," "Personal," and "Backup." When you change an icon's color, the icon and name take on the selected color shade. In List or Column view, the entire row takes on the color shade. In List view, you can sort files and folders quickly by color label. Sorting by color label also lets you create alphabetical groups within for color label in a single list. You can also use color labels with the Find command to search for files and folders with a particular color label.

Color a File or Folder Icon

1. Open the folder window with the file or folder icons you want to color.

2. Select the icons you want to color.

3. Click the **Action** button, and then click the color label you want.

 TIMESAVER *You can also use the File menu, or Control-click to access the color labels.*

4. When you're done, click the **Close** button.

Did You Know?

You can quickly take off a color.
Control-click the icon, and then click No Color (the x under Color Label).

See Also

See "Searching for Files Using the Find Window" on page 66 for information on searching for files and folders by color label.

Select a color

Blue color for icons

40

Sort a List View by Label

① Open the folder window with the file or folder icons you want to sort by color.

② Click the **List View** button.

③ Click the Label column heading.

The files and folder are sorted by color. Within each color, the files and folder are sorted in alphabetical order.

④ When you're done, click the **Close** button.

Name	Date Modified	Size
Photo Booth Library	May 2, 2011 9:38 AM	8 bytes
▶ 📁 Mission	May 12, 2011 4:32 PM	--
📁 iChat Icons	May 30, 2010 7:51 AM	47 bytes
▼ 📁 Garden	Oct 1, 2007 2:01 PM	--
Yellow Rose.jpg	Oct 9, 2003 1:39 PM	93 KB
White Flowers.jpg	Oct 9, 2003 1:41 PM	155 KB
Red Rose.jpg	Oct 9, 2003 1:40 PM	104 KB
Purple Flowers.jpg	Oct 9, 2003 1:41 PM	102 KB
Pink Rose.jpg	Oct 9, 2003 1:40 PM	127 KB
Iris.jpg	Jan 17, 2004 12:31 AM	75 KB
Flower Pond.jpg	Nov 17, 2007 8:06 PM	2.4 MB
Flower & Bug.jpg	Nov 17, 2007 8:07 PM	1.9 MB
Fish Pond.jpg	Nov 17, 2007 8:06 PM	2.3 MB
▶ 📁 Family	Oct 14, 2007 1:35 PM	--

14 Items, 118.47 GB available

Did You Know?

You need to display the label column before you can sort by color. In List view, click the View menu, click Show View Options, select the Labels check box, and then click the Close button.

Change Color Label Names

① Click the **Finder** menu, and then click **Preferences**.

② Click **Labels**.

③ Change the color names with ones that convey more meaning.

When you go back to List view, instead of seeing the color names, you'll see your new names (such as Personal, Work, In Progress).

④ Click the **Close** button.

Finder Preferences

General Labels Sidebar Advanced

Use these label names:

Final

In Progress

Work

Personal

Backup

Purple

Gray

Creating and Renaming Files and Folders

The keys to organizing files and folders effectively within a hierarchy are to store related items together and to name folders informatively. Creating a new folder can help you organize and keep track of files and other folders. In order to create a folder, you select the location where you want the new folder, create the folder, and then lastly, name the folder. You can also select files first, and then create a folder (**New!**). You should name each folder meaningfully, so that just by reading the folder's name you know its contents. After you name a folder or file, you can rename it at any time.

Create a Folder

1. Open the drive or folder where you want to create a folder.

 ◆ To create a folder with a selection, select the files you want to use.

2. Click the **File** menu, and then click **New Folder** or **New Folder with Selection (# Items)** (**New!**).

 TROUBLE? *If the New Folder command is grayed out, you don't have permission to create a folder in the folder. Click the File menu, and then click Get Info to change permissions.*

3. With the new folder name selected, type a new name.

4. Press Return.

Untitled new folder

Did You Know?

File names can be up to 255 characters. You can use spaces and underscores in names, but you can't use a colon (:). If you are going to use these files on a Windows PC, then don't use the following characters: * : < > | ? " \ or /. It's probably best to keep the name descriptive, but short. This allows you to view the file name in all view settings.

Rename a File or Folder

1. Open the drive or folder with the file or folder you want to rename.

2. Click the file or folder to select it.

3. To erase the entire current name, press Return.

 TROUBLE? *If you can't change the name of a file or folder, you may not have permission to make changes to the item. Click the File menu, and then click Get Info to change permissions.*

4. With the name selected, type a new name, or click to position the insertion point, and then edit the name.

 IMPORTANT *If extensions are showing, changing the name doesn't change the extension as long as the extension stays the same. If you change the extension, the file type changes and you may not be able to open the file with the application in which it was created.*

5. Press Return.

 The file may move to a location based on sort and view.

See Also

See "Showing or Hiding File Extensions" on page 79 for information on file extensions.

For Your Information

Correcting Your Most Recent Action in the Finder

Everyone makes mistakes and changes their mind at some point, especially when you make changes in the Finder. You can instantly correct your most recent action by using the Undo command (⌘+Z) on the Edit menu. If you change your mind about undoing an action, you can just as easily use the Redo command (⌘+Y) to restore the action you reversed.

Copying and Moving Files and Folders

Sometimes you'll need to move a file from one folder to another, or copy a file from one folder to another, leaving the file in the first location and placing a copy of it in the second. If the file or folder and the location where you want to move it are visible in a window or on the desktop, you can simply drag the item from one location to the other. When you drag multiple items, they flock together; the cursor indicates how many files (**New!**). Moving a file or folder on the same disk relocates it, whereas dragging it from one disk to another copies it so that it appears in both locations. When the destination folder or drive is not visible, you can use the Cut (to move), Copy, and Paste commands on the Edit menu to move or copy the items.

Copy or Move a File or Folder

1. Open the drive or folder containing the file or folder you want to copy or move.

2. Select the files or folders you want to copy.

3. Click the **Edit** menu, and then click **Cut** (to move) or **Copy**.

 TIMESAVER Press ⌘+X to move or press ⌘+C to copy.

4. Navigate to the drive or folder containing the folder where you want to copy or move the items.

5. Click the **Edit** menu, and then click **Paste**.

 TIMESAVER Press ⌘+V to paste.

 TROUBLE? If you can't copy a file or folder, click the File menu, and then click Get Info to change permissions.

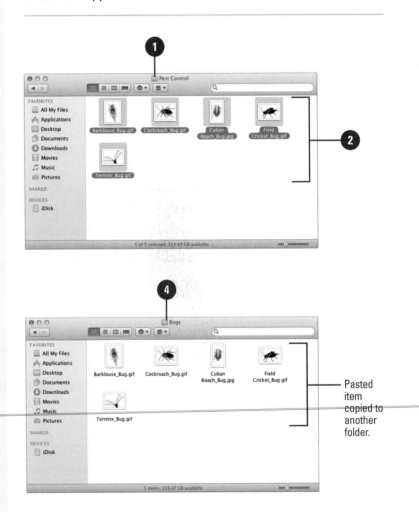

Pasted item copied to another folder.

Did You Know?

You need certain permissions to move or copy a file. You need Read Only or Read & Write permissions to the item you want to move or copy. You need Read & Write Only access to the location where you want to place it.

Copy or Move a File or Folder Using Drag and Drop

① Open the drive or folder containing the files and folders you want to move or copy.

② Drag the selection onto a folder, an icon in the Sidebar, or the desktop.

To copy files and folder, hold down the Option key while you drag.

When you drag multiple items, they flock together; the cursor indicates how many files (**New!**).

IMPORTANT *If you pause for a few moments on the destination folder (when spring-loaded folders is turned on) the destination folder automatically opens.*

③ Release the items.

④ If you add a file to a folder that contains a file of the same name (**New!**), click **Keep Both Files**, **Stop**, or **Replace**. Keeping both add "copy" to the end of the name.

⑤ If you add a folder to a folder that contains a folder of the same name (**New!**), click **Stop** or **Replace**.

See Also

See "Using Spring-Loaded Folders" on page 46 for information on copying and moving items using spring-loaded folders.

Flocking files

For Your Information

Moving and Copying Items Using Mission Control

Exposé in Mission Control can make it easier to move and copy files and folders using drag and drop. To move or copy items between open windows, start to drag the items (hold down the Option key to copy or hold down ⌘+Option to create an alias), press F9 (show all open windows) or F10 (show all open windows in the same application), point to the window where you want to move or copy the item, release F9 or F10, and then drag some more or release the items. A similar process works moving or copying items to the desktop using F11. The Mission Control shortcut keys can be changed, so check System Preferences if they are not working properly.

Using Spring-Loaded Folders

When you are moving or copying files and folders around, it can be tiresome to drag a selection to a folder, open the folder, and then continue to drag it to another folder. Spring-loaded folders allow you to drag a file or folder on top of another folder and it springs open to let you continue dragging the selection to another location in one continuous motion. When you drag a selection onto a folder (or even an icon in the Sidebar) and pause for a moment (with the mouse pressed), the window for the folder opens, so you can continue to drag to another folder as desired. You can use Finder Preferences to turn spring-loaded folders on and off, and set the delay setting for the amount of time you want to pause. If you set a long delay or turn off spring-loaded folders, you can press the Spacebar while you drag a selection to open the window immediately. The Spacebar method is useful because windows don't automatically open when you don't want them to, yet you still have the option to use spring-loaded folders when you need it.

Use Spring-Loaded Folders

1. Open the drive or folder containing the files and folders you want to move or copy.

2. To move, drag the selection onto a folder or an icon in the Sidebar. To copy, hold down the Option key while you drag.

3. Press the Spacebar, or pause for a few moments.

 The folder window automatically opens centered on your cursor:

 ◆ **In Icons view**, the new window replaces the previous window.

 ◆ **In List view**, a new window opens.

 ◆ **In Columns view**, a new column opens, displaying the new folder's contents.

Drag continues in spring-loaded folder.

Did You Know?

You can set the spring-loaded delay.
Click the Finder menu, click Preferences, click General, drag the Delay slider, and then click the Close button.

Sharing Files or Folders with Others

Mac OS X maintains a set of personal folders and options for everyone on your computer to make sure the contents remain private, unless you decide to share the contents with others. If you want the other users on your computer, or those connected to your computer over a network to have access to files, you can place those files in the Shared folder that each user can access. The Shared folder is located in the Users folder. It is set up with Read & Write permissions so that all users can open the files in this folder and copy files to the folder. If you want to share files with a specific user on your computer, you can use their Public folder. A Public folder is set up with Read Only permissions that allow others to see and copy its contents, but not change it. Each Public folder is located in the users' Home folder and also contains a Drop Box folder, which is set up with tighter permissions so other people can copy files to a Drop Box, but they cannot see its contents.

Share Files in the Shared Folder or a Public Folder

1. Open the drive or folder containing the files or folders you want to share.

2. Select the files or folders you want to share.

3. Click the **Edit** menu, and then click **Copy** or press ⌘+C to copy.

 TIMESAVER *Press ⌘+C to copy.*

4. Click the **Go** menu, click **Computer**, and then double-click the **Hard Disk** icon for your computer.

5. Double-click the **Users** folder.

6. Open the folder you want to use to share files:

 ◆ **Shared folder**. Double-click the Shared folder.

 ◆ **Public folder**. Double-click the user name, and then double-click the Public folder.

7. Click the **Edit** menu, and then click **Paste** or press ⌘+V to paste.

8. To use the Drop Box folder in a Public folder, drag the files and folder onto the Drop Box folder.

Users folder Shared folder for the computer.

Public folder resides in each users folder.

eyJmb290ZXJfbmF2aWdhdGlvbiI6dHJ1ZX0=

Deleting and Restoring Files and Folders

When you organize the contents of a folder, disk, or the desktop, you might find files and folders that you no longer need. You can delete these items or remove them from the disk. If you delete a file or folder from the desktop or from the hard disk, it goes into the Trash. The **Trash**, located on the right side of the Dock, is a temporary storage area for deleted files. The Trash stores all the items you delete from your hard disk so that if you accidentally delete an item, you can remove it from the Trash to restore it. You can use the Put Back command to restore a deleted item to it's original folder. Be aware that if you delete a file from a removable disk, it is permanently deleted, not stored in the Trash. The files in the Trash do occupy room on your computer, so you need to empty it to free up space.

Delete Files and Folders

1. Select the files and folders you want to delete.

 TROUBLE? *If an item is locked, you can't put it in the Trash. Click the File menu, and then click Get Info to unlock it.*

2. Drag the selection to the Trash in the Dock.

 TIMESAVER *Press ⌘+Delete key to delete selected items.*

3. Click the **Finder** menu, and then click **Empty Trash**.

 TIMESAVER *Click the Trash icon in the Dock, and then click Empty Trash, or press Shift+⌘ +Delete to empty the trash.*

4. Click **Empty Trash** to confirm the deletion.

 TIMESAVER *Press Shift+⌘ Option+Delete to empty the trash and skip the warning dialog.*

Are you sure you want to permanently erase the items in the Trash?

You can't undo this action.

Cancel Empty Trash

Restore Files and Folders

1 In the Dock, click the **Trash** icon.

2 Select the item or items you want to restore.

3 Click the **File** menu, and then click **Put Back** or drag the items back to their original folder or any other location.

The items are restored to their original location with the Put Back command or to a dragged location.

4 When you're done, click the **Close** button for the Trash window.

Did You Know?

You can uninstall software using the Trash. There's no uninstall program for Mac OS X. To uninstall a software, drag its folder from the Applications folder to the Trash icon in the Dock.

You can undo a deletion. If you accidentally delete a file, click the Edit menu, and then click Undo Delete. Mac OS X remembers your last three actions.

You can still recover deleted files after you empty the Trash in some cases. If you install special data recovery software, you still may be able to recover deleted files.

You can turn off the empty Trash warning. Click the Finder menu, click Preferences, click Advanced, clear the Show Warning Before Emptying The Trash check box, and then click the Close button.

For Your Information

Deleting Files Securely and Forever

If you are selling or giving away your computer, you can securely delete files and folders from your hard disk without any possibility of recovery. Drag the files and folders you want securely deleted into the Trash, click the Finder menu, click Secure Empty Trash, and then click Secure Empty Trash to confirm the deletion. Files securely deleted are completely overwritten by meaningless data, which may take a few moments or minutes to complete depending on the size of the files.

Getting and Setting File Information

You can get information about a hard disk, removable disk, network disk, application, folder, or file using the Info window. The Info window displays information about the kind, size, location, date created, and date modified. If you select a disk, the Info window also includes information about format, capacity, available space, and used space. In addition to displaying information, you can also use the Info window to add Spotlight text to enhance searches, create a stationery file, lock an item, change a files name and extension, determine which application to open a file with, change its ownership and permissions, and write a comment. When you set a file as stationery, the file opens as an untitled copy of the original, so the original file doesn't get changed. If you want to see information for different items without having to close the Info window, you can use Show Inspector to keep the Info window open while you select different items.

Display Info Window

1. Select the files, disks, folders, applications, or alias; don't select anything to get desktop info.

2. Use one of the following methods:

 ◆ **Separate window for each item**. Click the **File** menu, and then click **Get Info**.

 A separate Info window appears for each selected item. This is useful for comparing settings and information.

 ◆ **Single window for all items**. Hold down the Option key, click the **File** menu, and then click **Show Inspector**.

 A single Info window appears, displaying statistics (by type and size) about the selected items and options common to all the selected items. This is useful for setting the same option for a lot of items, such as locking or unlocking files.

3. Click the expand button (triangle) to display category options, or the collapse button (down arrow) to hide them.

4. When you're done, click the **Close** button.

Add text for use in Spotlight searches.

Separate window for each item.

Expanded pane

Single window for multiple items.

Collapsed pane

Set Info Window Options

① Select the files, disks, folders, or applications you want to set.

② Click the expand button (triangle) for a category.

③ Change the options you want:

◆ **Comments**. Add your own comments, which you can display in List view and use in Spotlight searches.

◆ **General**. View information about the selected items; create a Stationery Pad (a file opens as untitled); and lock or unlock a file.

◆ **More Info**. View information (varies) about the selected item.

◆ **Name & Extension**. Read and edit item name and extension; and hide extensions.

◆ **Content Index**. Index a disk or folder for better search results.

◆ **Memory**. Set memory options for Classic applications only.

◆ **Open With**. Specify which application opens when you double-click an icon.

◆ **Preview**. Display magnified picture thumbnails or play sounds and movies.

◆ **Languages**. Add or remove languages for an application.

◆ **Sharing & Permission**. Set read and write access privileges.

④ When you're done, click the **Close** button.

See Also

See "Setting File Access Permissions" on page 390 for information on setting file permissions and ownership.

Comments

General

Name & Extension

Open With

Sharing & Permissions

Creating a CD or DVD Using the Finder

The low cost and large storage size of CDs or DVDs (getting cheaper), and the popularity of recording hardware make using CDs and DVDs an effective approach to some file management tasks. For example, CDs or DVDs are an effective way to back up information or transfer information to another computer without a network or to a Microsoft Windows computer. Before you can create a CD or DVD, you must have blank CDs or DVDs and a CD-RW or DVD-RW drive (also known as a writer or burner) installed on your computer. You can copy or write files and folders to either CD-Rs or DVD-Rs (recordable) or CD-RWs or DVD-RWs (rewritable). With recordables, you can write files and folders only once and read them many times, but you can't erase them. With rewritables, you can read, write, and erase files and folders many times, just like a removable disk. When you write to, or **burn**, a CD or DVD, Mac OS X needs disk space on your hard disk to temporarily store files during the process, so make sure you have free hard disk space available for the size of the CD or DVD. Do not copy more files and folders to the CD or DVD than it will hold; anything beyond the limit will not copy. When the burn is complete, you can use the CD or DVD on a Macintosh or Windows PC appropriately equipped. You can also use other Mac OS X applications with disc burning features, such as iTunes, iPhoto, iDVD, or Disk Utility, to create specialized CDs or DVDs.

Prepare to Burn a CD or DVD

1. Insert a blank CD-R, CD-RW, DVD-R, or DVD-RW disc into your drive.

 If you insert a CD-RW disc that you previously recorded, the dialog doesn't appear; you need to erase the disc with Disk Utility before you can burn data on it again.

 TROUBLE? *If the dialog doesn't appear, click the Apple menu, click Preferences, click CDs & DVDs, select the options you want, and then click the Close button.*

2. Click the **Action** pop-up, and then click **Open Finder**.

3. Select or clear the **Make this action the default** check box.

4. Click **OK**.

 The blank disc appears on the desktop, where you can add and remove files and folders.

Add and Remove Files and Folders to a CD or DVD

1. Open a Finder window.

2. Navigate to the files and folders you want to add to the CD or DVD disc.

3. Drag the files and folders to the CD or DVD disc in the Sidebar, and then organize them.

 IMPORTANT *If you're using these files on a Windows PC, make sure the file names don't include \ / : * ? " < > |, otherwise you can't open them.*

4. To remove files and folders, click the CD or DVD disc in the Sidebar, or double-click the disc on the desktop, and then drag out the items you don't want.

Create a CD or DVD

1. If you want, rename the CD or DVD disc just like any other file.

2. Use any of the following methods to create a CD or DVD:

 ◆ **Drag to Trash.** When you drag a disk icon onto the **Trash** icon, it changes to a Burn icon.

 ◆ **Burn command.** Select the disk icon, click the **File** menu, and then click **Burn**.

 ◆ **Sidebar Burn button.** Click the Burn button in the Sidebar.

3. Type a name for the disc.

4. Click the **Burn Speed** pop-up, and then select a speed.

5. Select the Save **Burn Folder To** check box, and then type a name to create a burn folder.

6. Click **Burn**.

Burn command on File menu CD to burn

Sidebar Burn button Drag to Trash

Mounting and Ejecting Disks

When you insert a disk (such as a removable, CD, or DVD), its icon appears, or **mounts**, in the Computer window, in the Sidebar, and on the desktop (unless you've changed Finder Preferences) for you to open and use. When you no longer need a disk, you eject, or dismount, it from the drive. Mac OS X provides several different ways to eject a disk: drag the disk icon to the Trash (only happens for disks; a little strange, but its old time Mac functionality), use the Eject menu, select the Eject command, use the Sidebar, or hold down the Eject key. You can also use these methods to remove, or **unmount**, a network or FireWire drive, an iPod, or a disk image from your desktop.

Mount and Eject Disks

1. Insert the disk into the appropriate drive to mount the disk.

2. Use any of the following methods to eject a disk:

 ◆ **Drag to Trash.** When you drag a disk icon onto the **Trash** icon in the Dock, it changes to an Eject icon.

 ◆ **Eject command.** Select the disk icon, click the **File** menu, and then click **Eject**. You can also Control-click the disk icon, and then click **Eject**.

 ◆ **Eject menu.** Click the **Eject** menu, and then click **Eject "*disc name*"** or press F12.

 ◆ **Sidebar Eject button.** Click the **Eject** button in the Sidebar.

 ◆ **Eject key.** Press and hold down the Media Eject key in the upper-right corner of your keyboard (if available) for a moment, or press F12.

 TROUBLE? *If a CD or DVD doesn't eject, insert a straightened paper clip into the small hole on the front of the drive, or click the Apple menu, click Restart, and hold down the mouse button until it ejects before the restart.*

Eject menu

Eject button

54

Finding What You Want with Spotlight

3

Introduction

If you're looking for specific content on your computer or network and you don't know where to find it, you can use Spotlight to help you locate it. Spotlight not only searches the names of your files and folders, it also searches their content. In addition, Spotlight searches other information stored in files, known as **metadata**, which describes how and when and by whom a particular set of data was collected, or how the data is formatted. Examples of metadata include authors, page size, creation and modification dates, duration of music and movies, dimensions of graphics or PDF documents, exposure time of a camera lens for photographs, and names of layers in Photoshop.

Spotlight is conveniently located on the right side of the menu bar on your Mac screen. You can identify Spotlight by the blue icon with a magnifying glass. Spotlight performs a live search of your Home folder on your computer using the information you know. As you type in Spotlight, a menu appears displaying a list of everything Spotlight can find to match what you've typed so far. As you continue to type, the list changes. Spotlight searches for everything on your computer that matches what you've typed, which includes every file, folder, program, e-mail message, address book entry, calendar appointment, picture, movie, PDF document, music file, Web bookmark, Microsoft Office document, and System Preferences panel, and lists the 20 best matches divided into categories, which you can customize later.

When you start Mac OS X for the first time, Spotlight automatically starts collecting search information about your Home folder, known as **indexing**. The indexing process initially takes about 15 to 30 minutes to perform (the Spotlight icon pulses) and then updates take place as needed. Indexing the information on your computer reduces the time it takes to perform a search.

What You'll Do

Find Information Using Spotlight

Find Information in the Spotlight Window

Filter Spotlight Results

Group and Sort Spotlight Results

Work with Spotlight Results

Set Spotlight Preferences

Search for Files Using the Find Window

Search for Hard to Find Information

Work with Find Window Results

Create and Use Smart Folders

Get Help While You Work

Get Help Using Spotlight

Finding Information Using Spotlight

If you're looking for specific content on your computer and you don't know where to find it, you can use Spotlight to help you find it. Even if you can only remember part of the content. Spotlight performs a live search of your Home folder on your computer using the information you know. As you type in Spotlight, a menu appears displaying a list of everything Spotlight can find to match what you've typed so far. As you continue to type, the list changes. If you type two words, Spotlight finds items that contain both words. Spotlight searches for everything on your computer that matches what you've typed, which includes every file, folder, program, e-mail message, address book entry, calendar appointment, to-do item, picture, movie, PDF document, music file, Web bookmark, document, and System Preferences panel, and lists the 20 best matches divided into categories, which you can customize later. Spotlight not only searches the names of your files and folders, it also searches their content, and displays a preview of the material (**New!**) from the menu. In addition, you can drag items from the Spotlight menu (**New!**) for use in folder or on the desktop. You can search by typing phrases or metadata attributes, and using boolean operators.

Find Information Using Spotlight

1. Click the **Spotlight** (magnifying-glass) icon on the right side of the menu bar.

 TIMESAVER *Press* ⌘+Space bar to open Spotlight.

2. In the Spotlight field, start to type what you want to find. To find a specific phrase, place quotes around it.

 As you type, a menu begins to display a list of everything Spotlight can find to match what you've typed so far. As you continue to type, the list changes.

3. To preview an item (**New!**), point to the item in the list.

4. To copy an item (**New!**), drag the item off the Spotlight list.

5. To open an item, click the item or use the arrow keys to scroll down the list, and then press Return.

6. To clear or stop a search, click the **Close** button (x) in the Spotlight field.

Wikipedia

Preview of search item

Find Information with Metadata Using Spotlight

1 Click the **Spotlight** (magnifying-glass) icon on the right side of the menu bar.

TIMESAVER *Press* ⌘+Space bar to open Spotlight.

2 In the Spotlight field, type *code:keyword*. Use quotation marks around text to search for an exact phrase.

Where the code is a category, such as *kind*, *date*, *modified*, or *author*, and keyword is a specific type of category.

Here are some examples:

◆ ***kind:preference network*** displays the network system preference on your computer.

◆ ***kind:contact steve*** displays all the contacts with the name steve on your computer.

◆ ***kind:music by:"Bruce Springsteen"*** displays all music by Bruce Springsteen.

◆ ***date:today kind:email*** displays all the email for today on your computer.

Did You Know?

You can quickly cancel a Spotlight search. Press the Esc key to close the Spotlight menu and erase what you've typed. Now, you can type a new search. Press the Esc key again to cancel the entire search. To cancel the entire search in one step, press ⌘+Space bar again, ⌘+period, or ⌘+Esc.

Find Code and Keywords

Find	Code:Keyword
Program	kind:app, kind:application
Address book contact	kind:contact
Folder	kind:folder
Mail message	kind:email, kind:mail message
iCal appointment	kind:event
iCal task	kind:to do, kind:todo
Image, picture	kind:image
Movie	kind:movie
Music or Sound	kind:music, kind:audio
PDF file	kind:pdf
System Preference	kind:preference, kind:system preference
Safari bookmark	kind:bookmark
Font	kind:font
Presentation	kind:presentation
Week	date:this week, date:next week
Month	date:this month, date:next month
Year	date:this year, date:next year
Today	date:today
Tomorrow	date:tomorrow
Yesterday	date:yesterday

For Your Information

Using Boolean Operators to Help Your Search

If you can't find the information you are looking for using the Spotlight field or Search field, you can use boolean operators (AND, OR, NOT, and dash (-) for AND NOT to exclude items) to refine your help search. For example, typing **report AND proposal** finds both words, typing **report OR proposal** finds either *report* or *proposal*, while typing **report NOT proposal** finds *report*, but excludes *proposal*. If you type **report -proposal**, Spotlight finds *report* but not *proposal*. You can also use keywords in your search with boolean operators. For example, typing **kind:pdf report AND kind:presentation proposal**, finds PDF documents with *report* and presentation files with *proposal*.

Finding Information in the Spotlight Window

If you can't find what you're looking for on the Spotlight menu with the 20 most likely matches, you can click the Show All in Finder command at the top of the Spotlight menu to open the Spotlight window and view the complete list of matches organized by category. The Show All in Finder command displays the results of your search by retrieving content on your entire computer that matches the criteria. The Search bar, located below the toolbar, indicates the search location and type, which is "This Mac," folder or disk name, such as "Documents" or "All My Files" (**New**!), and "Shared" by default. You can search your entire computer (This Mac), your Home folder (All My Files), or shared network computer by the file name and the contents of a file.

Open and View the Spotlight Window to Locate Information

1. Click the **Spotlight** (magnifying-glass) icon on the right side of the menu bar.

 TIMESAVER *Press* Option+⌘+Space bar to open Spotlight window directly.

2. In the Spotlight field, start to type what you want to find.

3. Click **Show All in Finder** on the Spotlight menu.

 The Spotlight window opens, displaying the results of your search by category.

 If a search is currently in progress, a sprocket icon whirls around in the upper-left window corner.

4. To narrow or change the search, type the text you want to find in the Search field.

5. To open an item, double-click the item or use the arrow keys to scroll down the list, and then press Return.

6. To clear or stop a search, click the **Close** button (x) in the Search field.

7. When you're done, click the **Close** button.

Narrow Results in the Spotlight Window

1. Press Option+⌘+Space bar or click **Show All in Finder** on the Spotlight menu to open the Spotlight window.

 The Spotlight window opens, displaying the results of your search by category.

 If a search is currently in progress, a sprocket icon whirls around in the upper-left corner of the window.

2. In the Search bar, click the button with the search location you want:

 ◆ **This Mac.** Searches all the disks on your computer.

 ◆ **All My Files.** Searches your Home folder.

 ◆ **Server, Volume** or **Folder Name.** Searches only the currently opened server, volume, or folder. The item name appears in quotes in the Search bar.

 ◆ **Shared.** Searches shared folders on disks and computer.

3. To narrow or change the search, type the text you want to find in the Search field.

4. To open an item, double-click the item or use the arrow keys to scroll down the list, and then press Return.

5. To clear or stop a search, click the **Close** button (x) in the Search field.

6. When you're done, click the **Close** button.

For Your Information

Searching Made Easy

You can add text to the Spotlight Comments field in the Get Info dialog for a specific file or folder that you can quickly search for using Spotlight later. Control-click a file or folder, click Get Info, and then type the text you want in the Spotlight Comments field.

Filtering Spotlight Results

If the list of Spotlight results is too long to find the results you want, you can revise your search text in the Search field or use the Search bar to filter, or narrow down, the list. The Search bar allows you to filter down the Spotlight results by location and type. The left side of the Search bar provides buttons to filter the search results by where the information is stored, such as This Mac (your entire computer), All My Files (your Home folder), or Shared (your networked computers), if available. After you select where, you can select how. You can filter the result by whether the search criteria is in the content of a file or the file name of the results. If you want to further narrow down the Spotlight results, you can add other search criteria using file attributes.

Filter Spotlight Results

1. Press Option+⌘+Space bar or click **Show All in Finder** on the Spotlight menu to open the Spotlight window, and then perform or narrow a search.

 The Spotlight window displays the results of your search by category.

2. In the Search bar, click the button with the search location you want:

 ◆ **This Mac.** Searches all the disks on your computer.

 ◆ **All My Files.** Searches your Home folder.

 ◆ **Server, Volume** or **Folder Name.** Searches only the currently opened server, volume, or folder. The item name appears in quotes in the Search bar.

 ◆ **Shared.** Searches shared folders on disks and computer.

3. To clear a search, click the **Close** button (x) in the Search field.

4. When you're done, click the **Close** button.

Filtered results

Change Spotlight Criteria in the Spotlight Window

1. Press Option+⌘+Space bar or click **Show All in Finder** on the Spotlight menu to open the Spotlight window.

 The Spotlight window opens, displaying the results of your search by category.

 If a search is currently in progress, a sprocket icon whirls around in the upper-left corner of the window.

2. Click the **Action** button, and then click **Show Search Criteria**.

 The Spotlight items option appears in the first Search pop-up, indicating Spotlight results in the window.

3. Click the **Add** (+) button, and then specify the criteria you want.

4. Click the first **Search** pop-up of the second criteria item, and then select or type the search criteria.

 ◆ Select **Other** on the pop-up to display a complete list of searchable attributes.

5. Click the second **Search** pop-up of the second criteria item, and then select or type more specific search criteria.

6. To remove search criteria, click the **Remove** (-) button.

7. Click the **Action** button, and then click **Hide Search Criteria**.

8. To clear or stop a search, click the **Close** button (x) in the Search field.

9. When you're done, click the **Close** button.

Other available search criteria

Grouping and Sorting Spotlight Results

After you perform a search using the Spotlight window, you can use the Arrange By button, Arranged By submenu on the Action menu or the column header button in List or Cover Flow view to group and sort the results of your search to make it easier to find what you're looking for. Clicking on one of the column header buttons—such as Name, Kind, or Last Opened (default options)—in the search result window in either List or Cover Flow view, sorts the files and folders by the type of information listed in the column. If the columns are not organized in the order you want, you can use the mouse to quickly drag a column header to rearrange them.

Group and Sort Spotlight Results

1. Press Option+⌘+Space bar or click **Show All in Finder** on the Spotlight menu to open the Spotlight window, and then perform or narrow a search.

 The Spotlight window displays the results of your search by category.

2. Click the **List View** or **Cover Flow** button on the toolbar to display the search results in list form.

3. Click a column header name (default shown) to sort the file and folder in ascending or descending order:

 ◆ **Name.** List in alphabetical order by element name.

 ◆ **Kind.** List by kind of item, including applications, documents, or images.

 ◆ **Last Opened.** List by the date you last opened it.

4. To change the view options, click the **Action** button, click **Show View Options**, select options, and then click the **Close** button.

5. When you're done, click the **Close** button.

Select view options for Spotlight search results

Working with Spotlight Results

After you perform a search using the Spotlight window, you can Control-click an item to display a shortcut menu and get more information about an item in the Spotlight results. When you Control-click an item, the shortcut menu allows you to open the item, get information about the item from the Get Info dialog box, locate the item in the Finder, display a slide show for graphic items, or create an e-mail with attachments using Mail.

Work with Spotlight Results

① Press Option+⌘+Space bar or click **Show All in Finder** on the Spotlight menu to open the Spotlight window, and then perform or narrow a search.

The Spotlight window displays the results of your search by category.

② Control-click or right-click the item(s) you want, and then click the option you want:

- ◆ **Open.** Opens the selected item(s).

- ◆ **Open With.** Opens the selected item(s) with a specified application. Point to Open With, and then select an available application.

- ◆ **Open Enclosing Folder.** Displays the selected item(s) in a Finder window.

- ◆ **Get Info.** Opens the Get Info dialog box with basic file information for the selected item(s).

- ◆ **Quick Look.** View the contents of a file or folder without opening it.

③ When you're done, click the **Close** button.

Setting Spotlight Preferences

You can change Spotlight preferences to customize the way you use Spotlight. You can specify the categories, such as Applications, Documents, Folders, and so on, you want or don't want to include in a Spotlight search. In addition, you can change the order of the categories to prioritize the way the results appears. If you prefer different shortcut keys to display the Spotlight menu or open the Spotlight window, you can change them. When Spotlight performs a search, it looks every where on your computer (except for someone else's Home folder). If you want to keep certain disks, partitions, or folders private, you can add them to your privacy settings in Spotlight preferences. When you add an item to the privacy list, Spotlight removes them from the Spotlight index.

Set Spotlight Search Results Preferences

① Click the **System Preferences** icon in the Dock, and then click the **Spotlight** icon.

TIMESAVER *Click Spotlight preferences at the bottom of the Spotlight menu (after you've started a search).*

② Click the **Search Results** tab.

③ Select the check boxes you want to include in the search results or clear the check boxes you don't want to include in the search results.

④ To change the order to the search results categories, drag the categories to the location you want.

⑤ Click the **Close** button.

⑤ ④ ②

Spotlight

Show All

Spotlight helps you quickly find things on your computer. Spotlight is located at the top right corner of the screen.

Search Results | Privacy

Drag categories to change the order in which results appear.
Only selected categories will appear in Spotlight search results.

1 ☑ Applications
2 ☑ System Preferences
3 ☑ Documents
4 ☑ Folders
5 ☑ Messages & Chats
6 ☑ Contacts
7 ☑ Events & To Dos
8 ☑ Images
9 ☑ PDF Documents
10 ☑ Webpages
11 ☑ Music
12 ☑ Movies
13 ☑ Fonts
14 ☑ Presentations
15 ☑ Spreadsheets

③

☑ Spotlight menu keyboard shortcut: ⌘ Space
☑ Spotlight window keyboard shortcut: ⌥⌘ Space

Did You Know?

You can use Spotlight everywhere (almost). The Spotlight Search field is also available in the Finder, Mail, System Preferences, and Open and Save dialogs to name a few.

For Your Information

Selecting the Default Search Location

You can specify the default search location for Spotlight. Click the Finder menu, click Preferences, click Advanced, click the When performing a search pop-up, then click Search This Mac, Search the Current Folder, or Use the Previous Search Scope.

Set Spotlight Privacy Preferences

1. Click the **System Preferences** icon in the Dock, and then click the **Spotlight** icon.

2. Click the **Privacy** tab.

3. Drag the items (disks, partitions, or folders) to the list of non-searchable items from the desktop, or click the **Add** (+) button, navigate to the item, and then click **Choose**.

4. To delete an item, click the item, and then press Delete or click the **Remove** (-) button.

5. Click the **Close** button.

Set Keyboard Shortcuts for Spotlight

1. Click the **System Preferences** icon in the Dock, and then click the **Spotlight** icon.

2. Select the **Spotlight menu keyboard shortcut** check box, click the list arrow, and then select the shortcut you want.

3. Select the **Spotlight window keyboard shortcut** check box, click the list arrow, and then select the shortcut you want.

4. Click the **Close** button.

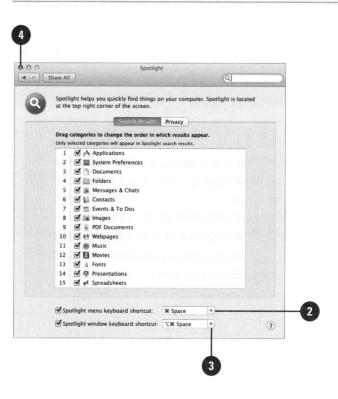

Searching for Files Using the Find Window

Spotlight provides a quick and easy way to search for files, but if you need to perform a more specific search, the Find window can help you search for what you need. The Find window lets you specify where and how you want to search—This Mac, All My Files or "folder or disk name," or Shared—with either file contents or name and make relevant suggestions as you type (**New!**). You can narrow your search by selecting or typing a specific list of criteria—such as name, location, size, or kind—available in the Find window. For example, you can search for all graphic files with the *.jpg* extension you created last month that contain *web*. After you complete a search, a separate results window opens. Unlike the Spotlight, you can change the criteria and perform a new search, and then compare the results.

Search for Files Using the Find Window

1. Open a Finder window.

2. Click the **File** menu, and then click **Find**.

 TIMESAVER *Press ⌘+F to open the Find window.*

3. In the Search field, type the text in which you want to search.

4. On the Search menu, select a suggestion, such as Filename contains "text" to narrow the search as desired. (**New!**)

5. Click the button with the search location you want:

 ◆ **This Mac.** Searches all the disks on your computer.

 ◆ **All My Files.** Searches your Home folder.

 ◆ **Server, Volume or Folder Name.** Searches only the currently opened server, volume, or folder. The item name appears in quotes in the Search bar.

 ◆ **Shared.** Searches shared folders on disks and computer.

6. To change the search, click the drop-down button, and then click **Filename** or **Everything**.

66

Narrow Search for Files Using the Find Window

1. Click the **File** menu, and then click **Find**.

2. In the Search field, type the text in which you want to perform an initial search.

3. Click the first **Search** pop-up, and then select or type the search criteria; options vary depending on the criteria.

 ◆ **Kind**. Finds files that are or aren't a certain kind.

 ◆ **Last Opened Date**. Finds files that you last opened.

 ◆ **Last Modified Date**. Finds files according to the date modified.

 ◆ **Created Date**. Finds files according to the date created.

 ◆ **Name**. Finds all or part of a file name (capitalization doesn't matter); select another option, such as Contains, Starts With, Ends With, or Is.

 ◆ **Contents**. Finds words inside your file; handy if you don't remember the name.

 ◆ **Other**. Finds files based on other selected attributes.

4. Click the second **Search** pop-up, and then select or type more specific search criteria.

5. To add search criteria, click the **Add** (+) button, and then specify the criteria you want.

6. To remove search criteria, click the **Remove** (-) button.

 The search results appear in the window.

7. To pause or stop a search in progress, click the **X** button.

For Your Information

Setting a Search Location Preference

In the Finder Preferences dialog, you can specify a search location preference. You can select any of the following options: Search This Mac, Search the Current Folder, or Use the Previous Search Scope. Click the Finder menu, click Preferences, click Advanced, click the When performing a search pop-up, and then select the option you want.

Searching for Hard to Find Information

In addition to searching for typical information, such as name, location, size, or kind, you can also search for file specific metadata, such as visibility (visible files, not hidden one used by Mac OS X), duration, dimensions, pixel height and width, device make, and layers. There are over 115 different metadata search attributes from which to choose. For example, you can select search attributes to find visible files (not hidden ones used by Mac OS X), the duration of music and movies, the dimensions of graphics or PDF documents, the device used to acquire a document, and the names of layers in Photoshop.

Search for Hard to Find Information

1. In the Finder, click the **File** menu, and then click **Find**.

 TIMESAVER *Press ⌘+F to open the Find window.*

 ◆ You can also use the Search field located in every Finder window.

2. In the Search field, type the text in which you want to search.

3. To display only matches with filename, select **Filename contains "text"** on the Search menu.

4. At the top of the window, click the button with the search location you want: **This Mac**, **All My files** or "folder or disk name," or **Shared**.

5. Click the first **Search** pop-up, and then click **Other**.

6. Select the search attribute you want to find.

7. Click **OK**.

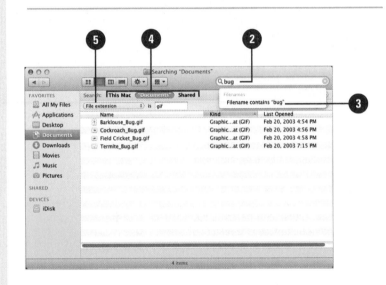

Working with Find Window Results

After you perform a search with the Find window, you can perform a variety of file management operations directly with the Find window results, which are similar to the ones you can perform in the Finder. For example, you can get file information, and move, copy, rename, or delete a file directly in the search results window. In addition, you can display the location of a file in the search results window, and then open its folder location or open the file.

Work with Find Window Results

After you perform a search with the Find window, you can use the following options to work with the results:

◆ **Find the location of a file.** Click a file to display the location in the Path bar at bottom of the window.

◆ **Open the location of a file.** Click the **File** menu, and then click **Open Enclosed Folder**.

◆ **Open a file.** Double-click the file icon.

◆ **Move or delete a file.** Drag the file to a new location or the Trash.

◆ **Rename a file.** Click its name, select the text, and then type a new name.

◆ **Copy a file.** Use the **Copy** and **Paste** commands on the **Edit** menu.

◆ **Get file information.** Click the File menu, and then click **Get Info**. Add criteria to Spotlight Comments for use in Spotlight searches.

◆ **Sort the result by category.** Click the column header.

◆ **Start a new search.** Change the text in the Search field, or click the Close (x) button in the Search field and type a new search.

◆ **Close the search.** Click the **Close** button or press ⌘+W.

Double-click to open Click column to sort

Path bar

Get info
spotlight comments

Creating and Using Smart Folders

A Smart folder is a self-updating folder that performs a search based on the search criteria you set and save in the Search dialog box. You can create a Smart folder by specifying a search in the Search dialog box and then saving it as a saved search. For example, if you set up a search for *Last Opened* and *This week*, and saved it as a Smart folder. In the Sidebar, you can click the Smart folder to perform the smart search, or Control-click it and click Show Search Criteria to edit it.

Create and Use a Smart Folder

1 Click the **File** menu, and then click **New Smart Folder**.

2 Use the **Add** (+) button to specify the search criteria you want to save as a Smart folder.

3 Click the **Save** button.

4 Type a name for the Smart folder.

5 Specify the location where you want to save the Smart folder.

The default location is the Saved Searches folder.

6 Select or clear the **Add To Sidebar** check box to either add or not add the Smart folder to the sidebar.

7 Click **Save**.

8 To use a Smart folder, click the Smart folder icon on the Sidebar, or navigate to the Saved Searches folder, and then double-click it.

◆ The Saved Searches folder is located in the Library folder, which is located in the Home folder.

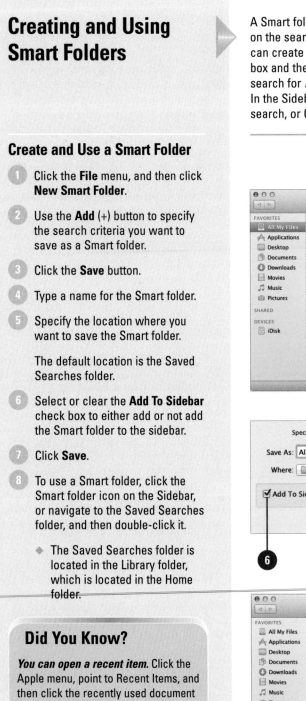

Did You Know?

You can open a recent item. Click the Apple menu, point to Recent Items, and then click the recently used document you want to open.

Smart folder

Edit a Smart Folder

1. Navigate to the Smart folder you want to edit; you can click Smart folder in the Sidebar to select to display it.

2. Click the **Action** menu, and then click **Show Search Criteria**.

3. Change the search criteria you want to modify.

4. Click **Save**.

5. Click the **Action** menu, and then click **Hide Search Criteria**.

Did You Know?

Where's the Smart folder? The Smart folder is located in the Saved Searches folder in the Library folder, which is located in the Home folder.

You can delete a Smart folder. Control-click the smart folder in the Sidebar, click Open Enclosing folder, and then drag the Smart folder you want to delete to the Trash icon.

You can remove a Smart folder from the Sidebar. Control-click the smart folder in the Sidebar, and then click Remove from Sidebar. The folder is removed from the sidebar, however it remains in the Save Searches folder.

You can add a Smart folder or other folder to the Sidebar. Select the folder in a Finder window or desktop, click the File menu, and then click Add To Sidebar.

Saved Searches folder

Items grayed out, not accessible.
Drag to trash to delete.

Getting Help While You Work

When you have a question about how to do something in Mac OS X, you can usually find the answer with several clicks of your mouse. Mac OS X Help is a resource of information to help you use Mac OS X. The Mac OS X Help Center is like an online book with a table of contents, complete with a search feature, and additional links to the Internet to make finding information a little bit easier. You can access help from the Help menu in the Finder as well as many other Mac OS X applications, such as Safari and iChat; you can even switch between the different help libraries using the Home button. If you see the Help button (question mark) in a window or dialog, you can click it to get feature related help. If you have an Internet connection, Help retrieves online updates to Mac OS X Help content as necessary. For additional help and support information, visit the Apple Web site at *www.apple.com*.

Browse for Help Information

1. In the Finder, or any other application, click the **Help** menu, and then click **Help Center** or **<application name> Help**.

2. To select another Help, click the **Help for all your apps** link, and then click a help library.

3. Click a link in the Help window until you find the topic with the information you're looking for.

4. Use the Help toolbar to navigation help topics:

 - Click the **Back** and **Forward** button to view previously viewed topics.

 - Click the **Action** button to change text size, find and highlight text on current page, or print current topic.

 - Click the **Home** button to return to the first page of the help.

 - Click the **Add Bookmark** button to add the current help topic to bookmarks. Click **Bookmarks** button to display the bookmark list to open, remove or email.

5. Click the **Close** button to quit Help.

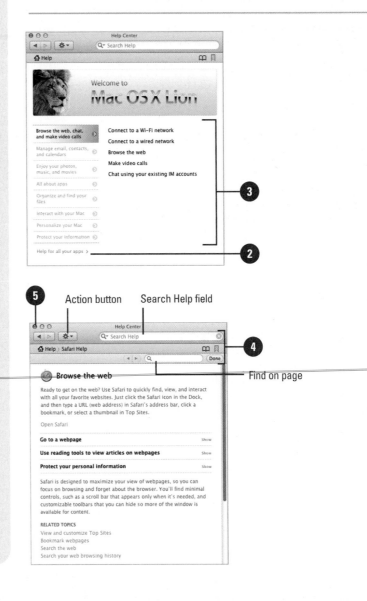

Action button Search Help field

Find on page

Search for Help Information

1. In the Finder, or any other application, click the **Help** menu, and then click **Help Center** or **<application name> Help**.

2. Click the magnifying glass in the Search field, and then click **Include Product Support Results** to check or uncheck it.

3. Click in the Search field.

 TIMESAVER *Press the Tab key to quickly go to the Search field.*

4. Type the words you want to find in the help topics, and then press Return.

 A list of matches appears with a Relevance column ranking the results by percentage.

5. Double-click the topic you want to read in the search results list.

6. Use the navigation buttons (**Back** and **Forward**) on the Help toolbar to move between help topics.

7. Click the **Close** button to quit Help.

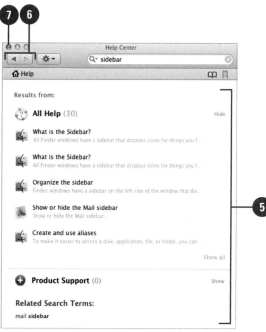

Did You Know?

You can start a new search in a new window. Click the File menu, click New, and then perform a new search.

You can print a help topic. Display the help topic in the Help window, click the Action button on the Help toolbar, click Print, and then click Print again.

You can change the size of Help text. Click the Action button on the Help toolbar, click Make Text Smaller or Make Text Bigger.

Getting Help Using Spotlight

In addition to using Spotlight to find files and other information on your computer, you can also use Spotlight to quickly find help information. When you click the Help menu, the Spotlight Search field appears at the top, where you can type the help information you want to find and display. You can access help from the Help menu in the Finder as well as many other Mac OS X applications, such as Safari and iChat. When you select a help topic from the Help menu, the Help window appears displaying the topic. If you want to display all the related help topics, click Show All Help Results. A complete search results appears, where you can double-click a topic to display it. If available, menu items appear on the Help menu, where you can select it to display an blue arrow pointing to the location of the menu.

Get Help Using Spotlight

1. Click the **Help** menu.

2. In the Spotlight Search field, start to type what you want to find. To find a specific phrase, place quotes around it. For example, "Preferences"

 As you type, a menu begins to display a list of everything Spotlight can find in Help to match what you've typed so far. As you continue to type, the list changes.

3. On the Help menu, select one of the following options:

 - ◆ **Display a Help Topic.** Click the Help topic item or use the arrow keys to scroll down the list, and then press Return to open the Help window.

 - ◆ **Show All Help Results.** Click **Show All Help Results** to display the search results for help topics, and then double-click the topic you want to open the Help window.

 - ◆ **Display a Menu Item.** Point to the Menu item name to display a blue arrow pointing to the location of the menu item.

4. Click the **Close** button to quit Help.

Display menu item

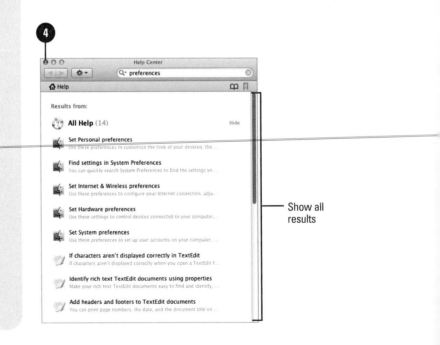

Show all results

Customizing the Finder

4

Introduction

Finder Preferences allow you to control how you interact with your desktop, windows, and icons. You can access Finder Preferences from the Finder menu. Finder Preferences are grouped into four main areas: General, Labels, Sidebar, and Advanced. The Finder Preferences window is a central location to set Finder related options. However, you can customize the Finder and the desktop in other places too.

In each of the Finder window views (Icon, List, and Column), you can set view specific options to customize the way you view icons. In addition to the predefined items in the Sidebar (the left pane in a Finder window), you can add your own items, including folders, documents, Web Internet Location files, to name a few. The Finder toolbar comes with a few standard buttons, and you can customize to add more. You can use the Customize Toolbar dialog to quickly drag button icons on and off the toolbar. You can set Dock preferences to adjust the Dock size and icon magnification (when you point to one), change the Dock position on the screen, apply a bounce effect to an icon when you launch an application, select a minimization special effect, and make it disappear when not in use.

To save some time, you can create shortcuts to the files, folders, or disks you use frequently, known as Aliases. An **alias** allows you to access the original folder or file from several different places. Mission Control with Spaces and Exposé let you view what's running on your computer and quickly move between windows to make it easier to work with windows in order to find, move, or copy files. If you have novice users who want to use your computer, you can set up a shared user account with Simple Finder, which is a simplified version of the Mac OS X Finder with fewer menus and icons. It's a great way for them to explore, yet keep your data safe.

What You'll Do

Understand Finder Preferences

Show Icons on the Desktop

Customize the Way Windows Open

Show or Hide File Extensions

Customize Finder Window Views

Customize the Toolbar

Customize the Sidebar

Customize the Dock

Create Aliases

Customize Mission Control

Use Simple Finder

Understanding Finder Preferences

Finder Preferences allow you to control how you interact with your desktop, windows, and icons. Finder Preferences are grouped into four main areas: General, Labels, Sidebar, and Advanced. You can open Finder Preferences by selecting Preferences from the Finder menu.

The **General preferences pane** allows you to display icons for local and network disks on the desktop, select options for opening new Finder windows, and enable spring-loaded folders and windows. The **Labels pref-**erences pane allows you to change the name of color labels for Finder items to more meaningful ones, such as work or project, which you can use as search criteria in the Find window. If you accidentally remove a Sidebar icon, you can use the **Sidebar preferences pane** to redisplay Finder specific icons, such as computer, hard disks, iDisk, network, desktop, and applications. The **Advanced preferences pane** provides options to show file extensions, a change file extension warning, an empty the Trash warning, empty the Trash securely, and where to perform a Spotlight search.

General

Labels

Sidebar

Advanced

Showing Icons on the Desktop

When you insert a removable disk, a CD, or DVD, or connect to a network server, an icon for the disk automatically appears on the desktop. Depending on your work style, you may or may not want icons to simply appear. You can use Finder Preferences to specify whether icons for hard and external disks, CDs, and network servers appear on your desktop. Having the icons on the desktop makes dragging them to the Eject icon in the Dock quick and easy, but the icons also add clutter to the desktop.

Show Volume Icons on the Desktop

1. Click the **Finder** menu, and then click **Preferences**.

2. Click **General**.

3. Select or clear the checkmarks for the icons you want to show or hide on the desktop.

 ◆ Hard disks

 ◆ External disks

 ◆ CDs, DVDs and iPods

 ◆ Connected servers (computers attached to a network)

4. Click the **Close** button.

4 **2**

Finder Preferences

General Labels Sidebar Advanced

Show these items on the desktop:
- ☑ Hard disks
- ☑ External disks
- ☑ CDs, DVDs, and iPods
- ☐ Connected servers

3

New Finder windows show:

📁 All My Files ▲▼

☐ Always open folders in a new window

☑ Spring-loaded folders and windows
Delay: ━━━━━━━━━◉━━━━━━━━
 Short Medium Long
Press the space bar to open immediately.

Customizing the Way Windows Open

When you create a new Finder window, you can specify options to always open folders in a new window or use spring-loaded folders and windows. Spring-loaded folders allows you to drag a file or folder on top of another folder, and it springs open to let you continue dragging the selection to another location. Instead of starting and stopping when you move or copy items from one folder to another, you can drag items continuously from folder to folder.

Customize the Way Finder Windows Open

1. Click the **Finder** menu, and then click **Preferences**.

2. Click **General**.

3. Click the **New Finder windows open** pop-up, and then select the window you want to open when you open a new Finder window.

4. Select or clear the **Always open folders in a new window** check box.

5. Select or clear the **Spring-loaded folders and windows** check box. If you select it, drag the slider to adjust the delay.

 TIMESAVER *When you drag an item to a folder with a spring-loaded folder, you can press the Spacebar to open the window immediately without the delay.*

6. Click the **Close** button.

Finder Preferences

General Labels Sidebar Advanced

Show these items on the desktop:
- ☑ Hard disks
- ☑ External disks
- ☑ CDs, DVDs, and iPods
- ☐ Connected servers

New Finder windows show:
All My Files

☐ Always open folders in a new window

☑ Spring-loaded folders and windows
Delay:
Short Medium Long
Press the space bar to open immediately.

Showing or Hiding File Extensions

A **file extension** is a three-letter suffix at the end of a document's file name that identifies the file type. For Windows operating system users, a file extension determines which application can open a file; the Mac doesn't use it. You might never have seen a document's file extension because your system might be set up to hide it. The file extension for simple text files is ".txt" (pronounced "dot t-x-t"), and many graphic files have the extension ".bmp" or ".jpg". This means that the full name for a text file named Memo is Memo.txt. If you double-click a document whose file name ends with the three-letter extension ".txt," Finder automatically opens the document with TextEdit, a word processing application. If you plan to exchange files with the Windows operating system, then show the file extensions, so Windows recognizes them. As a precaution, you can also set an option to display a warning before allowing an file extension change.

Show or Hide File Extensions

1. Click the **Finder** menu, and then click **Preferences**.

2. Click **Advanced**.

3. Select or clear the **Show all file extensions** check box.

4. Select or clear the **Show warning before changing an extension** check box.

5. Click the **Close** button.

Did You Know?

You can hide or show extensions one icon at a time. Select the icons you want to show or hide, click the File menu, click Get Info, select or clear the Hide Extension check box, and then click the Close button.

You can set an option to show a warning before emptying the Trash. Click the Finder menu, click Preferences, click Advanced, select the Show Warning Before Emptying The Trash check box, and then click the Close button.

Chapter 4 Customizing the Finder **79**

Customizing Finder Window Views

In each of the Finder window views (as Icons, as List, as Columns, and as Cover Flow, you can set view specific options to customize the way you view icons. For Icon, List, and Cover Flow views, you can select to apply your changes to the current window or to all Finder windows (a personal default). In Icon view, you can change icon size, label position, arrangement, and background. In List and Cover Flow views, you can change file size, date, and status related information. To make the display easier to view, you can display relative dates, such as "Today" and "Yesterday." In Column view, you can show icons and the preview column (summary information in the right column).

Change Icon View Options

1. In a Finder window, click the **View** menu, and then click **As Icons**.

2. Click the **View** menu, and then click **Show View Options**.

3. Select an **Arrange By** and **Sort By** option from the pop-ups (**New!**).

4. Drag the slider to change the icon size or the grid spacing.

5. To change the icon text size, click the pop-up, and then select a size.

6. Click the label position option (Bottom or Right) you want.

7. Select the options you want:
 - **Show item info**. Check to show item info under the icon name.
 - **Show icon preview**. Check to show a preview in the icon.

8. Click the **Background** option you want, and any related settings.

9. Click **Use as Defaults** to apply view changes to all windows.

10. Select the **Always open in icon view** check box to apply changes to the window; select the **Browse in icon view** check box to set default style to the view (**New!**).

11. Click the **Close** button.

Change List View or Cover Flow Options

1. In a Finder window, click the **View** menu, and then click **As List** or **Cover Flow**.

2. Click the **View** menu, and then click **Show View Options**.

3. Select an **Arrange By** and **Sort By** option from the pop-ups (**New!**).

4. Select an Icon size, and then select an icon text size.

5. Select or clear the check boxes you want to display in list form.

6. Click **Use as Defaults** to apply view changes to all windows.

7. Select the **Always open in <view>** check box to apply changes to the window; select the **Browse in <view>** check box to set default style to the view (**New!**).

8. Click the **Close** button.

Change Column View Options

1. In a Finder window, click the **View** menu, and then click **As Columns**.

2. Click the **View** menu, and then click **Show View Options**.

3. Select an **Arrange By** and **Sort By** option from the pop-ups (**New!**).

4. Click the **Text size** pop-up, and then select a point size.

5. Select or clear the check boxes you want to show previews.

6. Select the **Always open in column view** check box to apply changes to the window; select the **Browse in column view** check box to set default style to the view (**New!**).

7. Click the **Close** button.

Customizing the Toolbar

The Finder toolbar comes with a few standard buttons, but you can add more. You can use the Customize Toolbar dialog to quickly drag button icons on and off. The buttons include Path (navigation pop-up), Eject, Burn, Customize, Separator (designates groups), Space (adds a gap), Flexible Space (adds a gap that expands), New Folder, Delete, Connect, Get Info, iDisk, Search, and Quick Look. If you want the simple look again, you can drag the Default Set of buttons onto the toolbar to reset it. In addition to the button icons in the dialog, you can also drag icons, such as favorite folders, disks, or applications, from the desktop or any Finder folder onto the toolbar. You can also use the A key to cycle through size combinations of large and small icons and text labels.

Customize the Finder Toolbar

1. Click the **View** menu, and then click **Customize Toolbar**.

2. Click the **Show** pop-up, and then select a display option of **Icon Only**, **Icon & Text**, or **Text Only**.

 TIMESAVER *Control-click the toolbar (without the dialog open), and then click a display option.*

3. To add icons to the toolbar, drag them into place from the gallery.

4. To remove icons, drag them up or down off the toolbar.

5. To rearrange icons, drag them horizontally on the toolbar.

6. To reset the toolbar, drag the default set of items onto the toolbar.

7. When you're finished, click **Done**.

Did You Know?

You can access buttons that don't fit on a narrow window. You can either resize the window, or click the double arrow, and then select a toolbar item.

Add, Remove, or Rearrange Icons to the Toolbar

1. Display the icons you want to add to the Finder toolbar in the desktop or any folder window.

2. Drag icons from the desktop, or any folder window, directly onto the toolbar, and then pause before releasing the icon.

 TROUBLE? *If pausing doesn't work, use A while you drag.*

3. To remove an icon from the toolbar, hold down ⌘, and then drag the icon off the toolbar.

4. To rearrange an icon on the toolbar, hold down ⌘, and then drag the icon horizontally on the toolbar.

Icon added to toolbar

Change Toolbar Styles

1. Control-click a blank area of the toolbar, and then click **Icon and Text**, **Icon Only**, or **Text Only**.

Did You Know?

You can change toolbar styles in some applications too. You can also use ⌘ in Mac OS X applications, such as Mail, and many other applications.

Other toolbar styles

Customizing the Sidebar

In addition to the predefined items in the Sidebar, you can add your own items, including folders, documents, and Web Internet Location files, to name a few. When you click a volume or folder in the Sidebar, the Finder displays its contents in the window. When you click an application, document, or Web Internet Location file, the item opens in its own application window. If you accidentally remove a Sidebar icon, you can't undo it, but you can redisplay Mac OS X specific items using Finder Preferences, which includes categories for Favorites (**New!**), Shared, and Devices. Unfortunately, you have to recreate the ones you added.

Customize the Sidebar

◆ **Add items.** Drag the items to the lower section of the Sidebar.

 TIMESAVER *Select an item, and then press* ⌘+T, *or use the Add To Sidebar command on the File menu.*

◆ **Remove items.** Control-click the item, and then click **Remove from Sidebar**.

◆ **Rearrange items.** Drag the items up or down in the list.

◆ **Change the column width.** Position the mouse pointer over the divider between the Sidebar and the window contents, and then drag to change the width.

◆ **Hide and show the Sidebar.** Click the **View** menu, and then click **Hide Sidebar** or **Show Sidebar**.

Add item to Sidebar

Drag to change column width

Remove item from Sidebar

Change Sidebar Preferences

1. Click the **Finder** menu, and then click **Preferences**.

2. Click **Sidebar**.

3. Select or clear the check boxes with the items you want or don't want to see in the Sidebar.

 ◆ The items in Sidebar Preferences include icons for the categories Favorites (**New!**), Shared, and Devices.

4. Click the **Close** button.

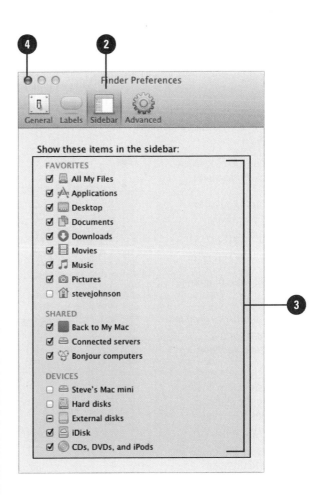

Customizing the Dock

After you have worked with the Dock for a while, you probably want to customize it to better suit your needs. You can set Dock Preferences to adjust the Dock size and icon magnification when you point to one, change the Dock position on the screen, apply a bounce effect to an icon when you launch an application, select a minimization special effect, and even make it disappear when not in use.

Customize the Dock

1. Click the **Apple** menu, point to **Dock**, and then click **Dock Preferences**.

 TIMESAVER *Control-click the divider in the Dock to quickly display the Dock submenu.*

2. Select the Dock options you want:

 ◆ **Dock Size**. Drag slider to change the Dock size.

 TIMESAVER *Point to the divider in the Dock, so it turns into a double-headed arrow, and then drag to size it.*

 ◆ **Magnification**. Select to enable it, and then drag the slider to magnify the icons when you point to them in the Dock.

 ◆ **Position on screen**. Click the Left, Bottom, or Right option.

 ◆ **Minimize using**. Select an animation effect.

 ◆ **Minimize windows into application icon**. Select to minimize windows into the application icon on the dock.

 ◆ **Animate opening applications**. Select to have the application icon bounce when you launch an application.

 ◆ **Automatically hide and show the Dock**. Select to auto hide/show the dock when not pointing or pointing to it.

 ◆ **Show indicator lights for open applications**. Select to show lights under dock icon (**New!**).

3. Click the **Close** button.

Magnifying icons

For Your Information

Displaying the Genie Effect

You can slow down the minimization of a window or application (a cool genie effect). Shift-click a window's Minimize button. The window collapses into the Dock about one-fifth the usual speed. You can also Shift-click the icon in the Dock to slowly unminimize the window. Unfortunately, you can't speed it up.

Add, Remove, and Rearrange Items in the Dock

◆ **Add an item.** Drag an icon from a Finder window to the Dock, and then position application icons to the left of the divider line and all other icons to the right.

◆ **Add an open application item.** Open the application to display the icon in the Dock, press and hold or Control-click the application icon, point to **Options**, and then click **Keep In Dock**.

◆ **Open a document using an application item.** Drag the document icon to the application icon in the Dock.

◆ **Move an item.** Drag the icon to the position you want in the Dock.

◆ **Remove an item.** Drag an icon out of the Dock.

> **TROUBLE?** *If you delete an application or document from your computer with an icon in the Dock, the Dock icon changes to a question mark, which you can remove.*

◆ **Open a folder stack.** Click a folder icon to display the stack list, and then click an item.

◆ **Customize a folder stack.** Control-click a folder icon to display a shortcut menu, and then click an option.

Add an item

Add an open application

Open a document

Remove an item

Customize a folder stack

Creating Aliases

It can take you a while to access a file or folder buried several levels down in a folder. To save some time, you can create shortcuts to the items you use frequently. **Aliases** are shortcuts that point to a folder or file. An alias allows you to access the original folder or file from several different places. When you create an alias to a folder or file, the icon includes a little arrow in the lower-left corner. You can't make an alias for an application. However, you can add an application into the Dock, which acts like an alias. When you double-click an alias icon, a folder opens with the contents of the original folder or a document opens using its associated application. If you delete an alias of a folder or file, the original folder or file is not deleted, just the alias.

Create an Alias

1. Open the Finder window with the icon in which you want to create an alias.

2. Select the icon.

3. Click the **File** menu, and then click **Make Alias**.

 TIMESAVER *Hold down ⌘+Option, and then drag a file or folder to create an alias.*

 The alias icon appears in the Finder window.

4. If you want, rename the alias icon, and then press Return.

5. Drag the alias icon to the desktop or another folder.

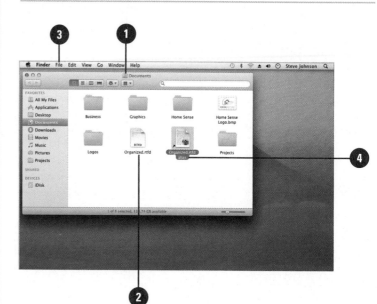

Did You Know?

You can quickly find the original file or folder of an alias. Select the alias file or folder, click the File menu, and then click Show Original. You can also press ⌘+R.

Create an Alias with the Title Bar

1. Open the application and document in which you want to create an alias.

2. Position the mouse pointer on the icon next to the document title in the title bar.

3. Drag the icon to the desktop, or on a folder or disk.

Did You Know?

You can drag the Title bar icon onto an application Dock icon. If you want to open a document created in one program (say TextEdit), and you want to open it up in another program (say Microsoft Word), you can drag the Title bar icon of a document in TextEdit to the Microsoft Word icon in the Dock to open it.

You can drag an alias icon into the Dock. Drag the alias icon into the Dock on the right side. When you release the mouse, the icon appears in the Dock.

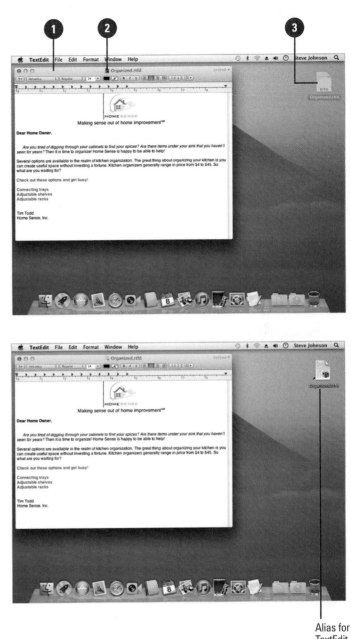

Alias for TextEdit document

Customizing Mission Control

In Mission Control (**New!**) preferences you can customize Exposé, Spaces, and Dashboard options. Exposé in Mission Control lets you quickly move windows out of the way temporarily to make it easier to work with windows to find, move, or copy files. The default way to move windows with Exposé is to use keyboard function keys. However, these function keys might already be taken by other applications, or your computer. You can customize them to move windows in three ways: screen corners, keyboard, and mouse. Use Hot Corners, you can trigger operation when you point to one of the screen corners. Using the keyboard pop-ups, you can change the keyboard shortcuts. When you display the pop-ups, you can press other modifier keys, such as Shift, Option, Control, or ⌘ to create a new shortcut. If you have a mouse with two or three buttons, you can change options to trigger them with your mouse. With Spaces, you can group and arrange windows to reduce desktop clutter and organize materials into unique spaces. You can also set options to show the Dashboard as a space, switch to a space with open windows for an application, and automatically reorder spaces.

Customize Exposé in Mission Control

1. Click the **System Preferences** icon in the Dock, and then click the **Mission Control** icon.

2. In the Keyboard and Mouse Shortcuts area, click the pop-ups for each operation, press a keyboard modifier (Shift, Control, Option, or ⌘) if you want, and then select a shortcut key, and then set a mouse button.

 ◆ **Mission Control**. Set to toggle between show/hide all open windows at once.

 ◆ **Application Windows**. Set to toggle between show/hide all open windows in the current application.

 ◆ **Show Desktop**. Set to toggle between hide/show all open windows and show/hide desktop.

3. To set active screen corners to activate operations, click **Hot Corners**, select corner operations, and then click **OK**.

4. Click the **Close** button.

Customize Spaces in Mission Control

1. Click the **System Preferences** icon in the Dock, and then click the **Mission Control** icon.

2. To automatically reorder spaces when they change, select the **Automatically reorder spaces based on most recent use** check box (**New!**).

3. Select or clear the **When switching to an application, switch to a space with open windows for the application** check box.

4. Click the **Close** button.

Customize Dashboard in Mission Control

1. Click the **System Preferences** icon in the Dock, and then click the **Mission Control** icon.

2. To show the dashboard as a space in Mission control, select the **Show Dashboard as a space** check box (**New!**).

3. In the Keyboard and Mouse Shortcuts area, click the Show Dashboard pop-up, press a keyboard modifier (Shift, Control, Option, or ⌘) if you want, and then select a shortcut key and/or a mouse button.

 ◆ **Show Dashboard**. Set to toggle between show/hide the dashboard.

4. Click the **Close** button.

Using Simple Finder

If you have novice users who want to use your computer, you should set up a user account with the Simple Finder in Parental Controls preferences. **Simple Finder** is a simplified version of the Mac OS X Finder with fewer menus and icons, and allows limited access to the items on your hard disk. The Dock contains only three folders: Documents, My Applications, and Shared. The Documents folder provides a place for users to save their documents, while the My Applications folder provides access to the applications you select for them in Parental Control preferences. If you want to share documents with them, they can access the items in the Shared folder.

Set Up the Simple Finder

1. Click the **System Preferences** icon in the Dock, and then click the **Parental Controls** icon.

2. Click the user account for the person you want to set up the Simple Finder. If necessary, click the Lock icon and enter user name and password, first. Also, click the Enable Parental Control button as needed.

3. Click the **System** tab.

4. Select the **Use Simple Finder** check box.

5. Select or clear the **Limit Applications** check box, and then select an **Allow App Store Apps** option (**New!**) to a specified limit.

6. Select or clear the applications you want to enable or disable for the account.

7. Click the **Close** button.

Simple Finder

Did You Know?

You can get administrative access while logged in to Simple Finder. Click the Finder menu, click Run Full Finder, and then type your name and password. When you're done, click the Finder menu, and then click Return To Simple Finder.

Setting System Preferences

5

Introduction

System Preferences allows you to customize various parts of Mac OS X, such as the appearance of your desktop, your computers date and time, the way CDs and DVDs start up when you insert them, or use speech recognition to convert a spoken voice into commands or electronic text. For those of you with a Mac laptop, you can manage power usage for your computer. Universal Access preferences make it easier for a person with a disability, such as difficulty seeing or hearing or controlling a mouse, to use a computer. If you have an ink device attached to your computer, you can use Ink Preferences to improve the recognition of ink to text.

You can access System Preferences from the Dock or the Apple menu. Many applications also have their own preferences, which you can access from the application menu within the application. System Preferences are organized into categories by default. Each category contains a set of icons, which you can open to set customization options in preference panes for different aspects of the Macintosh operating system.

Some System Preference panes are locked for security reasons. If preference settings are all grayed out, the preference pane is locked to prevent non- administrators from making changes. Check the Lock icon at the bottom of System Preferences. If the Lock icon is locked, you need an administrator name and password to unlock it and make changes. If you log in as an administrator, the Lock icon is unlocked, unless you set a security option to have the preference panes stay locked. When you close the preference pane, it locks automatically.

What You'll Do

Understand System Preferences

View System Preferences

Lock and Unlock Preference Settings

Change Appearance Options

Set Up the Desktop

Set Up Screen Savers

Set the Date and Time

Change Language Options

Change Text Substitution Options

Save Energy and Manage Power

Select a Startup Disk

Change the Way a CD & DVD Starts

Control Sound

Recognize Your Speech

Let Mac Do the Talking

Set Universal Access Options

Explore and Use VoiceOver

Set Ink Preferences

Understanding System Preferences

System Preferences allow you to customize system wide settings for various aspects of Mac OS X and your computer. The System Preferences window is organized alphabetically or by categories: Personal, Hardware, Internet & Network, and System. Each category contains preference areas that you can change to customize the way Mac OS X works. Only an administrator can change system settings that affect every account.

Personal

General. Change the look and feel of buttons, selected items, and scroll bars. See page 98.

Desktop & Screen Saver. Change the desktop background or select a visual screen effect to hide your desktop. See pages 100-102.

Dock. Change the location of the Dock, adjust the size of icons, set magnification, or hide the Dock. See pages 86-87 in Chapter 4.

Mission Control. Set keyboard shortcuts or mouse positions to show or hide all your windows at one time, or create unique spaces for projects. (**New!**) See page 90-92 in Chapter 4.

Language & Text. Change your computer to read or write with other languages and substitute text. See pages 104-106.

Security & Privacy. Protect your computer and the information on it, and adjust firewall settings to protect your computer from access over the Internet. (**New!**) See pages 397 and 400 in Chapter 16.

Spotlight. Select the categories and priority order you want used in Spotlight searches. See pages 64-65 in Chapter 3.

Universal Access. Set options for the visual or hearing impaired to make it easier to use the computer keyboard, mouse, and screen. See pages 118-125.

Hardware

CDs & DVDs. Set startup options when you insert a CD or DVD. See pages 111 and 318.

Displays. Set the screen size, resolution, color settings, and arrange multiple screens. See page 456-457 in Chapter 18.

Energy Saver. Set the computer to sleep and conserve power, and schedule automatic shutdown and startup. See page 108-109.

Ink. Set the computer to write text using a graphics tablet and stylus, recognize the ink, and turn it into words. (Available only if a graphics tablet or ink device is installed.) See page 126.

Keyboard. Change the speed of your keyboard, and customize universal keyboard shortcuts or application shortcuts. See page 453 in Chapter 18.

Mouse. Change the speed of your mouse, primary mouse button, or scroll wheel zoom. See pages 454 in Chapter 18.

Trackpad. Change the options related to using your internal or external trackpad. (**New!**) See pages 455 in Chapter 18.

Print & Scan. Add a printer, monitor print jobs, set up to receive scans and faxes, and share printers and a fax modem with other users. See pages 198-199 in Chapter 8.

Sound. Change computer sound volume, effects, and sound input or output devices. See pages 112-113.

Internet & Wireless

MobileMe. Create an online MobileMe account and set access options. See page 352 in Chapter 13.

Mail, Contacts & Calendar. Setup and manage accounts for internet services. (**New!**) See page 258 in Chapter 10.

Network. Create and manage network and Internet connection settings. See page 412 in Chapter 16.

Bluetooth. Control how to send and receive files between your computer and other Bluetooth devices. (Available if Bluetooth is enabled). See pages 413-415 in Chapter 16.

Sharing. Set sharing services for files, web, printer, internet, and bluetooth with others See pages 404-407 in Chapter 16.

System

Users & Groups. Set up accounts, access privileges, and log in and out settings to share your computer with others. (**New!**) See pages 387-388 in Chapter 15.

Parental Controls. Set limits on computer use, including content, Mail & iChat, and time, and create logs. See pages 392-393 in Chapter 15.

Date & Time. Set your computer's date, time, and time zone, or use a network time server. See pages 102-103.

Software Update. Set a schedule or options to check for updates automatically on the Internet. See pages 432-433 in Chapter 17.

Speech. Set the computer to speak the text on the screen or use spoken commands to control your computer. See pages 114-117.

Time Machine. Set options to back up everything on your computer. See page 478 in Chapter 20.

Startup Disk. Select the disk or drive you want to use to start up your computer. See page 111.

Adding or Removing Third-Party System Preferences

You can also add other System Preferences developed by other companies, known as third-party system preferences. To install a third-party preference, download the preference, double-click its icon, and then follow the on-screen instructions. To uninstall a third-party preference, use the method provided by the developer, or hold down the Control key, click the Preference icon, click Uninstall, and then follow the on-screen instructions.

Categories

Viewing System Preferences

System Preferences are organized into categories by default. Each category contains a set of icons, which you can open to set customization options in preference panes for different aspects of the Macintosh operating system. You can also view the icons in the System Preferences window alphabetically, depending on your preference. Simply click a preference icon to open it, and then make the changes you want. The preferences take effect when you quit or close System Preferences.

View System Preferences

1 Click the **Apple** menu, and then click **System Preferences** or click the **System Preferences** icon in the Dock.

2 To change preference organization, click the **View** menu, and then click **Organize By Categories** or **Organize Alphabetically**.

3 To open a preference, click the icon.

> **TIMESAVER** *Press the first letter of the preferences name to select the icon, and then press the Spacebar to open it.*

4 To switch to another preference, click the **View** menu, and then click the one you want to open.

> **TIMESAVER** *Click the Show All button on the toolbar to show all the preference icons.*

5 When you're done, click the **System Preferences** menu, and then click **Quit System Preferences**, or click the **Close** button.

Did You Know?

You can customize the System Preferences toolbar. To add a button to the toolbar in System Preferences, drag an icon to the toolbar. To remove a button, drag it out of the toolbar.

Locking and Unlocking Preference Settings

Some preference panes are locked for security reasons. If preference settings are all grayed out, the preference pane is locked to prevent non-administrators from making changes. Check the Lock icon at the bottom of System Preferences. If the Lock icon is locked, you need an administrator name and password to unlock it and make changes. If you log in as an administrator, the Lock icon is unlocked, unless you set a security option to have the preference panes stay locked. When you close the preference pane, it locks automatically.

Unlock a Preference Pane

1. Click the **System Preferences** icon in the Dock.

2. Click the preference pane icon (such as Security) that you want to lock settings.

3. Click the **Lock** icon.

4. To unlock, type an administrator name and password.

5. Click **OK**.

6. Click the **Close** button.

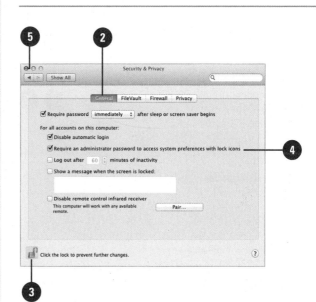

Set Preference Panes to Lock

1. Click the **System Preferences** icon in the Dock.

2. Click the **Security & Privacy** icon, and then click the **General** tab.

3. If settings are grayed out, click the **Lock** icon, type an administrator name and password, and then click **OK**.

4. Select the **Require an administrator password to access system preferences with lock icons** check box.

5. Click the **Close** button.

Changing Appearance Options

The General pane in System Preferences allows you to change the look and feel of Mac OS X in a few areas. You can change the color scheme for buttons, menus, and windows, and the highlight color for text and lists. Or if you're not comfortable using the scroll bars, you can change the way scroll bars work and the placement of the scroll arrows. If your text looks blurry or jagged, you can adjust the font smoothing, known as **anti-aliasing**, style to fix it (after you log out and back in). As you open files and applications, Mac OS X keeps a list in the Recent Items submenu in the Apple menu. In the Appearance pane, you can set the number of recent items that appear in the menu.

Change the Appearance Color and Scroll Bars

1. Click the **System Preferences** icon in the Dock, and then click the **General** icon.

2. Click the **Appearance** pop-up, and then select a color. If you select Other, the Color Picker palette appears so you can select a color.

3. Click the **Highlight Color** pop-up, and then select a color.

4. Click the **Automatically based on input device**, **When scrolling**, or **Always** option to select an how you want to show/hide overlay scroll bars (**New!**) as needed.

5. Click the **Jump to the next page** or **Jump to here** option to select an operation when you click in the scroll bar.

6. Select the **Use smooth scrolling** check box to avoid slight jumping when you click inside the scroll bar.

7. Select the **Double-click a window's title bar to minimize** check box to make it easier to minimize a window instead of using the yellow Minimize button.

8. Click the **Sidebar icon size** pop-up, and then select a size (**New!**).

9. Click the **Close** button.

Smooth Fonts

1. Click the **System Preferences** icon in the Dock, and then click the **General** icon.

2. Select the **Use LCD font smoothing when available** check box to enable font smoothing, which reduces jagged edges for some fonts.

3. Click the **Turn Off Text Smoothing For Font Sizes** pop-up, and then select a font size.

 All text in the font size or smaller is not smoothed, which makes it easier to read.

4. Click the **Close** button.

Change Number of Recent Items

1. Click the **System Preferences** icon in the Dock, and then click the **General** icon.

2. Click the pop-ups for the **Number of Recent Items**, and then select a number.

3. Select the **Restore windows when quitting and re-opening apps** check box (**New!**) to restore windows.

4. Click the **Close** button.

Did You Know?

You can clear the Recent Items sub-menu. Click the Apple menu, point to Recent Items, and then click Clear Menu.

Setting Up the Desktop

The desktop **background**, or wallpaper, is a picture that serves as your desktop's backdrop, the basic surface on which icons and windows appear. You can select a background picture from the ones provided (**New!**) with Mac OS X (which includes Nature, Abstract, Patterns, or Solid Colors, which allows you to create custom colors (**New!**)) or select one of your own in the Desktop & Screen Saver pane in System Preferences. You can select pictures in a variety of formats (such as JPEG, PICT, GIF, TIFF, PDF, or PSD) from your own Pictures folder, another folder you select, or even an iPhoto folder (Photo Library, Last Import, or iPhoto album), and then select options to display them on the screen. When you select a picture from a folder, you can display all the pictures at certain intervals in alphabetical or random order. In addition, you can turn on or off the translucent menu bar effect.

Select a Desktop Background

1. Click the **System Preferences** icon in the Dock, and then click the **Desktop & Screen Saver** icon.

2. Click the **Desktop** tab.

3. Click an image category folder in the left column.

4. Select a thumbnail.

5. If you want to use your own folder of pictures, click the **Add** (+) button, select the folder, and then click **Choose**.

 ◆ To remove one of your own added folders, select the folder, and then click the **Remove** (-) button.

6. To show all the pictures in a folder, select the **Change picture** check box, select an interval from the pop-up, and then select the **Random order** check box or clear it for random order.

7. Select the the **Translucent menu bar** check box to enable the menu effect or clear the check box disable it.

8. Click the **Close** button.

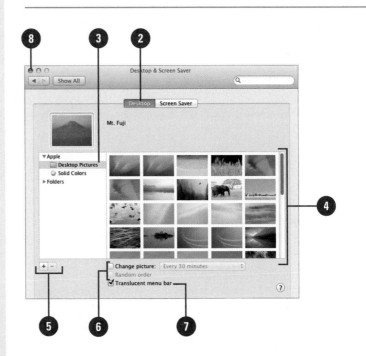

Setting Up Screen Savers

In the past, you needed a screen saver (a continually moving display) to protect your monitor from screen burn in. Those days are gone with the emergence of new display technology. Screen savers are more for entertainment than anything else. When you leave your computer idle for a specified wait time, a screen saver displays a continuous scene, such as an aquarium, until you move your mouse to stop it. If a security option is set in the Security & Privacy pane in System Preferences, your computer requires a password when you wake from a screen saver. You can select a screen saver from the ones provided with Mac OS X, or select a folder with pictures (all saved in the same format) or a published slideshow from a MobileMe account online or RSS feed, which gets downloaded to your computer. With iTunes Artwork, you can turn screen saver into a jukebox; just click an album (**New!**). With iPhoto, you can use onscreen controls to pause or flip through photos in an album (**New!**) .

Set Up a Screen Saver

1. Click the **System Preferences** icon in the Dock, and then click the **Desktop & Screen Saver** icon.

2. Click the **Screen Saver** tab.

3. Select a screen saver, using any of the following methods:

 - Click an Apple screen saver.
 - Click **Pictures Folder**, and then select one, or click **Shuffle** to shuffle through screen saver pictures.
 - Select the **Use random screen saver** check box to use different screen savers each time.
 - Select the **Show with clock** check box to show the clock.

4. Click **Options**, select the check boxes you want, and then click **OK**.

5. Drag the slider to determine when the screen saver starts.

6. To activate the screen saver with your mouse pointer, click **Hot Corners**, specify the options you want in the corner you want it.

7. Click **OK**.

8. Click the **Close** button.

Turns off screen saver

Setting the Date and Time

The date and time you set on your computer is very important. When you save a file or send and receive an e-mail, your computer uses the date and time you set in the Date & Time preference pane. You can set the date and time manually, or if your computer is connected to the Internet, you can have a time server set it automatically. If you have an Internet connect, such as DSL or cable, use the time server, otherwise you should set it manually. To make sure your files and e-mail times are not off by a few hours, you need to set your time zone, either manually or automatically. When you travel, Mac OS X can automatically change your time zone using Wi-Fi. You can also set the date and time to display as a digital (12:05 PM) or analog (round face with hands) clock in the menu bar, or have the computer speak, announcing the time at certain intervals.

Set the Date and Time

1. Click the **System Preferences** icon in the Dock, and then click the **Date & Time** icon.

2. Click the **Date & Time** tab.

3. To set the time automatically over the Internet, select the **Set date & time automatically** check box, and then use the pop-up to select a time server.

4. To set the date and time manually, use any of the following methods:

 ◆ Select the individual date and time fields, and then enter a number, or use the up and down arrows.

 ◆ Click a date in the calendar and drag the hands on the clock.

5. Click the **Time Zone** tab.

 ◆ To automatically set the time zone, select the **Set time zone automatically using current location** check box.

6. Click the part of the map closest to your location.

7. Click the **Closest City** pop-up, and then select the closest city to your location.

8. Click the **Close** button.

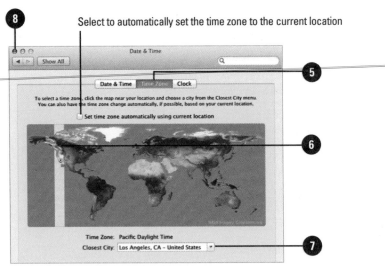

Select to automatically set the time zone to the current location

Set Date and Time Options

1 Click the **System Preferences** icon in the Dock, and then click the **Date & Time** icon.

2 Click the **Clock** tab.

3 Select the **Show date and time in menu bar** check box.

4 Select the view as (**Digital** or **Analog**) option you want.

5 Select or clear the following check boxes:

- ◆ **Display the time with seconds**. Check to add seconds to the time (Menu bar).

- ◆ **Flash the time separators**. Check to show a blinking colon.

- ◆ **Use a 24-hour clock**. Check to show military time (18:00 instead of 6:00 PM).

- ◆ **Show AM/PM**. Check to show AM or PM.

- ◆ **Show the day of the week**. Check to show the day of the week (Menu bar).

- ◆ **Show the date**. Check to show the date (Menu bar).

6 To speak the time, select the **Announce the time** check box, click the pop-up, and then select an interval.

To change the computer voice, click **Customize Voice**.

7 Click the **Close** button.

Menu bar

For Your Information

Using the Menu Bar Clock

When you display the clock in the menu bar, the time appears in analog form or as a clock icon with the current time. If you want to know the date, click the clock. A menu drops down displaying the complete date. The menu also allows you to switch between digital and analog clock types and open the Date & Time pane in System Preferences.

Changing Language Options

The Language & Text pane in System Preferences gives you options to use different languages for menus, dialogs, and the keyboard, as well as write text in other languages. The language you write can be different from the language for menus, dialogs, and the keyboard. The Language tab allows you to select a language that you use in application menus and dialogs, and write in an application. The Formats tab allows you to select international formats for dates, times, numbers, and measurement units. The Input Sources tab provides you with a list of languages that you can select a keyboard layout, which lets you type in other languages. If you're not familiar with the keyboard layout, you can use the Keyboard Viewer to show you what keys to press to display the keys you want in the input menu language. To make language selection easier, you can add the Input menu to the menu bar.

Set Input Sources Options

1. Click the **System Preferences** icon in the Dock, and then click the **Language & Text** icon.

2. Click the **Input Sources** tab.

3. Select the check box next to the language(s) you want to use.

4. To see what the characters look like on your keyboard, select the **Keyboard Viewer** check box.

 The Keyboard Viewer is available on the menu bar in the Input Menu.

5. Click **Keyboard Shortcuts**, select the keyboard shortcut or text matching options you want, and then click **OK**.

6. Select an option to use the same or different input sources.

7. To change input menu languages from the menu bar, select the **Show input menu in menu bar** check box.

8. Click the **Close** button.

 TIMESAVER *Press ⌘+ Spacebar to switch between the two most recent keyboard layouts. Press Option+⌘+Spacebar to cycle down the list of keyboards.*

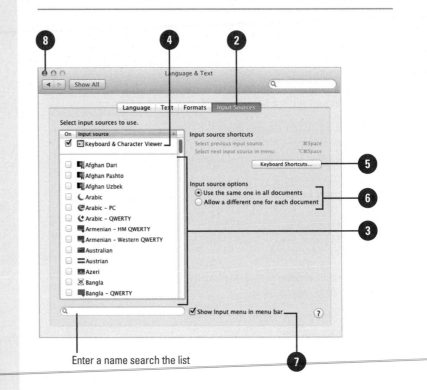

Enter a name search the list

Input menu

Keyboard Viewer

Set International Date, Time, and Number Formats

1. Click the **System Preferences** icon in the Dock, and then click the **Language & Text** icon.

2. Click the **Formats** tab.

3. Click the **Region** pop-up, and then select a region. If necessary, select the **Show all regions** check box to display your region.

4. Click **Customize**, specify the formats you want for Dates, Times, and Numbers, and then click **OK**.

5. Select a **Currency** and **Measurements Units** from the pop-ups.

6. Click the **Close** button.

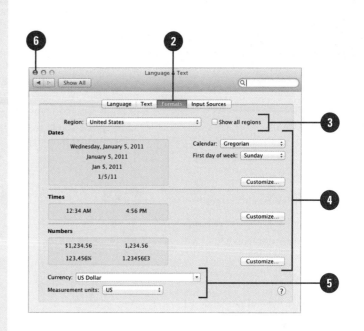

Change Language Options for Menus and Dialogs

1. Click the **System Preferences** icon in the Dock, and then click the **Language & Text** icon.

2. Click the **Language** tab.

 A list of available languages on your computer appears.

3. To add or remove languages, click **Edit List**, select or clear the check boxes, and then click **OK**.

4. Drag the language you want to the top of the list.

 If an application can't support the first language, it tries to use the second one, and so on.

5. Click the **Close** button.

 Changes take place the next time you launch the Finder or an application.

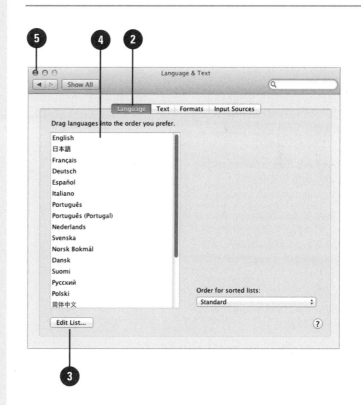

Changing Text Substitution Options

The Language & Text pane in System Preferences gives you options to automatically correct common spelling errors and insert symbols as you type. Mac OS X comes with a list of common text and symbol entries you can edit or remove. You can add words and phrases that you misspell, or add often-typed words and save time by just typing their initials. You can use text substitution to quickly insert symbols. For example, you can type (c) to insert ©. You can also set options to check spelling and select text by language, and automatically change double or single quotation marks.

Set Symbol and Text Substitution Options

1. Click the **System Preferences** icon in the Dock, and then click the **Language & Text** icon.

2. Click the **Text** tab.

3. Select the **Use symbol and text substitution** check box (**New!**) to enable the automatic substitution.

4. Select the check boxes you want to use for symbol and text substitution.

5. Select language and selection settings for the following options:

 ◆ Correct Spelling. Select the **Correct spelling automatically** check box to enable spell checking (**New!**).

 ◆ Spelling. Select **Automatic by Language** or a specific language to spell check.

 ◆ Word Break. Specifies how a word is highlighted when it's double-clicked. Select **Standard** or a specific language.

6. Select Smart Quote settings when you type double or single quotation marks.

7. To restore setting, click **Restore Defaults**.

8. Click the **Close** button.

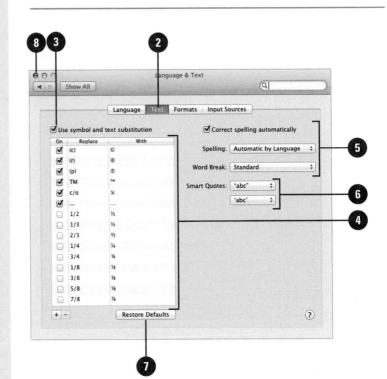

Add, Edit. or Remove a Text Substitution Entry

1. Click the **System Preferences** icon in the Dock, and then click the **Language & Text** icon.

2. Click the **Text** tab.

3. Do one of the following:

 ◆ **Add.** Click the **Add** (+) button, type a misspelled word or an abbreviation, press Tab, type the replacement text, and then press Return.

 ◆ **Edit.** double-click an entry, make a change, and then press Return.

 ◆ **Remove.** Select an entry, click **Remove** (-) button.

4. Click the **Close** button.

Add (+) and Remove (-) buttons

Replace Text as You Type

◆ To correct spelling errors or insert symbols automatically, continue typing until text substitution makes the required correction.

 ◆ **Enable Correct Spelling.** In the Language & Text Preferences dialog, select the **Correct spelling automatically** check box to enable automatic spell checking (**New!**) as you type.

See examples of text substitution in the following table.

Examples of Text Substitution

Type of Correction	If You Type	AutoCorrect Inserts
Common typos	can;t	can't
Common typos	windoes	windows
Superscript ordinals	2nd	2^{nd}
Stacked fractions	1/2	½
Smart quotes	" "	" "
Em dashes	Madison--a small city in Wisconsin--is a nice place to live.	Madison—a small city in Wisconsin— is a nice place to live.
Symbols	(c)	©
Symbols	(r)	®

Saving Energy and Managing Power

When you're not using your computer, you can save energy by putting it to sleep. When you put your computer to sleep, the power mode is set to low and the screen goes black to save energy. Your computer is still running, so it takes less time for it to wake up. You can use the Sleep command on the Apple menu to put your computer right to sleep, or you can put your computer and display to sleep automatically when it has been idle for a specific amount of time or when you schedule it at a regular time interval. You can also set the hard disk to sleep whenever possible to save more energy. If you have a Mac laptop, such as a MacBook, it automatically goes to sleep when you close the lid. You move your mouse or press a key to wake it up. If a security option is set in the Security pane in System Preferences, your computer requires a password when it wakes from a sleep. You can also schedule a computer restart or shutdown, at a regular time interval, or a restart after a power failure.

Set Sleep Options

1. Click the **System Preferences** icon in the Dock, and then click the **Energy Saver** icon.

2. Drag the slider to set a time interval for Computer sleep and Display sleep.

 IMPORTANT *To prevent your computer from sleeping at any time, drag the sliders for Computer and Display sleep to Never.*

 TROUBLE? *If the sleep time is less than the screen saver time, then increase the sleep time or click Screen Saver to change its time.*

3. To conserve energy, select the **Put the hard disk(s) to sleep when possible** check box.

4. Click the **Close** button.

Set a Sleep, Startup, or Shut Down Schedule

1. Click the **System Preferences** icon in the Dock, and then click the **Energy Saver** icon.

2. Click **Schedule**, and then click **Details**, if necessary.

3. Select or clear the **Start up or waker** check box. If so, select an interval from the pop-up, and then set a time.

4. Select or clear the bottom check box. If so, select an operation from the first pop-up menu, select an interval from the second pop-up, and then set a time.

5. Click **OK**, and then click the **Close** button.

Set Wake and Power Failure Restart Options

1. Click the **System Preferences** icon in the Dock, and then click the **Energy Saver** icon.

2. Select or clear the **Wake for Ethernet network access** check box.

3. Select or clear the **Allow power button to sleep the computer** check box.

4. Select or clear the **Start automatically after a power failure** check box.

5. Click the **Close** button.

Selecting a Startup Disk

Instead of starting from your local hard disk, you can start your computer from a CD or DVD, a network volume, another disk or disk partition (a single hard disk separated into two distinct areas), or another operating system, such as Microsoft Windows XP, Vista, or 7. Starting your computer with Windows is useful when you want to use applications that are not compatible with Mac OS X. When you start your computer in Windows, you need to use the Startup Disk Control Panel in the Apple menu to switch back to your Mac OS X startup disk. If Windows is not available in the Startup Disk preference pane, you need to have an Intel-based Mac and use Boot Camp Assistant to set up your computer. You can also restart you computer in Target Disk Mode, which allows you to connect to another computer using a FireWire cable and use it as a hard disk.

Select a Startup Disk

1. Click the **System Preferences** icon in the Dock, and then click the **Startup Disk** icon.

2. Click the icon of the system folder you want to use as the startup disk.

3. To restart your computer, click **Restart**.

 TIMESAVER *Hold down the Option key while you restart your computer, select a startup disk, and then click Restart.*

4. To restart your computer in order to connect to another computer using a FireWire cable, click **Target Disk Mode**, read the dialog for instructions, and then click **Restart**.

See Also

See Chapter 19,"Working with Mac OS X Along with Windows," on page 465 for information on starting your computer with Microsoft Windows XP, Vista, or 7.

Changing the Way a CD or DVD Starts

When you insert a CD or DVD into your computer, Mac OS X automatically performs an operation, such as opening iTunes and playing an audio CD. You can change what happens when you insert a CD or DVD in the CDs & DVDs preference pane in System Preferences. You can have Mac OS X open a dialog to ask you what to do, ignore it, run a script, or open an application, such as iTunes, iPhoto, iDVD, or Finder, to burn or play a disc. If you ignore a CD or DVD, the disc doesn't show up on the desktop or in a Finder window.

Change CD or DVD Start Settings

1. Click the **System Preferences** icon in the Dock, and then click the **CDs & DVDs** icon.

2. Click the pop-ups for each type of CD or DVD, and then select a startup option:

 ◆ **Ask what to do**. A dialog appears that asks you what to do with the disc.

 ◆ **Open an application**. Select Open Finder, Open application name or click Open An Application to select one.

 Mac OS X automatically opens the application you select.

 ◆ **Run Script**. Select and schedule a script to run.

 ◆ **Ignore**. Nothing happens.

3. Click the **Close** button.

Did You Know?

You can change Finder preferences to show CDs or DVDs on the desktop. Click the Finder menu, click Preferences, click General, select the CDs, DVDs, and iPods check box, and then click the Close button.

Controlling Sound

The Sound pane in System Preferences allows you to adjust input, output and alert volumes, change input and output sound devices, change alert sounds, and play Front Row, an entertainment system, and user interface sound effects, such as when you drag an icon to the Trash. You can use an input device, such as a microphone, to record your voice or give spoken commands on an output device, such as built-in or external speakers, to play music, words, and other sounds. If your computer has two stereo speakers, you can adjust the sound balance between them. If you don't want to hear sound from your speakers, you can turn on Mute, just like on your TV or stereo. If you use applications with volume controls, such as iTunes, the volume can only be equal to or less than the computer's output volume. To make volume control easier, you can add output volume to the menu bar.

Change Sound Effects

1. Click the **System Preferences** icon in the Dock, and then click the **Sound** icon.

2. Click the **Sound Effects** tab.

3. To change an alert sound, click a sound from the list.

4. Drag the **Alert volume** slider to adjust the alert volume, which is relative to the output volume.

 TIMESAVER *Hold down the Option key while you drag the main volume on the status menu bar to adjust the alert volume.*

5. To play Finder related sounds, select the **Play user interface sound effects** check box.

6. If you have volume keys on your keyboard, clear the **Play feedback when volume keys is changed** check box to disable the feedback option and use the volume keys.

7. To change output volume from the menu bar, select the **Show volume in menu bar** check box.

8. Click the **Close** button.

Volume on menu bar

Set Sound Output Options

1. Click the **System Preferences** icon in the Dock, and then click the **Sound** icon.

2. Click the **Output** tab.

3. Select a device for sound output.

 Options vary depending on the output sound device.

4. Drag the **Balance** slider to adjust the sound for the left and right speakers.

5. Drag the **Output volume** slider to increase or decrease the volume, or select the **Mute** check box to turn speaker sound off.

6. Click the **Close** button.

Set Sound Input Options

1. Click the **System Preferences** icon in the Dock, and then click the **Sound** icon.

2. Click the **Input** tab.

3. Select a device for sound input.

 Options vary depending on the input sound device.

4. Drag the **Input volume** slider to increase or decrease the volume.

 The Input level meter displays the sound level coming from the selected sound device.

5. Click the **Close** button.

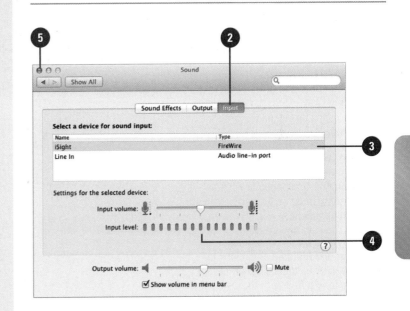

Recognizing Your Speech

The Speech pane in System Preferences allows you to initialize and customize speech recognition on your computer. **Speech recognition** is the ability to convert a spoken voice into commands or electronic text. However, Apple's speech recognition only does half the job; it only executes commands listed in the Speakable Commands window, which you can add or remove in groups, such as menu bar commands. You need another program, such as iListen (*www.macspeech.com*) to convert voice to text. After you turn on speech recognition, the Feedback window (a small circle microphone) appears, displaying the Esc key in the middle. Press and hold or press the Esc key, which you can change, to turn listening on and off. Now you can speak your commands.

Setup Listening Options

1 Click the **System Preferences** icon in the Dock, and then click the **Speech** icon.

2 Click the **Speech Recognition** tab, and then click the **Settings** tab.

3 Click the **Microphone** pop-up, and then select a microphone attached to your computer. Click **Calibrate** to improve recognition results, if necessary.

4 To change the listening key, click **Change Key**, enter a new key, and then click **OK**.

5 Click an option to listen while the listening key is pressed or while listening is turned on (by pressing the listening key).

If you select the second option, you can type a name and use the **Name** pop-up to specify whether the name must be spoken before each command.

6 Select the **Speak command acknowledgement** check box to have your computer repeat the command it heard.

7 Click the **Play this sound pop-up** to select a sound to play when your computer recognizes a spoken command.

8 Click the **Close** button.

Speech pane — Speech Recognition tab:
- Speakable Items: ● On ○ Off
- Settings | Commands
- Microphone: iSight — Calibrate...
- Listening Key: Esc — Change Key...
- Listening Method: ● Listen only while key is pressed ○ Listen continuously with keyword
- Keyword is: Required before each command
- Keyword: Computer
- Upon Recognition: ☐ Speak command acknowledgement
- Play this sound: Whit

Enable Speech Recognition and Select Commands

1. Click the **System Preferences** icon in the Dock, and then click the **Speech** icon.

2. Click the **Speech Recognition** tab.

3. Click the **On** option to display the Feedback window. To remove the window later, click the **Off** option.

4. Click the **Commands** tab.

5. Select or clear the check boxes with the groups of commands you want to enable or disable. If available, click **Configure** to specify other options.

6. Click a button or select the options you want:

 ◆ **Helpful Tips**. Click to display tips about speakable items.

 ◆ **Open Speakable Items Folder**. Click to open the Speakable Items folder.

7. Click the **Close** button.

Use Speech Recognition

1. Hold down the listening key or press it to turn listening on.

2. To display a list of commands, click the **Feedback window** triangle, and then click **Open Speech Commands Window**.

3. Say the name if necessary, and then say a command.

 Recognized commands appear above the Feedback window, while feedback appears below.

4. Release or press the listening key to turn listening off.

Spoken command

What Day Is It

Computer

It's Monday February 2

Computer response

Speech Commands
Standing By
Ready
What Day Is It

Commands you've spoken

Commands
Paste the clipboard here
Quit Speakable Items
Quit this application
Save this document
Show me what to say
Start screen saver
Tell me a joke
Turn on push to talk
What day is it?
What time is it?
▶ Application Switching

Available commands to speak

Letting Mac Do the Talking

Your Macintosh can speak to you as well as listen. Mac OS X can read aloud what appears on your screen, such as typed text, alert messages, window items, menus, and other interface items. It speaks using a synthesized voice, such as Pipe Organ, Cellos, or Junior. Some voices, such as Pipe Organ, are based on a song and sing the voice. Alex is a new synthesized English voice that uses advanced Apple synthesis to deliver a more natural speaking voice at a faster rate. You can use the Speech pane in System Preferences to select a default voice, set talking alert options for when alerts appear on the screen, and other spoken options for the user interface. Instead of just showing you, the Mac can tell you when an application needs your attention, such as when your printer is out of paper, or read buttons, icons, tabs, dialog options, and selected text in e-mails and documents when you point to it as well as read select text when you press a keyboard shortcut.

Set the Default Speaking Voice

1. Click the **System Preferences** icon in the Dock, and then click the **Speech** icon.

2. Click the **Text to Speech** tab.

3. Click the **System Voice** pop-up, and then select one of the voices from the list.

 ◆ Click **Show More Voices** at the bottom of the pop-up to display more voices from which to choose. Click **Show Fewer Voice** at the bottom of the pop-up to reduce the list.

 The computer speaks so you can hear the voice, and a description of the voice appears on the right.

4. To change the speed at which the voice speaks, drag the **Speaking Rate** slider.

5. To hear the select speaking voice at the current rate, click **Play**.

6. Click the **Close** button.

Set Spoken User Interface Options

1 Click the **System Preferences** icon in the Dock, and then click the **Speech** icon.

2 Click the **Text to Speech** tab.

3 Select the **Announce when alerts are displayed** check box, click **Set Alert Options**, specify the following alert options, and then click **OK**.

- ◆ **Voice.** Reads the contents of an alert dialog. Use the pop-up to select an alert voice.

- ◆ **Phrase.** Speak a certain phrase when an alert appears. Use the pop-up to select a phrase.

- ◆ **Delay.** Drag to set the delay between the alert and the computer speaking.

- ◆ **Play.** Click to display a sample of the alert.

4 Select the other spoken items options you want:

- ◆ **Announce when an application requires your attention**. Check to verbally announce when an application needs your attention, such as your printer is out of paper.

- ◆ **Speak selected text when the key is pressed**. Check to read any text you select when you press a key combination. In the dialog, press a keyboard shortcut or stop speaking selected text, and then click **OK**.

5 Click the **Close** button.

Setting Universal Access Options

Universal Access preferences make it easier for a person with a disability, such as difficulty seeing or hearing or controlling a mouse, to use a computer. You can set options to use VoiceOver so you can hear descriptions of screen items, have the screen flash when alert sounds occur, switch the screen to black and white for more visual contrast, zoom in on the screen to make images larger to see, use Sticky Keys or Slow Keys to help control the keyboard, and use Mouse Keys to make mouse functionality available on the numeric keypad. For the seeing impaired, screen zoom allows you to see the zoomed area in a separate window while keeping the rest of the screen at the default size (**New!**). The window can even follow the cursor or keep it in one place. If you're not sure where to find an option, you can use the Search field (**New!**).

Set Seeing and Hearing Options

1. Click the **System Preferences** icon in the Dock, and then click the **Universal Access** icon.

2. Click the **Seeing** tab.

3. Click the VoiceOver **On** or **Off** option.

4. Click the Zoom **On or Off** option, and then select the **Zoom in window** check box or clear to zoom in screen.

 ◆ Click **Options** to customize the way zoom works.

 TIMESAVER *Press* ⌘*+Option += (equal) to zoom in, or press* ⌘*+Option+- (minus) to zoom out.*

5. Click the **Black on White** or **White on Black** option.

6. Select or clear the **Use grayscale** check box.

7. Drag the slider to enhance the contrast as necessary.

8. Click the **Hearing** tab.

9. Select or clear the **Flash the screen when an alert sound occurs** check box.

10. Click the **Close** button.

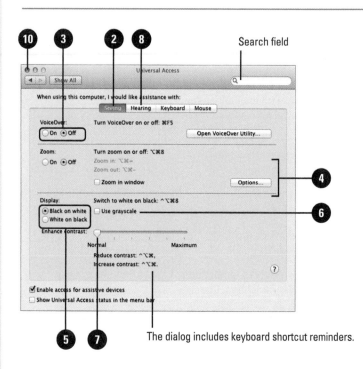

Search field

The dialog includes keyboard shortcut reminders.

Set Keyboard Options

1. Click the **System Preferences** icon in the Dock, and then click the **Universal Access** icon.

2. Click the **Keyboard** tab.

3. To press a group of modifier keys as a sequence, select the **On** option (Sticky Keys), select or clear the **Beep when a modifier key is set** check box, and then select or clear the **Display pressed keys on screen** check box. If so, white symbols appear when you press a modifier key.

4. To make the keyboard respond more slowly, click the **On** option (Slow Keys), drag the **Acceptance delay** slider, and then select or clear the **Use click key sounds** check box.

5. Click the **Close** button.

Set Mouse Options

1. Click the **System Preferences** icon in the Dock, and then click the **Universal Access** icon.

2. Click the **Mouse** tab.

3. Click the **On** option (Mouse Keys).

 Press 5 on the numeric keypad to click an item on the screen. Press 0 to press and hold, and then press 5 again to release, press and hold.

4. Set the slider options you want:

 - **Initial Delay.** Sets how the pointer moves when you press a key.

 - **Maximum Speed.** Sets the maximum pointer speed.

 - **Cursor Size.** Sets the cursor size.

5. Click the **Close** button.

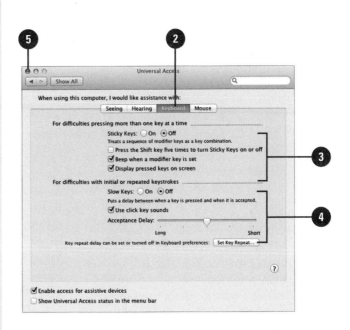

Having VoiceOver Read from the Screen

VoiceOver is a screen reader utility for Mac OS X that speaks the text in documents and windows. When you open accessible applications in VoiceOver, the application automatically speak text. For example, iChat speaks new text messages as they arrive.

When you move around your screen or within documents using VoiceOver, a dark rectangle appears, known as the VoiceOver cursor, to indicate the screen focus area for what to speak. You can use your mouse and keyboard with VoiceOver to move and configure the VoiceOver cursor. You can also let VoiceOver help you drag and drop. Simply mark the item you want to drag, then mark the destination and VoiceOver does the rest (**New!**). VoiceOver uses Apple synthesis to deliver a more natural speaking voice at a faster rate. Mac OS X includes built-in voices that speak 23 languages (**New!**), which you can customize to suit your needs. You can also download higher-quality versions of the languages (**New!**) from VoiceOver Utility.

VoiceOver also supports **Braille** (with greater display device support, including Bluetooth) and note-takers. If you have a supported Braille display connected to your computer, VoiceOver detects and configures it and can translate output into standard, Grade 2 contracted Braille for use in supported devices. A Braille display shows one line of screen content in a row of Braille cells. You can specify the default level at which you receive the content, known as the braille verbosity level (**New!**), as well as specific levels for individual controls, such as applications, check boxes, headings, images, and links. In addition, it supports more than 80 braille tables in a wide range of languages (**New!**).

Getting Started with VoiceOver

Before you can use VoiceOver, you need to turn it on in the Universal Access pane of System Preferences or use the keyboard shortcut ⌘+F5. In addition to turning on VoiceOver, it's a good idea to use the VoiceOver utility to customize VoiceOver so it works the way you want. You can set options in the following areas: General, Verbosity, Speech, Navigation, Web, Sound, Visual,

General

Speech

Commanders, Braille, and Activities. If you have an MobileMe account, you can use VoiceOver syncing to automatically update your VoiceOver preferences on all your Macs.

Working with VoiceOver

The easiest way to use VoiceOver is to use the VoiceOver keys, the Control and Option keys together. These are known as VO keys. When used together, the Control and Options keys allows you to control VoiceOver and move the VoiceOver cursor. However, it's easy to get lost. If you do get lost in VoiceOver and you're not sure where the focus is located, you can use the F1 through F6 keys with the VO keys to hear information about items where the VoiceOver cursor, keyboard, or mouse pointer is focused. If you are not sure what a key on the keyboard does in VoiceOver, you can use **keyboard help** to learn the names of the keys. After you start keyboard help, simply, press any key to hear its name. If you like to use the numeric pad on your extended keyboard, you can use **NumPad** and **Keyboard Commanders** to program the keys with VoiceOver com-

mands. If you prefer using menus instead of VO keyboard shortcuts, you can use one of the VoiceOver menu's to get help with or execute a command. The oversized white-on-black menu makes it easy to use.

In VoiceOver, you can navigate sequentially through a document or application or skip through by object. You can also create **hot spots** to monitor an object or area in a window and get notification when something changes. If you can't find what you're looking for, you can perform **smart searches** for objects and text in the current window.

When you're browsing the Web, VoiceOver can begin reading a Web page immediately when it's loaded. It also allows you to intelligently navigate around Web pages, including tables to important parts using Web spots.

If you use a trackpad, you can control VoiceOver by touching the pad. The surface of the trackpad acts as the active window with each corner representing absolute window coordinates. VoiceOver guides you through the process using voice commands.

Braille

Commanders

Setting VoiceOver Preferences

Before you can use VoiceOver, you need to turn it on in the Universal Access pane of System Preferences. In addition to turning on VoiceOver, you can also open the VoiceOver utility, which you can use to set a variety of different options. You can set options in the following areas: General, Verbosity, Speech, Navigation, Web, Sound, Visual, NumPad, Braille, and Activities (**New!**).

Set VoiceOver Preferences

① Click the **System Preferences** icon in the Dock, and then click the **Universal Access** icon.

② Click the **Seeing** tab.

③ Click the VoiceOver **On** or **Off** option.

TIMESAVER *Press ⌘+F5 to turn VoiceOver on and off.*

④ Click **Open VoiceOver Utility**.

TIMESAVER *Double-click the VoiceOver Utility icon in the Utilities folder.*

⑤ Select a category on the left, and then select the options you want.

◆ **General.** Enter a login greeting and select a portable preference option.

◆ **Verbosity.** Specify text and announcement options. Also includes general and instructional hint options. In the Braille tab (**New!**), you can specify the default level (amount of information you want to receive) for use with a refreshable braille display. You can also set levels for specific controls, such as headings, images, and links.

◆ **Speech.** Specify voice and pronunciation options. You can mute speech or customize the voice rate, pitch, or volume.

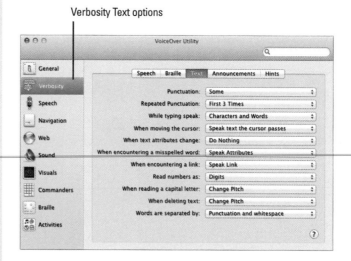

Verbosity Text options

◆ **Navigation.** Specify mouse and keyboard options. You can change VoiceOver cursor tracking options.

◆ **Web.** Specify Web navigation options, either DOM (Document Object Model) or Group (such as paragraph to paragraph).

◆ **Sound.** Mute sounds and enable positional audio.

◆ **Visuals.** Specify VoiceOver cursor, Caption and Braille panel, and menu options.

◆ **Commanders.** Enable NumPad Commander and Keyboard Commander, and customize commands. You can enable, assign, and use Quick Nav (**New!**) to navigate web pages and applications using only the arrow keys and navigate web pages using single keys.

◆ **Braille.** Specify display and input options.

◆ **Activities.** Set up activities and customize VoiceOver settings for specific users (**New!**). You can set up different voices, rates, and hot spots for different situations and applications. You can switch activities manually or have VoiceOver switch them for you based on the application in use.

⑥ Click the **Close** button.

Verbosity Announcements options

Navigation options

Visuals VoiceOver Cursor options

Using VoiceOver Commands

The easiest way to use VoiceOver is to use the VoiceOver keys, the Control and Option keys together. These are known as VO keys. When used together, the Control and Option keys allows you to control VoiceOver and move the VoiceOver cursor. If you're not sure what a keyboard key does, you can enable keyboard help, where you can press any key to hear its name as well as the name of the VoiceOver command. In addition to the VO keys, you can also use the standard keyboard shortcuts that work within Mac OS X. You can quickly turn VoiceOver on and off using a keyboard shortcut, ⌘+F5. If your using a menu instead of a VO keyboard shortcut, you can use one of the VoiceOver menu's to get help with or execute a command. The over-sized white-on-black menu makes it easy to use. In VoiceOver, you can create up to 10 hot spots to monitor an object or area in an accessible window and get notification when something changes.

Use VoiceOver Commands

1. To start or stop VoiceOver, press ⌘+F5.

2. Use the following keyboard shortcuts for help with VoiceOver.

 IMPORTANT *On a portable computer where function keys are used of other things, you need to press the Fn key first.*

 ◆ **VoiceOver menu.** VO+F7; use arrow keys to navigate

 ◆ **Item Chooser menu.** VO+I

 ◆ **Windows Chooser menu.** Lists all open windows: VO+F2 twice

 ◆ **Program Chooser menu.** Lists all open programs: VO+F1 twice.

 ◆ **VoiceOver Help.** VO+?; Help for an item: VO+H

 ◆ **Command menu.** Command menu for an item: VO+H+H

 ◆ **Select a menu.** Return

 ◆ **Stop an action or close a menu.** Esc

 ◆ **Keyboard help.** Hear key names on keyboard: VO+K

 ◆ **VoiceOver Utility.** VO+F8

VoiceOver Menu

③ Use the following common commands for VoiceOver.

◆ **What's on the screen.** Under mouse: VO+F5; keyboard highlight: VO+F4; VoiceOver cursor box: VO+F3

◆ **Read everything.** VoiceOver cursor: VO+A; In window, Dock, or desktop, VO+Shift+W

◆ **Pause/resume speech.** Press and release Control; press again to resume. Repeat phrase: VO+Z

◆ **Show/Hide caption panel.** VO+Command+F10

◆ **Show/Hide Braille panel.** VO+Command+F9

◆ **NumPad Commander on/off.** VO+Clear

◆ **Navigation.** VO+arrow keys; visible area top or bottom: VO+Home or VO+End

◆ **Links on a Web page.** VO+U

◆ **Text in a document.** Read all text: VO+A; read sentence: VO+S; read line: VO+L

◆ **Search.** Find text: VO+F; find hyperlink: VO+Command+L; find graphic: VO+Command+G

④ Use the following commands to create and use hot spots.

◆ **Create Hot Spot.** Select item, and then press VO+Shift+ [number key]

◆ **Go to Hot Spot.** Press VO+ [number key]

◆ **Hear Hot Spot.** Press VO+ Command+[number key]

◆ **Watch for Hot Spot Changes.** Press VO+ Command+Shift+ [number key]

VoiceOver Navigation menu

VoiceOver Commands menu

Setting Ink Preferences

If you have an ink device on your computer, you can use System Preferences to improve the recognition of ink to text. You can adjust Ink Preferences to your writing style, either widely or closely spaced, and to see how quickly your writing pen cursor changes back into a clicking device. You can improve recognition by adding words it may not know, such as names (like a custom dictionary for spell checking). As you write, Ink recognizes certain gestures or shapes, which get performed as commands, such as Undo, or pressed as keys, such as Delete or Space. The Gestures tab provides a list of gestures that you can turn on and off.

Set Ink Preferences

1. Click the **System Preferences** icon in the Dock, and then click the **Ink** icon.

2. Click the **On** or **Off** option to turn handwriting recognition on or off.

3. Click the **Settings** tab.

4. Specify the options you want:

 ◆ **My handwriting style is**. Drag slider to set spacing.

 ◆ **Allow me to write anywhere**. Check to use Anywhere mode.

 ◆ **Language**. Click to select a ink writing language.

 ◆ **Ink pad font**. Click to select a default recognition font.

 ◆ **Show ink window**. Check to use Ink Pad mode.

 ◆ **Show ink in menu bar**. Check to add the Ink menu commands to the menu bar.

5. Click the **Gestures** tab.

6. Select or clear the check boxes to turn gesture actions on and off.

7. Click the **Word List** tab.

8. Use the buttons to add or change uncommon words you use.

9. Click the **Close** button.

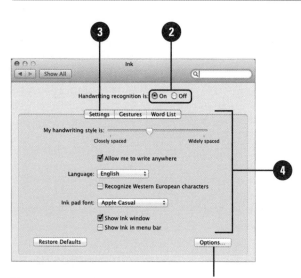

Click to adjust additional writing and mouse usage options.

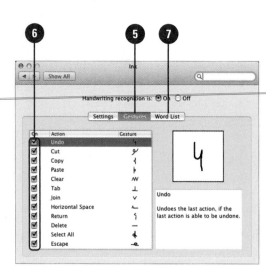

Using Mac OS X Applications

Introduction

Now that you know how to work with the graphical elements that make Mac OS X work, you're ready to work with applications. An **application**, also known as **app**, is software you use to accomplish a specific task, such as word processing or managing files on your computer.

Mac OS X comes with several small applications and utilities that are extremely useful for completing basic tasks, such as creating a written document or performing basic calculations. Its suite of applications let you organize your workflow and create sticky notes. You can even edit and create digital media for use on the Internet, CD, or burn it onto a DVD. In addition, Mac OS X makes setting up and communicating over the Internet easier than ever. And, if you happen to own an iSight (Macintosh Web camera), you can communicate with other web cam owners using audio and video. If you deal with a lot of fonts, Mac OS X comes packaged with a font management system second to none. The applications in Mac OS X are powerful tools for organization, gaming, controlling digital media, and Internet communication, just to name a few.

In addition to the applications that come with Mac OS X, you also have a multitude of applications developed by third-party developers. You can quickly access, purchase, download, and install these applications using the Mac App Store. If an app is not currently available at the App Store, you can also purchase it directly from the developer over the Internet using the company web site or other retail locations.

What You'll Do

Get Apps from the App Store

Download and Install Other Apps

Use Mac OS X Apps

Launch and Quit Apps

Open Applications and Files

View Full-Screen Apps

Switch Between Apps

Play Chess

Create and Edit an Address Book

Manage an Address Book

Perform Calculations and Conversions

Capture Images with a Digital Camera

Capture Screen Shots with Grab

Preview Images and PDF's

Use Apps with Auto Save

Create Sticky Notes

Manage Fonts with Font Book

Activate, Deactivate, and Customize Fonts

Work with Dashboard and Widgets

6

Getting Apps at the App Store

With the built-in Mac App Store (**New!**), you can quickly buy (many are free too!) and download Apps to your computer. When an update is available for an application, the developer can use the Apple Push Notification service to let you know. When you start an update, the App Store delivers only the data that is different from the previous version, so it uses internet bandwidth more efficiently. Before you can start using the Apple Store to make purchases and download software, you need to sign in with an Apple ID account, which includes iTunes, MobileMe, or Apple Support. If you don't have one, you can click the Sign In link in the App Store, click the Create Apple ID button, and then follow the on-screen instructions to quickly create one (**New!**). After you purchase an app, you can install it free on every Mac you own.

Find, Buy, Download, and Install an Application at the App Store

1. Click the **App Store** icon in the Dock.

2. Click **Sign In** in Quick Links, enter your Apple ID and password, and then click **Sign In**.

3. If you want to make a purchase using an iTunes gift card or other credit, click **Redeem**, enter your code, and then click **Redeem**.

4. Locate the application you want.

 ◆ Click the **Featured**, **Top Charts** or **Categories** button on the toolbar and then browse.

 ◆ Type a name in the Search bar on the toolbar, and then choose an item from the list.

5. Click the app's icon or name, and then click a price or **Free** for free Apps, and then click **Buy App** or **Install App**.

6. If prompted, enter an administrator's name and password, and click **Done** to download and install.

7. To get download and install status, click the **Purchases** button on the toolbar, or click the **Launchpad** icon in the Dock, and then view the app's icon and progress bar.

Sign In link

Work in the App Store

◆ **Pause or resume a download.**
Click the **Purchases** button, find
the app in the list, and then click
Pause, or **Resume**. In Launchpad,
click the application icon.

◆ **Cancel a download.** Click the
Purchases button, find the app in
the list, and then click **Cancel**.

◆ **Check for unfinished downloads.**
Click the **Store** menu, and then
click **Check for Unfinished
Downloads**.

◆ **Download and install a purchased
app on another Mac.** On the other
Mac, open App Store, sign in using
the Apple ID that purchased the
app, click the **Purchases** button,
find the app in the list, and then
click **Install**.

◆ **Update an app.** Click the **Update**
button, and then download and
install the updates at once, or
individually from the list. All of the
updates are free unless specified
by the developer as an upgrade for
purchase.

◆ **Delete an app from the App Store.**
In Launchpad, click and hold down
the app icon until all the icons
start to wiggle, and then click the
app's **Delete** button (x).

◆ **Review and change account
information.** When signed in, click
the **Store** menu, and then click
View Account, or click **Account** in
Quick Links.

See Also

See "Setting Parental Controls" on
page 392 for more information on set-
ting restrictions for the App Store.

Apps purchased Purchases button Status

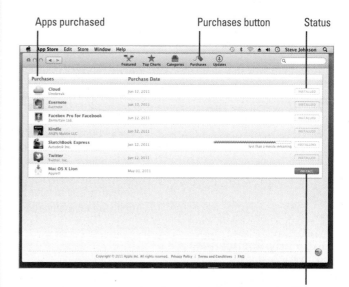

Install an app purchased on another Mac

Delete app from the App Store Launchpad

Click to switch between Launchpad pages

Downloading and Installing Other Apps

Mac OS X comes with a set of applications automatically loaded during the installation of the operating system, and appear on the hard drive within the Applications folder. All other third-party applications need to be installed separately. You can download applications using the App Store (**New!**). If an application is not currently available there, you can install a third-party application by inserting the software installation CD or DVD and following the instructions, or by downloading the software from the Web (**New!**) in your browser, such as Safari, to your hard disk, uncompressing the file if necessary, starting the installer (typically in a disk image file, .dmg, which mounts as a disk icon), and following the instructions. In some cases, an installer application is not used to perform an installation. In that case, all you need to do is simply drag the software files to your hard disk, typically in the Applications folder. To uninstall an application, simply drag the icon (or its folder) to the Trash.

Install Third-Party Applications Downloaded from the Internet

1. Download the software application from the Web.

 The file typically appears on your desktop. If you use Safari to download your application file, it automatically uncompressed it into a disk image file (.dmg), so you don't have to.

 Compressed files use these file extensions: **.sit** (standard Mac), **.zip** (standard Windows), **.tar** (tape archive Unix), **.gz** (standard Unix), **.tar.gz**, or **.tgz**

2. If the file is compressed, use the StuffIt Expander application (available at *www.download.com*) to uncompress the file.

3. Double-click the disk image file (**.dmg**).

 A disk icon from the disk image mounts on your desktop.

4. Double-click the mounted disk icon and the installer (as needed) to start the installer program, and then follow the instructions.

5. Drag the disk image file into the Trash to remove and eject it.

1 Use the Download button in Safari to displays downloads (**New!**)

Installer app icon

Using Mac OS X Apps

Mac OS X comes with several accessories, built-in applications that, while not as feature-rich as many applications sold separately, are extremely useful for completing basic tasks. A frequently used list of Mac OS X applications is provided here. However, you can view a complete list of installed applications in Launchpad or in the Applications folder. The Applications folder also contains a Utilities folder with additional applications you can use to perform specialized functions, which are detailed more in later chapters.

Frequently Used Mac OS X Applications

Program	Description
Address Book	Stores names, addresses, and other contact information
AppleScript	Automates tasks using a programming language
App Store (**New!**)	Provides a place to buy, download, and install applications
Automator	Automates tasks using workflows and no programming
Calculator	Performs arithmetic calculations
Dashboard	Provides a screen for mini-program called widgets
Dictionary	Provides an illustrated dictionary and thesaurus
Directory	Provides access to shared information about people, groups, location and resources
DVD Player	Plays sound, music, and video
FaceTime (**New!**)	Makes video calls to other Intel-based Mac computers, iPad2, iPhone 4, or iPod touch
Font Book	Installs, previews, and manages fonts and font collections
iCal	Keeps track of calendar appointments
iChat	Sends and receives instant messages to online contacts
Image Capture	Transfers images from your camera to your computer
iTunes	Plays digital sound files
Mail	Provides e-mail, newsgroup, and directory services
Mission Control (**New!**)	Shows everything running on the computer and organizes windows into spaces
Photo Booth	Takes pictures and adds visual effects
Preview	Views, rotates, resizes, crops, and converts image files
QuickTime Player	Plays and edits media located on your computer, a CD, or Internet
Safari	Displays Web (HTML) pages
Stickies	Creates notes for reminders, lists, and messages
TextEdit	Creates, edits, and displays text, Rich Text Format, and Word documents
Time Machine	Backs up everything on your computer

Launching Apps

All Mac OS X applications are automatically loaded during the installation of the operating system, and appear on the hard drive within the Applications folder. All other third-party applications need to be installed using the Mac App Store or separately with third-party installer. You can open, or launch, an application several ways. The quickest way is to use Launchpad (**New!**), which is a full-screen home page for all your applications. Launchpad is conveniently available in the Dock. Launchpad can contain multiple pages, where you can rearrange or move Apps, and organize Apps into folders. If you no longer want an app in Launchpad (that's not part of Mac OS X), you can uninstall it. In addition to Launchpad, you can also open Apps available in the Dock and the Applications folder.

Open, Move, or Delete an Application from Launchpad

1 Click the **Launchpad** icon in the Dock.

 TIMESAVER *Pinch three fingers and your thumb on the trackpad to start Launchpad* (**New!**).

2 To move to the next page of Apps, swipe left or right using two fingers, click the gray dots above dock (white is the current page), or press the arrow keys.

3 To open an app, click its icon.

4 To rearrange Apps, drag its icon to a new location.

 ◆ If the location is on another page, drag to the right edge of the screen, pause, let the next page appear, and then release at a new location.

 ◆ To add an app to the Dock, drag it to a Dock location.

5 To uninstall an app, click and hold an app's icon until all Apps wiggle, and then click the app's **Delete** button (x).

 ◆ If you want to app back, you need to download it again.

6 To close Launchpad, press Esc or click a blank area in Launchpad.

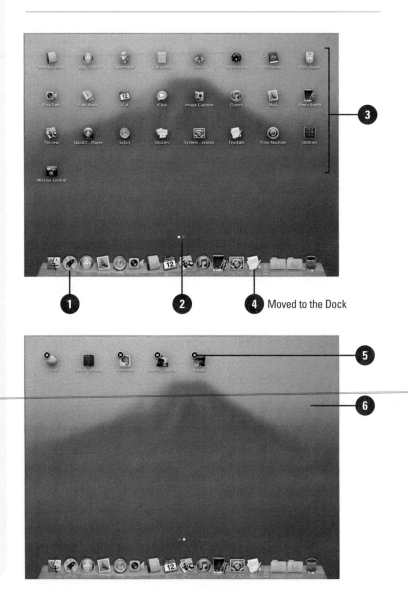

Moved to the Dock

Work with Folders in Launchpad

1 Click the **Launchpad** icon in the Dock.

2 Use any of the following folder operations.

◆ **Open a folder.** Click a folder icon.

◆ **Create a folder.** Drag one app's icon over another. Launchpad creates a folder and suggests a name.

◆ **Change a folder's name.** Click to open the folder, click the folder name, and then type a new name.

◆ **Move an app in a folder.** Drag the app onto the folder. Each folder can hold as many as 32 Apps.

◆ **Move an app out of a folder.** Click to open the folder, and then drag the app out of the folder.

Open folder Selected folder name

1

Folder contents; can hold as many as 32

Open an Application from a Finder Window

1 Double-click the hard drive icon on your desktop.

2 To change views, click a view button, such as View By Columns.

3 Click the **Applications** folder or navigate to the application folder.

4 Double-click on the application name, or application icon, to launch.

Application details are displayed

Opening Apps and Files

As you open applications and files, their names are kept in the Recent Items submenu in the Apple menu for easy access the next time you want to open a specific application or file. The Mac OS has always allowed you to double-click a document icon to launch the application used to create it and the document itself. If the Mac OS doesn't know what application created it (and gives you an error message), you can use drag and drop in the Dock to help you open the document. You can drag a document icon in the Dock on an application icon. If a document is stored in the Documents folder, you can click the Documents folder in the Dock and then click the document in the stack list to open it.

Open Recently Used Applications and Files

1. Click the **Apple** menu, and then point to **Recent Items**.

2. Click the recent application or file under the **Applications** or **Documents** listing.

3. To clear the recent list, click the **Apple** menu, point to **Recent Items**, and then click **Clear Menu**.

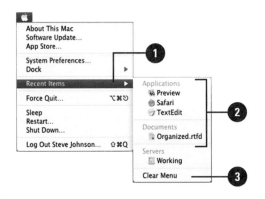

Open Applications and Files

◆ Double-click the document icon.

◆ Drag the document icon to the application icon in the Dock, either the one that created the document or one that will accept it. If the application can possibly open it, the application icon becomes highlighted. Release the icon to open the application and the document.

> **NOTE** *Hold down Option+⌘ while you drag a document icon into the Dock to force all applications to accept the icon. However, an error message may result.*

◆ Click the Documents folder in the Dock, and then click a document in the stack list.

Double-click to open Blank icon; no association

Drag icon onto an accepting application icon to open Documents folder

Viewing Full-Screen Apps

Mac OS X provides support for full-screen Apps (**New!**), such as iCal, Mail, Safari, Photo Booth, QuickTime, and Dashboard. Apps built to take advantage of the full-screen have a Full-screen button (diagonal double-arrows) in the window title bar. You can have multiple full-screen Apps open at the same time. A swipe of the trackpad takes you from full-screen to another or back to the desktop. When an app is full-screen, the menu bar is hidden, which you can access by pointing to the top of the screen. Dashboard is a full-screen app, which is available to the left of your desktop.

Work with Full-Screen Applications

◆ Open full-screen. Click the **Full-Screen** button in the right-corner of the window title bar.

◆ Unhide menu bar. Point to the top of the screen.

◆ Close full-screen. Point to the top of the screen to display the hidden menu, and then click the **Full-Screen** button.

◆ Move between full-screen Apps. Swipe left and right, or press the arrow keys.

Click the Full-Screen button to expand.

Point to top of the screen to display hidden menu.

Click the Full-Screen button to collapse.

Switching Between Apps

The Dock is initially located at the bottom of the desktop and is most often used to launch an application or switch from one application to another. When you launch an application, its icon appears in the Dock with a black arrow below it (when a General preference option is set). If an application is not available in the Dock, you can hide any open applications to display the desktop, open your hard disk, and then launch the application you want. If you arrange open application windows so that they are visible, you can switch among them simply by clicking in the window in which you want to work.

Hide and Show an Application

1. Click the application menu.

 In this case, the Chess menu.

2. Click **Hide *application name*** to hide the application.

 TIMESAVER *Press ⌘+H to hide the application.*

3. Point to the bottom of the screen to display the Dock. You'll see the hidden application in the Dock.

4. To show the application, click the application icon in the Dock.

Hide Other Applications

1. Click the application menu, and then click **Hide Others**.

 TIMESAVER *Press Option+ ⌘+H to hide all other applications.*

Did You Know?

You can bring forward an application and its windows and hide all other applications. Hold down Option+ ⌘, and then click the program icon in the Dock.

Chess	
About Chess	
Preferences...	⌘,
Services	▶
Hide Chess	⌘H
Hide Others	⌥⌘H
Show All	
Quit Chess	⌘Q

Switch Between Applications

Mac OS X provides several ways to switch between applications:

◆ Click a visible window in the other application.

◆ Display the Dock, and then click an application icon to show or launch the application.

◆ Press and hold down ⌘, and then repeatedly press the Tab key to highlight the Dock icon of an open application. (Use Shift+⌘+Tab to move backwards) Release both keys when you reach the one you want to open.

To leave without switching applications, press the Esc key.

TIMESAVER *Press ⌘+Tab once to open the application you used most recently. This is very useful when you are switching between two applications.*

◆ Press F11 (use Exposé) to hide all open windows, double-click the hard disk icon, open the Applications folder, and then double-click an application icon.

Did You Know?

You can quickly switch between windows within an application (including the Finder). Repeatedly press ⌘+~ (the Tilde key to the left of the number 1 key) to cycle through open windows in the application. Release both the keys to display the window you want.

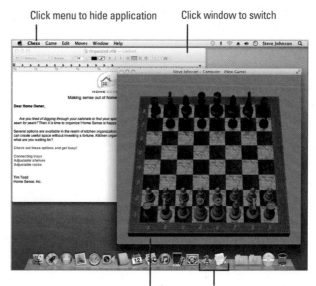

Click menu to hide application Click window to switch

Active window Click icon in the Dock to switch

Quitting Apps

When you're done working with an application, you should exit, or close it, to conserve your computer's resources. If an application stops responding while you work, Mac OS X provides you with the option to end the task. When you end a task, you'll probably lose any unsaved work in the problem application. If the problem persists, you might need to reinstall the application or contact product support to fix the problem.

Quit an Application

1. Click the application menu.

 In this case, the Chess menu.

2. Click **Quit** *application name*.

 TIMESAVER *Press ⌘+Q to quit an application.*

3. If necessary, click **Save** to save your changes.

Quit an Application That is Not Responding

1. Click the **Apple** menu, and then click **Force Quit**.

 TIMESAVER *Press ⌘+ Option+Esc to force a quit.*

2. Click the application name you want to force a quit.

3. Click **Force Quit**.

4. Click **Force Quit** again to confirm you want to force a quit.

5. Click the **Close** button.

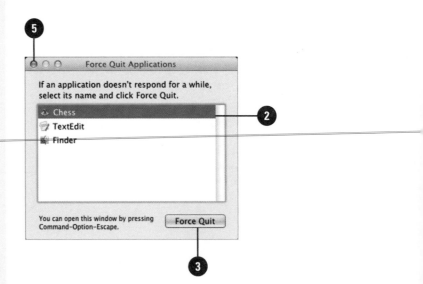

Playing Chess

CHECKMATE, oh how I love to hear those words, or at least when I'm the one saying them. Computers aren't just for business, worksheets, and documents. We all know that there are thousands of games available for computer systems, but one of the most challenging games in the world is available as soon as you load Mac OS X. Chess is available in Launchpad and the Applications folder and ready for you to play in full-screen (**New!**). Chess gives you more options, and even makes it quite a challenge to those who have moved beyond the beginner stage.

Play Chess

1. Click the **Launchpad** icon in the Dock, and then click the **Chess** icon.

2. To play in full-screen, click the **Full-Screen** button.

3. Click and drag a piece.

4. Black responds with a move.

5. Click the **Moves** menu, and then click **Take Back Move**, **Show Hint**, or **Show Last Move**.

6. Click the **Chess** menu, and then click **Preferences**. Select from the following options:

 ◆ Click the **Board** pop-up to select a new playing surface.

 ◆ Click the **Pieces** pop-up to select different playing pieces.

 ◆ Select the check boxes for Speech to use voice recognition to call your moves.

 ◆ Drag the **Computer Plays** slider to increase or decrease the computer's playing skills.

 ◆ Select the **Show Move in Title** check box to display the current move in the Title bar.

7. Click the **Close** button.

8. Click the **Game** menu, and then select a game option, such as New Game or Save Game.

9. Quit Chess.

Creating an Address Book

When you work with Address Book, you have the ability to create cards of information (**New!**). Each card can hold all the information you want to keep on a contact, no matter how many phone numbers and e-mail addresses a particular friend, or company might have. In addition, you can add a picture with a drag and a drop. Address Book comes packaged with a bunch of features such as: label generation, change of address notification, synchronization with MobileMe or iTunes, Google Contacts, or Yahoo! Address Book, view iChat Buddy status (**New!**), and even the ability to use speech recognition to look up and search the Address Book. With MobileMe or iTunes, you can sync across multiple computer or devices, including iPhone, iPad, or iPod touch (**New!**).

Create an Address Book

1. Click the **Address Book** icon in the Dock.

2. Click the **View** menu, and then click **Group** or click the **Groups** icon to display groups.

3. To create a group, click the **New Group** (+) button, give the new group a descriptive name, and then press Return.

4. Double-click the group or **All Contacts** you wan to use.

5. Click the **New Card** (+) button to add a new card.

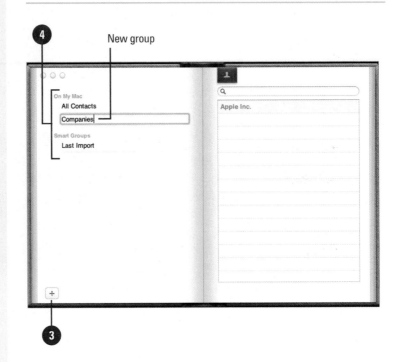

New group

Did You Know?

You can select and update your "me" card. Address Book automatically creates an address "me" card for you with information you entered when you set up your computer. Other applications, such as iCal, iChat, and Mail, use information from your "me" card. You can keep some or all of the information private and exclude it when you send your card to contacts. To display your "me" card, click the Card menu, and then click Go to My Card. To use another card as a "me" card, select the card, click the Card menu, and then click Make This My Card.

6 Type a Name, and then using the Tab key, type a Company Name (if necessary). If so, select the **Company** check box.

7 Press Tab or click in card fields to add information such as: Phone number, e-mail address, home address, Internet home page, and Instant Messaging user name (a MobileMe or AIM screen name).

If you enter an IM or AIM user name, you can view iChat Buddy status while browsing contacts in the Address Book.

8 To change a field name, click on the **Field** pop-up, and then select a field or click **Custom**.

9 To add a field, click the **Card** menu, point to **Add Field**, and then select a field type.

10 If a field is not needed, click the **Remove** button (-) to remove it.

11 Click **Done**.

12 Quit Address Book.

Did You Know?

You can archive your Address Book data. If your Address Book data is important, you can back up the data in case of a catastrophic failure. Open the Address Book application, click the File menu, point to Export, and then click Address Book Archive. The file name comes with the date of the archive. All you have to do is select where you'd like to save the archive, and then click Save. To restore the data, click the File menu, point to Import, and then click Address Book Archive. Select the file with the correct date, and then click Open.

For Your Information

Importing and Syncing Contacts from Yahoo!

Address Book lets you import and sync Yahoo! contacts by simply adding a Yahoo! account using the Add (+) button on the Accounts tab in Address Book Preferences. When you add a Yahoo! account, all your Yahoo! contacts are imported into Address Book (**New!**). When you make change to a Yahoo! contact in Address Book, the change is updated on your Mac and Yahoo! Address Book. You can view Yahoo! contacts separately from groups or with all contacts.

Importing Contacts into Address Book

Address Book creates and reads vCards, the standard method of exchanging data between applications. If you have vCards in another application, such as an e-mail application, you can import or export addresses with Address Book. To create a vCard, drag an address card out of the Address Book window. You can drag individual vCards in and out of the Address Book window. To import a set of vCards, click the File menu, point to Import, click vCards, select the file that contains the exported addresses, click Open, and then click OK (if you're updating contact information, click Review Duplicates to reconcile conflicts).

Editing an Address Book

Once a contact is placed within the Address Book, it's a simple matter to edit or add information concerning a contact. Editing or updating an Address Book contact involves the same skills learned in creating a contact, with the exception that the information is already there, so all you need to do is edit, add, or delete the contact. You can add, change, and remove fields—including yearless birthdays (**New!**)—as well as put a face with a name by inserting an existing or capture a new iPhoto picture (**New!**). In addition, you can also use the information in the Address Book to start other operations: click an address to see a Google map of the location, click a URL to open the website, click an email address to send an email or start a FaceTime video call (**New!**), press and hold an email to access social network profiles, such as Facebook (**New!**), or click the green circle (which indicates online status) next to a contact picture to invite a contact to text chats in iChat, AIM, or other chat application.

Edit an Address Book

1. Click the **Address Book** icon in the Dock.

2. Click the **View** menu, and then click **Group** or click the **Groups** icon to display groups.

3. Double-click the group or **All Contacts** you want to modify.

4. Select the Name from the available cards in the Group.

5. Click **Edit**.

 IMPORTANT *The Edit button is a toggle button, and once it's clicked, the name changes to Done.*

Search bar

2

All Contacts

Apple Inc.
Gene **Gadd**
Steve Johnson
Julie **Kenney**
Perspection, Inc.
Beth Teyler

Steve Johnson
Perspection, Inc.

home 925-555-1450
work stevej@perspection.com
home 3526 Valley Ave.
Pleasanton CA 94588
USA

note

+ Edit Share

4 **5**

6 Click in any of the fields to edit the existing information.

◆ **Change a field name.** Click on the **Field** pop-up, and then select a field or click **Custom**.

◆ **Add a field.** Click the **Card** menu, point to **Add Field**, and then select a field type.

◆ **Remove a field.** Click the **Remove** button (-) next to it.

7 To add a picture, double-click the picture frame, select a picture (Choose from a file, Import Face from iPhoto (**New!**), Capture from a video camera, or Apply an effect), and then click **Set**.

8 Click **Done**.

9 To remove a contact from the list, select a contact, press the Delete key, and then confirm your delete.

10 To use information to start other tasks, click the label next to the field, and then select a command (varies based on field type), such as Map this Address, Send Email, FaceTime, Search with Spotlight, or Open URL.

11 Quit Address Book.

Did You Know?

You can let the Address Book read a contact to you. Control-click an item in the contact window, point to Speech, and then click Start Speaking. To end the audio, Control-click, point to Speech, and then click Stop Speaking.

You can search for Address Book info in Google or Spotlight. Control-click a searchable item (such as name or phone) in the contact window, and then click Search in Google or Search in Spotlight.

Editing field

For Your Information

Printing from the Address Book

Address Book makes it easy to print a mailing list or print labels. The expanded Print dialog provides options to select a printing style and specify the specific fields from the Address Book you want to include in the printing. To print a mailing list or labels from Address Book, click the File menu, click Print, select a printer from the pop-up, select Lists or Mailing Labels from the Style pop-up, select a paper size from the pop-up, select an orientation, select or clear the attributes (fields) to display the information you want (such as phone, e-mail, address, Instant Messenger, photo, job title, etc.), select a font size from the pop-up, specify the number of copies, preview the results in the left pane, and then click Print.

Managing and Sharing an Address Book

Unlike paper address books, the address book in Mac OS X can create a very organized system... if you know what to do. You could create logical groups, and then use obvious naming conventions for each contact. You can name your groups by family, school, work, community service, kids sports teams just to name a few. Address Book has many features that helps you manage your groups and the contacts you create, and then share them with others. You can even use the vCard format to exchange contact information between various programs or set up synchronization and sharing with MobileMe or iTunes, Google Contacts, or Yahoo Address Book. With MobileMe or iTunes, you can sync across multiple computer or devices, including iPhone, iPad, or iPod touch (**New!**). In addition, you can add accounts and search for contacts and addresses using CardDAV, Microsoft Exchange 2007 or later, Yahoo! or LDAP (Lightweight Directory Access Protocol) servers.

Manage an Address Book

1. Click the **Address Book** menu, and then click **Preferences**.

2. Click **General** to organize the viewable screen.

3. Make any of the following changes: Display Order, Sort By, Address Format, and Font Size.

4. Click **Accounts** to create and synchronize your Address Book.

5. To create an account, such as Yahoo!, and then the **Add** (+) button, fill in the account information, and then click **Create**.

 ◆ **Account type.** Select an account type: CardDAV, Exchange, LDAP, or Yahoo!.

 Yahoo! imports all contacts in the account into Address Book.

 ◆ **User name and password.** Enter a username and password.

 ◆ **Server address.** Enter the server address.

6. To synchronize an account, click the check box for the account you want, click the **MobileMe** or **Configure**, and then follow the step by step instructions to use MobileMe, Yahoo!, or Google.

Added Yahoo! account

7. Click **Template** to organize the card data screen.

8. Make any of the following changes: Work and Mobile phone numbers, Email and Homepage information, Names, and Work address.

9. Click **Phone** to set the format for the phone number entry.

10. Click the **Formats** pop-up, and then select a phone number format.

11. Click **vCard** to set the preferences for vCards.

12. Make any of the following changes: vCard Format, vCard 2.1 Encoding, Enable Private 'Me' Card, Export Notes in vCards, and Export Photos in vCards.

13. Quit Address Book.

Click to add additional contact fields.

Did You Know?

You can notify contacts of changes to your address book information. Create a group of addresses, click the File menu, click Send Updates, select the group or groups you want to notify, type a subject and message, and then click Send.

You can subscribe to an address book. Click the File menu, click Subscribe to Address Book, enter the MobileMe e-mail address of the user you want, and then click OK.

You can exchange contacts in your Address Book with other Mac users. Select a contact, click the File menu, and then click Export vCard.

Performing Calculations and Conversions

Mac OS X comes with a great tool to help you perform common calculations and to do complex conversions. The Calculator application has been around for a long time, however, Mac OS X gave it a few powerful features, that just might make you want to reacquaint yourself with an old friend. If you're like most people, you probably have a dozen calculators laying about your home and office. If you're tired of all the mess, then take a look at the Mac's idea of a calculator. Not only does it help you add 2 + 2; it helps you convert miles into kilometers or the Euro dollar into American currency. The Calculator application gives you the ability to perform conversions on everything from currency to volume, from temperature to speed, and more.

Work with the Calculator

① Click the **Launchpad** icon in the Dock, and then click the **Calculator** icon.

② Click the buttons on the calculator to perform standard calculations.

③ Click the **Window** menu, and then click **Show Paper Tape** to display a Paper Tape dialog, which shows all of your calculations.

④ Click **Clear** to clear the tape, or click **Recalculate Totals** to have the calculator refigure the total.

⑤ Click the **File** menu, and then click **Print Tape** to have a paper copy of your calculations.

⑥ Click the **View** menu, and then click **Scientific** to have access to a scientific calculator.

⑦ Quit Calculator.

Did You Know?

You can use the keypad with the Calculator. If you have a 10-keypad, instead of trying to click the calculator buttons, just use the keypad. The Calculator automatically reads the keypad objects, and display the results in the calculation window.

Work with Conversions

1. Click the **Applications** folder in the Dock, and then click the **Calculator** icon.

2. Enter a value into the calculation window.

3. Click the **Convert** menu, and then click **Currency**.

4. Click the **Convert** pop-up, and then click **Currency**. If you need to change the convert type, click the Convert pop-up and make your change.

5. Click the **From** and **To** pop-ups to select currency countries.

6. If available, click **Update Currency Rates** to access the latest exchange rate (requires an Internet connection).

7. Click **OK**.

 The conversion results display in the calculation window.

8. Quit Calculator.

Did You Know?

You can save calculation results in memory. Click the M+ (memory add) button to save a calculation result or to add a calculation result to the value residing in memory. At any time during the calculation, if you want to use that result, click the MR (Memory Recall) button and the number reappears. In addition, you can use the M- (memory subtract) to subtract a displayed result from the value in memory, or the MC (Memory Clear) button to clear out the memory.

Conversion results

Capturing Images with a Digital Camera

Mac OS X has provided you a way to directly access your digital camera and organize your images and even sounds. Just plug in your digital camera or scanner directly, and import your pictures or sounds from any application that supports Services and Rich Text Format (most digital cameras and scanners). Image Capture (**New!**) lets you download all or selected contents from your digital camera, rotate images, and even delete unwanted pictures from your camera. You can even use Image Capture to take a picture using the Take Picture command on the File menu or scan an image when a compatible device with a camera or scanner—with an automatic document-feeder or flatbed—is connected to your computer (**New!**). In addition, you can use the images to create a slideshow or format them for printing.

Capture Images with a Digital Camera

1. Plug a digital device into your computer.

2. If necessary, click the **Launchpad** icon in the Dock, and then click the **Image Capture** icon.

3. If necessary, select the device you want to use.

4. Click the **Import To** pop-up, and then select a location to download the images.

5. To select some images to import or modify, hold down ⌘, and then click the individual images you want or hold down the Shift key and then click a start and end image to select a range.

6. To rotate or delete selected images, click **Rotate Left**, **Rotate Right**, or **Delete** buttons.

7. To delete images after import, select the **Delete after import** check box.

8. Click **Import** to move only selected images or click **Import All** to move all the images from the digital device to your destination.

9. Quit Image Capture.

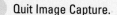

Capturing Screen Shots with Grab

If there is something on your computer screen, such as an error dialog, window, or desktop, that you want to capture as a picture to show someone, you can use a built-in utility called Grab to get the job done. Grab is useful for taking pictures of different parts of the screen, like the ones in this book. This may not be a tool you'll use everyday (unless you are a computer trainer or book author), but it may come in handy one day.

Capture Screen Shots with Grab

1. Display the screen you want to capture.

2. Click the **Launchpad** icon in the Dock, click the **Utilities** folder, and then click the **Grab** icon.

3. Click the **Capture** menu, and then select the command with the method you want to use:

 ◆ **Selection.** Drag to select a capture area.

 ◆ **Window.** Click the **Choose Window** button, and then click a window.

 ◆ **Screen.** Click a screen.

 ◆ **Timed Screen.** Click the **Start Timer** button, display a screen, and then wait 10 seconds.

4. Click the **File** menu, and then click **Save**.

5. Select the drive and folder in which you want to save the file.

6. Type a name for the file, and then click **Save**.

7. Quit Grab.

Did You Know?

You can show a pointer in a screen capture. Click the Grab menu, click Preferences, click a pointer type or the blank one for no pointer, and then click the Close button.

Grab app in Applications folder

Selection method

Window method

Screen method

Timed Screen method

Previewing Images and PDF's

Need a quick way to view images, or possibly a Portable Document File (PDF)? No problem, the built-in PDF viewer, Preview, lets you quickly view graphics and PDF files as a full-screen app (**New!**) with the click of a button. Preview works to open images or documents, which are not identified by another program, regardless of type. You can open iWork documents and most Microsoft Office document (**New!**). When you open a PostScript or EPS (Encapsulated PostScript) file, Preview converts the file into the PDF format. You can open multiple PDFs in a single document window or import scan images in Preview. You can also open and view multiple image files as a contact sheet. When you've opened a PDF file, Preview lets you perform an improved indexed search with a sidebar display (**New!**), select text and embedded images and copy it to the clipboard (**New!**), and even view FAX documents. If you want to add comments, annotations, or even signatures (**New!**)—using an iSight or FaceTime camera from a handwritten signature—to a PDF, you can get easy access to the tools you need by using the Annotation toolbar. With the Smart Magnify tool (**New!**), you can focus on a specific part of an image or PDF. If you want to adjust image size or color levels, including highlights and shadows (**New!**), you can use the Adjust Size or Adjust Color commands on the Tools menu for high-quality results. As you make changes to a file, Preview periodically saves it as you work, however, you can also explicitly save (**New!**) snapshot versions, which you can browse and revert to as desired (**New!**) like Time Machine.

Set Preview Preferences

1. Click the **Preview** icon in the Dock.

2. Click the **Preview** menu, and then click **Preferences**.

3. Click any of the following icons to set Preview preferences:

 ◆ **General.** Sets options to open files in a single or separate windows.

 ◆ **Images.** Sets options for scaling images.

 ◆ **PDF.** Sets options to for scaling PDFs, opening and viewing documents, and annotations.

 ◆ **Bookmarks.** Allows you to remove bookmarks.

 ◆ **Signatures.** Allows you to scan a signature (**New!**) with an iSight or FaceTime camera.

4. Click the **Close** button.

Signatures tab in PDF preferences

iSight camera

Preview Images and PDF's

1. Click the **Preview** icon in the Dock.

2. Click the **File** menu, click **Open**, select one or more document or image files, and then click **Open**.

3. To view or change the Sidebar display, click a view button: **Contents Only**, **Thumbnails**, **Table of Contents**, or **Contact Sheet**.

4. To move between pages in a PDF or images, click an item in the Sidebar.

5. To increase or decrease the viewing size of the image, click the **Zoom In** or **Zoom Out** buttons. To use Smart Magnify, click the **Tools** menu, and then click **Show Magnifier** or **Hide Magnifier** (**New!**).

6. To select a portion of a document or image, click a selection tool button (**Move**, **Text**, or **Select**), and then drag to select it.

7. To modify a selected image, click the **Tools** menu, and then click **Adjust Size** or **Adjust Color** (**New!**).

8. To draw or add notes, signatures on the document, click the **Annotate** button to display the Annotation toolbar, and then use the tools.

 ◆ To create or insert a signature, click the **Signature** button, and then click **Create Signature from <device>** or a signature (**New!**).

9. To print, display the document or select a portion of it, click the **File** menu, and then click **Print**.

10. To save a version (**New!**), click the **File** menu, and then click **Save a Version**. To revert to an earlier version, click the **File** menu, click **Revert to Saved**, scroll through list and select a document, and then click **Restore**. Click **Done** to cancel.

11. Quit Preview.

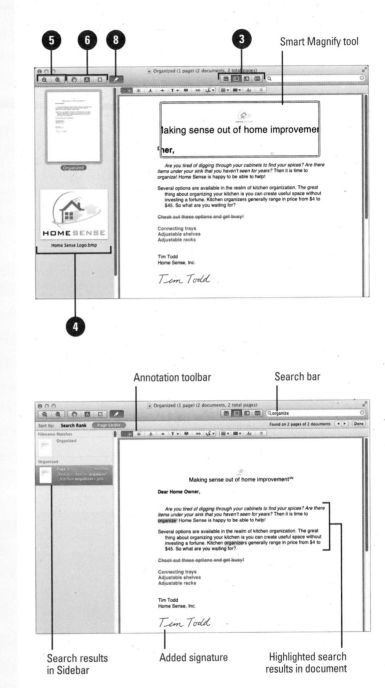

Smart Magnify tool

Annotation toolbar Search bar

Search results in Sidebar Added signature Highlighted search results in document

Using Apps with Auto Save

Some Apps—including Preview, TextEdit, and Automator—in Mac OS X come with Auto Save (**New!**), which automatically saves document changes as you work. Auto Save works in the background to save only your changes, so you don't need to do anything unless you want to. Auto Save adds only the changes directly into the file, so there's only one file to manage. If you don't want your changes, you can revert to a previous version using a Time Machine timeline (**New!**). Saved versions get pruned as needed to keep them manageable. If you need a copy of a document, you can make a duplicate. If you don't want others to make changes to a document, you can lock it. If you don't make changes to a document for two weeks, Mac OS X automatically locks the document for you. When you open it again, it asks if you want to unlock it.

Use Auto Save and Versions

1. Open the app with Auto Save, and then open or create a document.

 The current document is saved and then Auto Saved every hour.

2. Click the **File** menu, and then click **Save a Version**.

3. If a document is locked, the click **Unlock**. To duplicate a locked document, click **Duplicate**.

4. Use the following to lock or duplicate a document.

 ◆ **Lock/Unlock a document.** Click the document name arrow, and then click **Lock** or **Unlock**.

 ◆ **Duplicate a document.** Click the document name arrow, and then click **Duplicate**.

5. Use the following to revert to a previous version of a document.

 ◆ **Revert to saved.** Click the **File** menu, click **Save a Version**. Select the version you want on the right, and then click **Restore**. To cancel, click **Done**.

 ◆ To delete a version, click the document name arrow, and then click **Delete This Version**.

 ◆ **Revert to the last saved.** Click the document name arrow, and then click **Revert to Last Saved Version**.

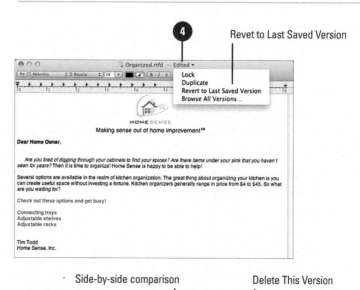

Revert to Last Saved Version

Side-by-side comparison Delete This Version

Current version 5 Use to select versions

Creating Sticky Notes

The Sticky Notes application is not new to Mac OS X, however it does give you the ability to tack notes onto your desktop; where they stay until removed. Just think, no longer do you need to worry about the sticky note on your monitor losing its "stick" and falling off. You can use your desktop the way Apple intended—to help with everyday life. Once you create a sticky note, you can change the color of the note, change the color and size of the text, or even have your sticky note talk to you by turning on the speech mode through the Edit menu.

Create Sticky Notes

1. Click the **Launchpad** icon in the Dock, and then click the **Stickies** icon.

 When you first open the Stickies application, you'll see 3 pre-written stickies notes.

2. Click the **File** menu, and then click **New Note**.

3. Type the text into the note area.

4. To increase or decrease the note size, drag the lower-right corner of the sticky note.

5. Click the **Font** menu, and then select from the font options.

6. Click the **Note** menu, and then select between **Floating Windows** or **Translucent Windows**.

7. To change the color of the selected note, click the **Color** menu and make your change.

8. Click the **File** menu to import or export notes, archive your notes, and to print or save your notes.

9. Click the **Close** button to quit without saving.

10. Quit Stickies.

It's easy to customize your notes.

Make your notes stand out and get noticed.

- Format text using different **fonts** and font sizes
- Add emphasis with **bold** and *italic* text styles or color.
- Include graphics 🖼.

Stickies has lots of other great features, including a spell checker, import and export features, and other ways to arrange and customize your notes. Plus, you'll find a "Make New Sticky Note" service in many applications.

Look in Help to find out more about

Make a note of it!

Stickies lets you keep notes (like these) on your desktop. Use a Stickies note to jot down reminders, lists, or other information. You can also use notes to store frequently used text or graphics.

- To close this note, click the close button.
- To collapse this note, double click the title bar.

Your current notes appear when you open Stickies.

Make plans for the family vacation for this summer.

Managing Fonts with Font Book

Most of us have fonts...a whole lot of fonts. Mac OS X organizes fonts into main folders: User and Computer. Fonts in the User folder reside in your Home folder for private use, while fonts in the Computer folder are available for all users. Besides these folders, you can also organize your fonts into specific user-defined folders, known as collections, and then activate those folders, or specific fonts within the folder without having to restart your application. In addition, Font Book gives you a window to view the font, and change its viewing size. Mac OS X now includes Damascus, PT Sans, and Kefa fonts (**New!**) as well as language support in the Indian subcontinent (**New!**).

Manage Fonts with Font Book

1. Click the **Launchpad** icon in the Dock, and then click the **Font Book** icon.

2. Click the **Add Collections** (+) button, type a name, and then press Return.

3. Click the **Add Fonts** (+) button.

4. Select the fonts you want to add to the New Collection (active folder).

5. Click **Open**.

6. Select a collection from the Collection column, and then click on a font to view a sample.

7. To increase or decrease the view of the font in the window, drag the view slider up or down.

8. To copy a font, click and drag a font from the Font window into another Collection.

9. If necessary, type search criteria to locate specific fonts.

10. To remove a font from a Collection (this does not delete the file from the hard drive), select a font, and then press the Delete key.

11. Quit Font Book.

Type collection here

Activating, Deactivating, and Customizing Fonts

Once you've created a series of font collections, it'll be necessary to instruct the Font Book application as to what fonts you want to use, and what fonts you want to turn off. It's important to understand that fonts consume memory on your computer. For example, if you have hundreds of fonts active (and that's not unusual), it takes more RAM memory to maintain those fonts; even if you're not using them. That's where font management comes into play. Using Font Book, you can decide what fonts you need, and what fonts can be retired, or disabled, for the remainder of the work session.

Activate and Deactivate Fonts

1. Click the **Launchpad** icon in the Dock, and then click the **Font Book** icon.

2. To deactivate a collection or a font, select the collection or font, click **Disable**, and then click **Disable** to confirm.

 IMPORTANT *The Enable button is a toggle, when a font is active, it displays the word On, and when a font is disabled it displays the word Off.*

3. To activate selected fonts, select one of more fonts from the Font column, and then click **Enable**.

 If a font is disabled, it says Off to the right of the font.

4. Quit Font Book.

Did You Know?

You can find duplicate fonts. If a dot appears next to a font family, it means you have a duplicate. You can correct the problem by disabling the one you don't want. Select the version you want, click the Edit menu, and then click Resolve Duplicates.

You can locate a font on your computer. Select the font, click the File menu, and then click Reveal In Finder.

Disabled Font window

Selected font

Working with Dashboard

Dashboard is a Mac OS X screen that gives you quick access to widgets, such as news headlines and updates, slide shows, weather information, traffic maps, Internet radio streams, and slide shows of online photo albums. **Widgets** are mini-applications that can connect to Web services, such as an RSS feed (which automatically delivers Web content to your desktop), or integrate with many of your applications, such as viewing your calendar. You can customize Dashboard to suit the way you work by using the Widget bar. Mac OS X comes with a set of widgets to get you started. However, you can easily download more widgets online. You can quickly open Dashboard by pressing the F12 key. If you prefer a different shortcut key, you can select the one you want in the Mission Control pane (**New!**) of System Preferences.

Work with Dashboard

◆ **Show or Hide Dashboard.** Press F12.

◆ **Open Widget Bar.** Click the **Open** (+) button in the lower-left corner of Dashboard or press ⌘+= (equal).

◆ **Close Widget Bar.** Click the **Close** (x) button or press ⌘+= (equal).

◆ **Scroll the Widget Bar.** Click the Left or Right Arrow buttons or press ⌘+Left Arrow or ⌘+Right Arrow.

◆ **Reload Current Widget.** Press ⌘+R.

Did You Know?

You can make widgets available to all users. Move or copy the widget into the Widgets folder in the Library folder for your computer from the similar Library folder in your Home folder. All the Mac OS X pre-installed widgets are stored in the Widgets folder for your computer.

Dashboard widgets

Click to open widget bar

Change Dashboard Preferences

1. Click the **Apple** menu, and then click **System Preferences**.

2. Click the **Mission Control** icon.

3. Select the **Show Dashboard as a space** check box or clear it to hide the Dashboard in Mission Control (**New!**).

4. Click the **Show Dashboard** pop-up, press a keyboard modifier (Shift, Control, Option, or ⌘) if you want, and then select the shortcut key you want.

 If you want to see more shortcut options, hold down the Shift, Control, Option, or Command keys, or a combination of the keys, while you view the pop-up menu.

5. If you have a Mighty Mouse, Magic Mouse, or other multi-button mouse, you can use the other pop-up to set mouse button shortcuts.

6. Click the **Close** button.

Did You Know?

You can update all your Macs with widgets using MobileMe. With an MobileMe account, you can use Dashboard syncing to automatically update all the widgets on all your Macs. Click the System Preferences icon on the Dock, click the MobileMe icon, click the Sync tab, select the Synchronize With MobileMe check box, select the Dashboard Widgets check box, and then click the Close button.

6

Mission Control

◀ ▶ Show All Q

Mission Control gives you an overview of all your open windows, thumbnails of your full-screen applications, and Dashboard, all arranged in an unified view.

☑ Show Dashboard as a space ——————————————————————— **3**
☑ Automatically rearrange spaces based on most recent use
☑ When switching to an application, switch to a space with open windows for the application

Keyboard and Mouse Shortcuts

With a single keystroke, view all open windows, windows of the current application, or hide windows to locate an item on the desktop that might be covered up.

Mission Control: F9 ⬍ — ⬍
Application windows: F10 ⬍ — ⬍
Show Desktop: F11 ⬍ — ⬍
Show Dashboard: F12 ⬍ — ⬍
(for additional choices press Shift, Control, Option, or Command)

Hot Corners... ?

4 **5**

Using Dashboard Widgets

Dashboard comes with a wide variety of widgets pre-installed with Mac OS X. Dashboard displays the Calculator, Weather, World Clock, and iCal widgets by default. However, you can add other pre-installed widgets to the Dashboard, which include Address Book, CI Filter Browser, Dictionary, ESPN, Flight Tracker, Movies, People, Ski Report, Stickies, Stocks, Tile Game, Translation, Unit Converter, and Web Clip. In fact, you can add more than one of the same widget, such as two World Clocks for two different times around the world. Some of the widgets are linked with applications and allow you to access information or functionality without opening the application. For example, the Weather widget displays Web-based content on the Dashboard without opening a Web browser.

Show or Hide Widgets on the Dashboard

1. Press F12 to open Dashboard.

2. Click the **Open** (+) button in the lower left corner to display the Widget bar.

3. To hide a widget from the Dashboard, click the **Close** (x) button in the upper-left corner of the widget.

 TROUBLE? *If you don't see a Close button, press Option and move the pointer over the widget.*

4. To show a widget on the Dashboard, click the widget you want on the Widget bar.

5. To move a widget on the Dashboard, drag it to another location.

6. Click the **Close** (x) button in the Widget bar.

6 Toggles between (t) and (x).

Use Pre-installed Widgets

◆ **Widgets.** use to manage widgets, where you can show/hide or sort them, or add new ones.

◆ **Address Book.** Type a name, or click the arrow buttons.

◆ **Calculator.** Use the numeric pad or click buttons to enter numbers.

◆ **CI Filter Browser.** Use to apply filters to images.

◆ **Dictionary.** Type a word to view a definition.

◆ **ESPN.** Click the Info (i) button to select a sport. Click New or Scores to change the display.

◆ **Flight Tracker.** Enter flight information, and then click Find Flights.

◆ **iCal.** Use the arrow buttons or arrow keys to move around the calendar. Click the today's date pane to expand/collapse it.

◆ **Movies.** Click the Info (i) button to enter your zip code to view theaters near you.

◆ **Ski Report.** Click the Info (i) button to type the name of a resort.

◆ **Stickies.** Type notes. Click the Info (i) button to change color and font.

◆ **Stocks.** Type a company. Click the Info (i) button to view a graph.

◆ **Tile Game.** Click a tile that borders the empty space to move it.

◆ **Translation.** Select a language, and then type the word or phrase.

◆ **Unit Converter.** Select a Convert category, select the unit converted and the unit converted to.

◆ **Weather.** Click the Info (i) button to check the weather forecast.

◆ **Web Clip.** Click the Info (i) button to access Web clips using Safari.

◆ **World Clock.** Click the Info (i) button to change the city.

Calculator Weather World Clock

iCal calender

Click to scroll through available widgets

Adding and Removing Dashboard Widgets

Even though Mac OS X comes with a wide range of commonly used widgets, there is always room for more. Developers are continually creating new widgets, which you can download from the Internet and install onto your computer. If you no longer use a widget on the Dashboard, you can remove a pre-installed widget from the Widget bar or remove a widget you installed from your computer.

Install a Dashboard Widget

1. Press F12 to open Dashboard.

2. Click the **Open** (+) button in the lower left corner to display the Widget bar.

3. Click **Manage Widgets**.

4. Click **More Widgets**.

5. Browse the widget Web site to find the widget you want to download and install.

6. Click the widget's Download button.

 The installer should automatically start. If it doesn't, double-click the downloaded file. If the file is compressed, you need to uncompress it first.

7. Click **Install**.

8. Click **Keep** to keep the widget or click **Delete** if you decide not to keep it.

9. Click the **Close** button.

Remove a Dashboard Widget

1. Press F12 to open Dashboard.

2. Click the **Open** (+) button in the lower left corner to display the Widget bar.

3. Click **Manage Widgets**.

4. To remove (disable) a widget from the Widget bar, clear the check box next to the widget name you want to remove.

5. To remove a widget you installed, click the widget's **Remove** (-) button, and then click **OK**.

6. To close a widget from the screen and remain in the Widget bar, click the **Close** (x) button.

7. Click the **Close** button.

Did You Know?

You can customize a widget. When you point to a widget on the Dashboard and a small info (i) button appears, you can customize the widget. Click the small info (i) button to display the settings you can change. The available options vary depending on the widget.

You can sort widgets on the Widget bar. Press F12, click the Open (+) button, click Manage Widgets, click the Sort pop-up, click Sort By Name or Sort By Date, and then click the Close button.

Creating a Web Clip Dashboard Widget

You can also create your own widgets by using Web Clips or Dashcode. A Web Clip widget is a container for a Web page you can add to the Dashboard. When you open the Web Clip widget in Dashboard, the Web page associated with it opens. If you're a developer with a basic knowledge of HTML, JavaScript, and CSS, you can create your own Dashboard widget using Dashcode. Dashcode is out of the scope of this book. For more information on Dashcode, go to the Apple Developer Connection Web site.

Create a Web Clip Dashboard Widget

1. Launch Safari, and then display the Web page you want to make into a Web Clip widget.

2. Click the **File** menu, and then click **Open in Dashboard**.

3. Move the page to highlight the area you want to use, and then click the mouse button.

4. To reposition the highlighted area, drag the area. To resize it, drag the circular handles on the edges of the box.

5. Click **Add**.

6. To customize the widget, point to it, click the small info (i) button, and then specify the options you want:

 ◆ Edges. Displays thumbnails of different edge styles. Click the style you want.

 ◆ Only Play Audio in Dashboard. Select or clear the check box to play or not play audio in Dashboard.

 ◆ Edit. Click to select a different highlighted area.

7. When you're finished, click **Done**.

Working with Documents

Introduction

Mac OS X comes with a word processing application, called TextEdit, you can use to create basic documents. TextEdit is designed especially for working with text, so it's a snap to create and edit letters, or any other word-based communication. TextEdit contains all the tools and features you need to produce interesting documents that say exactly what you mean, and have the look to match.

TextEdit is a versatile word-processing application. You can use TextEdit to view, create, and edit documents containing multi-lingual text, graphics, movies, and other document files. If you are working with HTML code (document as they appear in a Web browser), TextEdit makes the perfect editor. If you have speakers connected to your Macintosh, you can hear documents read aloud by your computer. When you're done working with a document, you can save it in multiple formats, such as plain text, Rich Text Format (RTF), Microsoft Word, and Portable Document File (PDF).

Tools, such as the Spelling Checker and Dictionary, help you present your thoughts accurately, clearly, and effectively. When your text is complete, you can quickly add formatting elements, such as bold type and special fonts, to make your documents look professional. Each document contains simple styles that have common design elements. Apply the existing styles for headings, titles, body text, and so forth. Then modify the styles, or create your own to better suit your needs. Make sure you get the look you want by adding emphasis using italics, boldface, and underline, changing text alignment, adjusting line and paragraph spacing, setting tabs and indents, creating bulleted or numbered lists, and adding tables. When you're done, your document is sure to demand attention and convey your message in its appearance.

What You'll Do

Create and Open a Document

Edit Text

Recognize Handwriting Ink

Make Corrections

Make Text Substitutions

Check Spelling and Grammar

Look Up Words with Dictionary

Find and Replace Text

Format Text

Display Rulers

Set Paragraph Tabs and Indents

Change Character Spacing

Change Line Spacing

Add Lists and Tables

Apply and Create a Style

Insert Special Characters

Add Pictures, Movies, or Files to a Document

Save and Close a Document

Set TextEdit Preferences

Creating and Opening a Document

A **document** is a file you create using a word processing program, such as a letter, memo, or resume. When you start TextEdit, a blank document appears in the work area, known as the document window. You can type information to create a new document and save the result in a file, or you can open an existing file (using the Sidebar and List or Column view) in various formats, and save the document with changes. You can also add pictures, movies, and files in your documents.

Create a Document

1. Click the **Launchpad** icon in the Dock, and then click the **TextEdit** icon.

 If TextEdit is already open, click the **File** menu, and then click **New**.

2. To change the file format, click the **Format** menu, and then click **Make Plain Text** or **Make Rich Text**.

3. Type your text.

 ◆ **Character picker.** To quickly use an accented letter (**New!**), hold down the letter to display a dialog, and then press a number with the one you want.

4. Press Return when you want to start a new paragraph.

5. When you're done, save and close the document.

Document window

Character picker

Press and hold "e" to display the character picker.

See Also

See "Setting Up Page Options" on page 204 for information on selecting paper size, orientation, and printer scaling and format.

Did You Know?

You can set the file format for all new documents. Click the TextEdit menu, click Preferences, click the Plain Text or Rich Text option, and then click the Close button.

For Your Information

Understanding Document Formats

You can open and edit plain text, HTML (HyperText Markup Language, which displays Web pages in a browser), Rich Text Format (RTF), Rich Text Format Directory (RTFD), and Microsoft Word files in TextEdit. However, you can only save files in the plain text, RTF, and Word format. Plain text files use the file extension **.txt**, RTF files use **.rtf**, and Word files use **.doc**. If you add graphics to an RTF file, the file extension changes to **.rtfd**. The RTF and Word formats can include formatting, pictures, and other embedded files, while the plain text format can only include nonformatted text. In a plain text document, you cannot change preset tabs and font styles and colors are not saved. Since Microsoft Word is a full featured word processing application, not all Word features, such as tables, are supported in TextEdit.

Open an Existing Document from Within an Application

1. Click the **File** menu, and then click **Open**.

2. Select the hard drive and the folder in which you want to open the file.

3. Click the document you want to open.

 If available, scroll through the preview the entire document in Preview pane (**New!**).

4. If the document contains one or more languages, click the **Plain Text Encoding** pop-up, and then select **Unicode** (for multiple languages) or a specific language.

5. If you want to open a HTML document or create a plain text document, select the **Ignore rich text commands** check box.

6. Click **Open**.

Where pop-up

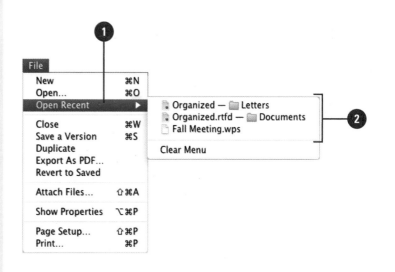

Open a Recent Document

1. Click the **File** menu, and then point to **Open Recent**.

2. Click the recently opened document you want to re-open.

Did You Know?

You can remove all recently used documents from the Open Recent sub-menu. Click the File menu, point to Open Recent, and then click Clear Menu.

Editing Text

One of the advantages of using a word processing program is that you can edit a document or change the contents without re-creating it. In the TextEdit work area, the mouse pointer changes to the I-beam pointer, which you can use to reposition the insertion point (called navigating) and insert, delete, or select text. Before you can edit text, you need to highlight, or select, the text you want to modify. Then you can delete, replace, move (cut), or copy text within one document or between documents even if they're different programs. When you cut or copy an item, it's placed on the Clipboard, which stores only a single piece of information at a time. You can also move or copy selected text without storing it on the Clipboard by using drag-and-drop editing.

Select and Edit Text

1. Open a document, and then move the I-beam pointer to the left or right of the text you want to select.

2. Click, and then drag the pointer to highlight the text.

 TIMESAVER *Double-click a word to select it; triple-click a paragraph to select it.*

3. Perform one of the following editing commands:

 ◆ To replace text, type your text.

 ◆ To delete text, press the Delete key.

Insert and Delete Text

1. Click in the document to place the insertion point where you want to make the change.

 ◆ To insert text, type your text.

 ◆ **Character picker.** To quickly use an accented letter (**New!**), hold down the letter to display a dialog, and then press a number with the one you want.

 ◆ To delete text, press the Delete key.

Move or Copy Text

1. Select the text you want to move or copy.

2. Click the **Edit** menu, and then click **Cut** or **Copy**.

 TIMESAVER *Press ⌘+X to cut or press ⌘+C to copy.*

3. Click where you want to insert the text.

4. Click the **Edit** menu, and then click **Paste**.

 TIMESAVER *Press ⌘+V to paste.*

Move or Copy Text Using Drag and Drop

1. Select the text you want to move or copy.

2. Point to the selected text, and then click and hold the mouse button.

 If you want to copy the text to a new location, also press and hold the Option key. A plus sign (+) appears in the pointer box, indicating that you are dragging a copy of the selected text.

3. Drag the selected text to the new location, and then release the mouse button (and the Option key, if necessary).

4. Click anywhere in the document to deselect the text.

Untitled

Dear Home Owner,

Are you tired of digging through your cabinets to find your spices? Are there items under your sink that you haven't seen for years? Then it is time to organize! Home Sense is happy to be able to help!

Several options are available in the realm of kitchen organization. The great thing about organizing your kitchen is you can create useful space without investing a fortune. Kitchen organizers generally range in price from $4 to $45. So what are you waiting for? Check out these options and get busy! — 1

Tim Todd
Home Sense, Inc.

3

Dear Home Owner,

Are you tired of digging through your cabinets to find your spices? Are there items under your sink that you haven't seen for years? Then it is time to organize! Home Sense is happy to be able to help!

Several options are available in the realm of kitchen organization. The great thing about organizing your kitchen is you can create useful space without investing a fortune. Kitchen organizers generally range in price from $4 to $45. So what are you waiting for? Check out these options and get busy! — 1

Check out these options and get busy!

Tim Todd
Home Sense, Inc.

3

Dear Home Owner,

Are you tired of digging through your cabinets to find your spices? Are there items under your sink that you haven't seen for years? Then it is time to organize! Home Sense is happy to be able to help!

Several options are available in the realm of kitchen organization. The great thing about organizing your kitchen is you can create useful space without investing a fortune. Kitchen organizers generally range in price from $4 to $45. So what are you waiting for?

Check out these options and get busy! —

Tim Todd
Home Sense, Inc.

4

Recognizing Handwriting Ink

Although typing information into an document or e-mail through the keyboard is fast and efficient, you may find that you need to enter information in handwritten form, known as **ink**. Programs that accept ink, such as TextEdit or Mail, provide handwriting recognition to help you convert handwriting into text. Before you can insert handwritten text into a document, you need to have an ink device, or a handwriting tablet, such as Wacom, attached to and installed on your computer. With handwriting recognition turned on in the Ink pane in System Preferences, you can write in two ink modes: Anywhere or Ink pad. Anywhere mode is useful for writing in a word processing document. As you write in Anywhere mode, your ink strokes appear in a yellow lined translucent overlay. As the Mac recognizes the writing, it converts the ink to text, inserts it in the open document, and erases it from the overlay. When you need to use the mouse, you need to turn off Anywhere mode. Ink pad provides a floating window in which you can use the stylus to write ink and to perform commands as the mouse. Using ink can be tricky at first, but over time you'll get the hang of it.

Insert Handwritten Text Anywhere into a Document

1. Open a program, such as TextEdit, that accepts ink.

2. Turn on handwriting recognition (Ink icon in System Preferences).

 The Ink toolbar appears.

3. Write your text in the yellow lined overlay. After recognition, the text that you write appears in the document.

4. To turn Anywhere mode off to use the mouse, click the **On/Off** button on the Ink toolbar.

5. When you're done, turn off handwriting recognition, and close any open documents.

See Also

See "Setting Ink Preferences" on page 126 for information on turning handwriting recognition on and off, as well as other options.

Use buttons to perform keyboard shortcuts.

Shift key
Control key
Command key
Option key

Recognized text

Insert Handwritten Text Using the Ink Pad

1. Open a program, such as TextEdit, that accepts ink.

2. Turn on handwriting recognition (Ink icon in System Preferences).

 The Ink toolbar appears.

3. Click the **Show Ink Pad** button on the Ink toolbar.

4. Click the **A** button to input text, or click the **Star** button to create a drawing.

5. Write your text or draw with the pen in the Ink Pad window.

 TROUBLE? *If Ink makes a mistake, hold down the Option key, tap the word, and then select a transcription option.*

6. Use the Ink toolbar buttons (Command, Shift, Option, or Control) to perform keyboard shortcuts.

7. Click **Send** to have your text or drawing pasted into the open document behind it.

8. When you're done, turn off handwriting recognition, and close any open documents.

Ink drawing

Click to clear Ink pad.

Did You Know?

You can recognize gestures in Ink pad.
As you write, Ink recognizes certain gestures, or shapes, which get performed as commands, such as Undo, or pressed as keys, such as Delete or Space. A list is available on the Gestures tab in the Ink pane in System Preferences.

For Your Information

Handwriting in Chinese and Other Languages

Mac OS X supports displaying and typing vertical text used by Chinese and Japanese languages (**New!**). If you have a Multi-Touch trackpad on your Mac, you can draw Chinese characters in your documents. When you draw on the trackpad, the Chinese characters appear in an input window, which recommends closely matched characters from an extended Simplified Chinese recognizer with Roman symbols, punctuation, and a small set of additional characters (**New!**) and allows you to choose the one you want. The input window—which is movable (**New!**)—also provides suggestions for subsequent characters based on what you chose. It supports filtering by tones, ordering and filtering by radical or stroke count and improved pinyin-had conversion accuracy (**New!**).

Making Corrections

Everyone makes mistakes and changes their mind at some point, especially when creating or revising a document. With TextEdit you can instantly correct typing errors by pressing a key. You can also reverse more complicated actions, such as typing an entire word, formatting a paragraph, or creating a chart. If you need to undo several actions, you can use the Undo command multiple times. With the Undo command, if you change your mind, you can just as easily use the Redo command to restore the action you reversed.

Undo or Redo an Action

◆ Click the **Edit** menu, and then click **Undo** to reverse your most recent action, such as typing a word or formatting a paragraph.

TIMESAVER *Press ⌘+Z to undo.*

◆ Click the **Edit** menu, and then click **Redo** to restore the last action you reversed.

TIMESAVER *Press ⌘+Shift+Z to redo your undo.*

NOTE *The Undo and Redo commands may change based on the action that was last performed (such as typing or dragging).*

Click to undo
Click to redo

Edit	
Undo Typing	⌘Z
Redo Drag	⇧⌘Z
Cut	⌘X
Copy	⌘C
Paste	⌘V
Paste and Match Style	⌥⇧⌘V
Delete	
Complete	⌥⎋
Select All	⌘A
Insert	▶
Edit Link...	⌘K
Find	▶
Spelling and Grammar	▶
Substitutions	▶
Transformations	▶
Speech	▶
Special Characters...	⌥⌘T

Correct Typing Errors Using the Keyboard

To Delete	Press
One character at a time to the left of the insertion point	Delete
One word at a time to the left of the insertion point	Option+Delete
Selected text	Delete

Making Text Substitutions

Text substitution allows you to correct words and phrases that you misspell or insert symbols. For example, you can type "teh" to change to "the" or type (c) to insert ©. Suggested words for text substitution appear below the word (**New!**), where you can press Return to accept the change or click the X to keep the current spelling. You can add words, phrases, and symbols to the Symbol and Text Substitution list in Language & Text preferences (**New!**). In TextEdit, you can use Smart Copy/Paste to adjust text formatting during a copy and paste, Smart Dashes to automatically replace a sequence of dashes to typographical dashes, Smart Quotes to replace quotes and apostrophes to typographical ones, and Smart Links to convert URLs into links. TextEdit also uses **data detectors** to analyze what you type to detect specialized text, such as dates and addresses, so you can take smart actions, such as create a contact, create an iCal event, or map an address depending on the type of information.

Select Substitution Options

1. Click the **Edit** menu, point to **Substitutions**, and then select or deselect any of the following options:

 ◆ **Show Substitutions.** Opens the Substitutions dialog where you can enable or disable text substitution options (*ones listed below*), open the Language & Text preferences dialog, or make text replacements.

 ◆ **Smart Copy/Paste.** Adjusts the formatting for text when you copy and paste.

 ◆ **Smart Quotes.** Replaces quotes and apostrophes to typographical ones

 ◆ **Smart Dashes.** Replaces a sequence of dashes to typographical dashes

 ◆ **Smart Links.** Converts URLs into links

 ◆ **Data Detectors.** Analyzes text, such as dates and addresses, in order to take smart actions.

 ◆ **Text Replacement.** Replaces text using the list in Language & Text preferences.

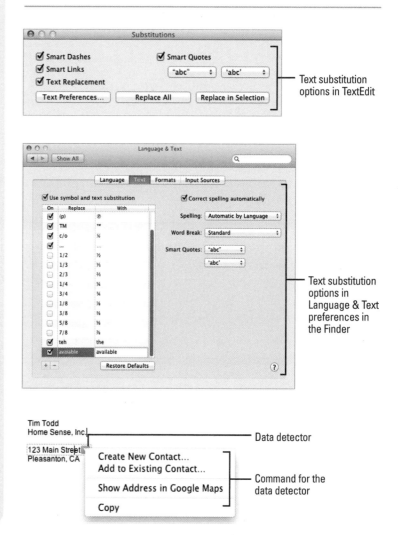

Text substitution options in TextEdit

Text substitution options in Language & Text preferences in the Finder

Data detector

Command for the data detector

Checking Spelling and Grammar

As you type, a red wavy line appears under words not listed in TextEdit's dictionary (such as misspellings or names) or duplicated words (such as the the). You can correct these errors as well as grammatical problems as they arise or after you finish the entire document. For common spelling errors, such as "teh," TextEdit can automatically correct the mistake as you type. TextEdit uses symbol and text substitution options in Language & Text preferences to make the correction. Before you print your final document, use the Spell and Grammar Checker to ensure that your document is error-free.

Correct Spelling and Grammar as You Type

① Select the spelling and grammar commands to enable the options.

◆ **Check Spelling.** Click the **Edit** menu, point to **Spelling and Grammar**, and then click **Check Spelling While Type**.

◆ **Correct Spelling.** Click the **Edit** menu, point to **Spelling and Grammar**, and then click **Correct Spelling Automatically**.

◆ **Check Grammar.** Click the **Edit** menu, point to **Spelling and Grammar**, and then click **Check Grammar With Spelling**.

② Control-click a word with a red dotted underline.

③ Click a substitution, or click **Ignore Spelling** to skip any other instances of the word.

Did You Know?

You can add a familiar word to your dictionary. Control-click the wavy line under the word in question, and then click Learn Spelling. The wavy line disappears and you've added the word or name to the dictionary.

Correct Spelling and Grammar

1. Click at the beginning of the document or select the text you want to correct.

2. Click the **Edit** menu, point to **Spelling and Grammar**, and then click **Show Spelling and Grammar**.

 As it checks each sentence in the document or your selection, TextEdit selects misspelled words or problematic sentences and provides appropriate alternatives.

3. If necessary, click the **Language** pop-up, and then select a language.

4. To check grammar, select the **Check grammar** check box.

5. Select an option:

 ◆ Click a suggestion, and then click **Change** to make a substitution.

 ◆ If no suggestion is appropriate, click in the document and edit the text yourself. Click **Find Next** to continue.

 ◆ Click **Ignore** to skip the word.

 ◆ Click **Learn** to add the word to the dictionary.

 ◆ Click **Define** to look up the word in the dictionary.

 ◆ Click **Guess** to suggest possible corrections.

 The Spell Checker will beep when the process is done.

6. Click the **Close** button to return to the document.

Spelling and Grammar dialog

Suggestion window

Looking Up Words with Dictionary

The Dictionary application, located in the Applications folder, gives you the ability to search for words and definitions as a stand-alone program or from any application, such as TextEdit. Within an application, you can view words in a Quick Look Dictionary panel (**New!**) or open the Dictionary application. You can also use the Dictionary widget in Dashboard to look up and find the definitions you need. Dictionary provides several different sources for you to reference, including English and other language dictionaries, an Apple terms dictionary, a thesaurus (second edition), and Wikipedia, which is a free online encyclopedia. You can select which sources you want to use as well as set parental controls to limit access to some works for specific users.

Look Up Words with Dictionary

1. Start the Dictionary application as a stand-alone program or in another application:

 ◆ **Stand Alone.** Click the **Launchpad** icon in the Dock, and then click the **Dictionary** icon.

 ◆ **In an Application.** Hold down the Control key and click the word you want, click **Look Up "word"** from the menu to display the word in the Dictionary panel.

2. In an application, view the Quick Look Dictionary panel (**New!**), and then click an item to find out more. Click the **Return** (arrow) button to go back.

 To open the Dictionary app and expand the search, click **Dictionary**, **Thesaurus**, or **Wikipedia** in the Quick Look.

3. Select the source you want to search: **All**, **Dictionary**, **Thesaurus**, **Apple**, or **Wikipedia**.

4. Type the search word or phrase you want, if necessary.

5. Click a link to find out about an item.

6. Click the **Close** button.

Set Dictionary Preferences

1. Click the **Dictionary** menu, and then click **Preferences**.

2. Select or specify the various options you want to use:

 ◆ **Sources.** Select the check boxes for the dictionaries and thesaurus' you want to use, and then select the reference resource you want to set additional options.

 ◆ **Pronunciation.** If available, select the pronunciation option you want.

 ◆ **Font Size.** Click the up and down arrows to set the font size.

3. Click the **Close** button.

4. Quit Dictionary.

Did You Know?

You can look up information with a gesture. (**New!**) Double-tap with three fingers to select a word or phrase in any OS X app to look it up. Results from dictionary, thesaurus, and web are displayed inline under the selected item.

You can set parental controls for dictionary use. As the administrator, click the System Preferences icon in the Dock, click the Parental Control icon, enter your administrator password, select the user you want to set limits, click Content, select the check box next to Dictionary, and then click the Close button.

You can view recent dictionary searches. To see previously viewed words, use the Back and Forward buttons. To skip to a specific word, hold down the Back or Forward buttons to see a menu of recent words, and then click the one you want.

For Your Information

Speaking Text in a Document

TextEdit can speak all or part of the text in a document. To speak text in a document, deselect all text to speak the entire document or select the text you want to hear, click the Edit menu, point to Speech, and then click Start Speaking. To make the speaking stop, click the Edit menu, point to Speech, and then click Stop Speaking. The voice you hear is set in the Speech pane of System Preferences. To change the sound of the computer's voice, click the Apple menu, click System Preferences, click Speech, click the Default Voice tab, select a voice, and then click the Close button.

Finding and Replacing Text

The Find and Replace commands make it easy to locate or replace specific text or formulas in a document using the Find and Replace toolbar (**New!**). For example, you might want to find each reference to a individual or company name in a long report to verify that it's properly used. Or you might want to replace all references to a special character in your document with another one. If you only know part of a word you want to find, you can use the Contains option—with the Search bar arrow (**New!**)—to help you locate what you're looking for. If you are looking for a case sensitive text with upper and lower case characters, turn off the Ignore Case option. To make sure you check the entire document no matter where you start, turn on the Wrap Around option. When you search for text in a document, all occurrences of the text are highlighted in yellow for easy identification (**New!**).

Find Text

1. Click at the beginning of the document, or select the text you want to find.

2. Click the **Edit** menu, point to **Find**, and then click **Find**.

3. Type the text you want to find.

 Inline find highlights all word occurrences in yellow.

4. Click the **Search bar** arrow, and then select other options:

 ◆ **Ignore Case.** Check to ignore upper and lower case letters.

 ◆ **Wrap Around.** Check to wrap back to the beginning or end of the document.

 ◆ **Contains.** Select a search option: **Contains**, **Starts With**, or **Full Word**.

 ◆ **Insert Pattern.** Select to search for special characters (**New!**).

5. Click **Previous** or **Next** on the Find toolbar until the text you want to find is highlighted.

6. To clear the search, click the **Close** button (x) in the Search bar.

7. When you're done, click the **Done** button on the Find toolbar.

Replace Text

1. Click at the beginning of the document, or select the text you want to replace.

2. Click the **Edit** menu, point to **Find**, and then click **Find and Replace**, or click **Find**, and then click the **Replace** check box.

3. Type the text you want to find.

 Inline find highlights all word occurrences in yellow.

4. Type the text you want to replace.

5. Click the **Search bar** arrow, and then select other options:

 - **Ignore Case.** Check to ignore upper and lower case characters.

 - **Wrap Around.** Check to wrap back to the beginning or end of the document.

 - **Contains.** Select a search option: **Contains**, **Starts With**, or **Full Word**.

 - **Insert Pattern.** Select to search for special characters (**New!**).

6. Click one of the Replace buttons:

 - **All**. Click to substitute text throughout the entire document.

 - **Replace**. Click to substitute the replacement text and find the next occurrence.

7. Click **Previous** or **Next** on the Find and Replace toolbar until the text you want to find is highlighted.

8. To clear the search, click the **Close** button (x) in the Search bar.

9. When you're done, click the **Done** button on the Find and Replace toolbar.

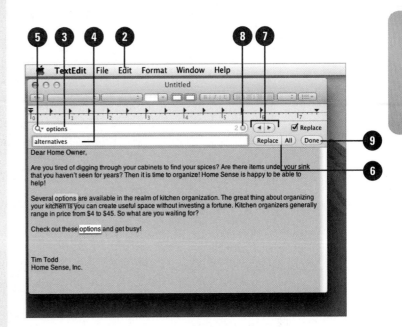

For Your Information

Using Bidirectional Text

If you use different languages in the same document, the mixing of the text can sometimes cause problems. For example, if you use one language, such as Hebrew or Arabic, written from right to left and another language, such as English, written from left to right, the flow of text between the to may not look right. With bidirectional text, you can mix languages with the results you want. You can also use a split-cursor to help show you the right direction of the text at the boundary between right-to-left and left-to-right text. that shows the right direction.

Formatting Text

When you are working with Rich Text Format (RTF) and Word Format documents, you can change the format or the appearance of text and graphics in a document so that the document is easier to read and more attractive. A quick and powerful way to add emphasis to parts of a document is to format text using bold, italics, underline, or color. For special emphasis, you can combine formats, such as bold and italics. In addition, you can change the font style and size. A **font** is a set of characters with the same typeface or design that you can increase or decrease in size, such as Arial or Times New Roman. Font size is measured in points; one point is 1/72 of an inch high. You can quickly access these formatting options on the Formatting toolbar (**New!**).

Format Text

① Select the text or click in the paragraph you want to format.

② Select any of the formatting options on the Formatting toolbar:

- ◆ **Font Family, Typeface, and Size.** Click a pop-up, and then select a font family, typeface, or size. Click **Show Fonts** to make multiple options at once.

- ◆ **Font Color and Background Color.** Click the **Color** box, and then select a color. Click **Show Colors** to select a specific or custom color.

- ◆ **Bold, Italic, and Underline Text.** Click the **Bold**, **Italic**, or **Underline** button.

③ Click an alignment button: **Left**, **Center**, **Justify**, and **Right**.

④ Click in the document to unselect the newly formatted text.

Color palette

Fonts dialog

Colors dialog

Select options for font, typeface, and size.

Select a text color

Did You Know?

You can make text upper case, lower case or capitalize. Select the text, click the Edit menu, point to Transformations, and then click Make Upper Case, Make Lower Case, or Capitalize.

Displaying Rulers

The TextEdit ruler does more than just measure. The horizontal ruler above the document shows the length of the typing line and lets you quickly adjust left and right margins, indents, and set tabs. You can hide the ruler to get more room for your document. When you press Return to start a new paragraph, TextEdit continues to use the same ruler settings. As you work with a document, ruler settings change. Instead of resetting ruler settings each time, you can copy and paste them.

Show and Hide the Ruler

① Click the **Format** menu, point to **Text**, and then click **Show Ruler**.

TIMESAVER Press ⌘+R to show or hide the ruler.

A check mark next to the command indicates the ruler is shown. A non check mark indicates the ruler is hidden.

Copy and Paste the Ruler

① Click in the line to place the insertion point or select the lines with the ruler settings you want to copy.

② Click the **Format** menu, point to **Text**, and then click **Copy Ruler**.

TIMESAVER Press Control+ ⌘+Z to copy ruler.

③ Click in the line to place the insertion point or select the lines in which you want to paste the ruler.

④ Click the **Format** menu, point to **Text**, and then click **Paste Ruler**.

TIMESAVER Press Control+ ⌘+Z to paste ruler.

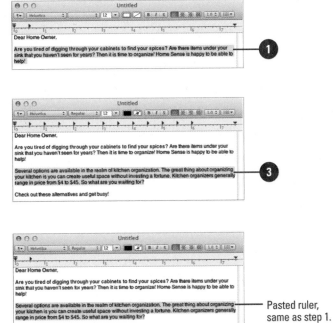

Pasted ruler, same as step 1.

Setting Paragraph Tabs

Tabs set text or numerical data alignment in relation to the edges of a document. A **tab stop** is a predefined stopping point along the document's typing line. Default tab stops are set every half-inch on the ruler, but you can set multiple tabs per paragraph at any location. Each paragraph in a document contains its own set of tab stops. The default tab stops do not appear on the ruler, but the manual tab stops you set do appear. Once you place a tab stop, you can drag the tab stop to position it where you want. If you want to add or adjust tab stops in multiple paragraphs, simply select the paragraphs first.

Create and Clear a Tab Stop

1. Select the text or click in the paragraph you want to format.

2. Click a position on the ruler to insert a tab stop.

3. To change the tab stop, Control-click the tab stop, and then select a tab style (**New!**): **Left tab**, **Center tab**, **Right tab**, or **Decimal tab**.

 TIMESAVER *Double-click a tab stop to cycle through the different types.* (**New!**)

4. To move a tab, drag the tab stop to position it where you want.

5. To clear a tab stop, drag it off the ruler.

See Also

See "Setting Up Page Options" on page 204 for information on changing the paper size.

Tab Stops

Tab Stop	Name	Description
▶	Left tab stop	Aligns tab text to the left
◆	Center tab stop	Aligns tab text to the center
◀	Right tab stop	Aligns tab text to the right
●	Decimal tab stop	Aligns numbers to the decimal point

Setting Paragraph Indents

When you indent a paragraph, you move its edge in from the left or right margin. You can indent the entire left or right edge of a paragraph or just the first line. The markers on the ruler control the indentation of the current paragraph. The ruler has three markers. The top rectangle, called the **paragraph indent marker**, controls where the first line of the paragraph begins. The bottom triangle, called the **left indent marker**, controls where the remaining lines of the paragraph begin. The triangle on the right side of the ruler, called the **right indent marker**, controls where the right edge of the paragraph ends.

Change Paragraph Indents

Select the text or click in the paragraph you want to format.

◆ To change the left indent of the first line, drag the Paragraph Indent marker.

◆ To change the indent of the second and subsequent lines, drag the Left Indent marker (under the Paragraph Indent marker).

◆ To change the left indent for all lines, drag the Left Indent marker, and the Paragraph Indent marker to the same point.

◆ To change the right indent for all lines, drag the Right Indent marker.

As you drag a marker, the dotted guideline helps you position the indent accurately.

Paragraph Indent marker Right Indent marker

Left Indent marker

For Your Information

Changing Text Wrap

By default, TextEdit wraps lines of text based on the width of the window. If you change the width of the window, the lines of text get shorter or longer. If you widen the window, the text gets smaller. When you print the document, TextEdit reduces the font size of the text to match the printed document to what you see on the screen, which might not be the results you want to achieve. To avoid this, you can change the text to wrap to the paper size. TextEdit uses the paper size and orientation you set in Page Setup, to determine the point in which the text line wraps. To change text wrap, click the Format menu, and then click Wrap to Page or Wrap to Window. When you change the text wrap to Wrap To Page, a rectangle appears in the window indicating the margins of the document.

Changing Character Spacing

Kerning is the amount of space between each character that you type. Sometimes the space between two characters is larger than others, which makes the word look uneven. You can expand or condense the spacing to create a special effect for a title, or re-align the **baseline**, which is the position of characters to the bottom edge of the text—this is helpful for positioning the copyright or trademark symbols.

Change Character Spacing

1. Select the text you want to format.

2. Click the **Format** menu, point to **Font**, and then point to **Kern**.

3. Click any of the following options:

 ◆ **Use Default**. Uses default kerning.

 ◆ **Use None**. Removes kerning.

 ◆ **Tighten**. Moves the characters together slightly; you can repeat the command.

 ◆ **Loosen**. Moves the characters slightly apart; you can repeat the command.

Change Character Baseline

1. Select the text you want to format.

2. Click the **Format** menu, point to **Font**, and then point to **Baseline**.

3. Click any of the following options:

 ◆ **Superscript**. Moves the text above the level of normal text.

 ◆ **Subscript**. Moves the text below the level of normal text.

 ◆ **Raise**. Moves the text up only a little bit; you can repeat the command.

 ◆ **Lower**. Moves the text down only a little bit; you can repeat the command.

Changing Line Spacing

The lines in all TextEdit documents are single-spaced by default, which is appropriate for letters and most documents. But you can easily change your document line spacing to double or you can specify to allow extra space between every line. This is useful when you want to make notes on a printed document. Sometimes, you'll want to add space above and below certain paragraphs, for headlines, or indented quotations to help set off the text. To set specialized line spacing settings, use the Other command on the Spacing pop-up. You can select options for line height, inter-line spacing, and paragraph spacing. **Line height** is the distance from the top of a line to the top of the line below it; **inter-line spacing** is the distance from the bottom of a line to the top of the line below it; and **paragraph spacing** is the distance from the bottom of a paragraph to the top of the first line in the paragraph below it.

Change Line Spacing

1. Select the text you want to change.

2. Click the **Spacing** pop-up on the Formatting toolbar, and then select a spacing option:

 - Click an available line spacing option from 0.5 (half a line) to 1.0 (single line) to 2.0 (double line).

 - Click **Show More**, specify the exacting options you want, and then click **OK**.

Specify exacting line spacing options

Adding Lists and Tables

The best way to draw attention to a list is to format the items with bullets or numbers. You can even create multi-level lists. For different emphasis, change any bullet or number style to one of TextEdit's many predefined formats. For example, switch round bullets to check boxes or Roman numerals to lowercase letters. You can also customize the list style or insert a picture as a bullet. If you move, insert, or delete items in a numbered list, TextEdit sequentially renumbers the list for you. A **table** neatly organizes information into rows and columns. The intersection of a column and row is called a **cell**. Enter text into cells just as you would anywhere else in TextEdit, except that pressing the Tab key moves you from one cell to the next. You can format a table just like you format any other text in TextEdit.

Create a Numbered or Bulleted List

1. Select the text you want to change or click the place the insertion point where you want to start a list.

2. Click the **Lists** pop-up on the Formatting toolbar, and then select the numbered or bulleted list option you want.

3. For a new list line, type a list item, and then press Return.

 ◆ To add to an existing list, place the insertion point at the end of the line, and then press Return.

4. To indent a list, place the insertion point at the beginning of the line, and then press Tab.

 ◆ To go back to the previous indent level, hold down the Shift key and press Return.

5. To finish a list, press Return twice.

Add a Table

1. Place the insertion point where you want to insert a table.

2. Click the **Format** menu, and then click **Table**.

3. Type the number of rows and columns you want or use the arrow buttons.

4. Set any of the following table options:

 - **Alignment**. Left, Center, Justified, Right, or Top, Baseline, Middle, or Bottom.

 - **Cell Border**. Use the arrow button to set the pixel border.

 - **Cell Background**. Click the pop-up to select **None** or **Color Fill**. Click the color box, click a color, and then click the **Close** button.

5. Click the **Close** button in the Table dialog box.

6. To adjust the height or width of a row or column, position the pointer over a cell border, and then drag the border.

Formatted table

Did You Know?

You can merge cells in a table. Select the cells you want to merge, click the Format menu, point to Text, click Table, click Merge Cells, and then click the Close button.

You can create a table in a table. Select the cell you want to insert a table, click the Format menu, point to Text, click Table, click Nest Table, and then click the Close button.

Applying and Creating a Style

When you want to apply multiple groupings of formatting, such as font type, size and color, use a style. A **style** is a collection of formatting settings saved within a document or favorites list that you can apply to text. TextEdit keeps track of all the styles in the current document. If you want to save a style for use in all documents, you can add it to a favorites list. TextEdit provides a few basic favorite styles. But you can add your own to create the exact look you want. If you need a quick way to apply a single instance of formatting, you can copy and paste it.

Apply a Favorite Style

1. Select the text you want to apply a style.

2. Click the **Styles** pop-up on the Formatting toolbar.

3. Click the style you want to apply.

Apply a Document Style

1. Select the text whose formatting you want to save as a style.

2. Click the **Format** menu, point to **Font**, and then click **Styles**.

3. If necessary, click the **Document Styles** option.

4. Click the arrow buttons to select the style you want to apply.

5. Click **Apply**, and then when you're done, click **Done**.

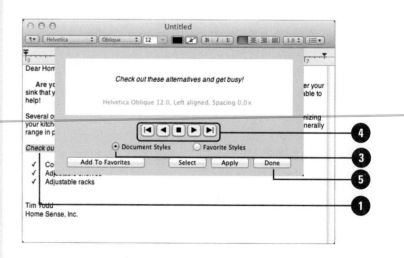

Add a Style to Favorites

① Select the text whose formatting you want to save as a style.

② Click the **Format** menu, point to **Font**, and then click **Styles**.

③ Click **Add To Favorites**.

④ Type a name for the style.

⑤ Select or clear the check boxes to include the font or ruler as part of the style.

⑥ Click **Add**.

Did You Know?

You can remove a style favorite. Click the Format menu, point to Font, click Styles, click the Favorite Styles option, click the pop-up, select the style favorite, and then click Remove From Favorites.

Copy and Paste Formatting

① Select the text in which you want to copy the formatting.

② Click the **Format** menu, point to **Font**, and then click **Copy Style**.

 TIMESAVER *Press Option+ ⌥⌘+Z to copy ruler.*

③ Select the text to which you want to apply a style.

④ Click the **Format** menu, point to **Font**, and then click **Paste Style**.

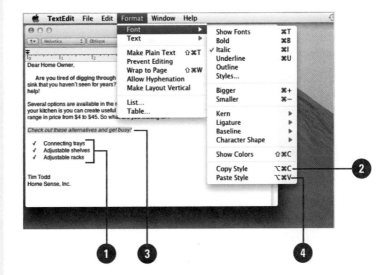

Inserting Special Characters

When you need to insert special characters such as ©, ™, or ® that don't appear on your keyboard, you can use a special accessory called Special Character to do the job. Special Character is available in Mac applications and displays all the characters that are available for each of the fonts on your computer. You can insert special characters in a variety of symbol fonts (**New!**), including arrows, punctuations, currency symbols, pictographs, bullets/stars, math symbols, letterlike symbols, emoji (emoticons), and latin. Each one of the fonts also includes style variations (**New!**).

Insert a Special Character

1. Click in the text to place the insertion point where you want to insert a special character.

2. Click the **Edit** menu, and then click **Special Characters**.

3. Select a category, click **Recently Used**, or click **Favorites** to select from your favorites.

4. Click a subcategory, if necessary, and then click the special character you want to insert.

5. Click a font variation, if desired.

6. To add the character to a favorites list, click **Add To Favorites**.

7. To insert a special character into a document, double-click the character.

8. Click the **Close** button.

See Also

See "Making Text Substitutions" on page 171 for information on quickly inserting symbols using text substitution while you type.

List of favorites

Adding Pictures, Movies, or Files to a Document

If you have a picture, movie, or another file, (such as another text file, spreadsheet, or PDF), you can place them within a TextEdit document. Before you can add a picture, movie, or files to a TextEdit document, the file needs to be converted to the Rich Text Format (RTF). Pictures and movies appear in the document as embedded graphics, while files appear as embedded icons. With embedding, a copy of the file becomes part of the TextEdit file. If you want to edit the embedded file, you make changes in the TextEdit file, and the original file remains intact. You can double-click the embedded graphics or icons to open and view the files.

Add a Picture, Movie, or File to a Document

1. Click the **Format** menu, and then click **Make Rich Text**.

2. Switch to the Finder, and then open the folder containing the picture, movie, or file you want to add.

3. Display the picture, movie, or file icon in the Finder and the TextEdit document on the screen where you can view them both.

4. Drag the picture, movie, or file icon from the Finder to the document window where you want to place it.

 The image is placed in your document.

 ◆ To insert a file, you can also click the **File** menu, click **Attach Files**, browse and select the file and then click **Open**.

5. Close the Finder window.

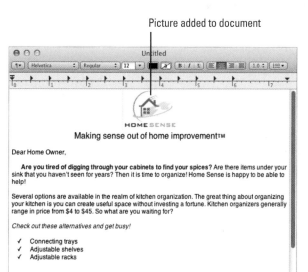

Picture added to document

Saving and Closing a Document

Saving your files frequently ensures that you don't lose work during an unexpected power loss. With TextEdit you don't have to worry, because the program automatically saves your work with Auto Save (**New!**). Even though TextEdit saves your work, it's important to name your Untitled document. You specify a file name and folder and a file format in the Save As dialog. The Save As dialog appears in a compact view (useful for saving in the same place) and an expanded view (useful for saving in a different location or creating a new folder). Expanded view includes the Sidebar, and List and Column view. If you want to change a file's name or location, you can use the Duplicate command on the File menu to create a copy of the original file. To conserve your computer's resources, close any file you are not working on.

Save an Untitled Document as Rich Text or Microsoft Word

1. For plain text only, click the **Format** menu, and then click **Make Rich Text**.

2. For an Untitled document, click the **File** menu, and then click **Save**.

 ◆ To save a version, click the **File** menu, and then click **Save a Version**. (**New!**)

3. Type a name for the file, or use the suggested name.

4. Select the hard drive and folder in which you want to save the file.

5. To change the format of a file, click the **File Format** pop-up, and then click **Rich Text Format** or one of the Word formats.

6. Click **Save**.

Compact view

Click to expand dialog to show Sidebar and file list.

Save As: Untitled.rtfd
Where: Letters
File Format: Rich Text Format with Attachments
Cancel Save

Did You Know?

TextEdit can save documents as a PDF file. Click the File menu, click Save As PDF, type a name, navigate to a folder in which you want to save the file, and then click Save. *See "Previewing Images and PDF's" on page 150-151 for more information on working with PDF (Portable Document File) files.*

For Your Information

Protecting Documents

If you have content in your TextEdit document that you don't want users to change, you can make the document read-only. This is useful for documents, such as "read me" files, contracts, and any other document you want users to read, but not accidentally change. To prevent others from changing your TextEdit documents, click the Format menu, and then click Prevent Editing. To allow users to make changes to a read-only document, click the Format menu, and then click Allow Editing. Another way to protect a document is to lock it. When you lock a file, users can make changes to the file, but the application prevents them from saving it. To lock a file (**New!**), click the document name arrow in the title bar in TextEdit, and then click Lock; to unlock it (**New!**), click the document name arrow, and then click Unlock.

Save an Untitled Document as Plain Text

1. For plain text only, click the **Format** menu, and then click **Make Plain Text**.

2. For an Untitled document, click the **File** menu, and then click **Save**.

 ◆ To save a version, click the **File** menu, and then click **Save a Version**. (**New!**)

3. Type a name for the file, or use the suggested name.

4. Select the hard drive and folder in which you want to save the file.

5. Click the **Plain Text Encoding** pop-up, and then select an encoding format.

6. Click **Save**.

Compact view **3** Click to expand dialog.

Save As: Untitled.txt

Where: Letters

Plain Text Encoding: Unicode (UTF-8) — **5**

☑ If no extension is provided, use ".txt".

Cancel Save

4

6

Close a Document

1. Click the **Close** button.

2. If the document is Untitled, type a name, select a location, select a format, and then click **Save**.

3. Quit TextEdit.

Did You Know?

You can revert to a previously saved document. Before you save, click the File menu, and then click Revert To Saved. (**New!**) *See "Using Apps with Auto Save" on page 152 for more information on working with Auto Save and restoring document.*

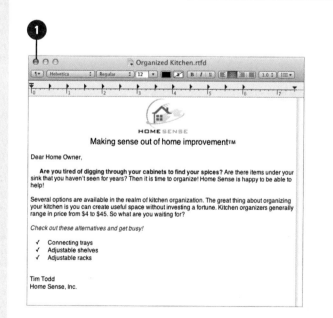

1

Organized Kitchen.rtfd

HOME SENSE
Making sense out of home improvement™

Dear Home Owner,

 Are you tired of digging through your cabinets to find your spices? Are there items under your sink that you haven't seen for years? Then it is time to organize! Home Sense is happy to be able to help!

Several options are available in the realm of kitchen organization. The great thing about organizing your kitchen is you can create useful space without investing a fortune. Kitchen organizers generally range in price from $4 to $45. So what are you waiting for?

Check out these alternatives and get busy!

✓ Connecting trays
✓ Adjustable shelves
✓ Adjustable racks

Tim Todd
Home Sense, Inc.

Using TextEdit for Web Design

You can use TextEdit to create and edit HTML code documents. You can open an existing HTML file or create a new one using plain text or RTF Rich Text Format. If you want to add graphics to your RTF document, you cannot save it as an HTML file. However, you can save it as a Web archive file. In addition, you can insert a link to an URL address into a document.

Create Plain HTML Code Files

1. For plain text only, click the **Format** menu, and then click **Make Plain Text**.

2. Write the HTML code.

3. For an Untitled document, click the **File** menu, and then click **Save**.

 ◆ To save a version, click the **File** menu, and then click **Save a Version**. (**New**!)

4. Add the .html extension at the end of the file name.

5. Click **Save**.

6. Click **Use .html**.

Did You Know?

You can set preferences to save HTML files. Click the TextEdit menu, click Preferences, click the Open and Save tab, select a document type, a setting for cascading style sheets (CSS), and an encoding. If you want to include code to preserve blank areas, select the Preserve White Space check box, and then click the Close button.

Open an HTML Document

1. Click the **File** menu, and then click **Open**.

2. Select the hard drive and the folder in which you want to open the file.

3. Click the document you want to open.

4. Select the **Ignore rich text commands** check box.

5. Click **Open**.

Add a Link

1. Select the text you want for the link.

2. Click the **Edit** menu, and then click **Add Link**.

3. Type or paste the URL link address in the Link Destination box.

4. Click **OK**.

Did You Know?

You can edit or remove a link. To edit a link, select the link, click the Edit menu, click Edit Link, edit the link text, and then click OK. To remove a link, select the link, click the Edit menu, click Edit Link, and then click Remove Link.

Setting TextEdit Preferences

TextEdit preferences help you configure some of the more common features of the program. You can set preferences for new documents, default fonts, rich text processing, default plain text encoding, editing, and saving. These preference areas allow you to turn features on and off as well as customize the way TextEdit works.

Set General Preferences

1. Click the **TextEdit** menu, and then click **Preferences**.

2. Click the **New Document** tab.

3. Select or specify the various options you want to use:

 ◆ **Format.** Select options for document format and text wrapping.

 ◆ **Window Size.** Specify the width and height you want.

 ◆ **Font.** Click **Change** to select the default fonts you want.

 ◆ **Properties and Options.** Enter document properties and check or clear to enable or disable the editing options.

4. Click the **Open and Save** tab.

5. Select or specify the various options you want to use:

 ◆ **When Opening a File.** Check or clear to ignore or allow rich text commands.

 ◆ **When Saving a File.** Check or clear the options you want.

 ◆ **Plain Text File Encoding.** Click the Open or Save pop-ups to select a text encoding default.

 ◆ **HTML Saving Options.** Click the pop-ups to select a default HTML type, styling, and encoding.

6. Click the **Close** button.

Printing and Faxing

Introduction

Let's face it, you work all day on a computer, but sooner or later, you're going to have to get your one-of-a-kind project, text document, or photograph off the computer. Computer data finds itself in the most unlikely places. For example, you could save a text document onto a CD or DVD, and then store the CD or DVD away; never to be seen again. Probably the most common place you find computer data is on paper. It might be nice to talk of a paperless society, however, most people prefer the satisfying feel of paper in their hands, as opposed to a cold computer monitor. That's where Mac OS X steps in and makes your life easy. Not only does Mac OS X give you all the standard ways to print to paper or fax, it also gives you hundreds of printer drives; supporting the vast majority of printers in the market. In addition, you can save paper by previewing your jobs—using Mac OS X's print preview feature—which shows you a color-accurate on-screen version of your print job.

If you fax documents, then Mac OS X is an operating system tailor-made expressly for your needs. Mac OS X integrates its faxing features with a state-of-the-art printing system. Just open the Print & Scan pane in System Preferences, and you can set up your computer to receive faxes. Then, when you go to print a document from virtually any application, you'll see a Fax button in the Print dialog. In addition, if you have a large print job that you would rather print after work, or a fax that has to be sent at a specific time; Mac OS X lets you schedule a time to print a document, or fax with the click of a button.

What You'll Do

Understand Printers

Understand Printer Drivers

Add or Remove a Printer

Set Print Settings

Share a Printer

Set Up Page Options

Set Basic Print Options

Preview Documents

Save Documents as PDF Documents

Manage Print Queues

Create a Cover Page

Scan Documents

Send Fax Documents

Receive Faxes Automatically

Understanding Printers

Although there are many different kinds of printers, there are two main categories: ink-jet and laser. An **ink-jet printer** works by spraying ionized ink on a sheet of paper. Ink-jet printers are less expensive and considerably slower than laser printers, but they still produce a good quality output. A **laser printer** utilizes a laser beam to produce an image on a drum, which is rolled through a reservoir of toner and transferred to the paper through a combination of heat and pressure. Laser printers are faster and produce a higher quality output than ink-jets, but they are also more expensive. Ink-jet and laser printers are combined with other hardware devices, such as a copier and scanner, into a multi-function device. A **multi-function device** provides common device functionality at a lower cost than purchasing each device separately. Printers are classified by two main characteristics: resolution and speed. Printer resolution refers to the sharpness and clarity of a printed page. For printers, the resolution indicates the number of dots per inch (dpi). For example, a 300-dpi printer is one that is capable of printing 300 distinct dots in a line one-inch long, or 90,000 dots per square inch. The higher the dpi, the sharper the print quality. Printer speed is measured in pages per minute (ppm). The speed of printers varies widely. In general, ink-jet printers range from about 4 to 10 ppm, while laser printers range from about 10 to 30 ppm. The speed depends on the amount of printer memory (the more the better) and the page's contents: if there is just text or the page has only one color, the ppm is in the high range, but when a page contains graphics and/or has multiple colors, the ppm rate falls to the low range.

Ink-jet printer

Laser printer

Multi-function device

Understanding Printer Drivers

Printer drivers are lines of code designed to help an operating system communicate with a specific printer. No two printer models are created equal: Some have two paper trays, while others have one; some are ink-jet, while others are laser; some are color and some black and white. Although there are generic printer drivers available, most printers have a driver program, designed specifically for that make and model. Mac OS X installs all of the printer drivers onto your hard drive when you run the Mac OS X installation program.

The drivers become available when you attach your printer and run the Printer Setup Utility. The good news is that the process of hooking up your printer, and being able to print is easy to do. Mac OS X comes bundled with almost every conceivable printer driver; however, new printers and updates are being released all the time. When you plug in a new printer, Mac OS X downloads the appropriate driver. Periodically, it checks to make sure it has the lastest driver using Software Update as needed. It's always a good idea to keep the CD or DVD that came with your printer handy; it contains a driver for that particular model of printer. In addition, the Web sites for the printer companies such as *www.epson.com* or *www.hp.com*, contain the latest updates and patches for their printers. You can visit them to see if any updates are available.

Since you'll only need one or two printer drivers, you can delete the others. All those unused drivers take up over a gigabyte of space on your hard drive. Once you've installed the necessary printers, select the Library folder (located on the main hard drive), click Printers folder, and then delete the unused drivers. If necessary, you can always reinstall them from the OS X install disks.

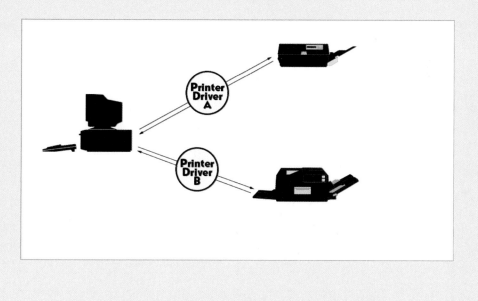

Adding or Removing a Printer

Setting up a printer use to be a difficult and time-consuming process. There were all kinds of questions to answer, driver files to find, and after all that time, you might still have problems. With Mac OS X, setting up a printer is easy. Adding a printer can be as simple as plugging it into your computer. In most cases that's all you need to do. Mac OS X automatically tries to autoconfigure almost any USB, FireWire, or Bluetooth connection. If you want to install a network printer, such as Bonjour, or your printer doesn't appear in the printer list, you can add it manually in the Print & Scan pane in System Preferences. If you no longer use a printer, you can quickly remove it while your in Print & Scan preferences.

Add or Remove a Printer

1. To add a printer, follow the printer setup instructions to install any necessary software, and then connect it to your computer using a USB or FireWire connection.

 Mac OS X automatically tries to install the printer. In most cases, the printer is available in any Print dialog box.

 If the printer is not available, continue.

2. Click the **System Preferences** icon in the Dock, and then click the **Print & Scan** icon.

 The printer appears in the left column. If your printer doesn't appears in the list, follow the instructions to add a printer manually on the next page.

3. To remove a printer, select the printer you want to remove, click the **Remove** (-) button, and then click **OK**.

4. Click the **Close** button.

Add a Printer Manually

1. Click the **System Preferences** icon in the Dock, and then click the **Print & Scan** icon.

2. Click the **Add** (+) button.

 TIMESAVER *In a Print dialog box, click the Printer pop-up, and then click Add Printer.*

3. Use the toolbar buttons to specify the information required to display (if necessary) and select the printer you want to add:

 ◆ **Default.** Displays available autoconfigured printers

 ◆ **Fax.** Displays available autoconfigured faxes.

 ◆ **IP.** Provides options to setup a network printer using an IP (Internet Protocol) address, such as 192.160.1.170.

 Also can provide options to setup special-case printers, such as Canon IJ Network, Epson FireWire or TCP/IP, or HP IP Printing.

 ◆ **Windows.** Displays network printers using Windows and an Ethernet connection.

4. Click **Add**, and then click **Continue**, if necessary.

5. Click the **Close** button in the Add Printer window.

6. Click the **Close** button.

Default

IP

Setting Print Settings

Using your Macintosh to print and fax is an obvious extension of the normal, everyday computing process. You write and create documents, and send them to paper; you take a photograph using a digital camera and send it to a photo-quality printer. You can use the Print & Scan pane in System Preferences to modify many of the aspects of printing. For example, you can set the default printer, the one that automatically appears when you want to print, and the default paper size. If you want to find out the available options for a specific printer, you can use Options and Supplies, where you can find printer information, change a printer name, select a different driver, and check out printer supplies available online, such as ink and toner.

Set Default Printer Settings

1. Click the **System Preferences** icon in the Dock, and then click the **Print & Scan** icon.

2. Click the **Default Printer** pop-up, and then click **Last Printer Used** or select a default printer to appear first in the Print dialogs of all your applications.

3. Click the **Default Paper Size in Page Setup** pop-up, and then select a paper size to be used as a default in the Print dialogs of all your applications.

4. Click the **Close** button.

Set Printer Specific Settings

1. Click the **System Preferences** icon in the Dock, and then click the **Print & Scan** icon.

2. Select the printer you want to change print settings.

3. Click **Options & Supplies**.

4. Click the tab for the area in which you want to change settings, such as General, Driver, or Supply Levels. The tabs vary depending on the printer.

 ◆ **General.** Displays printer information (queue and host name, and driver version). You can change the name and location of the printer.

 ◆ **Driver.** Allows you to select a different driver.

 ◆ **Supply Levels.** Allows you to access a Web site that lets you order more supplies, such as ink or toner. Click **Supplies** to open the Web site.

5. Click **OK**.

6. Click the **Close** button.

See Also

See "Using Network Sharing Services" on page 404-405 for more information on setting Sharing Preferences.

| General | Driver | Supply Levels |

Name: HP LaserJet 3050

Location: Steve's Mac mini

Queue Name: HP_LaserJet_3050

Driver Version: 17.5

Cancel OK

For Your Information

Selecting a Printer's PPD File

A PostScript Printer Description (PPD) file specifies a printer's options and features. When you add a printer to your computer, Mac OS X selects a PPD for you. If you have another PPD for your printer (typically provided by the printer manufacturer), you can use it instead. Click the System Preferences icon in the Dock, click the Print & Scan icon, select your printer, click Options & Supplies, click the Driver tab, click the Print Using pop-up, click Other, select the PPD file you want, click OK or Open, and then click OK.

Sharing a Printer

If you have a printer connected to your computer and your computer is connected to a network, you can share your printer with other network users. Before you can share a printer, you need to turn on printer sharing in the Sharing pane in System Preferences and then enable sharing for each printer in the Print & Scan pane. After you share a printer, other users—with Mac OS X, UNIX, or Windows computers—connected to your network can use your printer; you can also connect to other shared printers—including an AirPort base station— available on your network. For security purposes, if you want to share your printer with a Windows user via SMB/CIFS, you need to set Firewall options to allow all incoming connections on the Firewall tab of Security preferences. If a Windows user has Bonjour installed, the user can use the Bonjour wizard to connect to your printer on a Mac. After you share your printer, if a user connected to your network still cannot access your printer, you can provide them with your Mac IP address (available in Network preferences for the network connection, such as Built-in Ethernet) and queue name (available in Print & Scan preferences in Options & Supplies) to make the connection to the shared printer.

Share a Printer

1. Click the **System Preferences** icon in the Dock, and then click the **Print & Scan** icon.

2. Select the printer you want to change print settings.

3. Select the **Share this printer on the network** check box.

4. If printer sharing is turned off, click **Sharing Preferences**, select the **Printer Sharing** check box, and then click the **Close** button.

 ◆ You can also click the **System Preferences** icon in the Dock, and then click the **Sharing** icon.

5. To share your printer with Windows users via SMB/CIFS, click **Show All**, click the **Security** icon, click **Firewall**, click **Start**, click **Advanced** (if you want to set other options), and then click the **Back** button.

6. Click the **Close** button.

Click to add a shared printer

Access a Shared Printer

1. Click the **System Preferences** icon in the Dock, and then click the **Print & Scan** icon.

2. Click the **Add** (+) button.

3. Use the toolbar buttons to specify the information required to display and select the printer you want:

 - **IP.** Provides options to setup a network printer using an IP (Internet Protocol) address, such as 192.160.1.170.

 Also can provide options to setup special-case printers, such as Canon IJ Network, Epson FireWire or TCP/IP, or HP IP Printing.

 - **Windows.** Displays network printers using Windows and an Ethernet connection.

4. Click **Add**.

5. Click the **Close** button in the Print & Scan Browser window.

6. Click the **Close** button.

For Your Information

Using AirPort Base Station to Share a Printer

If you have an AirPort Extreme or AirPort Express base station, you can share a USB printer with other computers on your network. When you use an AirPort Express base station, you may not see error or status messages, such as *Out of Paper*. To use the AirPort base station, you need to follow setup instructions to install any software, connect the printer to your computer, print a test page, and then connect the printer to the AirPort base station. You can also print to shared Windows printers over a network or share your own printer with Windows users.

Setting Up Page Options

With few exceptions, Macintosh applications give you the ability to print a document to paper. Programs such as: Microsoft Word, Corel WordPerfect; even TextEdit—Macintosh's proprietary word processing application—give you the option to print what you have committed to type. When you select the Print option (located under the File menu), you're instructing the application to use an output device (the printer) to place your words on paper. Since all printers have options, it's important to be able to set those options before printing. You might be using a specific size paper or printing orientation. For this operation, you'll use the Page Setup command, located within the File menu of most applications.

Set Up Page Options

1. Open a document, such as a text document.

2. Click the **File** menu, and then click **Page Setup**.

3. Click the **Settings** pop-up, and then select from the following options:

 ◆ **Page Attributes**. This option lets you select a printer, specific paper size, orientation, and print scale.

 ◆ **Custom Paper Size**. Click **New** to create a customized paper size by entering height, width, and margin values into the appropriate input fields.

 ◆ **Document Specific Option**. This option gives you specific options for the current application.

 ◆ **Summary**. Click **Summary** to see an outline of your options.

 ◆ **Save As Default**. Click this option to save your current settings as default for future printing operations.

3

| Settings: | Page Attributes | ⬍ |

| Format For: | Any Printer | ⬍ |

| Paper Size: | US Letter | ⬍ |

8.50 by 11.00 inches

Orientation: [icons]

Scale: 100 %

(?) Cancel OK

Click the **Format for** pop-up, and then select a printer from the available options.

Click the **Paper Size** pop-up, and then select a paper size from the available options.

Click the **Orientation** buttons, and then select from the following:

- **Portrait**

- **Landscape**

Enter in a printing scale percentage.

Click **OK**.

If necessary, save the file and close the application.

Settings: Page Attributes

Format For: Any Printer — 4

Paper Size: US Letter — 5
8.50 by 11.00 inches

Orientation: — 6

Scale: 100 %

? Cancel OK — 8

7

Setting Basic Print Options

All applications that allow you to send a document to a printer, give you the ability to set up specific printing parameters. Some print options are generic, such as how many pages to print, and some are more specific, such as what paper tray to use (in a multi-tray printer). Regardless of the options, they're all located in one specific location, the Print command of the opened application. When you select the Print command, a dialog opens displaying a preview of the pages (**New!**) with all the options associated with the default printer; including the ability to change the default printer, and any other printing values.

Set Basic Print Options

1. Open a document.

2. Click the **File** menu, and then click **Print**.

3. Click the **Printer** pop-up, and then select a printer from the available options.

 The Print dialog displays a preview of the page (**New!**). You can click buttons below the print preview to scroll through pages.

4. Click **Show Details,** if necessary, to expand the Print dialog box.

5. Click the **Presets** pop-up, and then select a user-defined print setting.

6. Specify the following standard print options:

 ◆ **Preview Image.** Click the arrows below the preview image to view the document.

 ◆ **Copies.** Type the number of copies you want. Select or clear the **Collated** check box. Selected prints 1, 2, 3, 1, 2, 3. Cleared prints 1, 1, 2, 2, 3, 3.

 ◆ **Pages.** Click the **All** option or the **From** option, and then enter the print range you want.

 ◆ **Paper Size.** Select the paper size you want.

 ◆ **Orientation.** Select the portrait or landscape option you want.

Print preview

⑦ Click the **Options** pop-up, and then select from the available options:

◆ **Application Specific Options.** If you're using Microsoft Word, this option lists specific options for that specific application.

◆ **Layout.** When printing large documents, allows you to select how many pages per sheet, the layout direction, border options, and two-sided printing.

◆ **Color Matching.** Gives you access to Macintosh's ColorSync management system, and the ability to apply the new Quartz Filters to the printed document.

◆ **Paper Handling.** Select to print in reverse order (page 1 prints last), whether to print all, odd, or even pages, and scale a document to fit the paper.

◆ **Paper Feed.** Select the paper tray for all pages or a different paper tray for the first and remaining pages.

◆ **Cover Page.** Lets you select options to print a cover page, such as standard, classified, unclassified, or confidential.

◆ **Color/Quality Options.** Lets you set printer resolution options.

◆ **Finishing.** Let you set printing to different media types, such as as paper weight.

IMPORTANT *The print settings on the Options pop-up vary depending on the selected printer.*

⑧ To save your print settings, click the **Presets** pop-up, click **Save Current Settings as Presets**, type a name, and then click **OK**.

⑨ Click **Print**.

Previewing Documents

One of the most frustrating things is looking at a document on your monitor, clicking the Print command, and then deciding that what you see on the paper is not what you wanted. Unfortunately, a monitor is not a piece of paper, and the term What You See is What You Get (WYSIWYG), is a phrase that most computer users do not take very seriously. Once again, Macintosh comes to the rescue with a preview (**New!**) in the Print dialog and a more detailed display in Preview utility that targets your default printer. If you see what you like, you can print a single copy directly from the Preview dialog, or you can close the preview, and then print using the standard Print option.

Preview Documents

1. Open or create a document in an application.

2. Click the **File** menu, and then click **Print**.

 The Print dialog display a preview of the document (**New!**). You can click buttons below the print preview to scroll through pages.

3. To open in Preview, click the **PDF** button, and then click **Open PDF in Preview**.

4. In Preview, select from the following options:

 ◆ **Zoom In or Zoom Out**. Click to increase or decrease the viewing size of the image.

 ◆ **Move**. Click to move around the current page.

 ◆ **Text**. Click to select text on the current page.

 ◆ **Select**. Click to select a portion of the current page.

 ◆ **Annotate**. Click to display the Annotation toolbar.

 ◆ **View**. Click to display a view: Content Only, Thumbnails, Table of Contents, or Contact Sheet.

5. Click **Cancel** to close or **Print** to print the document.

6. Quit Preview.

Print preview

Click to scroll thru pages

Saving Documents as PDF Documents

The PDF (Portable Document File) format is undoubtedly the most successful multi-platform format ever created by any company. Designed by Adobe, it has become the standard for transferring text and graphics documents, spreadsheets; even creating interactive forms, that can be filled out by a visitor, and then sent back to the owner for processing. The reason for the success of the PDF format is Adobe's tight control over the Adobe Acrobat application (used to create PDF's), and the Acrobat Reader application (used by visitors to read PDF's). Once a PDF document is properly saved, it can be opened by virtually anyone that has Acrobat Reader, regardless of computer or operating system. And the good news is that the Reader application is a free download, just point your browser to *http://www.acrobat.com*, and then click Download Reader to obtain the latest version of the Acrobat Reader application, tailored for your specific operating system.

Save Documents as a PDF

① Open or create a document in an application.

② Click the **File** menu, and then click **Print**.

③ Click **PDF**, and then select the type of PDF you want to create:

◆ **Save as PDF.** Creates a PDF document. Enter a name, specify a location, and then click **Save**.

◆ **Fax PDF.** Creates and faxes a PDF document.

◆ **Add PDF to iTunes.** Creates and adds a PDF document to iTunes. (**New!**)

◆ **Mail PDF.** Creates and attaches a PDF document in an e-mail.

◆ **Save PDF to Web Receipts Folder.** Creates and stores a PDF document in your Web Receipts folder; great for saving Web site receipts.

③ Specify PDF settings; options vary

A PDF document viewed in Acrobat Reader.

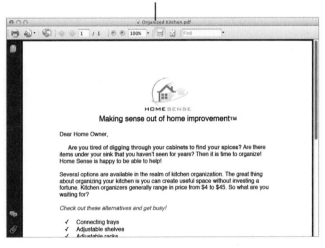

Managing Print Queues

The definition of a queue is a line. In Great Britain the term is used to describe a line of people waiting to get into a movie or restaurant. In printing terms a **queue** is a group of documents all waiting to be printed on the same printer. Mac OS X handles the queue like a master conductor; keeping everything in order, as it smoothly instructs the printer to print each document in turn. However, sometimes problems can occur that the Print Queue utility doesn't quite know how to handle. For example, it's possible that you want to place a job on hold while other jobs print (preferably yours), or you many want to delete a job. In fact, you can even instruct the printer to stop printing altogether.

Manage Print Queues

1. Open the Printer window with the print jobs you want to manage:

 - ◆ Click the **System Preferences** icon in the Dock, click the **Print & Scan** icon, select the printer, and then click **Open Print Queue**.

 - ◆ Double-click the printer's icon in the Dock while the document is printing.

 - ◆ Double-click the printer's icon as a desktop printer.

2. Select a job, and then click one of the following:

 - ◆ **Delete**. Deletes the job from the queue.

 - ◆ **Hold/Resume**. Stops or resumes the printing of the selected job.

 - ◆ **Info**. Opens the Options & Supplies dialog box.

 - ◆ **Pause/Resume Printer**. Pauses or resumes the printer.

3. To view information about completed print jobs, including the print time and date, click the **Jobs** menu, and then click **Show Completed Jobs**.

4. Click the **Close** button.

Click to change printer setup options

Current print job

Paused printer

Creating a Cover Page

When you print a document, Mac OS X allows you to create a cover page. When you work with secure information, you can print a cover page that indicates the private nature of a document. For example, you can add a cover page with the following tags: classified, confidential, secret, top secret, and unclassified. Many companies require a cover page to be sent with sensitive documents. Since the decision to use a cover sheet is dependent on the document, Mac OS X gives you the choice to add a cover sheet each time you print a document.

Create a Cover Page

1. Open a document that you want to print a cover page.

2. Click the **File** menu, and then click **Print**.

3. Click the **Printer** pop-up, and then select a printer from the available options.

4. Click the **Options** pop-up, and then click **Cover Page**.

5. Click the print cover page option you want: **None**, **Before document**, or **After document**.

6. Click the **Cover Page Type** pop-up, and then select the print cover page option you want.

7. Click **Print**.

Scanning Documents

If you have a scanner or a printer with a scanner, you can scan images and documents to your computer, typically without any other special software. Simply, plug-in and play. If you have a flatbed scanner, you can scan many images at once (make sure there is empty space between the images), store each one in it's own file, and straighten any images that were crooked on the scanner bed. If you have a scanner with an automatic feeder, you can scan multiple pages at once. If you're in an application, like Preview, you can import from a scanner; click the File menu, point to Import from Scanner, and then select a scanner.

Scan Documents

1. Click the **System Preferences** icon in the Dock, and then click the **Print & Scan** icon.

2. Select the printer/scanner or scanner device you want to use, and then click the **Scan** tab, if necessary.

3. Click **Open Scanner**.

4. Place the document or image you want to scan in the scanner.

5. Select from the following options:

 ♦ Scan Size. Select a specific size, or let the scanner do it: click **Detect Separate Items** or **Detect Enclosing Box**.

 ♦ Scan To. Select the program you want to use to open and display the scan.

6. Click one of the from the following buttons:

 ♦ **Scan.** Scans and creates the document using the default settings.

 The scanned document is stored in the Pictures folder.

 ♦ **Show Details.** Performs an overview prescan to show you the initial scan. You can set the scan options you want before actually scanning the documents.

212

7. Select from the available options (setting may vary depending on the scanner):

- ◆ **Kind.** Select a document type: Text, Black & White, or Color.

- ◆ **Colors.** Select the range of colors: Millions or Billions.

- ◆ **Resolution.** Specify the dpi (dots per inch).

- ◆ **Use Custom Size.** Select to specify a custom size and use auto selection.

- ◆ **Size and Rotation Angle.** Specify a scan size and any rotation.

- ◆ **Orientation.** Select Portrait or Landscape.

- ◆ **Scan To.** Select the program you want to use to open and preview the scan.

- ◆ **Name.** Enter a name for the scan document.

- ◆ **Format.** Select a file format.

- ◆ **Image Correction.** Set to manual to specify brightness, tint, temperature, or saturation.

- ◆ **Descreen.** Select to remove screen moire patterns.

- ◆ **Color Restoration.** Select to restore faded color.

- ◆ **Adaptive Lighting.** Select to auto-adjust exposure levels.

- ◆ **Sharpen.** Select to increase sharpness.

8. Click **Overview** to perform a prescan with the current settings or click **Scan** to perform a scan and create the document using the current settings.

The scanned document is opened in the specified application. The scanned document is stored in the Pictures folder.

Adjust resize handles to change scan area

Scanned document in Preview

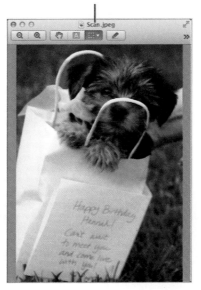

Sending Fax Documents

Using your Mac to print and fax is an obvious extension of the normal, everyday computing process. You have a document, and you need to fax it to a co-worker or friend. Once you've decided whom the fax is to be sent to, and what the fax number is, the next step is to send the fax. When you fax a document, Mac OS X allows you to create a cover page. A cover page indicates to the person receiving the fax, the number of pages in the fax, who is sending the fax, the date and time the fax was sent, and a short text paragraph. Since the decision to use a cover sheet is dependent on the document, Mac OS X gives you the choice to add a cover sheet each time you generate a fax.

Send Fax Documents

1. Open a document that you want to fax.

2. Click the **File** menu, and then click **Print**.

3. Click the **PDF** button, and then click **Fax PDF**.

4. If necessary, click the **Printer** pop-up, and then select your fax modem.

5. Specify the specifics for the fax job (copies, pages, paper size, and orientation).

6. Click the **Options** pop-up, and then select from the following options:

 ◆ **Fax Information**. Type the fax number in the To field. Enter any prefixes into the Dialing Prefix field, such as 9 to get an outside line. Select the **Use Cover page** check box to add a fax cover sheet, and then type the subject and message text you want to display on the Cover Page.

 IMPORTANT *You cannot create a new paragraph while typing the cover page text. The Return key only sends the fax prematurely. To get around this, create the cover page text in another application, and then copy and paste it into the field.*

For Your Information

Addressing Faxes from the Address Book

When you send a Fax, you need a document, and a fax number to send it. Do you need to open the Address Book, and write that number down? No. Mac OS X gives you the ability to pull that information directly from the address card. Remember that in order for an address card to be used for faxing, it must first have a fax number entered into the card. In the Print dialog, click the PDF button, click Fax PDF, click the Options pop-up, and then click Fax Information. Click the Address Book button, select a name from your address list, click the To button to add the name and fax number to the current fax request, select a name, and then click the Close button.

◆ **Fax Modem**. Select between tone or pulse phones, whether to hear the dialing through your computer speakers, and if you want the modem to wait for a dial tone before beginning the fax process.

◆ **Layout**. When printing large documents, allows you to select how many pages per sheet, the layout direction, border options, and two-sided printing.

◆ **Paper Handling**. Select to print in reverse order (page 1 prints last), and whether to print all, odd, or even pages.

◆ **Scheduler**. Lets you schedule a time for faxing the document.

◆ **Printer Features**. Select between low and high quality output.

7 Click **Fax**.

8 Close your document.

Did You Know?

You can let other users send faxes through your computer. Click the System Preferences icon in the Dock, click the Print & Scan icon, select the fax modem you want to share, select the Share This Fax On The Network check box, and then click the Close button. The fax is now available for other to use.

You can view fax information about completed jobs. Click the System Preferences icon in the Dock, click the Print & Scan icon, double-click the fax modem icon in the Fax list, click the Jobs menu, and then click Show Completed Jobs.

Fax modem options

7

For Your Information

Checking the Status of a Fax

You can check the status of a fax. Click the fax modem icon in the Dock while a document is being sent. To pause the printer, click the Pause Printer button; to resume the printer, click the Resume Printer button. To put a fax on hold, select it, and then click the Hold button; to resume the fax, select it, and then click the Resume button.

Saving your Fax Print Options

If you have a combination of faxing options that you frequently use, you can save it as a Preset. After selecting your options, click the Presets pop-up menu, click Save As, and then type a name for the new options. If you want to use the new options to fax a document, click the Presets pop-up, select its name from the Presets pop-up menu, and then click Fax.

Receiving Faxes Automatically

It's actually pretty easy to set up your computer to receive faxes automatically. All you need is a phone line, and your Mac. You can set up the Fax to answer after a certain number of rings, and you don't have to be logged in; however, your Mac needs to be on and not in sleep mode, which you can set in Energy Saver preferences. To make it easier to work with faxes, you can set the option to show the Fax status menu in the menu bar for easy access. After you send and receive some faxes, you can view information about the completed job. You can manage the fax queue just like the print queue. You can also manually receive faxes. Wait for the phone to ring, click the Fax status menu, and then click Answer Now.

Receive Faxes Automatically

1. Click the **System Preferences** icon in the Dock, and then click the **Print & Scan** icon.

2. Select the fax modem you want to use.

3. To use the Fax status menu, select the **Show fax status in menu bar** check box.

4. Enter your fax number into the field, exactly as you would dial the number.

5. Click **Receive Options**.

6. Select from the following options:

 ◆ **Receive faxes on this computer**. Select the check box to receive faxes.

 ◆ **When a fax arrives answer After**. Enter how many rings are required before the Fax answers the phone.

 ◆ **Save to**. Select the check box, and then select where to save the faxes.

 ◆ **Email to**. Select the check box, and then select where to e-mail the faxes.

7. Click **OK**.

8. Click the **Close** button.

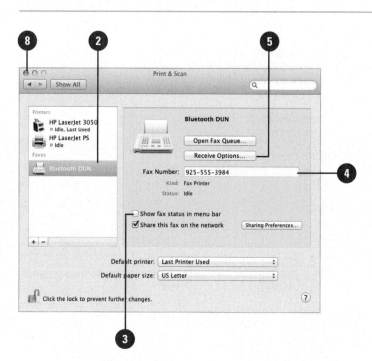

216

Exploring the Internet

9

Introduction

The **Internet** is a global collection of more than a billion computers (and growing) linked together to share information. The Internet's physical structure includes telephone lines, cables, satellites, and other telecommunications media. Using the Internet, computer users can share many types of information, including text, graphics, sounds, videos, and computer programs. The World Wide Web (also known as the Web or www) is a part of the Internet that consists of Web sites located on different computers around the world.

History of the Internet and the World Wide Web

The Internet has its roots in the Advanced Research Projects Agency Network (ARPANET), which the United States Department of Defense started in 1969. In 1986, the National Science Foundation formed NSFNET, which replaced ARPANET. NSFNET expanded the foundation of the U.S. portion of the Internet with high-speed, long-distance data lines. In 1991, the U.S. Congress expanded the capacity and speed of the Internet further and opened it to commercial use. The Internet is now accessible in almost every country in the world. The World Wide Web was developed in Switzerland in 1991 to make finding documents on the Internet easier. Software programs designed to access the Web, known as Web browsers, use point-and-click interfaces. The first such Web browser, Mosaic, was introduced at the University of Illinois in 1993. Since the release of Mosaic, Microsoft Internet Explorer, Netscape, and AOL have become some of the most popular Web browsers.

What You'll Do

Connect to the Internet

Set Up a Modem, Ethernet, or Wi-Fi Wireless Connection

Set Up Multiple Connections

Make an Internet Connection

Understand Web Sites and Browsers

Start and Customize Safari

Browse the Web

Change the Home Page

View a History List

Bookmark a Web Page

Work with Bookmarks

View and Bookmark RSS Feeds

Fill Out Forms on the Web

Search the Web

Print and Save a Web Page

Save Pictures or Text from a Web Page

Download Files from the Web

Set Safari Preferences

Block Pop-Up Windows

Connecting to the Internet

Universities and large companies are most likely connected to the Internet via high-speed wiring that transmits data very quickly. Home computer owners usually rely on a modem and the phone lines already in place. In some areas, however, several faster connection options are becoming available and affordable. There are **DSL** (Digital Subscriber Lines), wires that provide a complete digital connection; **cable modems**, which use cable television lines; and **wireless**, which doesn't use wires or phone lines. DSL and cable modems, also known as **broadband** connections, are continually turned on and connected to an Ethernet network so you don't need to establish a connection using a dial-up modem. Data travels more slowly over phone wires than over digital lines and cable modems. Wireless provides a mobile connection to the Internet using an Wi-Fi connection anywhere there is a wireless base station, such as a router or a network hub. Whether you use a phone line, a DSL line, a cable modem, or a wireless device, Mac OS X can help you establish a connection to the Internet.

Before you start the process to set up an Internet connection, you need to select an ISP (Internet Service Provider), which is a company that sets up an Internet account for you and provides Internet access. ISPs maintain servers connected directly to the Internet 24 hours a day. You pay a fee, sometimes by the hour, but more often a flat monthly rate. To connect to the Internet, you need to obtain an Internet account and connection information from your ISP or your system administrator. Each type of Internet connection requires certain connection information, including:

◆ **ISP Phone Number.** A number to create a dial-up connection.

◆ **Account Name.** A user name for the Internet account.

◆ **Password.** A security password for the Internet account.

If your ISP needs it, you may also need the following information:

◆ **IP Address.** An IP (Internet Protocol) address is a unique identifier of your computer on the Internet.

◆ **Subnet Mask.** A filter that helps your computer differentiate between computers on a local network and the Internet.

◆ **Router.** A device address that sends and receives information over the Internet.

◆ **Domain Name Server** (DNS). A computer that translates a Web site name into an IP address.

◆ **Proxy.** A computer your Macintosh uses to access the Internet.

When you have the connection information from your ISP or network administrator, you can use the Network pane in System Preferences to set up, configure, and display status for all your network connections, such as Modem, Ethernet, and Wi-Fi.

Network pane in System Preferences

Get assistance

218

Getting Internet Connection Assistance

At the bottom of the Network pane is the **Assist Me** button. When you click the Assist Me button, it starts the Network Setup Assistant, which asks you a series of questions to help you set up your Internet Connection.

Creating Multiple Connections

If you have a mobile computer, such as a MacBook, you can set up multiple connections for different locations. Setting up multiple connections allows you to connect to the Internet at home using a dial-up connection, at the office using an ethernet connection, or on the road using a wireless connection.

If you have a dial-up modem or AirPort card, you can use the Internet Connect application located in the Applications folder to help you quickly create an Internet connection to different configurations in your current location.

Protecting your Computer from the Internet

When you connect to the Internet, you can access Web sites and information on the Internet, but other users on the Internet can also access information on your computer. You can prevent this by activating a firewall, another security layer of protection. A **firewall** is a security system that creates a protective barrier between your computer or network and others on the Internet. The firewall monitors all communication between your computer and the Internet and prevents unsolicited inbound traffic from the Internet from entering your private computer. The firewall discards all unsolicited communication from reaching your computer unless you specifically allow it to come through. If your computer is directly connected to the Internet, you should activate a firewall. If you are sharing an Internet connection on your network to provide Internet access on multiple computers, you should activate the firewall on the computer connected to the Internet only to avoid creating network communication problems. For more information and instructions on setting up a firewall, see "Configuring an Internet Firewall," on page 409 in Chapter 16.

Sharing an Internet Connection

If you have an Internet connection and work on a network, you can share the Internet connection with other computers on your local area network. For more information and instructions on sharing an Internet connection, see "Sharing an Internet Connection," on page 408 in Chapter 16.

Setting Up a Modem Connection

If you have a dial-up modem installed on your computer, you can set up and use a modem connection to access the Internet or another computer. You only need to set up a dial-up connection once. After you set up the dial-up connection, you can use the Show Modem Status menu to easily connect and disconnect from the Internet or network, and show modem connection information. When you are connected, the Finder displays a connection icon and connects information in the menu.

Set Up a Modem Connection

1. Click the **System Preferences** icon in the Dock, and then click the **Network** icon.

2. Click **Modem** in the list.
 - If a modem is not in the list, click the **Add** (+) button, click Modem from the Interface pop-up, and then click **Create**.

3. Click **Advanced**.

4. Click the **PPP** tab, and then specify your user name, password, and ISP phone number.
 - Specify PPP Options to redial a busy connection, automatically connect when starting TCP/IP applications, and automatically disconnect if you select Log Out from the Apple menu.

5. Click the **TCP/IP** and **DNS** tabs, and then specify any settings provided by your ISP, such as IP Address, Subnet Mask, Router, and DNS Servers.

6. Click the **Proxies** tab, and then specify any settings provided by your ISP.

7. Click the **Modem** tab, and then specify any settings specific to your computer's modem.

8. Click **OK**.

9. Click **Apply**.

Modem

PPP TCP/IP DNS Proxies Modem

Service Provider: ISP (Optional)
Account Name: Perspec
Password: ••••
Telephone Number: 925-555-1234
Alternate Number: (Optional)
☑ Save password

(PPP Options...)

(Cancel) (OK)

Modem

PPP TCP/IP DNS Proxies Modem

Modem: Apple Internal 56K Modem (v.90) ⟳
☑ Enable error correction and compression in modem
☑ Wait for dial tone before dialing
Dialing: ⦿ Tone ○ Pulse
Sound: ⦿ On ○ Off
Country Setting: United States (Change...)

(Cancel) (OK)

Setting Up an Ethernet Connection

If you have a DSL or cable modem, you can set up and use an ethernet connection to access the Internet. In addition to connecting to the Internet, you also use ethernet to connect to a local area network (LAN). When you set up an ethernet connection using a cable modem or on a corporate network, some settings are typically configured automatically by a **BOOTP** (boot protocol) or **DHCP** (Dynamic Host Configuration Protocol). If your network supports ones of these services, you can use the Configure IPv4 pop-up in the TCP/IP area to select a protocol. If your ISP uses **PPPoE** (Point to Point Protocol over Ethernet), you need to specify your account and password. Check with your ISP or network administrator to determine if this applies to you.

Set Up an Ethernet Connection

1. Click the **System Preferences** icon in the Dock, and then click the **Network** icon.

2. Click **Ethernet** in the list.

3. If you want assistance, click **Assist Me**, and then follow the instructions.

4. Click **Advanced**, if needed.

5. Click the **TCP/IP** and **DNS** tabs, and then specify any settings provided by your ISP, such as IP Address, Subnet Mask, Router, and DNS Servers.

 TROUBLE? *If your Internet connection is having problems, click Renew DHCP Lease to refresh your IP address.*

6. Click the **Proxies** tab, and then specify any settings provided by your ISP.

7. Click the **Ethernet** tab, and then select a configuration (automatic or manual) and specify settings.

8. Click **OK**.

9. Click **Apply**.

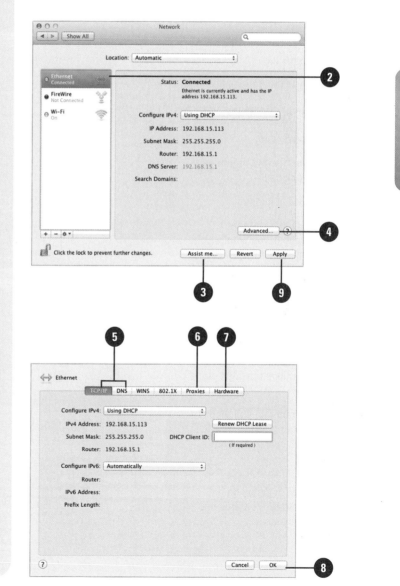

Setting Up a Wireless Connection

If you have an AirPort card on your computer and are within range of a wireless base station, such as a router or network hub, you can set up and use an wireless connection to access the Internet. An AirPort card is Apple's 802.11b-based wireless networking device that enables you to connect to the Internet without using network wires or phone lines. Wireless networks are identified by a network name. You can join a specific network or select one of the detected wireless networks. You can join a wireless network quickly with the Wi-Fi status menu, which includes signal strength for all visible wireless networks.

Set Up a Wireless Connection

1. Click the **System Preferences** icon in the Dock, and then click the **Network** icon.

2. Click **Wi-Fi** in the list.

3. Click **Turn Wi-Fi On**, if needed.

4. Click the **Network Name** pop-up, and then select a wireless network and enter a password.

5. Select or clear the **Ask to join new networks** check box.

6. Click **Advanced**, if needed.

7. Click the **Wi-Fi** tab, and then specify the options you want, such as add or remove a network.

8. Click the **TCP/IP** and **DNS** tabs, and then specify any settings provided by your ISP, such as IP Address, Subnet Mask, Router, and DNS Servers.

9. Click the **Proxies** tab, and then specify any settings provided by your ISP.

10. Click the **Ethernet** tab, and then select a configuration (automatic or manual) and specify settings.

11. Click **OK**.

12. To show the Wi-Fi status menu, select the **Show Wi-Fi status in menu bar** check box.

13. Click **Apply**.

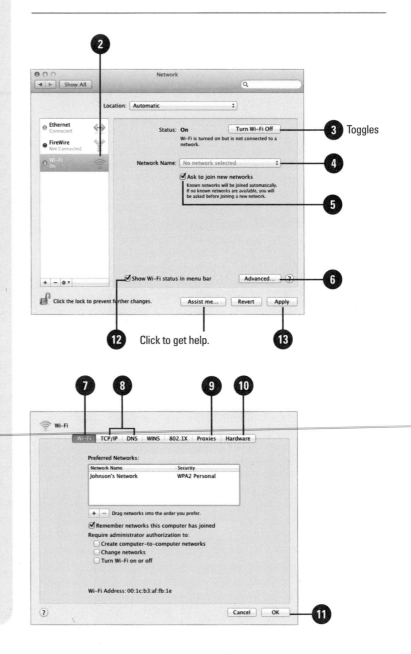

222

Setting Up Multiple Connections

If you have a mobile computer, such as a MacBook, you can set up multiple connections. For example, you can use a laptop to access the Internet at home using a dial-up modem, go to work and connect to a network using ethernet, or relax at a coffee shop and browse the Web using Wi-Fi. Each set of network connections is called a **network port configuration**. You can create different port configurations with unique priorities for different locations, which makes switching from one location to another easier. You can quickly access different locations using the Location submenu on the Apple menu.

Set Network Port Configurations and Locations

1 Click the **System Preferences** icon in the Dock, and then click the **Network** icon.

2 Click the **Location** pop-up, and then select one of the following options:

◆ **Automatic**. Default location.

◆ **A location name**. Switches to the location name.

◆ **Edit Location**. Creates a new location or modifies an existing location.

3 Select the network you want to disable or enable, click the **Action** button, and then click **Make Service Inactive** or **Make Service Action**.

4 Click **Apply**.

For Your Information

Understanding Infrared Wireless Communication

Infrared wireless communication technology allows you to transfer files between computers, typically laptops, with infrared ports even when no formal network is available. IrDA is an infrared wireless communication protocol, a set of rules, that enables computer-to-computer interaction.

Making an Internet Connection

After you set up your connection in the Network Preferences pane, you can also use the pane to connect to the Internet. This is not always convenient, so Mac OS X provides status menus on the right side of the menu bar. The status menus makes it easy to quickly log into different configurations in your current location for dial-up modem, Bluetooth, and Wi-Fi connections. You can use the Network Preferences pane to enable the menus.

Use Status Menus to Connect to the Internet

◆ **Bluetooth.** Click the **Bluetooth** icon on the menu, and then click a command:

 ◆ **Turn Bluetooth On or Off.**

 ◆ **Discoverable, Send File, Browse Device, Set Up Bluetooth Device,** or **Open Bluetooth Preferences.**

◆ **Wi-Fi.** Click the **Wi-Fi** icon on the menu, and then click a command:

 ◆ **Turn Wi-Fi On or Off.**

 ◆ **Join Other Network, Create Network,** or **Open Network Preferences.**

◆ **Modem.** Click the **Modem** icon on the menu, and then click a command:

 ◆ **Connect.**

 ◆ **Show time connected, Show status while connecting,** or **Open Network Preferences.**

Bluetooth Status menu

Bluetooth: On
Discoverable: Off
Turn Bluetooth Off

Send File...
Browse Device...

Set Up Bluetooth Device...
Open Bluetooth Preferences...

Wi-Fi Status menu

Wi-Fi: On
Turn Wi-Fi Off

No network selected
Johnson's Network
Perspection2

Join Other Network...
Create Network...
Open Network Preferences...

Modem Status menu

Modem: Idle
Connect
✓ Default

✓ Show time connected
✓ Show status while connecting

Open Network Preferences...

Understanding Web Sites and Browsers

A **Web site** contains Web pages linked together to make searching for information on the Internet easier. **Web pages** are documents that contain highlighted words, phrases, and graphics, called **hyperlinks** (or simply **links**) that open other Web pages when you click them. Some Web pages contain frames. A **frame** is a separate window within a Web page that lets you see more than one Web page at a time. **Web browsers** are software programs that you use to "surf the Web," or access and display Web pages. Browsers make the Web easy to navigate by providing a graphical, point-and-click environment. Safari 5.1 is a browser from Apple that is built into Mac OS X Lion. Microsoft Internet Explorer, Mozilla Firefox, and Netscape Navigator are other popular browsers. With a Web browser, you can display Web pages from all over the world, use links to move from one Web page to another, play audio and video clips, search the Web for information, bookmark Web pages for easy access, and print text and graphics on Web pages.

Web browser

Web site

Web page

Link

Starting and Customizing Safari

Safari is a Web browser that you use to search the World Wide Web. You can start the Safari application using the Safari button in the Dock or the Safari icon in the Applications folder. After you start Safari, you might need to enter a user name and password when you use a dial-up modem to establish a connection to the Internet. After you establish a connection to the Internet, you are ready to explore Web pages on the Internet. The elements of the Safari window allow you to view, print, and search for information on the Internet. You can customize the Safari window display to conform to the way you work. The View menu allows you to turn on and off different display elements.

Start the Safari Application and Customize the Window

1. Click the **Safari** icon in the Dock.

2. If necessary, click **Connect** to dial your ISP. If prompted, type your user name and password.

 The Safari window opens.

3. Click the **View** menu.

4. Click the menu item with the element you want to show or hide in the Safari window.

 - ◆ **Toolbar**
 - ◆ **Customize Toolbar**
 - ◆ **Bookmarks Bar**
 - ◆ **Tab Bar**
 - ◆ **Status Bar**
 - ◆ **Reader** (**New!**)
 - ◆ **Reading List** (**New!**)
 - ◆ To change the display view, select a zoom commands: **Actual Size**, **Zoom In**, **Zoom Out**, or **Zoom Text Only**.

 TIMESAVER *Double-tap to zoom in and double-tap again to return to the original state.* (**New!**)

 - ◆ **Enter Full Screen.** (**New!**) Point to the top of the screen to show menu bar. Click **Full Screen** button (right corner) or press Esc to exit.

3

View	
Hide Toolbar	⌘ \|
Customize Toolbar...	
Hide Bookmarks Bar	⇧⌘B
Show Tab Bar	⇧⌘T
Show Status Bar	⌘ /
Show Reader	⇧⌘R
Show Reading List	⇧⌘L
Stop	⌘ .
Reload Page	⌘R
Actual Size	⌘0
Zoom In	⌘ +
Zoom Out	⌘ −
Zoom Text Only	
View Source	⌥⌘U
Text Encoding	▶
Enter Full Screen	^⌘F

4

For Your Information

Selecting a Text Encoding

Text encoding determines how characters appear in a Web page. When a Web page doesn't specify text encoding, Safari uses the default text encoding specified in the Appearance pane of Safari preferences. Sometimes when the Safari default text encoding doesn't correspond with the desired Web page text encoding, you can see garbled text. If the text in a Web page is garbled, use the View menu to select a text encoding that corresponds to the language used in most of the Web pages you visit. This may fix the problem.

Viewing the Safari Window

Menu bar
Contains all the commands you need to access and move around Web pages, customize Safari, and get Help.

Address bar
Provides buttons to locate and move around Web pages, as well as a place to enter or display the address of the current Web page.

Full Screen
Provides ability to work as a full-screen application. (**New!**)

Bookmarks bar
Contains buttons for quick access of favorite Web sites.

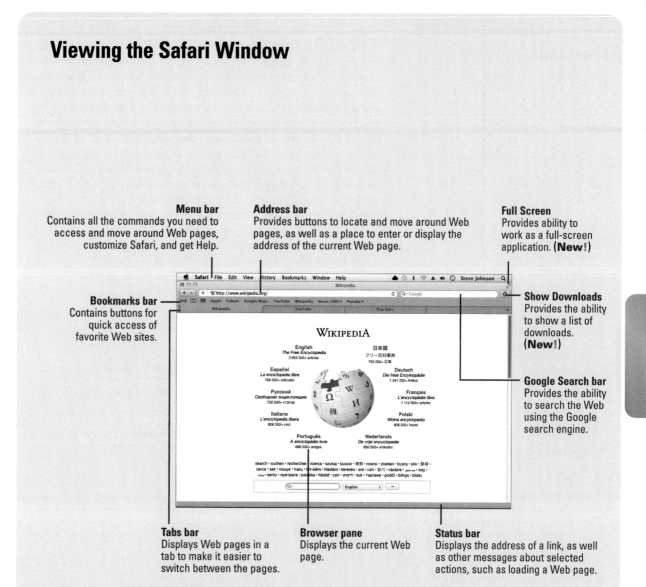

Show Downloads
Provides the ability to show a list of downloads. (**New!**)

Google Search bar
Provides the ability to search the Web using the Google search engine.

Tabs bar
Displays Web pages in a tab to make it easier to switch between the pages.

Browser pane
Displays the current Web page.

Status bar
Displays the address of a link, as well as other messages about selected actions, such as loading a Web page.

Browsing the Web

A **Web address** (also known as a **URL**) is a unique place on the Internet where you can locate a Web page. With Safari, you can browse sites on the Web with ease by entering a Web address or by clicking a link on a Web page to access a new site. When you type a Web address in the Address bar, Safari tries to find a recently visited page that matches what you've typed so far. If Safari finds a match, it fills in the rest of the address. As Safari opens the Web page, the Address box shows a blue-shaded progress bar as the page loads. If the page opens too slowly or if you decide not to access it, you can stop it. If a Web page loads incorrectly or you want to update page information, you can reload, or refresh the page. As you browse the Web, you can move backward or forward one location at a time to show sites you've previously visited in this session. Safari also stores information about Web sites you visit and information you've entered, which other users can view. You can prevent this by using Private Browsing, which clears the history list, Downloads window, AutoFill information, searches, and cookies are deleted. It's as if you never used Safari.

Open and View a Web Page

Use any of the following methods to display a Web page:

- In the Address box, type the Web address, and then press Return.

 If you have recently entered the Web page address, Safari remembers it and tries to complete the address for you. The suggested match is highlighted. Click the correct address in a list of possibilities or continue to type until the address you want appears in the Address list.

- Click any link on the Web page, such as a picture or colored, underlined text. The mouse pointer changes to a hand when it is over a link.

- Browse Privately. Click the **Safari** menu, click **Private Browsing**, and then click **OK**. To skip the confirmation, Option-click the Private Browsing command.

 - To turn it off, click the **Safari** menu, and then click **Private Browsing**.

Type a Web address

Click a link

Navigation Basics

◆ To move back or forward one Web page at a time, click the **Back** button or the **Forward** button on the Address bar.

> TIMESAVER *To move back, press ⌘+[(left bracket). To move forward, press ⌘+] (right bracket).*

◆ To stop a page from loading, click the **Stop** button on the Address bar during the load, or click the **View** menu, and then click **Stop**.

> TIMESAVER *Press ⌘+. (period).*

◆ To reload a page, click the **Reload** button on the Address bar, or click the **View** menu, and then click **Reload**.

> TIMESAVER *Press ⌘+R.*

◆ To go to the Home page, click the **History** menu, and then click **Home**.

> TIMESAVER *Press ⌘+Shift+H.*

Did You Know?

You can open a Web page on your hard disk or network server. Click the File menu, click Open File, type the complete path and file name of the Web page, and then click Open.

You can open a Web page from a document in another application. Select the Web address, click the application menu (such as TextEdit), point to Services, and then click Open URL.

Back button

Forward button

Reload button

For Your Information

Understanding a Web Address

The address for a Web page is called a URL (Uniform Resource Locator). Each Web page has a unique URL that is typically composed of four parts: the protocol (a set of rules that allow computers to exchange information), the location of the Web site, the name that maintains the Web site, and a suffix that identifies the type of site. A URL begins with a protocol, followed by a colon, two slashes, the location of the Web site, a dot, the name of the Web site, a dot, and a suffix. The Web site is the computer where the Web pages are located. At the end of the Web site name, another slash may appear, followed by one or more folder names and a file name. For example, in the address, http://*www*.perspection.com/downloads/main.htm, the protocol is *http* (HyperText Transfer Protocol), the location of the Web site is *www* (World Wide Web), the name of the Web site is *perspection*, and the suffix is *com* (a commercial organization); a folder at that site is called */downloads*; and within the folder is a file called *main.htm*.

Browsing the Web Using Tabs

When you open a Web page, it opens in the same window you are using. If you want to view more than one page at a time in a single window, you can open Web pages in separate tabs or new windows. You can also bookmark a set of tabs for easy access in the future or revert to the tabs that were open the last time you used Safari. Before you start opening Web pages in tabs, you can set tab browsing options to specify the way you want to use tabs in Safari. When you open a page in a tab, the Tab bar appears (below the Bookmarks bar) with the name of the Web page along with a box you can use to close the tab. You can also use the View menu to show the Tab bar. If you select a Web page from the History or Bookmarks menu, the page opens in the current tab. When you use the Back and Forward buttons in the Address bar, Safari displays Web pages previously viewed in the current tab.

Set Tabbed Browsing Options

1. Click the **Safari** menu, and then click **Preferences**.

2. Click **Tabs**.

3. Click the **Open pages in tabs instead of windows** pop-up, and then select an option (**New!**): **Never**, **Automatically**, or **Always**.

4. Select the ⌘-**click opens a link in a new tab** check box to open a link in a new tab; clear it to open a link in a new window.

5. Select the **When a new tab or window opens, make it active** check box to open new tabs in front of the current tab.

 IMPORTANT *Some keyboard shortcuts change depending on the tab options you select. The bottom of the Tab Preferences window displays the new shortcuts. The shortcuts change revert back when you disable the options.*

6. Click the **Close** button.

Shortcuts to use when working with tabs.

Open and View a Web Page in a Tab

◆ To show or hide the Tab bar, click the **View** menu, click **Show/Hide Tab Bar**.

◆ To open a Web page in a tab, click the **File** menu, click **New Tab**, type the Web address, and then press Return.

◆ To open a link or bookmark in a tab, hold down ⌘, and then click the item.

◆ To open a bookmark collection in the Bookmarks bar in tabs, hold down the Control key, click the collection in the Bookmarks bar, and then click **Open In Tabs**.

◆ To open a folder of bookmarks in the Bookmarks Library in tabs, click the **Bookmarks** menu, click **Show All Bookmarks**, hold down the Control key, click the folder in the right pane, and then click **Open In Tabs**.

◆ To switch between Web page tabs, click the tab in the Tab bar.

◆ To close a tab, point to the tab, and then click the **Close** box on the tab.

TIMESAVER *Hold down the Option key and click the Close box to show the Web page and close all other tabs.*

Did You Know?

You can change the size of text on a Web page. Click the View menu, and then click Zoom Text Only. You can also click the View menu, and then click Zoom In (⌘++) or Zoom Out (⌘+-). To view the page at 100%, click the View menu, and then click Actual Size (⌘+0).

Close box Active tab

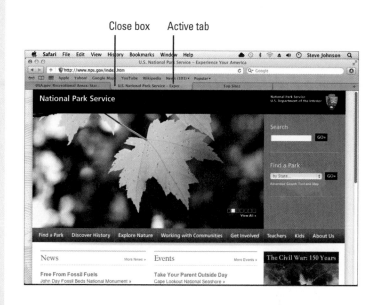

Opening a Web Page in a Different Window

You can open a Web page in a different window. Click the File menu, click New Window, type the Web address, and then press Return. To open a Web page in a new window using a link, hold down the Control key, click a link or bookmark, and then click Open Link In New Window. To find out the address of a link, point to it, and then view the Status bar. To switch between open windows, use the Window menu.

Using Gestures to Navigate Web Pages

If you have a Multi-Touch trackpad, you can use gestures in Safari to quickly get around the Web. You can navigate through the pages of a website by simply swiping (**New!**). When you swipe to the left, the next page slides into view. When you swipe to the right, you go back to the previous page. You can also zoom in and out with gestures. You can double-tap to zoom in on a column of text or an image. The text and images scale up smoothly, and then text remains sharp. You can double-tap again to zoom out. You can also zoom in and out on text and images more precisely with a pinch (**New!**).

Using the Reader and Reading List

If you find yourself bookmarking web sites so you can come back to read information later, Safari provides a Reading List (**New!**) to make it easier for you manage and keep track of the information. Safari's Reader allows you to view news stories and other text-based articles in a window that's optimized for easy reading. Reader connects articles that are continued over multiple pages and broken up by ads, graphics, and other elements. When a web page contains a text-based article, the Reading button (**New!**) appears in the Address bar, like the RSS button. When you click the Reader button, a viewer appears, similar to a PDF reader, where you can easily read your article without any distractions.

Use the Reader

1. Open a web page with a text-based article, such as a news site.

 A Reading button appears in the Address bar, like the RSS button.

2. Click the **Reading** button (**New!**) in the Address Bar.

3. Read and scroll down the article.

4. To navigate the screen, point to the bottom middle of the Reader to display a toolbar.

 ◆ **Zoom in and out.** Click to zoom in and out.

 ◆ **Mail this page.** Click to mail this page using your e-mail program.

 ◆ **Print this page.** Click to print this page.

 ◆ **Close Reader.** Click to close the Reader.

Did You Know?

You can view a RSS version in Reader. If a Reader article can also be viewed in RSS, hold down the Reader button, and then click Show RSS.

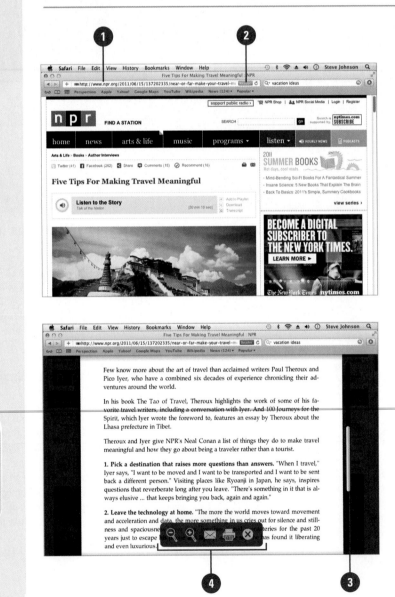

Use the Reading List

1. Open the web page you want to add to the Reading List.

2. Click the **Reading List** button (**New!**) on the Bookmarks Bar.

3. Click **Add Page**.

 ◆ You can also Shift-click a link to quickly add it to the list.

 ◆ You can also Click the **Bookmarks** menu, and then click **Add to Reading List**.

4. To view the Reading List in different ways, click **All** or **Unread**.

 After you have read an item, it get removed from the Unread reading list, however it remains in the list of all items.

5. To remove a page from the list, point to the item to display a **Remove** button (x), and then click it.

 ◆ To remove all items in the list, click **Clear All**.

6. Click the **Reading List** button again to close it.

Clear All

Point to item to display Remove button.

Viewing Top Sites

Top Sites is a visual preview of your favorite Web sites. Safari tracks the sites you visit the most and ranks your favorites, displaying up to 24 thumbnail previews. Simply, click the Show Top Sites button to view and select a Web site to visit. If you don't see a site, you can use the History tab (**New!**) or Search History box to visually find it using Cover Flow. You can also add or remove sites, mark or unmark sites as permanent, rearrange sites, and change the view to customize Top Sites.

View and Use Top Sites

◆ **View Top Sites.** Click the **Show Top Sites** button, and then click a thumbnail to visit the page, or use one of the navigation buttons.

> **TIMESAVER** *To view Top Sites, press Shift+⌘+1.*

◆ **View History.** In Top Sites, click the **History** tab (**New!**), and then drag the slider to flip through Web pages. Click the **Top Sites** tab to exit.

◆ **Search Top Sites.** In Top Sites, click in the **Search History** box, type keywords to search or drag the slider to flip through Web pages. When you're done, click the **Close** (x) button in the Search History box to exit.

◆ **Add Sites.** In Top Sites, click **Edit**, type the URL site address in Address bar, drag it to the window, and then click **Done**.

◆ **Remove Sites.** In Top Sites, click **Edit**, click the **Never include as top site** button (the X button), and then click **Done**.

◆ **Mark as Permanent Site.** In Top Sites, click **Edit**, click the **Mark as permanent top site** button (the Pin button), and then click **Done**.

◆ **Arrange Sites.** In Top Sites, click **Edit**, click **Small**, **Medium**, or **Large**, and then click **Done**.

◆ **Change View.** In Top Sites, click **Edit**, drag a thumbnail to another location, and then click **Done**.

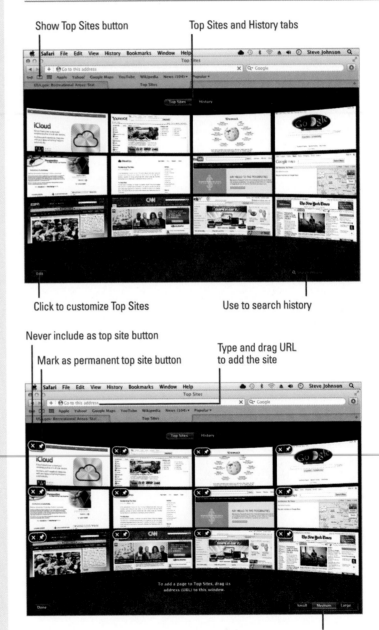

Show Top Sites button — Top Sites and History tabs

Click to customize Top Sites — Use to search history

Never include as top site button

Mark as permanent top site button — Type and drag URL to add the site

Click to change the view

Changing the Home Page

Your **home page** in Safari is the page that opens when you start the program. When you first install Safari, the default home page is the startpage for the Apple Web site. If you want a different page to appear when you start Safari and whenever you click the Home button, you can change your home page. You can select one of the billions of Web pages available throughout the Internet. When you open a new window or tab in Safari, you can specify the default page that you want to view, such as home page, Top Sites, empty page, same page, or bookmarks.

Change the Home Page

① Open the Web page you want to be the new home page.

② Click the **Safari** menu, and then click **Preferences**.

③ Click **General**.

④ Click **Set to Current Page**.

⑤ To specify the page that appears when you open a new window or tab, do any of the following:

◆ New Window. Click the **New windows open with** pop-up, and then select a page option.

◆ New Tab. Click the **New tabs open with** pop-up, and then select a page option.

⑥ Click the **Close** button.

Did You Know?

You can type a Web address for your home page. Click the Safari menu, click Preferences, click General, type a Web address in the Home Page box, and then click the Close button.

Viewing a History List

Sometimes you run across a great Web site and simply forget to add it to your Bookmarks list. With Safari there's no need to try to remember all the sites you visit. The History list keeps track of where you've been for a week organized by the date. Safari deletes Web pages from the History list older than a week. If you no longer need the pages in the History list, you can clear the entire list. To view the History list, click the History menu, and then point to a day or click Show All History. When you show all history or bookmarks, you can visually browse and search sites using Cover Flow.

Open a Web Page from the History List

1 Click the **History** menu, and then click **Show All History**.

◆ To quickly open a Web page, click the **History** menu, point to a date if desired, and then click a Web page.

2 Click the **Expand** arrow to display the bookmarks you want to view.

3 Scroll through the list in Cover Flow or use the Search box to locate the one you want.

4 Double-click the Web page.

Cover Flow Full search

Did You Know?

You can delete individual entries in the History list. Click the History menu, click Show All History, click History in the Collections column, select the entry you want to remove, press Delete, and then click the Close button.

You can clear the entire History list. Click the History menu, and then click Clear History.

You can clear the entire History list automatically on a regular basis. Click the Safari menu, click Preferences, click General, click the Remove History Items pop-up, select the interval option you want, and then click the Close button.

For Your Information

Emptying the Cache

As you open Web pages, Safari saves the page content in a temporary location on your local hard disk, known as the **cache**, to make it faster to open the same pages next time. Anytime you display new content, the cache continues to increase in size, taking up valuable hard disk space. You can empty the cache at anytime to remove the local version of the Web page content and free up hard disk space. To empty the cache, click the Safari menu, click Empty Cache, and then click Empty.

Bookmarking a Web Page

Rather than memorizing URLs or keeping a handwritten list of Web pages you want to visit, you can use the Bookmarks Library to store and organize the addresses. When you display a Web page or a set of tabs that you want to display again at a later time, you can add the Web page or tab set to your Bookmarks Library. After you add the bookmark to the Bookmarks Library, you can quickly return to it by using the Bookmarks bar or Bookmarks menu to select it. If you have bookmarks in other browsers, such as Internet Explorer, Netscape Navigator, and Mozilla Firefox, you can import the bookmarks in the Bookmarks Library using the Import Bookmarks command on the File menu.

Create Bookmark Pages

1. Open the Web site you want to add to your Bookmark list.

2. Click the **Bookmarks** menu, and then click **Add Bookmark** or **Add Bookmark For These Tabs**.

 TIMESAVER *Click the Add Bookmark button in the Address bar or drag the icon in the Address box to the Bookmarks bar to quickly add a bookmark.*

3. Click the pop-up, and then select a location, either the Reading List (**New!**), Top Sites, Bookmarks Bar, Bookmarks Menu, or a collection of bookmarks in folders.

4. Type the name for the bookmark, or use the default name supplied.

5. Click **Add**.

6. To quickly return to a bookmark, use the Bookmarks bar or Bookmarks menu.

Add Bookmarks button

Click to go to the Bookmarks Library.

Did You Know?

You can drag a bookmark to move or delete it. Drag a bookmark to another place on the Bookmarks bar to move it, or outside the Safari window to delete it. You can also drag bookmarks and folders from the Bookmarks Library to the Bookmarks bar.

Working with Bookmarks

If your list of bookmarks grows long, you can use the Bookmarks Library to delete bookmarks you don't visit anymore or move bookmarks into folders to make them easier to find. The Bookmarks Library shows your collections of bookmarks in the left column, and the Cover Flow display at the top and the names and addresses of bookmarks and folders at the bottom in the right column. You also use the Bookmarks Library to work with Web sites from cards in your Address Book, RSS Feeds, and History and Bonjour Web sites. Safari uses Bonjour to find any Web sites on your local network or subnet. Before you can work with the Address Book and Bonjour, you need to enable the options in the Bookmarks pane of Safari preferences.

Create a Bookmark Folder

1. Click the **Bookmarks** menu, and then click **Add Bookmark Folder**.

 The Bookmarks Library opens, displaying a new untitled folder with the name selected.

2. Type a name for the folder, and then press Return.

3. Display the bookmarks you want to move in the folder in the right column.

4. Drag the bookmarks to the folder.

5. Click the **Bookmarks Library** button on the Bookmarks bar to close it.

 The folder appears on the Bookmarks bar with a triangle next to the name.

Cover Flow Full search

Organize Bookmarks in the Bookmarks Library

◆ **Show and hide Bookmarks Library**. Click the **Bookmarks** menu, and then click **Show All Bookmarks** or **Hide All Bookmarks**.

◆ **Create a collection**. Click the **Add** button (+) at the bottom of the Collections column.

◆ **Rename a collection**. Double-click the name, type a new name, and then press Return.

◆ **Add a folder to a collection**. Select a collection, and then click the **Add** button (+) at the bottom of the Bookmark column.

◆ **Rename a bookmark or folder**. Control-click the name, click **Edit Name**, type a new name, and then press Return.

◆ **Remove a collection, folder, or bookmark**. Select the item, and then press Delete.

◆ **Move or rearrange a collection, folder, or bookmark**. Locate the item, and then drag its icon to the location or icon where you want to place it. To copy it, hold down the Option key as you drag the icon.

Click a collection to display folders and bookmarks

Click to add a folder Click name and type to change rename item

Click to add a collection

Did You Know?

You can add Address Book home pages to the Bookmarks bar or menu. Click the Safari menu, click Preferences, click Bookmarks, select the Include Address Book check box where appropriate, and then click the Close button.

Viewing and Bookmarking RSS Feeds

A **feed** delivers frequently updated Web content to your browser on a continuous basis. A feed, also known as RSS (Really Simple Syndication) feed, XML feed, syndicated content, or Web feed, is usually offered on a subscription basis and typically free of charge. A feed can deliver text content in the form of news headlines or blogs, or digital content in the form of pictures, audio, and video. When audio content is delivered usually in the MP3 format, it's referred to as a podcast. When you visit a Web site, Safari checks for available feeds. If it discovers a feed, Safari puts an RSS icon at the right end of the address bar. You can view an individual feed or subscribe to one to get content automatically. When you subscribe to a feed, Safari checks the Web site and downloads new content so you always stay updated with the latest site content.

Customize RSS Feeds

① Click the **Safari** menu, and then click **Preferences**.

② Click the **RSS** button on the toolbar.

③ Specify any of the following options:

◆ **Default RSS Reader.** Select a default reader, such as Safari or Mail.

◆ **Update Articles.** Select the **Bookmarks Bar** and/or **Bookmarks Menu** check boxes to specify where to be notified of automatic updates.

◆ **Mark as Read.** Click **After viewing the RSS page** or **After clicking them** option.

◆ Select or clear the **Highlight unread articles** check box.

◆ **Check Updates.** Select an interval: **Never, Every Day, Every Hour,** or **Every 30 minutes.**

◆ **Remove Articles.** Select an interval or click **Remove Now.**

④ Click the **Close** button.

View and Bookmark a RSS Feed

1. Visit a Web site with a feed.

 The RSS button appears in the Address bar.

2. Click the **RSS** button.

 If multiple feeds are available, a list of feeds appears. You can click the **RSS** button again to close it.

3. If available, click the feed you want to see.

4. Click the **Add** (+) button on the toolbar to add an individual or folder bookmark.

 ◆ A bookmark folder shows the total number of new articles.

 TIMESAVER *Press ⌥⌘+click a bookmark folder to show all feeds.*

5. Type the name for the bookmark, or use the default name supplied.

6. Click the pop-up, and then select **Bookmarks Bar**, **Bookmarks Menu**, or a collection of bookmarks in folders.

7. Click **Add**.

8. To view all RSS articles, click the **Bookmarks** menu, and then click **View All RSS Articles**.

Added RSS feed

Filling Out Forms on the Web

Safari can use information in your Address Book or data you previously entered in an online form to automatically complete online forms you need to fill out in the future. AutoFill is a service that helps you complete online forms and log in to Web sites with a user name and password and information from your Address Book (**New!**). You use the AutoFill pane of the Safari preferences to select, modify, or delete which information AutoFill uses to complete a form or log in. When you use AutoFill to automatically fill in information, Safari highlights the data in yellow so you can see the changes. Safari keeps your information private until you choose to send it (**New!**). If you no longer need the AutoFill service, you can keep Safari from automatically completing forms and log ins. If you run out of room in a text field, you can now resize text fields on any Web page by dragging the corner of the field to make more room and reflow the Web page.

Set AutoFill Preferences

1. Click the **Safari** menu, and then click **Preferences**.

2. Click **AutoFill**.

3. Select or clear the **Using info from my Address Book card** check box to enable or disable AutoFill from information in your Address Book.

4. Select or clear the **User names and passwords** check box to enable or disable AutoFill from Web site log in information you've entered.

5. Select or clear the **Other forms** check box to enable or disable AutoFill based on data from other online forms.

6. For any of the selected check boxes, click **Edit** to view or remove information stored by AutoFill.

7. Click the **Close** button.

Did You Know?

You can resize text fields on a Web page. Drag the corner of a text field to resize it and reflow the Web page.

User name and password Autofill data

Address Book Autofill data

Fill Out Forms in Web Pages

1 Select AutoFill data and options in the AutoFill pane of Safari preferences; click the **Safari** menu, click **Preferences**, and then click **AutoFill**.

2 Use any of the following methods to fill out forms using AutoFill:

◆ **Complete user name and password in a log in.** Display a log in screen, enter a user name and password, and then click **Yes** to save the log in information so you don't have to do it again; click **Not Now** to defer saving the log in information until later; and click **Never for this website** to not save log in information for this Web site.

◆ **Complete a Web form.** Open the Web page, and then click the AutoFill button in the Address bar.

◆ **Complete individual boxes in a form.** Open the Web page, select a text box, and then start typing. If AutoFill retrieves a match, a menu appears (**New!**). Select the correct item and then click AutoFill. to bypass the menu, press Return.

Enter user name and password

Click an AutoFill save option

Did You Know?

You can display an alert before you send a non-secure form. Click the Safari menu, click Preferences, click Security, select the Ask Before Sending A Non-Secure Form To A Secure Website check box, and then click the Close button.

For Your Information

Checking Spelling and Grammar in Safari

You can't spell check the content of a Web page, but you can spell check any text you enter in a text box on a page. For example, if you type a word in a text box on a form or in the Google box in the Address bar, you can check its spelling before you complete the form or start the search. To check spelling and grammar, click in a text box, click the Edit menu, point to Spelling and Grammar, and then click Check Document Now. If your computer doesn't recognize a word, a dialog opens, asking you to correct, ignore, or add the word to a dictionary. You can also check spelling as you type, like many word processing programs. When you select the Check Spelling While Typing command on the Spelling and Grammar sub-menu located on the Edit menu, Safari displays a wavy red line under any term your computer doesn't recognize. You can also select the Check Grammar With Spelling to check grammar on demand.

Searching the Web

You can find all kinds of information on the Web. The best way to find information is to use a search engine. A **search engine** is a program you access through a Web site and use to search through a collection of Internet information to find what you want. Safari comes with the Google search engine built-in to the program. When performing a search, the search engine compares keywords with words that it finds on various Internet Web sites. **Keywords** are words or phrases that best describe the information you want to retrieve. If the search engine finds your keywords in the stored database, it lists links to the matched sites. When you open a link from the results, you can use the SnapBack button to quickly return to your search results. In addition, you can search for text that either contains or starts with the text you type (**New!**) within a Web page to display the found count and highlight matching terms within a page.

Search for Information

1. Click the **Google Search** box, type a word or phrase you want to find, and then press Return.

2. Click a link in the list of search results to open a Web page.

3. To return to the last page of Google search results, click the SnapBack button in the Google Search box.

4. To repeat a previous search, click the magnifying glass in the Google Search box, and then select the search term you want.

Search Within a Page

① Click the **Edit** menu, point to **Find**, and then click **Find**.

② Click the Find bar arrow, and then click **Contains** or **Starts With** (**New!**).

③ Click in the Find bar, and then type the word or phrase you want to find on the current page.

Displays the found count and highlights matching terms within the page.

④ Click the left and right arrows on the Find bar to highlight the matching terms.

⑤ When you're done, click **Done**.

Highlighted find word Currently selected find

Did You Know?

You can revisit search results using SnapBack. Type a search term or phrase in the Search box, press Return, visit some Web pages, and then click the SnapBack button in the Search box to return to the search results.

Printing a Web Page

Web pages are designed for viewing on a computer screen, but you can also print all or part of one. Before you print, you should preview the page to verify that it looks the way you want. When you are ready to print, Safari provides many options for printing Web pages. If the Web page consists of frames, you can print the specific frame you want to print. You can also use the Print dialog to create a PDF of a Web page or send a Web page as a PDF fax or PDF mail attachment.

Print a Web Page

1. Open the Web page you want to print, click the **File** menu, and then click **Print**.

2. Click the **Printer** pop-up, and then select from the available printers.

3. Click the **Presets** pop-up, and then select from the available preset options.

4. Click the **Show Details** button to expand the dialog.

5. Click the **Print Options** pop-up, and then select from the available print options, such as Safari.

6. Choose the various print options you want.

7. Click the following options to finalize your print: **PDF**, **Cancel**, or **Print**.

Did You Know?

You can print a frame of a Web page. Hold down the Control key, click the frame you want to print, click Print Frame, specify the options you want, and then click Print.

See Also

See Chapter 8, "Printing and Faxing," on page 195 for information on setting up and printing a page.

Viewing PDF Files

In Safari, you can display a PDF file in the browser window along with a toolbar and sidebar to make it easier to view the file. When you point to the middle of an open PDF page, near the bottom, of the Safari window, a toolbar with PDF tools appears. You can use the tools to zoom in and out to view the screen, open the PDF in Preview, and save the PDF to the Downloads folder. When you no longer want to use the toolbar, simply move the pointer off it.

PDF document in the browser window

View PDF Files in the Browser Window

1. Open the Web page with the link to the PDF you want to view.

2. Click the link for the PDF file.

3. Use any of the following PDF tools:

 ◆ **View Toolbar.** Point to the middle of the PDF page, near the bottom.

 If you move the pointer off the toolbar, it disappears.

 ◆ **View Sidebar.** Click the triangle at the left of the toolbar.

 ◆ **Move Pages.** Click the arrow buttons in the toolbar or click a page in the sidebar.

 ◆ **Zoom In or Out.** Click the Zoom In (+) or Zoom Out (-) buttons.

 ◆ **Open PDF in Preview.** Click the button on the toolbar to open the PDF in the Preview application.

 ◆ **Save PDF to Download Folder.** Click the button on the toolbar to quickly save the file to the Downloads folder in the Home folder.

 ◆ **Single or Two Pages.** Control-click the page, and then click Single Page, Single Page Continuous, Two Pages, or Two Pages Continuous.

Saving a Web Page

You can save a Web page, and view it later from your local hard drive or use it as source for HTML (HyperText Markup Language) code, which instructs the browser how to display the Web page. When you save a Web page, Safari can save only the HTML text content of the current page, or all the elements on the page, which includes text and images. Before you save a Web page you can view the HTML code to determine if you need it.

Save Web Page Text

1. Open the Web page you want to save, click the **File** menu, and then click **Save As**.

2. Type a name for the file, or use the suggested name.

3. Select the hard drive and folder in which you want to save the file.

4. Click the **Format** pop-up, and then select a Web format: Web Archive.

 ◆ **Page Source.** Saves only the source text of this page.

 ◆ **Web Archive.** Saves text, images, and other content on this page.

5. Click **Save**.

Click to expand or collapse.

Export As: Apple – Support – Manuals

Where: Documents

Format: Web Archive

Saves text, images, and other content of this page.

Cancel Save

Did You Know?

You can view the HTML code of a Web page. Open the Web page, click the View menu, and then click View Source. When you are done viewing, click the Close button.

See Also
See "Saving and Closing a Document" on page 190 for more information on using the Save As dialog.

Saving Pictures or Text from a Web Page

If you find information on a Web page that you want to save for future reference or share with others, you can copy and paste it to another document or save it on your computer. When you copy information from a Web page, make sure you're not violating any copyright laws.

Save a Picture from a Web Page

1. Open the Web page with the picture you want to save.

2. Control-click the picture, and then click **Save Image As**.

 TIMESAVER *Control-click the picture, and then click Save Image to "Downloads" to quickly save an image to the Downloads folder.*

3. Type a name for the file.

4. Select the drive and folder in which you want to save the file.

5. Click **Save**.

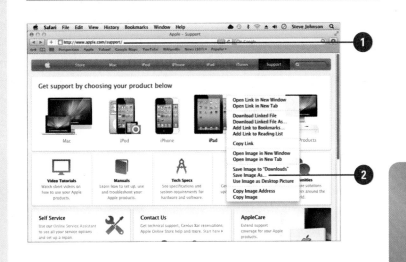

Copy Text from a Web Page

1. Open the Web page with the text you want to copy.

2. Select the text you want to copy.

3. Control-click the selected text, and then click **Copy**.

4. Switch to where you want to paste the text.

5. Click the **Edit** menu, and then click **Paste**.

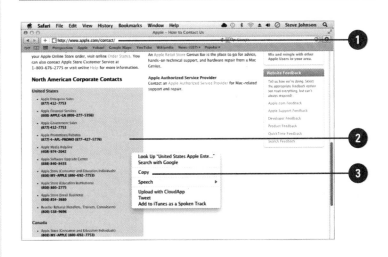

Downloading Files Safely from the Web

There are thousands of sites on the Internet offering all sorts of files you can download to your computer, from trailers to the latest game demos. You can download files from any Web site by finding the file you want, and then clicking the download link. Safari automatically downloads the file to the location specified in the General pane of Safari preferences. When a file is downloading, the Downloads panel (**New!**) in Safari displays a progress and status information. You can stop downloading a file, view a downloaded file in the Finder, and clear the Downloads panel when it gets too full.

Download a File from a Web Page

1. Open the Web page that you want to download a file.

2. Click a download link, or Control+click the link pointing to the actual file, and then click:

 ◆ **Download Linked File** to download the file to the Downloads folder.

 ◆ **Download Linked File As** to specify a download location.

3. Click the **Show Downloads** button c on the Address Bar.

 The Downloads panel appears, displaying the estimated time to download the file, along with the estimated transfer time, and a list previous file downloads.

4. Click the **Show Downloads** button on the Address Bar again to close the Downloads panel.

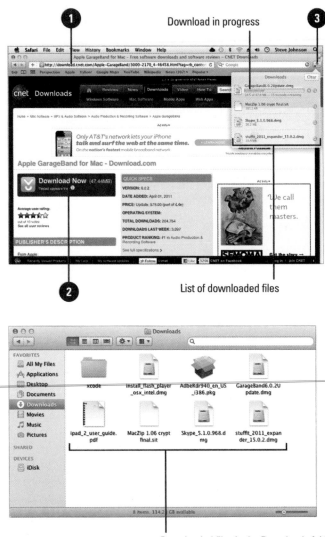

Download in progress

List of downloaded files

Downloaded files in the Downloads folder

Work with Files in the Downloads Window

1 If necessary, click the **Window** menu, and then click **Downloads**.

◆ The Downloads folder is located in the Home folder. You can click the **Go** menu, click **Home**, and then double-click the **Downloads** folder.

2 Perform any of the following operations.

◆ **Stop a downloading file.** Click the **Stop** icon to the right of the file name; to restart the download, click the icon again.

◆ **View a downloaded file.** Click the **Magnifying Glass** icon to the right of the file name.

◆ **Clear the Downloads window.** Click the **Clear** button. Clearing the window does not clear files that are being downloaded.

◆ **Remove a downloaded file.** Control-click the file name, and then click **Remove From List**.

3 Click the **Close** button.

See Also

See "Setting Safari Preferences" on page 252 for information on selecting the download file location and specifying when to remove downloaded items from the Downloads window.

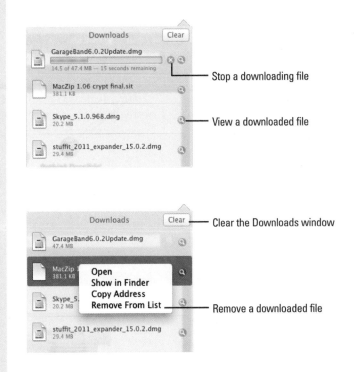

Stop a downloading file

View a downloaded file

Clear the Downloads window

Remove a downloaded file

For Your Information

Downloading Disk Images and Installing Software

When you download a disk image, Safari decompresses the file and in some cases mounts a volume, and opens an installer program (if available). There are several different types of disk images. Safari works a little differently for each type. If you download a disk image in the MacBinary, BinHex, or gzip file format, Safari decompresses the file and opens an installer (if available). If you download an Internet Disk Image, Safari decompresses the file, opens an installer (if available), and moves the disk image to the Trash. If you download a disk image file, Safari decompresses the file, mounts the disk image volume, and opens an installer (if available).

Setting Safari Preferences

Safari preferences help you configure browser features and functionality in ten sections: General, Appearance, Bookmarks, Tabs, AutoFill, Security, Privacy (**New!**) and Extensions (**New!**), and Advanced. These preference areas allow you to turn features on and off as well as customize the way Safari works. In Extensions (**New!**), you can install third-party functions, such as Twitter and Facebook, to Safari to show custom HTML content in a borderless window from the extension's toolbar, or when you click an icon in the extension's toolbar.

Set General Preferences

1. Click the **Safari** menu, and then click **Preferences**.

2. Click **General**.

3. Select or specify the various options you want to use:

 ◆ **Default Web Browser.** Select a default browser.

 ◆ **Default search engine.** Select a default search engine (**New!**).

 ◆ **New Windows open with** or **New tabs open with.** Click the pop-up, and then click Home Page, Same Page, Empty Page, or Bookmarks.

 ◆ **Home page.** Specify a Web address.

 ◆ **Remove history items.** Click pop-up to specify an interval.

 ◆ **Save downloaded files to.** Click the pop-up, and then select Desktop or Choose Other to specify another location.

 ◆ **Remove download list items.** Click the pop-up, and then click Manually, When Safari Quits, or Upon Successful Download.

 ◆ **Open "Safe" files after downloading.** Check to automatically activate safe downloaded files, such as movies, pictures, sounds, PDF and text documents.

4. Click the **Close** button.

For Your Information

Setting Advanced Preferences

Safari also provides advanced preferences for specialized circumstances, such as Universal Access, style sheets, proxies, data storage, and developer menu display. To access preferences, click the Safari menu, click Preferences, and then click Advanced. Click the Style Sheet pop-up, and then click None Selected or select a style sheet, which specifies a uniform format for the appearance of Web pages. Click Change Settings to modify settings for a proxy server. See your ISP or network administrator for settings. Specify a database storage amount allowed before asking. Use this option when a web site stores documents as databases on your computer; set the option to adjust the storage size. Select the Show Development menu in menu bar check box to use Web development related-commands. When you're done, click the Close button.

Set Appearance Preferences

1. Click the **Safari** menu, and then click **Preferences**.

2. Click **Appearance**.

3. For the Standard Font, click **Select** to choose a font for Web pages that don't specify one.

4. For the Fixed-Width Font, click **Select** to choose a fixed-width font for Web pages when you need to align text in a specific way.

5. Select or clear the **Display images when the page opens** check box.

6. Click the **Default Encoding** pop-up, and then select a character encoding set, which tells your browser how to interpret and display characters in a Web page.

7. Click the **Close** button.

Set Extensions Preferences

1. Click the **Safari** menu, and then click **Preferences**.

2. Click **Extensions (New!)**.

3. To enable or disable extensions, slide the switch to **On** or **Off**.

4. To get extensions, click **Get Extensions**, find the extension you want from the Apple Web site, and then click **Install Now**.

5. To set options for an extension, select the extension, and then set the options you want..

6. To get automatic updates, click **Updates**, and then select the **Install Updates Automatically** check box.

7. Click the **Close** button.

Setting Security Preferences

When you browse the Internet, you can access and gather information from Web sites, but Web sites can also gather information about you and store documents as databases without your knowledge. When you visit a Web site, the site creates a file on your computer, known as a **cookie**, which stores information, such as your Web site preferences or personal information, including your name and e-mail address. Not all cookies are harmful; many cookies save you time re-entering information on a return visit to a Web site. Safari's Security and Privacy (**New!**) options allow you to block, permit, or remove (**New!**) cookies; however, when you block cookies, you might not be able to access all Web site features. You can also get a warning when you visit a fraudulent sites.

Set Security Preferences

1. Click the **Safari** menu, and then click **Preferences**.

2. Click **Security**.

3. Select the **Warn when visiting a fraudulent website** check box to get a warning message.

4. Select the Web Content check boxes you want to enable:

 ◆ **Enable plug-ins**. A software module that provides additional functionality outside of HTML.

 ◆ **Enable Java**. A programming language for writing interactive Web pages.

 ◆ **Enable JavaScript**. A programming language for displaying interaction.

5. Select or clear the **Ask before sending a non-secure form to a secure website** check box.

6. Click **Privacy**.

7. Click **Remove All Website Data** (**New!**) to delete all cookies or click **Details** to remove individual ones.

8. Click the Accept Cookies option you want: **From third parties and advertisers**, **Always**, or **Never**.

9. Click an option (**New!**) to limit website access to location services.

10. Click the **Close** button.

Click the Details button to display dialog, where you can remove individual or all cookies on your computer.

Blocking Pop-Up Windows

When you open or close a Web page, some pages display pop-up windows to advertise products and services or request login and other information. Pop-up windows can be extremely annoying. Most of the time you end up closing them. To avoid the continual borage of pop-up windows, you can block them in Safari. When you set Safari to block pop-up windows, the program only stops pop-up windows that appear when you open or close a page, but not when you click a link.

Block Pop-Up Windows

① Click the **Safari** menu, and then click **Preferences**.

② Click **Security**.

③ Select the **Block pop-up windows** check box.

> **TIMESAVER** *Click the Safari menu, and then click Block Pop-up Windows to display a check mark on the menu.*

④ Click **Block** to confirm the option selection to block pop-up windows.

⑤ Click the **Close** button.

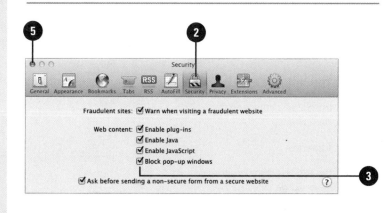

Did You Know?

You can check security when browsing secure Web sites. When you enter sensitive information on the Web, you can make sure it's secure. To check security, look for the lock icon in the upper-right corner of the Safari window, or make sure the Web sites address begins with "https," not "http."

For Your Information

When Web Pages Don't Work

If you are getting error messages or having problems displaying all or part of a Web page, your security settings may be the cause of the problems. To potentially correct the problems, click the Safari menu, click Preferences, click Security, select the check boxes to use plug-ins, Java, and JavaScript, clear the Block Pop-Up Windows check box, and then click the Close button. A **Plug-in** is a software module developed by a third-party for use with Safari to provide additional functionality outside of HTML. Safari works with common plug-ins including Java, QuickTime and Shockwave Flash. To view which plug-ins recognized by Safari are installed on your computer, click the Help menu, and then click Installed Plug-Ins.

Selecting a Default Browser

Mac OS X comes with Safari as the default Web browser and Google as the default search engine. If you prefer to use another browser as your default, you can remove Safari from your computer, install another browser, such as Microsoft Internet Explorer, Mozilla Firefox, or Netscape Navigator, and set it as your default Web browser program. When you click links in other applications, such as Mail messages, or double-click a Web Internet Location file icon, your default browser launches and opens the Web page in a new window or tab in the current window. If you prefer to use another search engine as your default, you can change it to another one (**New!**), such as Bing or Yahoo!.

Select a Default Browser

1. Click the **Safari** menu, and then click **Preferences**.

2. Click **General**.

3. Click the **Default Web Browser** pop-up, and then select a Web browser.

4. Click the **Default Search Engine** pop-up, and then select a search engine (**New!**).

5. Click the **Close** button.

See Also

See "Downloading Files Safely from the Web" on page 250 for information on adding or removing applications.

For Your Information

Reset Safari Settings

If you use a shared or public computer, you might want to reset Safari to prevent other people from seeing what you have been doing. When you reset Safari, the Web browser program clears the history list, Google search entries, and the Downloads window; removes all cookies saved by Safari and other related applications, such as any saved AutoFill data, such as user names and passwords; and empties the cache. To reset Safari, click the Safari menu, and then click Reset Safari.

Exchanging Messages Using Mail

Introduction

If you're like many people today who are using the Internet to communicate with friends and business associates, you probably have piles of information (names, e-mail addresses, phone numbers, etc) that you need often. Unless this information is in one convenient place, and can be accessed immediately, the information becomes ineffective and you become unproductive. Apple's Mail application solves these problems by integrating management and organization tools into one simple system. Mac OS X Lion includes Mail 5.0, a powerful application for managing **electronic mail** (known as e-mail), and contact information like names, and e-mail addresses.

Using Mail with an Internet connection allows you to accomplish several tasks:

- ◆ Create and send e-mail messages
- ◆ Manage multiple e-mail accounts with different Internet service providers
- ◆ Use the Address Book to store and retrieve e-mail addresses
- ◆ Add stationery to your e-mail messages
- ◆ Add a personal signature to your e-mail messages
- ◆ Attach a file to an e-mail message
- ◆ Organize e-mail messages by conversation
- ◆ Block junk e-mail messages
- ◆ Print e-mail messages
- ◆ Get RSS feeds in e-mail messages

What You'll Do

Set Up Accounts in One Place

Start Mail

Set Up and Manage Accounts

View the Mail Window

Compose and Send an E-Mail

Address an E-Mail

Add Stationery to E-Mail

Format Message Text

Add an E-Mail Signature

Create Notes

Receive and Read E-Mail

Respond to E-Mail

Send and Retrieve a File

Manage and Delete E-Mail

Save E-Mail

Search E-Mail for Text

Block and Bounce E-Mail

Divert Incoming E-Mail to Mailboxes

Create a Smart Mailbox

Get RSS Feeds in E-Mail

Setting Up Accounts in One Place

In System Preferences you can use the Mail, Contacts & Calendars pane (**New!**) to set up your accounts to use with Address Book,, iCal, iChat, Mail, and other apps. It's a one stop shop for all your Internet communication accounts. You can setup accounts for Microsoft Exchange, MobileMe, Gmail, Yahoo, AOL, and more. In most cases, all you need is your e-mail address and password and the system does the rest. If you need to specify more account detail, you need to go into the related application, such as Mail, where you can set account options in Mail Preferences. After you setup an account, you can enable and disable the available features you want to use, such as Mail, Contacts, Calendars, and Chat. If you no longer need an account, you can quickly delete it. When you first log in to your Google, Yahoo!, or AOL accounts in Safari, you'll have the option to use them with Mail, iCal, Address Book, iChat, and other applications on your Mac (**New!**).

Set Mail, Contacts & Calendars Preferences

1. Click the **System Preferences** icon in the Dock.

2. Click the **Mail, Contacts & Calendars** icon.

3. To add an account, click **Add Account**, and then continue as follows:

 ◆ Click the type of account you want: Microsoft Exchange, MobileMe, Gmail, Yahoo, AOL, or Other.

 If you click **Other**, you can create an account for specific types, including Mac Mail, iChat, CalDAV, CardDAV, LDAP, and Mac OS X server.

 ◆ Enter your name, user ID, password, and then click **Set Up**.

4. To enable or disable feature options, click the account, and then select or clear the check boxes for the individual features, such as Mail, Contacts, Calendars, and Chat.

Add and Remove buttons ③ Other accounts

Starting Mail

Whether you want to exchange e-mail with colleagues and friends or join news feeds to access ideas and information, Mail provides you with all the tools you need. When you install Mac OS X, an icon for Mail appears in the Dock. The first time you start Mail, you need to set up an e-mail account by simply entering your e-mail address and password and letting Mail do the rest. If you are switching from another e-mail application to Mail, you can import your mailboxes and e-mail messages into Mail by answering a few questions. You can set Mail as your default e-mail application so that whenever you click an e-mail link on a Web page or select the mail command in your Web browser, Mail opens. If you have unread messages after you set up your mail accounts, a red circle with the number of unread messages appears on the Mail icon in the Dock.

Start Mail

① Click the **Mail** icon in the Dock.

If you have a MobileMe account, Mail automatically creates an e-mail account using your MobileMe information.

② When you start Mail for the first time, the application asks you:

◆ If you don't have an e-mail account, follow the one step instruction, enter your e-mail address and password.

◆ If prompted and you want to import mailboxes from another e-mail client. If so, click **Yes**, and then follow the on-screen instructions (see details on the next page). Otherwise, click **No**.

Did You Know?

You can set options to start Mail from your Web browser. Click the Mail menu, click Preferences, click General, click the Default Email Reader pop-up, click Mail (5.0), and then click the Close button.

For Your Information

Importing Mailboxes and E-Mail

If you are switching from another e-mail application to Mail, you can import your mailboxes and e-mail messages into Mail by answering a few questions. To start, click the File menu, and then click Import Mailboxes. In the dialog, click an option to select the importing application (use Other for Windows or UNIX), and then click Continue. Follow the on-screen instructions; the steps to import mailboxes and e-mail vary between applications. **Import from Apple Mail**. Mailboxes are located in Library/Mail/Mailboxes in your home folder. **Import from Windows or UNIX**. Use Standard mbox, except for Eudora or Netscape, which use their own. Microsoft Outlook, and Outlook Express for the PC are not supported. Some options require that you have the importing application, such as Entourage, open. The imported mail appears in the new Import mailbox.

Setting Up an Account

Before you can set up an e-mail account, you need your account name, password, e-mail server type, and the names of your incoming and outgoing e-mail servers from your ISP or network administrator. You can use Add Account to help you set up an e-mail account by answering a series of questions, which is available in the Accounts pane in Mail preferences. Mail allows you to send and retrieve e-mail from different types of **e-mail servers** (including MobileMe and Microsoft Exchange 2010 (**New!**)), which are the locations where e-mail is stored before you access it. MobileMe is an IMAP mail server type, while Microsoft Exchange is a POP or IMAP mail server type. MobileMe and Exchange allow you to have all your messages (in Mail), meetings (in iCal), and contacts (in Address Book) in one place. You can set up Mail to receive e-mail from multiple accounts where each one can have multiple e-mail addresses.

Set Up an E-Mail Account by Answering Questions

1. Click the **Mail** menu, and then click **Preferences**.

2. Click **Accounts**.

3. Click the **Add** (+) button.

4. Type the information requested (ask your ISP as needed), and then click **Continue**.

 ◆ **Full Name**. The name used in outgoing e-mail.

 ◆ **E-mail Address**. The From address in outgoing e-mail. You can type multiple addresses, each separated by a comma.

 ◆ **Password**. The method that provides secure access to the mail server. If you prefer to type a password every time you check mail, leave this empty.

5. Type the information requested (ask your ISP as needed), and then click **Continue**.

 ◆ **Account Type**. POP, IMAP, Exchange 2007 or 2010 (**New!**), or Exchange IMAP.

- ◆ **Description**. The account name (appears in mailbox list).
- ◆ **Incoming Mail Server**. The POP or IMAP name.
- ◆ **User Name and Password**. The name and password that identifies you to the mail server.

6 Type the information requested (ask your ISP as needed), and then click **Continue**.

- ◆ **Incoming Mail Security**. Select the Use Secure Sockets Layer (SSL) check box, and then select an authentication option.

7 Type the information requested (ask your ISP as needed), and then click **Continue**.

- ◆ **Outgoing Mail Server**. The SMTP name.
- ◆ **User Name and Password**. The name and password that identifies you to the mail server.

8 Upon completion, click the **Create**.

Review the account information in the Accounts pane in Mail preferences.

Did You Know?

You can create a new mail account using a mail script. Click the Scripts (S) menu, point to Mail Scripts, and then click Create New Mail Account. You can also start the script from the AppleScript Editor (in the Utilities folder). Click an account type, and then click OK. Type the information requested (ask your ISP as needed), and then click OK, or click Yes or No to the question.

For Your Information

How Do I Select an E-Mail Server?

Mail supports three types of incoming e-mail servers: **POP** (Post Office Protocol), **IMAP** (Internet Message Access Protocol), and **Microsoft Exchange 2010 (New!)**. A **protocol** is a set of rules that control the transmission of content, format, sequencing, and error management for information over the Internet or network much like rules of the road govern the way you drive. POP servers allow you to access e-mail messages from a single Inbox folder (requires you to log in and download messages), while IMAP servers allow you to access e-mail messages from multiple folder locations or different computers (messages stay on server). An example of an incoming e-mail server is *mail.server.com*. When you use POP or IMAP e-mail servers, you also need to provide an outgoing e-mail server. **SMTP** (Simple Mail Transfer Protocol) is used to send messages between e-mail servers. An example is *smtp.server.com*.

Managing Accounts

You can set up Mail to receive e-mail from multiple e-mail accounts and from different computers. As you work with multiple accounts, you can use the Accounts pane in Mail preferences to change the order, rename, or delete accounts. Account order indicates the mailbox list order and helps determine which account (if not specified) Mail uses to send an e-mail message. If an account changes, or you no longer need it, you can rename or delete it. If you're using an IMAP or a MobileMe account, mail stays on the mail server so you can access it from any computer. If you're using a POP account, mail downloads to your computer unless you select an Accounts pane option to keep a copy on the mail server.

Manage E-Mail Accounts

1. Click the **Mail** menu, and then click **Preferences**.

2. Click **Accounts**.

3. Select the account you want to manage.

4. To change the order in which accounts are listed in the Mailbox list, drag the account names.

5. To delete an e-mail account, click the account name, click the **Delete** button (-), and then click **OK**.

6. To rename an e-mail account, click the **Account Information** tab, and then change the name in the Description field.

7. Click the **Close** button, and then click **Save**.

Did You Know?

You can view a list of all account and preference information. Click the Scripts menu, point to Mail Scripts, and then click Display All Accounts And Preferences. An e-mail appears with the information.

Set Advanced Account Options

1 Click the **Mail** menu, and then click **Preferences**.

2 Click **Accounts**.

3 Click the **Advanced** tab.

4 Select from the following options:

◆ **Enable this account.** Check or clear to turn this account on or off.

◆ **Include when automatically checking for new mail.** Check or clear to check or exclude this account from automatic mail checking.

◆ **Keep copies of messages for offline viewing (IMAP only).** Click the pop-up to download e-mail to your computer for offline viewing.

◆ **Remove copy from server after retrieving a message (POP only).** Check to check e-mail from different computers, and then specify a removal duration.

◆ **Prompt me to skip messages Over ___ KB (POP only).** Check to skip retrieval of large e-mail.

◆ **Use SSL.** If your mail provider supports Secure Sockets Layer (SSL), check for increased security.

◆ **Authentication.** Click the pop-up to specify a security access method. Typically, Password.

5 Click the **Close** button, and then click **Save**.

IMAP specific options

POP specific options

Viewing the Mail Window

Favorites bar
The Favorites bar contains buttons to your mail folders. (**New!**)

Mail toolbar
The Mail toolbar contains buttons for the most commonly used commands you need to work with mail messages. (**New!**)

Full Screen
Provides ability to work as a full-screen application. (**New!**)

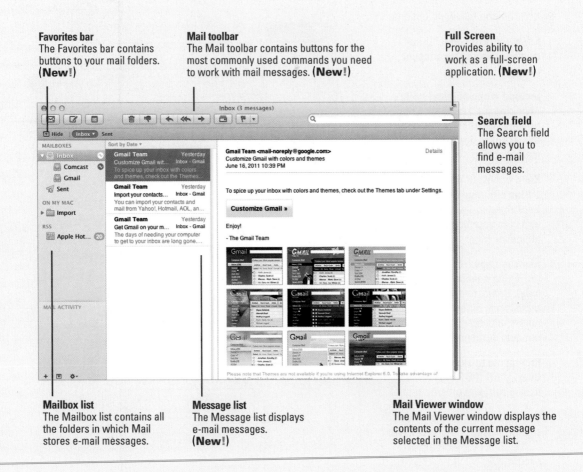

Search field
The Search field allows you to find e-mail messages.

Mailbox list
The Mailbox list contains all the folders in which Mail stores e-mail messages.

Message list
The Message list displays e-mail messages. (**New!**)

Mail Viewer window
The Mail Viewer window displays the contents of the current message selected in the Message list.

Composing and Sending an E-Mail

E-mail is becoming the primary form of written communication for many people. E-mail messages follow a standard memo format, with fields for the sender, recipient, date, and subject of the message. To send an e-mail message, you need to type the recipients e-mail address, type a subject, then type the message itself. You can send the same message to more than one individual, to a contact group, or to a combination of individuals and groups. If you type multiple addresses, you must separate the addresses with a comma (,). If you have multiple accounts, you can select which account you want to use to send the e-mail message.

Compose and Send an E-Mail

1. Click the **New Message** button on the Mail toolbar.

2. Type the e-mail addresses or names of each recipient or groups.

3. Type the e-mail addresses or names for those recipients or groups who should receive a carbon copy of the message.

4. Type a subject that indicates the purpose of the message.

5. Select a From e-mail address and outgoing server.

6. To add custom mail options, click the **Customize** button, and then click an option.

 ◆ **Bcc Address Field.** An address not included in recipients' list.

 ◆ **Reply-To Address Field.** An alternate address for replies.

 ◆ **Priority.** Add mail priority.

 ◆ **Customize.** Use to select from multiple accounts.

7. Type the content of your message.

8. If a red dotted line appears under a word, Control-click the word, and then click the correct spelling.

9. Click the **Send** button on the toolbar.

 Messages are sent out, and then copies appear in the Sent mailbox.

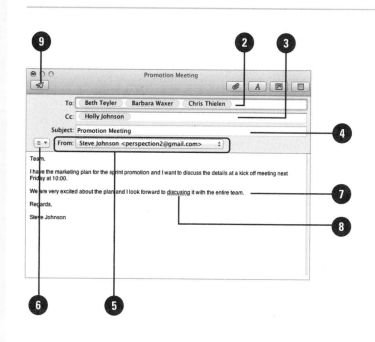

For Your Information

Checking the Spelling and Grammar in E-Mail

Before you send an e-mail message, you should spell check the text and grammar to make sure your content is accurate. To start the spell check, click the Edit menu, point to Spelling and Grammar, and then click Show Spelling and Grammar. To have Mail spell check all of your e-mail messages as you type, click While Typing on the Check Spelling submenu (on the Spelling and Grammar submenu) to enable or disable the option. If a word appears with a dotted red line under it, you can Control-click the word, and then click the correct spelling, or other options, such as Ignore or Learn. To include grammar checking, click Check Grammar with Spelling on the Spelling and Grammar submenu.

Addressing an E-Mail

Mail gives you several ways to address an e-mail. You can type the address manually by typing it in the To or Cc field, or you can select or drag an address from your Address Book. When you begin to type an e-mail address, Mail looks up the name and address in your Address Book, followed by your Previous Recipients list, and then followed by names in the LDAP database (typically for corporate use if specified in the Composing pane of Mail preferences). If Mail finds a match, it automatically completes the recipients name. If you type multiple addresses, you must separate the addresses with a comma (,). You can make addressing easier to view by using Smart Addresses, which displays the recipient name only without the e-mail address for those in your Address Book and Previous Recipients list. You can display the Previous Recipients list to remove addresses you misspelled or don't need anymore, or add addresses to your Address Book.

Select Names Using Address Complete

1. In the New Message window, type the first few letters of a name, address, or group.

 Mail suggests possible matches.

2. Click the name you want to enter.

Did You Know?

You can use Smart Addresses to show names. Smart Address are names and addresses in your address book, Previous Recipients list, or any LDAP server. Any names not found in your Address Book or Previous Recipients list still appear in full. To enable it, click the Mail menu, click Preferences, click Viewing, select the Use Smart Addresses check box, and then click OK.

See Also

See "Creating an Address Book" on page 140 for information on creating a group of recipients.

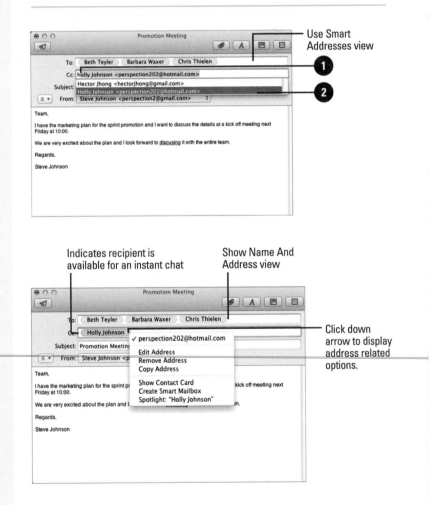

Use Smart Addresses view

Indicates recipient is available for an instant chat

Show Name And Address view

Click down arrow to display address related options.

Work with the Previous Recipients List

1. Click the **Window** menu, and then click **Previous Recipients**.

2. Select an address.

3. To remove the address, click **Remove From List**.

4. To add the address to the Address Book, click the **Add To Address Book**.

5. Click the **Close** button.

Did You Know?

You can set addressing preferences. Click the Mail menu, click Preferences, click the Composing button, select or clear the following check boxes: Automatically Complete Addresses, When Sending To A Group, Show All Member Address, and Mark Addresses Not In This Domain, and then type a domain name such as *apple.com* to mark it as safe when using LDAP.

You can change the use of a mailbox for an IMAP account. Select a mailbox, click the Mailbox menu, point to Use This Mailbox For, and then click Drafts, Sent, Trash, or Junk.

For Your Information

Creating and Working with Notes

Instead of jotting notes down on paper, you can use Mail to create notes and then to help you organize and track them so the things you need done, get done. You can include formatted text, graphics, and attachments in a note. After you create a note, you can also send it to another person as an e-mail message. Click the Note button on the Mail toolbar, and then type the note text you want in the Note window. Mail uses the first line of the note as the subject. To format the note, use the Attach or Fonts on the Note toolbar. To send the note as an e-mail, click the Send Note button on the Note toolbar, address the e-mail, and then click the Send button. In the note, click the Close button on the Note toolbar. To view notes, expand Reminders in the Mailbox list, and then click Notes. To delete an item from Mail, select it, and then click the Delete button.

Adding Stationery to E-Mail

Instead of using a standard white background for your e-mail, you can spruce it up with some stationery. If you want to send an e-mail message for a special occasion, such as a birthday, thank you, get well, or just for fun, you can quickly create the look you want by applying stationery templates with professionally designed layouts, fonts, and colors. If you want to use your own photos, you can use the Photo Browser in Mail to find photos in your iPhoto library or Photo Booth, and insert them into your e-mail messages.

Add Stationery and Photos

1. Open the message you want to apply a stationery.

2. Click the **Stationery** button on the toolbar to show it (toggle button).

3. Click a category.

4. Click the thumbnail of the template you want. To change the background for some templates, click the thumbnail again.

5. To add images, use any of the following methods:

 - **Photo Browser.** Click the Photo Browser button, select/drag the images to the e-mail.

 - **Finder.** Drag an image file from the desktop or Finder window.

6. To remove a template, click the **Stationery** category, and then click **Original**.

7. To add a template to your favorites list, drag it to the Favorites category. To remove it, click the **Delete** (x) button in Favorites.

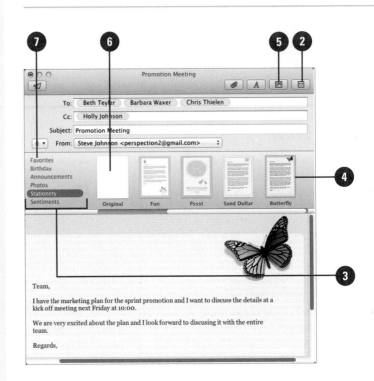

Did You Know?

You can have message text read aloud. Select the text you want to have read, click the Edit menu, point to Speech, and then click Start Speaking or Stop Speaking.

For Your Information

Using Data Detectors to Manage Information

Mail tries to recognize different types of data, such as an address or a date, so you can effectively manage and use it. When you place your pointer over data in messages, such as an e-mail address, street address, or date and time, you can use the data to create a new contact in your Address Book, map street directions on the Web, or create an event in iCal. In Mac OS X, data detectors can identify flight numbers, which takes you to the Dashboard Flight Tracker widget.

Formatting Message Text

You can specify a file format for message text. The Plain Text format is one that all e-mail programs recognize, but it doesn't support text formatting. The Rich Text format allows text formatting, but it's not always supported. However, most programs that don't recognize Rich Text, convert the message to plain text. When you use Rich Text, you can use formatting tools, such as bold, italicize, underline, numbered and bulleted lists, indentations, and color text and backgrounds, on the Format bar (**New!**), Format menu and in the Fonts and Color dialogs to help draw the reader's attention to key words and emphasize the meaning of your message.

Format the Message Text

1. Open the message you want to format.

2. Click the **Format** menu, and then click **Make Rich Text**, if available.

3. Select the text you want to format.

4. Click the **Format Bar** button on the toolbar to show it. (**New!**)

5. Use the Format bar (**New!**) to change any of the following:

 ◆ **Font and Size.** To use the dialog settings (type, size, style, and effects), click the **Font** button, and then click **Show Fonts**.

 ◆ **Color.** To use the dialog color wheel to select a color, click the **Color** button, and then click **Show Colors.**

 ◆ **Bold, Italic, and Underline.**

 ◆ **Alignment.**

 ◆ **Lists and Indention.**

Did You Know?

You can set font preferences. Click the Mail menu, click Preferences, click Fonts & Colors, select default fonts for the message list, message text (Rich Text), and plain text, and then click the Close button.

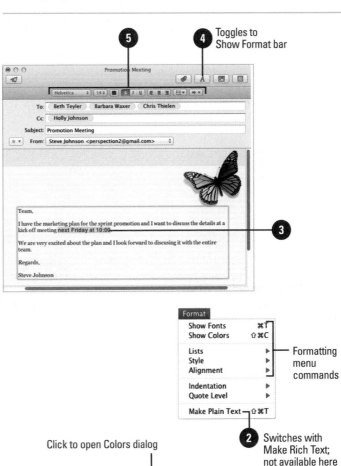

Toggles to Show Format bar

Formatting menu commands

Click to open Colors dialog

Switches with Make Rich Text; not available here

Select several font attributes at once.

Adding an E-Mail Signature

If you type the same information at the end of each e-mail message, such as Best Regards and your name, then you can automate that task by creating a signature. You can add one signature to all messages or create several and select one when you compose a message. You can customize your signature with a variety of formatting styles, such as font type, size, and color, and you can even include a picture or attach your virtual business card, known as a **vCard**, from your Address Book.

Create a Signature

1. Click the **Mail** menu, click **Preferences**, and then click **Signatures**.

2. Select an account or **All Signatures**.

3. Click the **Add** (+) button.

4. Type a title for the signature.

5. Type/modify the signature text.

6. For a Rich Text signature, use the **Format** menu to change the text font, color, style, or alignment.

7. If you want, drag a picture or vCard, and then click **OK**.

8. Click the **Choose Signature** pop-up, and then select a signature, **None**, or an option.

9. Select or clear the **Place signature above quoted text** check box to place the signature above or below the quoted text.

10. To remove a signature, select it, and then click the **Remove** (-) button.

11. Click the **Close** button.

Did You Know?

You can add your signature to e-mail quickly. In an e-mail message, click where you want the signature, click the Signature pop-up, and then click a signature.

Customizing the Mail Window

The Mail window is broken down into 4 main areas: toolbar and favorites bar (**New!**), sidebar, message list, and message preview. The Mail window provides flexibility and ease of use. The Favorites bar gives you easy access to mail folders in a horizontal layout and options to hide/show the sidebar. The message list (**New!**) displays a compact preview of each message (**New!**), which includes the first two lines of the e-mail, along with contact photos. These options are all customizable in Mail Viewing preferences (**New!**); you can even display the classic view (the default from Mail 4.0). When you point to the header in a message, convenient inline controls (**New!**) appear for ease of use. You can display the Mail window in full-screen view (**New!**), which give you more screen area to read, respond, and manage to your e-mail messages.

Customize the Mail window

- Show/Hide Toolbar. Click the **View** menu, and then click **Show Toolbar** or **Hide Toolbar**.

- Show/Hide Favorites Bar. Click the **View** menu, and then click **Show Favorites Bar** or **Hide Favorites Bar**. (**New!**)

- Show/Hide Sidebar. Click the **Show Sidebar** or **Hide Sidebar** button on the Favorites bar. (**New!**)

- Add/Remove from Favorites Bar. Drag the item on or off the Favorites bar. (**New!**)

- Sort Messages. Click the **Sort by** button in the Message list, and then select a sort by option. (**New!**)

- Viewing Preferences. Click the **Mail** menu, click **Preferences**, click **Viewing**. Select options to use classic layout, show to/cc or contact photos in the message list. (**New!**)

- Full Screen. Click the **Full Screen** button in the title bar. To return, point to the top of the screen to display the menu bar, and then click the **Full Screen** button. (**New!**)

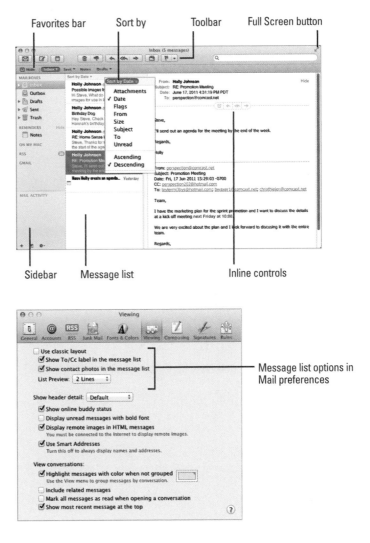

Favorites bar Sort by Toolbar Full Screen button

Sidebar Message list Inline controls

Message list options in Mail preferences

Receiving and Reading E-Mail

You can receive e-mail anytime day or night—even when your computer is turned off. You can retrieve your e-mail manually or set Mail to do so automatically by setting options in Mail preferences. When you start Mail, the application checks for new e-mail. It continues to check periodically, based on preferences, while the application is open. New messages appear in the Inbox along with any messages you haven't stored elsewhere or deleted. A blue dot appears next to unread messages. The Message list displays the subject line of a message and other information, such as date received, senders name, attachments, and priority flags, which you can customize to display the information you need.

Check for New E-Mail

1. Click the **Mail** menu, and then click **Preferences**.

2. Click **General**.

3. Click the **Check for new messages** pop-up, and then select a duration.

4. Click the **New messages sound** pop-up, and then select a sound.

5. Click the **Dock unread count** pop-up, and then select the mailboxes included in the unread mail count on the Mail icon in the Dock.

6. Click **Accounts**.

7. Select an account, and then click the **Advanced** tab.

8. Select the **Include when automatically checking for new messages** check box.

9. Click the **Close** button.

10. To check for mail manually, click the **Get Mail** button on the Mail toolbar, or click the **Mailbox** menu, point to **Get New Mail**, and then click **In All Accounts** or an account name.

Open and Read an E-Mail

1. Click the **Inbox** icon in the Mailbox list or on the Favorites bar to view new messages.

2. Click an e-mail message to read it in the Mail Viewer window.

3. Double-click an e-mail message to open it in its own window.

Did You Know?

You can add a sender to the Address Book. Select the message in the Message list, click the Message menu, and then click Add Sender To Address Book.

Change the Message List View

1. Click the **View** menu, and then point to **Columns**.

2. Select a column to display:

 ◆ **Attachments.** Displays a paper clip for attachments.

 ◆ **Buddy Availability.** Displays buddy status information.

 ◆ **Date Received.** Displays date received.

 ◆ **Date Sent.** Displays date sent.

 ◆ **Flags.** Displays a priority flag.

 ◆ **From.** Displays sender name.

 ◆ **Mailbox.** Displays name/ account.

 ◆ **Number.** Displays sequential numbers next to the messages.

 ◆ **Size.** Displays size of a message or mailbox.

 ◆ **To.** Displays recipient name.

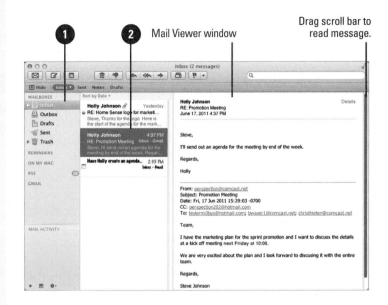

Mail Viewer window

Drag scroll bar to read message.

Status (always available)

Buddy Availability

Drag a column header to change positions.

Attachments

Classic layout; available in Mail preferences

Responding to E-Mail

You can respond to a message in three ways: reply to it, which creates a new message addressed to the sender(s) and other recipients; forward it, which creates a new message you can send to someone else; or redirect it, which creates a new message from the original sender you can send to someone else (useful when you receive a message by mistake). When you reply or forward a message, the original message appears in the message response. You can reply to the sender only, or to all the people who received the original message.

Reply to an E-Mail

① Select the e-mail message you want to reply to.

② If you want, select a portion of the text to include as quoted text.

③ Click the **Reply** button to respond to the sender only, or click the **Reply All** button to respond to the sender and all recipients listed in the e-mail.

④ Add or delete names from the To or the Cc field.

⑤ Type your message.

⑥ Click the **Send** button on the Message toolbar.

A curved arrow appears in the Status column next to messages you reply to.

Click to toggle between addresses for Reply All and Reply.

Quoted text

Did You Know?

You can reply with an instant message. If you're logged into iChat, Mail displays a green dot indicator next to messages from buddies who are online, or a yellow dot indicator when the person is idle. Click the Mail menu, click Preferences, click the Viewing button, select the Show Online Buddy Status check box, and then click the Close button. Select a message in the Message list, click the Message menu, and then click Reply With iChat.

For Your Information

Quoting Text in E-Mail

When you reply to an e-mail message, you can include all or part of the original message, known as **quoted text**. The original message appears with a single quote bar to the left of the text. If the original message contained quoted text, you see an additional quote bar. To use quoted text, click the Mail menu, click Preferences, click the Composing button, select the Quote The Text Of The Original Message check box, and then click the Include Selected Text If Any, Otherwise Include All option. To change the color of quoted text, click Fonts & Colors, select the Color Quoted Text check box, and then select colors from the pop-up for Levels One, Two, and Three. When you're done, click the Close button. You can use the Quote Level submenu on the Format menu to change the number of quote bars.

Redirect an E-Mail

1. Select the e-mail message you want to redirect.

2. Click the **Message** menu, and then click **Redirect**.

3. Type or select names in the To or the Cc field.

4. Click the **Send** button on the Message toolbar.

 A segment arrow appears in the Status column next to messages you redirect.

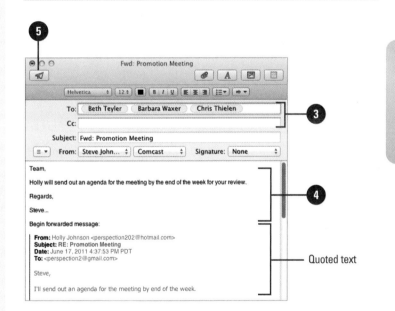

Message text redirected without a quote bar.

Forward an E-Mail

1. Select the message(s) or open a message you want to forward.

2. Click the **Forward** button on the toolbar.

3. Type or select names in the To or the Cc field.

4. Type your message.

5. Click the **Send** button on the Message toolbar.

Quoted text

Did You Know?

Attachments aren't sent on replies.
When you reply to a message that has an attachment, the attachment isn't returned to the original sender. You can forward the message to the original sender if you need to send the attachment back.

Sending and Retrieving a File

You can easily share a file, such as a picture, document, vCard (virtual business card from your Address Book), sound, or movie by attaching it to an e-mail message. Some ISPs have trouble sending attachments greater than 5 megabytes MB, so it's a good idea to check with your ISP for limits on file size. Upon receiving the e-mail, the recipient can view it with Quick Look, open the file in the application that created it, or save it on a disk for use in other applications from the Mail Viewer window. The Message list displays the number and size of the attachments. If you send an e-mail to a Windows user, the attachment is automatically compressed in a standard zipped (gzip) format so it can be read.

Send a File with an E-Mail

1. Compose a new message or reply to an existing message.

2. Click the **Attach** button on the Message toolbar.

3. Select the drive and folder that contains the file, and then select it.

4. Select or clear the **Send Windows-Friendly Attachments** check box.

5. Click **Choose File**.

6. For images, click the **Image Size** pop-up, and then select a size (**New!**). The message size appears on the Status bar.

7. Click the **Send** button on the Message toolbar.

Attached file

Did You Know?

You should compress large files before you send them. Select the file or files you want to compress in the Finder, click the File menu, and then click Compress. Rename the compressed file with a *.zip* extension as necessary.

You can send a Web link in an e-mail message. Type or paste the full URL, including "http://" in the body of the message. Your recipients can click the link to go directly to the Web page.

View or Open a File in an E-Mail

① Select the message with the attached file.

② Click **Quick Look** in the message header.

◆ You can also click the **File** menu, and then click **Quick Look Attachments**, or Control-click the attached file, click **Open Attachment**, or point to **Open With**, and then select a program.

> ## Did You Know?
>
> *You can remove attachments from an e-mail.* Select the e-mail, click the Message menu, and then click Remove Attachments.

Attachment icon

Quick Look
in Preview

Save Files in an E-Mail

① Select the message with the attached file.

② Use one of the following methods:

◆ **Save All.** Click the **File** menu, and then click **Save Attachments**, or click **Save** in the message header.

◆ **Save Individual.** Click and hold **Save** in the message header, and then click file name. You can also Control+ click the attached file, and then click **Save to Downloads Folder** (by passes Steps 3 and 4).

③ Select the drive and folder where you want to save the files.

④ Click **Save**.

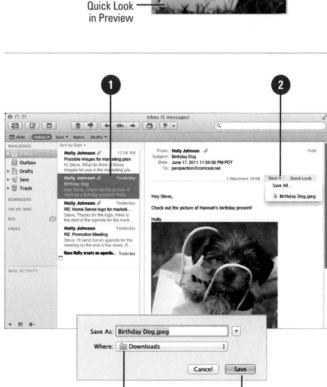

Managing E-Mail

A common problem with using e-mail is an overcrowded Inbox. To keep your Inbox organized, you should move messages you want to save to other mailboxes and subfolders (a mailbox inside another mailbox), delete messages you no longer want, and create new mailboxes as you need them. A mailbox can store messages on your computer, within a specific account, or within an existing mailbox. When a mailbox contains both messages and other mailboxes, the mailbox icon appears in blue. Mail automatically groups related messages together, known as a conversation (**New!**), with each message streamlined and numbered, so you can identify and read messages in sequence. Since the messages are grouped, it's easy to find, reply, or even delete (**New!**). Mail also hides quoted text to reduce repeated information for easy reading (**New!**).

Create a New Mailbox

① To create a subfolder in a mailbox, select the existing mailbox.

② Click the **Add** (+) button at the bottom of the Mailbox list, and then click **New Mailbox**.

③ Click the **Location** pop-up, and then select **On My Mac** (local computer) or an IMAP account (online mail server).

④ Type a name for the new mailbox.

⑤ Click **OK**.

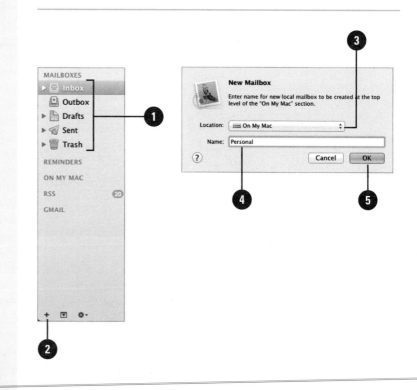

Did You Know?

You can show and hide the Mailbox list. Click the View menu, and then click Show/Hide Mailbox List.

You can move items in the Mailbox list. Drag the sidebar item to a new location in the Mailbox list.

You can delete a mailbox. Control+ click it, click Delete Mailbox, and then click Delete.

You can rename a mailbox. Control+ click the mailbox, click Rename Mailbox, change it, and then press Return.

For Your Information

Learning About the Standard Mailboxes

Mail comes with several standard mailboxes: Inbox, Drafts, Sent, and Trash. **Inbox** stores messages you have received from others; the Drafts mailbox stores messages you have written and saved, but not sent; and the Sent mailbox stores copies of messages you have sent. The Trash mailbox stores all your deleted messages.

Organize E-Mail in Mailboxes

1. Select the e-mail message you want to move. If necessary, press and hold down ⌘, and click to select multiple e-mail messages.

2. Drag the e-mail message(s) to the new folder.

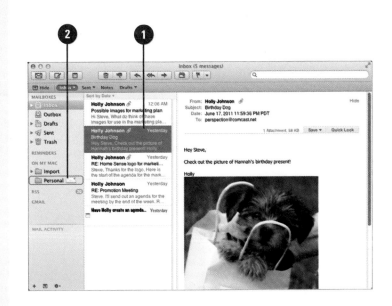

Organize E-Mail by Conversation

1. Open the mailbox with the e-mail you want to view as threads.

2. Click the **View** menu, and then click **Organize By Conversation** (**New!**) to display a check mark.

 ◆ To expand or collapse all conversations, click the **View** menu, and then click **Expand All Conversations** or **Collapse All Conversations**. (**New!**)

3. To show or hide the related messages in a conversation, click the message, and then click **Related Messages** button (**New!**) on the Mail toolbar.

4. To show or hide the names in a related message, click the message number arrow (**New!**).

5. To ungroup, click the **View** menu, and then click **Organize By Conversation**.

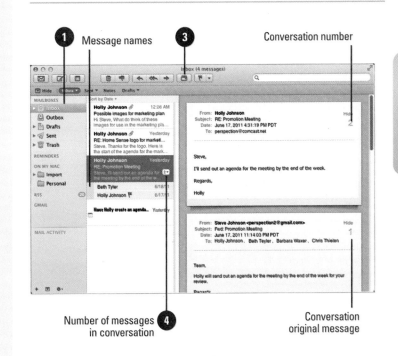

Message names

Conversation number

Number of messages in conversation

Conversation original message

Deleting E-Mail

Deleting unwanted messages makes it easier to see the new messages you receive and to keep track of messages to which you have already responded. When you delete an e-mail message, Mail simply moves it into the Trash mailbox. If you want to recover a deleted message, you just have to retrieve it from the Trash mailbox. To get rid of a message permanently, you need to open the Trash mailbox, select the message, and then click Delete. Mail automatically places e-mail messages in the Sent mailbox every time you send them. You'll want to periodically open the Sent mailbox and delete messages so your mail account doesn't get too large. You can also set account options to help you delete messages.

Delete Unwanted E-Mail

1. Click a mailbox icon in the Mailbox list with the e-mail you want to delete.

2. Click the unwanted e-mail.

3. Click the **Delete** button on the Mail toolbar.

4. To erase messages in the Trash mailbox, click the **Mailbox** menu, point to **Erase Deleted Items**, click **In All Accounts** or a specific account, and then click **Erase**.

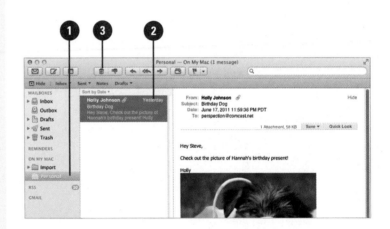

Recover E-Mail from the Trash

1. Click the Trash mailbox in the Mailbox list.

2. Select the e-mail message you want to retrieve.

3. Drag the e-mail message to another folder.

Did You Know?

You can resend a message. Select the message in the Sent mailbox, click the Message menu, click Send Again, add or change recipients, and then click the Send button.

Change E-Mail Delete Options

1. Click the **Mail** menu, and then click **Preferences**.

2. Click **Accounts**.

3. Select an account.

4. Click the **Mailbox Behaviors** tab.

5. Select any of the following:

 ◆ **Move deleted messages to the trash mailbox**. Check to move deleted messages to the Trash.

 ◆ **Store deleted messages on the server**. Check to keep deleted messages on the mail server for an IMAP account.

 ◆ **Permanently erase deleted messages when**. Click the pop-up, and then select based on the duration you want.

6. Click the **Close** button, and then click **Save**.

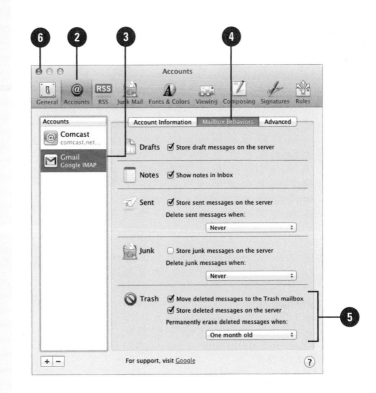

Did You Know?

You can save sent messages on the mail server. Click the Mail menu, click Preferences, click Accounts, click the Mailbox Behaviors tab, select the Store Sent Messages On The Server check box, and then click the Close button.

You can print e-mail messages. Select the message(s) you want to print, click the File menu, click Print, and then click Print. If you select multiple messages, the e-mails are combined into a single document in the order you selected them in the Message list.

For Your Information

Backing Up E-Mail

The information in your e-mail messages is important, so making a backup, or **archive**, of a mailbox is a good way to protect it. In Mail, select the mailboxes you want to back up, click one or more messages to archive, click the Message menu, and then click Archive (**New!**). Mail creates an archive mailbox for each account whose message you archive. The archived messages remain in the Archive mailbox until you delete or move them. Mail backs up the mailboxes as .mbox packages.

Another method is to drag a mailbox from an IMAP account to On My Mac to copy it on your computer. Likewise, you can drag a mailbox from On My Mac to an IMAP account to copy it to your mail server online. To create a copy of a mailbox, drag the mailbox from the Mailbox list to your desktop.

Saving E-Mail

If you have not finished composing a message, you can save it in the Drafts mailbox and work on it later. If you quit Mail with an open message, Mail automatically saves it as a draft. If you want to use the text from a message in a word processing application, such as TextEdit, you can save a message as a separate file in the Rich Text or Plain Text format. You can also save one or more messages in the Raw Message Source (mbox) format, which is a standard mail message format; you can import mbox into other mail applications, including Mail.

Save a Draft E-Mail

1. Open a new or a reply to an existing e-mail message, and then type a message.

2. Click the **File** menu, and then click **Save**.

3. Close the e-mail message.

4. Click the **Drafts** mailbox in the Mailbox list.

5. Double-click the e-mail message to view and change it.

6. Click the **Send** button.

Save an E-Mail as a File

1. Open a new or a reply to an existing e-mail message, and then type a message.

2. Click the **File** menu, and then click **Save As**.

3. Select the hard drive and folder where you want to save the file.

4. Type a name for the file.

5. Click the **Format** pop-up, and then select a format.

6. Click **Save**.

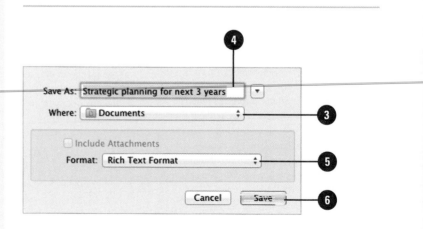

Searching E-Mail for Text

If you're looking for an e-mail message with specific information, you can use the Mail Search field to search for text in a message, in all messages in a mailbox, in all messages for a specific account, or in all mailboxes. In the Search field, you can search for people, text in the subject and message, or attachments using it's filename or it's content (**New!**). Mail finds messages containing the same beginning letters as you type with the most relevant match, yet it also makes search suggestions, such as people or subjects, in the Search field menu based on the content (**New!**). To refine your search, use the words "and," "or," "not," and parentheses in the Search field. If you frequently search for the same text, you can create a Smart Mailbox to make it quick and easy to find in the future. In addition to the search field, you can also use Spotlight to find e-mails or text in Mail.

Search E-Mail for Text

1. To search in selected mailboxes, select the mailboxes or accounts.

2. Click in the Search field, and then type the text you want to find.

 To narrow the search, select an option or suggestions on the Search field menu (**New!**).

 TIMESAVER *Press ⌘+Option +F to quickly place the insertion point in the Search field.*

 As you type, Mail starts the search and displays the results.

3. Click **All** or a specific mailbox on the Search bar to narrow the results (**New!**).

4. To save the search as a Smart Mailbox, click the **Save** button on the Search bar, enter a name, and then click **OK**.

5. To broaden the search, click the **Spotlight** icon on the menu bar, type the text you want, and then click the search result you want on the menu.

 TIMESAVER *Press ⌘+F to find or replace text in an open e-mail.*

Search field menu

Search suggestions

Search Techniques

Technique	Example
Use descriptive words	Home improvement
Place phrases in quotes	"Home Sense"
Use AND to find all words	"meeting and promotion"
Use OR to find at least one word	"meeting or promotion"
Use NOT to find the first one but not the second one	"meeting not promotion"
Use () to find combinations	"meeting and (promotion or fall)"

Blocking and Flagging E-Mail

You can have Mail handle junk e-mail for you. You can specify what should be considered junk e-mail and how Mail should handle that e-mail. You can ensure that e-mail which might seem to be junk e-mail, but is actually from a person or site that you are interested in, gets to you. You can mark messages as junk mail to help train Mail (set rules) to more effectively distinguish between junk and non junk. If you receive an e-mail that you want to follow up on later, you can color-code (**New!**), or flag, it for future reference. It's quick and easy. Simply select the one or more message you want to mark, click the Flag button on the Mail toolbar, and then select a flag. Mail creates folders for your flagged messages for easy access (**New!**). You can rename the color-code flags (**New!**)—which you use for searching—as well as clear flags from messages.

Change Junk E-Mail Options

1. Click the **Mail** menu, and then click **Preferences**.

2. Click **Junk Mail**.

3. Select the **Enable junk mail filtering** check box.

4. Click the option to leave it in my Inbox and change the text color or move it to the Junk mailbox.

5. Select the check boxes to exempt e-mail from junk filtering:

 * **Sender of message is in my Address Book**
 * **Sender of message is in my previous recipients**
 * **Message is addressed using my full name**
 * **Filter junk mail before applying my rules**

6. Click **Advanced**.

 The default junk mail rule appears, which you can customize.

7. Use the pop-ups, fields, and buttons to specify the criteria for the junk rule to apply to messages.

8. Click **OK**.

9. Click the **Close** button.

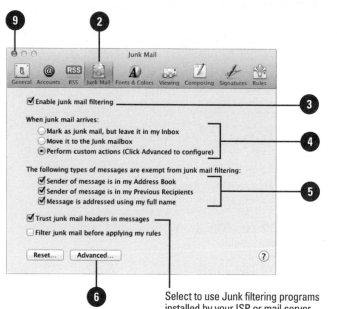

Select to use Junk filtering programs installed by your ISP or mail server along with Mail.

Mark E-Mail as Junk or Not Junk

1. Select the e-mail you want to mark as junk or not as junk.

2. Click the **Junk** button or **Not Junk** button on the Mail toolbar.

 The button toggles between Junk and Not Junk.

3. To erase messages in the Junk mailbox, click the **Mailbox** menu, click **Erase Junk Mail**, and then click **Erase**.

Did You Know?

You can reset junk mail rules to the default. Click the Mail menu, click Preferences, click Junk Mail, click Reset, click Reset, and then click the Close button.

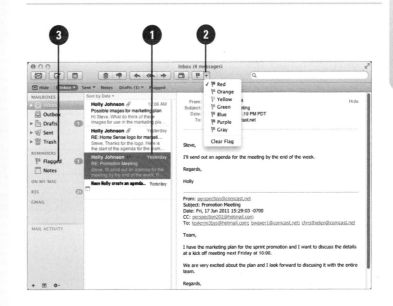

Click to mark not as junk

Junk icon

Message currently marked as Junk mail

Flag an E-Mail

1. Select the e-mail message you want to flag.

2. Click the **Flag** button arrow on the Mail toolbar, and then select a flag.

3. To view flagged messages, show **Reminders** in the Sidebar, and then click **Flagged**.

4. To rename a flag, double-click a flag in the Sidebar (under Reminders), type a new name, and then press Return.

5. To clear a flag from a message, select the message, click the **Flag** button arrow, and then click **Clear Flag**.

Diverting Incoming E-Mail to Mailboxes

Mail can direct incoming messages that meet criteria to other mailboxes in the Mailbox list rather than to your Inbox. You can set message rules to store any messages you receive from a friend in a different folder so they won't clutter your Inbox. When you are ready to read the messages, you simply open the mailbox and access the messages just as you would messages in the Inbox. You can also set rules to automatically reply to incoming messages, which is useful when you are *out of the office*, or forward incoming messages with additional message text. You can also color-code the messages that you send to or receive from particular people for quick and easy recognition.

Set Rules for Incoming E-Mail

1. Click the **Mail** menu, and then click **Preferences**.

2. Click **Rules**.

3. Click **Add Rule**.

4. Type a name for this rule.

5. Click the pop-up, and then click **Any** or **All** to set initial criteria.

6. Use the pop-ups and fields, to specify the criteria for the rule to apply to a message.

7. Click the **Add** (+) button or **Remove** (-) button to add or remove criteria.

8. Under the Perform The Following Actions area, use the pop-ups and fields to specify the actions you want to be taken if the criteria is met.

9. Click the **Add** button (+) or **Subtract** button (-) to add or remove actions.

10. Click **OK**, and then click **Apply** or **Don't Apply**.

11. To edit, duplicate, or remove a rule, select a rule, and then click **Edit**, **Duplicate**, or **Remove**.

12. Click the **Close** button.

Select to activate or clear to deactivate.

Creating a Smart Mailbox

A Smart Mailbox displays e-mail messages or to-do items based on a search criteria in an easy to use folder in the Mailboxes list. The message or to-do items are not moved to the Smart Mailboxes. Each time you select a Smart Mailbox, Mail performs a search to create an up-to-date list of results. A Smart Mailbox is like a Smart Folder for Mail. You can create a Smart Mailbox for RSS articles, specific content, or from a specific sender.

Create a New Smart Mailbox

1. To create a subfolder in a mailbox, select the existing mailbox.

2. Click the **Add** (+) button at the bottom of the Mailbox list, and then click **New Smart Mailbox**.

3. Type a name for the new mailbox.

4. Specify the criteria you want for the Smart Mailbox:

 ◆ **Contents.** Select **messages** or **to-do's**.

 ◆ **That Match.** Select **any** or **all**.

 ◆ **Conditions.** Use the pop-ups to specify the criteria you want for the Smart Mailbox.

 ◆ **Add or Remove Conditions.** Click the **Add** (+) or **Remove** (-) buttons. You can add as many as you want.

5. Select or clear the **Include messages from trash** or **Include messages from sent** check boxes.

6. Click **OK**.

7. To edit a Smart Mailbox, select the mailbox, click the **Mailbox** menu, and then click **Edit Smart Mailbox**.

8. To delete a Smart Mailbox, select the mailbox, click the **Mailbox** menu, click **Delete Mailbox**, and then click **Delete** to confirm.

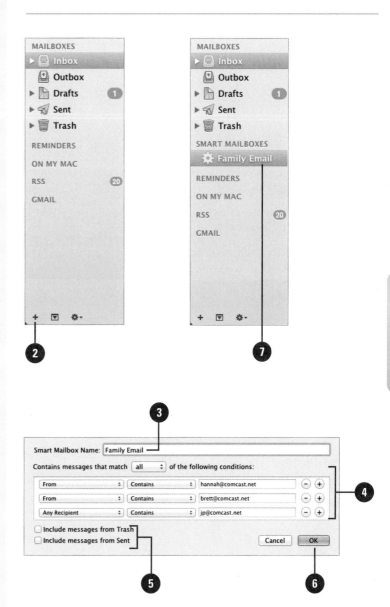

Getting RSS Feeds in E-Mail

Since e-mail is an important form of communication, you can use Mail to subscribe to RSS (Really Simple Syndication) feeds and display them in your inbox. A feed delivers frequently updated Web content to your browser on a continuous basis. A feed, is usually offered on a subscription basis and typically free of charge. A feed can deliver text content in the form of news headlines or blogs, or digital content in the form of pictures, audio, and video. When you get feeds in e-mail, a line or two of each articles content and a link to the full article appears for you to quickly and easily view.

Subscribe to RSS Articles

1. Click the **Add** (+) button at the bottom of the Mailbox list, and then click **Add RSS Articles**.

2. Browse and select a feed from the ones you bookmarked in Safari, or enter a Web address for a new feed.

 ◆ **Find Feeds.** Use the Search field to locate the feeds you want.

 ◆ **Multiple Feed.** Use Shift-click or Command-click to select multiple feeds.

3. Select the **Show in Inbox** check box to include the feeds in your inbox.

4. Click **Add**.

5. Click the RSS feed you want to view in the Source pane.

RSS feeds RSS article

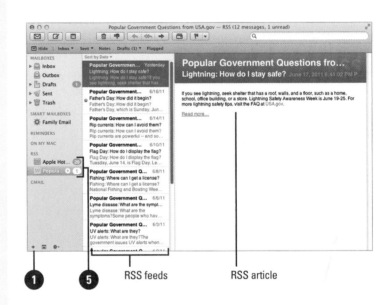

Did You Know?

You can RSS feed preferences in Mail.
Click the Mail menu, click Preferences, click RSS, use the pop-ups to select a Default RSS Reader, Check For Updates (Interval), and Remove Articles (Manually or Automatically), and then click the Close button.

Conducting Live Chats and Video Conversations

Introduction

Mac OS X makes communicating with other computers over the Internet easier than ever with iChat 6.0. You can talk to others over the Internet (like you do on a telephone), use full screen video to see and be seen by others while you converse, share programs and files, and collaborate on documents.

You can use iChat to exchange instant messages with a designated list of buddies over the Internet. An **instant message** is an online typewritten conversation in real-time between two or more buddies. Unlike an e-mail message, instant messages require both parties to be online, and the communication is instantaneous.

iChat makes setup effortless. The first time you launch iChat, a setup screen appears to walk you step-by-step through the process. During the setup process, you need to create or provide a screen name, which is your instant messaging address. If you already have an Apple ID (me.com or Mac.com), AOL Instant Messenger (AIM), Google Talk, Yahoo, or Jabber account, you can use it with iChat. Otherwise, you can setup a me.com or Mac.com account to get a screen name. To use the AV features of iChat, you need to have a microphone (for audio only) or FireWire compatible video camera (for audio and video) installed on your computer and a fast Internet connection. iChat automatically identifies other local users who are logged in, and lets you send messages or files to each other.

In addition to using iChat over the Internet, you can also use it on your local network—known as **bonjour messaging**—at the office, school, or home. If you want to communicate with users on an iPad 2, iPhone 4, iPod Touch (4th generation with iOS 4.1 or later), or another Mac, you can use FaceTime to make video calls.

What You'll Do

Create an Instant Message Account

Start iChat

View iChat

Change My Status

Use the iChat Status Menu

Add a Buddy

Change a Buddy Picture

Create and Manage Buddy Groups

Send and Receive Instant Messages

Block a Buddy

Send a File During an Instant Message

Have a Audio and Video Chat

Enhance a Video Chat

Chat on a Local Network

Change the Appearance of a Chat

Get Notification Alerts

Get Started with FaceTime

Make a Video Call with FaceTime

Creating an Instant Message Account

The first time you launch iChat, a setup screen opens to walk you step-by-step through the process. To complete the process, you need to provide or create a screen name (your instant messaging address) to send and receive instant messages with iChat. If you already have a me.com (MobileMe) or Mac.com (old .Mac) account, an AOL Instant Messenger (AIM) screen name, Jabber ID, Google Talk, or Yahoo! (**New!**), you can use it with iChat. A me.com screen name is your e-mail address, such as perspection@me.com, or an AIM screen name is a handle, such as perspection. If you don't have a screen name, you can sign up for a me.com or Mac.com account at during the setup process to get one. If you have multiple accounts, you can switch between them or use them separately. If you are using iChat over a local network for Bonjour messaging, you don't need a screen name.

Create an Instant Message Account the First Time

1. If necessary, install a microphone or compatible video camera according to product instructions.

2. Start iChat for the first time; display the Dock on the desktop, and then click the **iChat** icon.

3. Read the Welcome screen, and then click **Continue**.

4. Type your first and last name, if needed.

5. Click the **Account Type** pop-up, and then select an account: **AIM, me.com, Mac.com, Jabber, Google Talk**, and **Yahoo! (New!)**.

 TROUBLE? *If you don't have an account, click Get An iChat Account to get an AIM account.*

6. Type your Account Name and Password, and then click **Continue**.

7. Select options to setup audio and video for iChat, and then click **Continue**.

8. Click **Done**.

Create and Enable Accounts

1 Click the **iChat** menu, and then click **Preferences**.

2 Click **Accounts**.

IMPORTANT *If multiple people use a computer with separate accounts, they use their own screen names.*

3 To create another account, click the **Add** (+) button, select an account type (**AIM**, **me.com**, **Mac.com**, **Google Talk**, **Jabber**, and **Yahoo!** (**New!**)), enter account name and password, and then click **Done**.

Your password is added to your keychain.

4 Click the **Account Information** tab.

5 Select one of the following options:

◆ **Enable this account.** Select to enable and display this account.

◆ **Allow multiple logins for this account.** Select to use multiple logins for this account.

6 Click the **Close** button.

Did You Know?

You can get the latest version of iChat online. Visit the Apple Web site at *www.apple.com* to get updates.

You can get or change your password and account information. Visit the AOL Instant Messenger Web site at *www.aim.com*, or visit the me.com Web site at *www.me.com*.

For Your Information

Installing and Selecting AV Hardware

Before you can start or join a video chat, you need to connect and install a microphone, a FireWire based video camera, such as iSight by Apple, built-in USB, and a broadband Internet connection (384 Kbps or faster), such as cable or DSL, to your Macintosh computer. If you have a Digital Video (DV) camcorder with a FireWire cable, you can also use it with iChat. Once you attach and install (if necessary) your audio and video equipment, you can set options in the Video pane of iChat Preferences. If you are using a camera with a built-in microphone, iChat automatically uses the camera microphone unless you change it to another one you have attached to your computer.

Starting iChat

iChat is an instant messaging program that allows you to exchange instant messages with a designated list of buddies over the Internet. An **instant message** is an online typewritten conversation in real time between two or more buddies. Instant messages require both parties to be online, and the communication is instantaneous. After you start iChat, you sign in to let others online know you are connected. When you're done, you sign out.

Start iChat and Sign In and Out

1. Click the **Launchpad** icon in the Dock, and then click the **iChat** icon.

 A Buddy List window opens, displaying a "Connecting" message. Upon completion, the Buddy List expands to list your buddies and their online status.

2. If you're not automatically signed in, click the **iChat** menu, and then click **Log In To <account>**.

3. To sign out, click the **iChat** menu, and then click **Log Out Of <account>**.

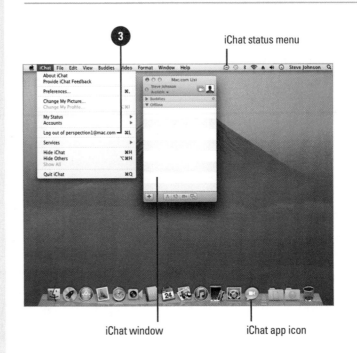

iChat status menu

iChat window

iChat app icon

Did You Know?

You can stop signing in automatically. Click the iChat menu, click Preferences, click Accounts, select an account, clear the Enable This Account check box, and then click the Close button.

Your buddies might need to upgrade their AIM software. If your buddies are using older versions of the AOL Instant Messaging software, they might need to get a newer version to send messages to your me.com or Mac.com screen name.

You can get help specific to iChat. Click the Help menu, and then click iChat Help. The application help system works just like Spotlight help.

For Your Information

Using Chat Service Plug-ins

If you would like more functionality when you chat, you should check out chat service plug-ins. Chat service plug-ins from third-party developers allow you to add new chat services to iChat (**New!**). Simple perform an Internet search on iChat service plug-ins. After you find the one you want, download it to your computer, and then double-click it to install it like any other app. Read the third-party documentation for information on use of the service plug-in.

Viewing iChat

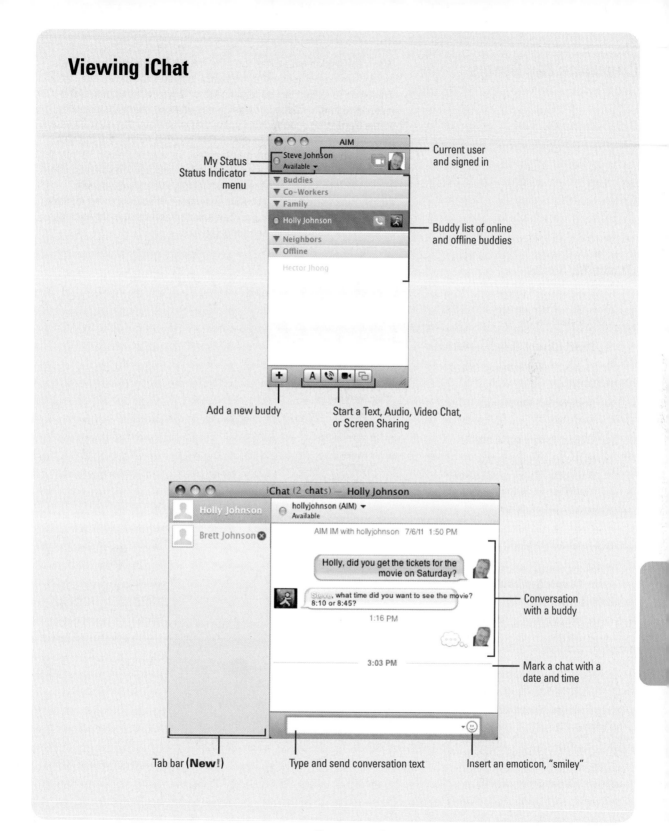

My Status
Status Indicator
menu

Current user
and signed in

Buddy list of online
and offline buddies

Add a new buddy

Start a Text, Audio, Video Chat,
or Screen Sharing

Conversation
with a buddy

Mark a chat with a
date and time

Tab bar (New!)

Type and send conversation text

Insert an emoticon, "smiley"

Changing My Status

When you sign in with iChat, the program notifies buddies currently online from your Buddy list that you are available to chat (green status). While you're signed in, you might need to leave your computer for a meeting or lunch. Instead of signing out, you can change your online status (red) to let your buddies know that you're busy, away from your desk, on the phone, or out to lunch. When you're away, your buddies see that you're idle, and any message you receive is waiting for you. If you don't want your buddies to see or send messages to you, you can go offline. If you don't see the status message you want, you can quickly customize one to suit your own needs. If you are using multiple Accounts at the same time, you can have different status for each one or the same status for all accounts (**New!**).

Change My Status

1. Click the Status Indicator.

2. Click a status type.

 - **Status (Green).** Online available.
 - **iTunes.** Online listening to a song.
 - **Status (Red).** Online not available.
 - **Offline.** Offline not available.
 - **Use Same Status for All Accounts.** Check to set same status for all accounts. (**New!**)

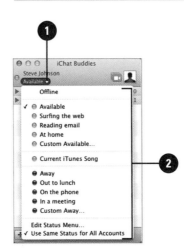

Create a Custom Status Message

1. Click the Status Indicator, and then click **Custom Available** or **Custom Away**.

2. Type a custom message, and then press Return.

Did You Know?

You can change items from the Status Indicator menu. Click the Status Indicator menu, click Edit Status Menu, click the Add (+) or Remove (-) buttons, double-click items to edit, or drag items to order, and then click OK.

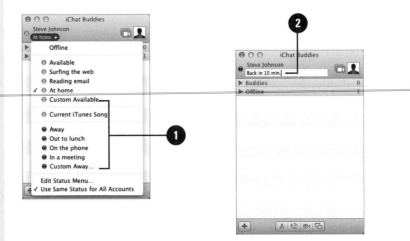

Using the iChat Status Menu

The iChat Status menu appears as a chat balloon icon on the right side of the menu bar for all applications. When the balloon icon is empty, you're online; when there is a line in the middle, you're away or offline. If you turn on the iChat Status menu, you can still receive instant messages, view online buddies, and change your status when you quit the iChat program. You can turn the Status menu on in the General pane of iChat Preferences, where you set other status options when you switch users or your computer is inactive. When the Status menu is turned off and you quit iChat, you're logged out of AIM and Bonjour messaging.

Turn On the iChat Status Menu

1. Click the **iChat** menu, and then click **Preferences**.

2. Click **General**.

3. Select the **Show status in menu bar** check box.

4. Select or clear the **When I Quit iChat, set my status to offline** check box.

5. Select or clear the **Set my status to Away after the computer is inactive** check box.

6. Set additional status options after your computer is inactive.

7. Click the **Close** button.

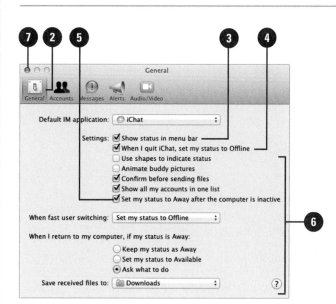

Use the iChat Status Menu

1. Click the **iChat Status** menu, and then select an available option:

 ◆ **A status.** Click Offline, Invisible (**New!**), Available, or Away; you can also select custom available or away messages.

 If you don't want to be seen offline, you can go invisible (**New!**).

 ◆ **A buddy.** Click the name of an online buddy.

 ◆ **Buddy List.** Click to display your Buddy List.

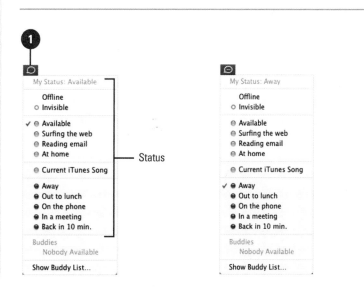

Adding a Buddy

Before you can send instant messages to other people, they need to be in your Buddy list. Your Buddy list shows you a unified list (**New!**)—no matter what the chat service—of who's currently online and offline, their audio and video capabilities, and if they are available for chatting. You can add a person who has a screen name from one or more chat accounts (**New!**) to your Buddy list. You can add as many buddies as you like to your Buddies list. You can add them from your Address Book or type new ones. When you add a new person to your Buddy list, a new card is added to your Address Book. Your Buddy list is stored on an instant message server, so you can log in to your account from any computer and see if your buddies are online.

Add a Buddy

1. If necessary, click the **Window** menu, and then click **Buddy List** to display the Buddy List window.

2. Click the **Add** (+) button in the Buddy List window, and then click **Add Buddy**.

3. Type an account name, select a group, type the first and last screen name for the person, or click the **Expand/ Collapse** button, and then select an address from the Address Book.

 TIMESAVER *If your buddy uses more than one screen name, you can type more than one by separating each with a comma.*

4. Click **Add**.

Did You Know?

You can quickly delete a buddy from your Buddy list. Click a buddy in the Buddy list, press Delete, and then click OK. People who are removed from your list can still contact you unless you block them.

You can view and edit information about a buddy. Select a buddy in the Buddy list, click the Buddies menu, and then click Show Info. The information shown is typed by your buddy.

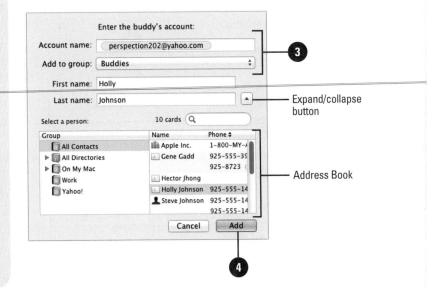

Expand/collapse button

Address Book

Changing a Buddy Picture

You can change the picture that appears next to your name in the Buddy List and in message windows, along with the ones that appear next to your buddies. The picture is known as the Buddy icon. The Buddy icon you select appears in the Buddy List of those in which you have a chat. To change your Buddy icon, drag an image file—64 x 64 pixels is recommended—to your name in the Buddy List. In addition to an image file, you can also use an animated picture, also known as a GIF or animated GIF, as a buddy picture, which you can also create using Photo Booth or iPhoto (**New!**).

Change a Buddy Picture

1. If necessary, click the **Window** menu, and then click **Buddy List** to display the Buddy List window.

2. Select the buddy you want to change.

3. Click the **Buddies** menu, and then click **Show Info**.

4. Click the **Address Card** tab.

5. Clear the **Always use this picture** check box.

6. Drag the image or animated GIF you want to the picture box.

 ◆ **Enable Buddy Picture Animation.** Click the **iChat** menu, click **Preferences**, click **General**, select the **Animate Buddy Pictures** check box, and then click the **Close** button.

7. Select the **Always use this Picture** check box.

8. Click the **Close** button.

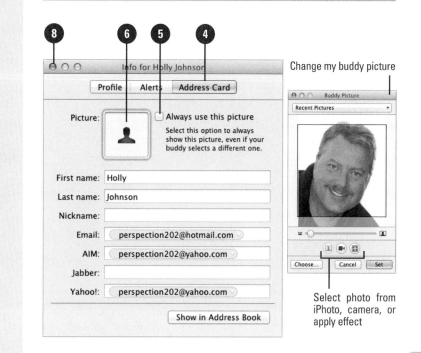

Change my buddy picture

Select photo from iPhoto, camera, or apply effect

For Your Information

Creating an Animated GIF in Photo Booth

If you don't have an animated GIF, you can create one using Photo Booth. Open Photo Booth from the Applications folder, and then click the button for four-up picture format. If you want to add effects, click the Effects button and then select a video effect. Click the Camera button to take a series of four pictures, select the animation, and then export it as a file or set it as a buddy picture. To export it, click the File menu, click Export, specify a name and folder, and then click Save. To set it as a buddy picture, click the Buddy Picture button, specify the size, and then click Set.

Creating and Managing Buddy Groups

As your Buddy list grows, you may want to organize your buddies into groups. iChat makes it easy to create your own groups and use the one predefined group called Buddies that comes with iChat. Once you have organized your groups, you can simply drag buddies from one group to another. You can use the triangles next to the group name to hide and display buddies in a group. If a group changes, you can rename it, if a group is not where you want it, you can drag to move or merge it, or if you no longer need a group, you can remove it. You can also quickly search for buddies using the Search field (**New!**).

Turn On or Off the Use of Groups and Offline Groups

1. Click the **View** menu.

2. Click **Use Groups** or **Use Offline Group**.

 TIMESAVER *Press Shift+⌘+H.*

3. To turn off the use of Groups or Offline Groups, click the **View** menu, and then click **Use Groups** or **Use Offline Group** again.

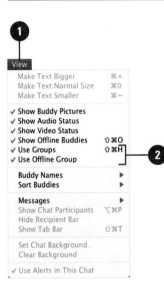

Create a Buddy Group

1. If necessary, click the **Window** menu, and then click **Buddy List** to display the Buddy List window.

2. Click the **Add** (+) button in the Buddy List window, and then click **Add Group**.

3. Type a name for the group.

4. Click **Add**.

Manage Buddies and Groups

1. If necessary, click the **Window** menu, and then click **Buddy List** to display the Buddy List window.

2. Select from the following options:

 ◆ **Search for buddies.** Press +F, enter a name or part of a name. As you type, iChat filters your buddy list (**New!**). Select a buddy from the results. Click **Done** to exit it.

 ◆ **Display all group members.** Click the **View** menu, and then click **Use Groups** or **Use Offline Groups**.

 ◆ **Display group members.** Click the arrow next to the group name.

 ◆ **Move a buddy into a group.** Drag the buddy to a group.

 ◆ **Copy a buddy into a group.** Press and hold down the Option key while you drag the buddy to each group.

 ◆ **Move a group.** Drag the buddy group to a new position.

 ◆ **Merge groups.** Drag the buddy group onto another one.

 ◆ **Delete a group.** Click the **Add** (+) button, click **Edit Group**, select the group, click the **Delete** (-) button, and then click **OK**.

 You can't delete a group with buddies in multiple groups, but you can delete a group with the only one buddy in it. You can't delete the last group in the list; you need to always have at least one.

 ◆ **Rename a group.** Click the **Add** (+) button, click **Edit Group**, select the group, click the group again, type a new name, and then click **OK**.

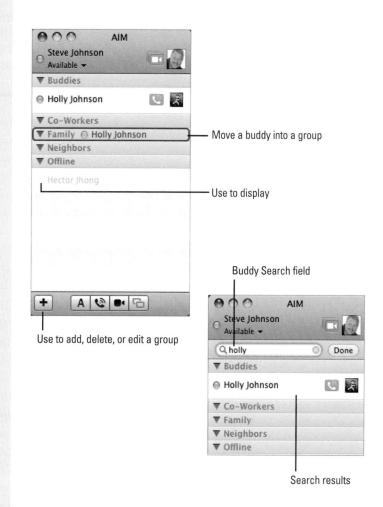

Move a buddy into a group

Use to display

Use to add, delete, or edit a group

Buddy Search field

Search results

Sending and Receiving Instant Messages

An instant message is an online typewritten conversation in real-time between two or more buddies. As you type an instant message, you can format your messages by using fonts and color and by inserting graphical symbols called **emoticons**, or "smiley," such as a happy face, which help convey your emotions. You can have instant message conversations with several different buddies at once. When you send a instant message to a group, all participants receive the message and all responses are visible to everyone involved. If a buddy has multiple accounts, you can select the one you want to use to send to and from. If you have multiple chat windows open at the same time, you can merge them all together into a single tabbed window or move them to new windows (**New!**).

Send and Receive Instant Messages

1. To start a chat, select one or more names in the Buddy list, and then click the **Start A Text Chat** button.

 TIMESAVER *Double-click a person in your buddy list to start a chat session.*

 To respond to a text chat invitation, click the invitation window, type a message, and then click **Accept**.

2. If the buddy has multiple accounts, click the **Account** menu, and then select a **To** or **From** account.

3. Type your message in the box. To start a new line, press Shift+Return.

4. Press Return, and then wait.

5. Click the **View** menu, and then click **Show Tab Bar**. (**New!**)

6. To add another person to the chat, click the **View** menu, click **Show Chat Participants**, click the **Add** (+) button, and then click a buddy.

7. To move or merge chat windows, click the **Window** menu, and then click **Move Chat to New Window** or **Merge All Chat Windows**. (**New!**)

8. When you're done, click the **Close** button to end the session.

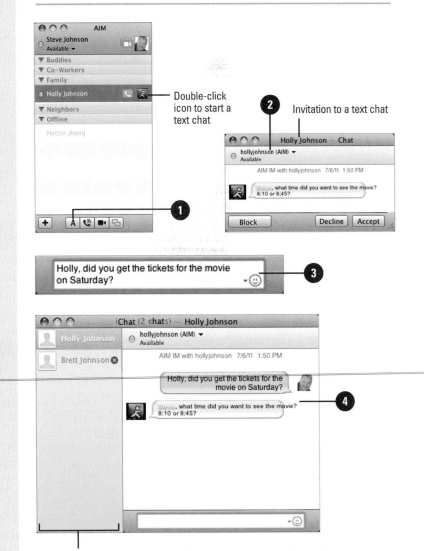

Double-click icon to start a text chat

Invitation to a text chat

Tab bar with all two Chat windows merged into one (**New!**)

Format Message Text

1. Type and then select the text you want to format.

2. Click the **Format** menu, and then click the **Show Fonts**.

3. Specify the font, font style, size, color, and effect you want, and then preview the result in the sample box.

4. Click the **Close** button, and then send the formatted message.

Insert Emoticons

1. In the Chat window, click the **Emoticons** button.

 TIMESAVER *Type a smiley using the keyboard, such as ":-)" and iChat inserts a corresponding graphic. Point to a smiley to view its type.*

2. Type your text, and then click the icon you want to insert into the conversation.

3. Press Return.

Emoticon in chat

Did You Know?

You can collect all open chats into a single tabbed window. Click the iChat menu, click Preferences, click Messages, select the Collect Chats Into A Single Window check box, and then click the Close button.

You can auto-reply when you're away. Click the iChat menu, click Preferences, click Messages, select the Auto-reply With My Away Message check box, and then click the Close button.

For Your Information

Adding Date and Time Stamps

During a long chat, you can insert your date and time stamp to mark a transcript. In a chat, click the Edit menu, and then click Mark Transcript. To clear a chat, click the Edit menu, and then click Clear Transcript. This is helpful when you automatically save a transcript for review later. Click the iChat menu, click Preferences, click Messages, select the Automatically Save Chat Transcripts To check box, and then click the pop-up to select a folder location. To specify the number of messages to save, select the In new chat window, show check box, click the pop-up to select an option.

Blocking a Buddy

If you no longer want to receive instant messages from a specific buddy, you can block the buddy from sending you instant messages. When you block a buddy, you appear to be offline to the person, who doesn't know blocking is turned on. Blocking a buddy moves them from your Allow list to your Block list in the Privacy pane of iChat Preferences.

Block or Unblock a Buddy

1. Click the **iChat** menu, and then click **Preferences**.

 TIMESAVER *Select the buddy in the Buddy list, click the Buddies menu, click Block buddy name, and then click Block.*

2. Click **Accounts**, and then select the account with the buddy you want to block.

3. Click the **Security** tab.

4. Click a privacy option:

 ◆ **Allow anyone**. Click to unblock everyone.

 ◆ **Allow people in my Buddy List**. Click to unblock buddies in my Buddy List.

 ◆ **Allow specific people**. Click the option, and then click Edit List to select buddies.

 ◆ **Block everyone**. Click to block everyone.

 ◆ **Block specific people**. Click the option, and then click Edit List to add and remove buddies.

5. Select or clear the **Block others from seeing that I am idle** check box.

6. Click the **Close** button.

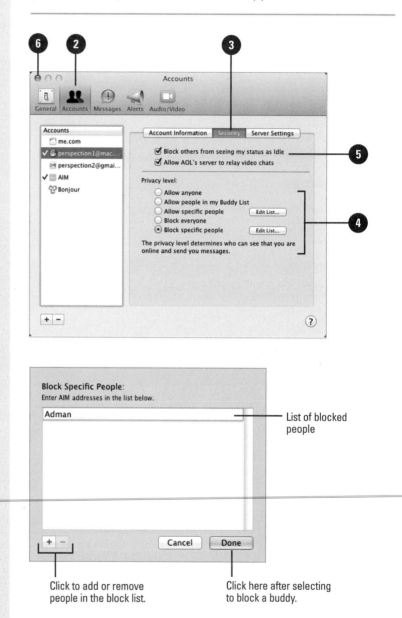

List of blocked people

Click to add or remove people in the block list.

Click here after selecting to block a buddy.

Did You Know?

You can search for a buddy in Spotlight. Select the buddy in the Buddy list, click the Buddies menu, and then click Search in Spotlight.

Sending a File During an Instant Message

While you are conversing in iChat, you can send a buddy a file or hyperlink. You can send many different types of files, including pictures, documents, and music. When you send a picture, it's displayed right beside your text in the Chat window, which you can instantly preview with Quick Look. When you send any other type of file, a request to transfer the file is sent to your buddy. You are notified when your buddy accepts or declines your request. Before you receive files over the Internet, make sure you have virus protection software to protect your computer. You can also send a hyperlink that points to a Web site. When your buddy receives a message with a link, the person can click it to open the Web address in their Web browser.

Send a File or Hyperlink

1 Start a chat with the buddy to whom you want to send the file or hyperlink.

2 Type your message in the box at the bottom of the window.

3 Click the **Edit** menu, and then click one of the following:

◆ **Send a File.** Click **Attach File**, navigate to and select the file you want to send (for best results, use JPEG or GIF), and then click **Open**. A small icon appears to indicate the picture.

TIMESAVER *Drag the picture file to the area where you type your message.*

◆ **Send a Hyperlink.** Click **Add Hyperlink**, type a Web address, and then click **OK**.

4 Type any additional text if you want, and then press Return.

If you're sending a picture, the image appears in the chat window; if it's a file, wait for the recipient to accept or decline the file; or if it's a hyperlink, the link appears in the chat window.

5 To open a file or hyperlink, click the file (to preview in Quick Look) or link in the chat window.

Send a picture

Send a file

Send a hyperlink

For Your Information

Checking File Status

You can send or receive files from your buddies. File transfers with iChat don't have a size limit, so you can send large files. However, large files can take awhile. To help you manage the file transfers, you can use the File Transfers manager in iChat. The File Transfers manager displays a list of transferred files and status for any current file transfers, just like the Downloads manager. To send a file, select the buddy you want to send the file, click the Buddies menu, click Send, select the file you want, and then click Send. Your buddy can accept or reject the file. You can send only one file at a time. If you want to send multiple files, compress them together into a single file.

Having an Audio and Video Chat

With iChat, you can talk to others over the Internet as you do on a regular phone, and you can use video to see others and let others see you as you converse. Once you set up your computer hardware and software, you're ready to communicate over the Internet. You have two communication choices: audio only, or audio and video. With audio only, you speak into a microphone and hear the other person's response over your speakers. With audio and video, you send video to others so they receive live images as well as sound. If the buddies you call don't have a video camera, they'll see you, but you won't see them. iChat supports only one video or audio chat at a time.

Have a Audio or Video Chat

1. If necessary, click the **Window** menu, and then click **Buddy List**.

2. To start a chat, select a name in the Buddy list, and then click the **Start A Video Chat** button or **Start An Audio Chat** button.

 To respond to an audio or video chat invitation, click the invitation window, and then click **Accept**.

 To decline or block a chat invitation, click **Decline** or **Block**.

3. Start talking.

4. Use video controls on the Video menu or use the following:

 ◆ Size Video Window. Click the double arrow button to switch between normal and full-screen modes. You can also drag the bottom right corner of the video window.

 ◆ Invite. Click the **Invite** button to invite another person to chat.

 ◆ Pause Video. Option+click the **Microphone** button. Click the button again to start it.

 ◆ Mute Audio. Click the **Microphone** button.

5. When you're done, click the **Close** button to end the session.

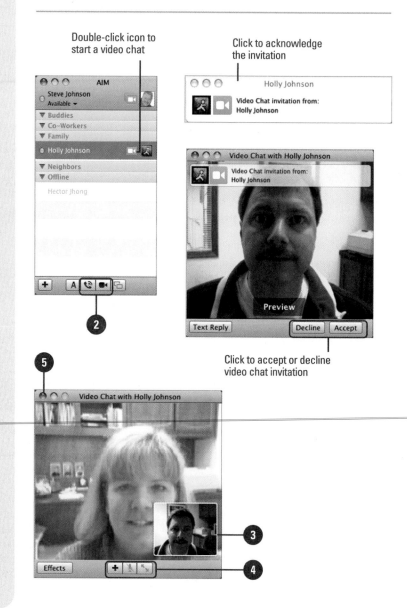

Double-click icon to start a video chat

Click to acknowledge the invitation

Click to accept or decline video chat invitation

Change Video Bandwidth Speed and Preferences

1. Click the **iChat** menu, and then click **Preferences**.

2. Click **Audio/Video**.

3. If available, click the **Camera** pop-up, and then select an installed camera.

4. Click the **Microphone** pop-up, and then select an installed microphone.

5. Click the **Bandwidth Limit** pop-up, and then select a video speed option for your computer's performance and quality.

6. Select or clear the check boxes to automatically open iChat when the camera is turned on or play repeated ring sound when invited to a chat.

7. Click the **Close** button.

Did You Know?

You can monitor a video chat. Click the Video menu, and then click Connection Doctor. The frame rate shows the number of frames the video plays per second (fps). The Bit Rate setting show the average number of bits that one second of video data consumes in kilobits per second (kbps). The call duration shows how long the chats lasts.

You can take a picture of your video chat. ⌘+click the video chat window and drag the image (a JPEG file) out of the window to a buddy icon in your Buddy list or a location on your hard disk. You can also press ⌘+C to copy a picture of your chat and then press ⌘+V to paste it in another document.

iChat Performance and Quality

Option	Standard	Enhanced	High
Window Size	352x288 to Full Screen	352x288 to Full Screen	352x288 to Full Screen
Video Resolution	176x144	176x144	352x288
Frames Per Second (fps)	15	20	20/30
System Required	> 600 Mhz G3 or 350 Mhz G4	> 1Ghz G4	> dual 800 Mhz G4 and any G5
Bandwidth	100-500 Kbps	100-500 Kbps	Above 500 Kbps

Enhancing a Video Chat

As you hold a video conversation in iChat, you can enhance your experience by adding video effects or backdrops to the video window. The video effects are provided by Photo Booth and the backdrops are professionally designed by Apple. You can use the ones provided, download new ones, or create your own. If you have Mac OS X and a fast broadband Internet connection (300 Kbps or faster), you can host an iChat theater presentation that contains photos, keynote presentation slides, or movies with high resolution 640 x480 from your desktop while your buddies view it on their computer in an iChat video window.

Enhance an Audio or Video Chat

1. Start a video chat with one or more buddies.

2. Click **Effects**.

3. To view the video effects and backdrops, click the left and right arrow buttons.

4. Click the video effect thumbnail you want to use.

 ◆ **Photo Booth Effects.** Unique video effects, such as X-Ray, Thermal Camera, and Pop Art.

 ◆ **Backdrops.** Backgrounds you can be in front of.

5. To add your own backdrop, drag it from the desktop or Finder window to a blank backdrop placeholder (User Backdrop 1, etc.) in the Video Effects window.

6. To remove the video effect, click the **Original** thumbnail.

7. When you're done, click the **Close** button to close the Video Effects window.

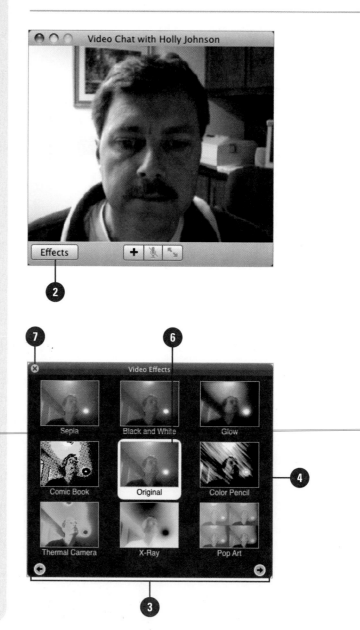

Host an iChat Theater Presentation

1. Start a video chat with one or more buddies.

2. Click the **Invite** button, and then click **Share a File With iChat Theater** or **Share iPhoto With iChat Theater**.

 TIMESAVER *With an open video chat, you can drag the presentation item to the video chat window.*

3. Select the items you want to present:

 ◆ **Photos, Text, and Other Files.**

 ◆ **QuickTime Movies.**

 ◆ **iPhoto Album Slide Shows.**

 ◆ **Keynote Slide Shows.**

 If you can open an item as a Quick Look, you can use it in iChat Theater.

4. Click **Share**.

5. Deliver the presentation.

6. When you're done, click the **Close** button to end the presentation.

7. Click the **Close** button to end the session.

Did You Know?

You can record a video chat. Start a video chat, click the Video menu, click Record Chat, and then click the Stop button or close the video chat window to stop recording. The recorded chat is saved to the iChats folder in the Documents folder by default.

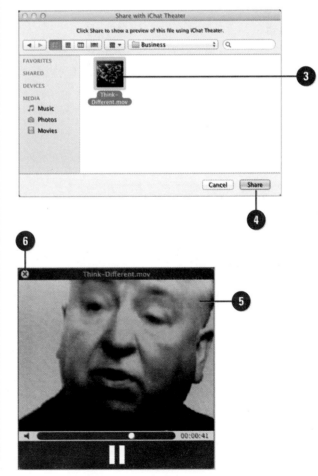

Chatting on a Local Network

If you don't have an instant message account or server, you can still use iChat to chat with others on your local network. Instead of communicating with a central Internet server, each computer communicates directly with each other over network cables. iChat also works with a wireless connection using AirPort over a local network or the Internet. Bonjour allows you to chat with people on your local network or wireless local community. You can't add a Bonjour user to your Buddy list. The user names are based on the log-in settings on each person's computer and are not AIM screen names. Unlike regular instant message, when you type a Bonjour instant message, each character you type is sent immediately unless you turn off the default setting in the Messages pane of iChat Preferences.

Turn On Bonjour Instant Messaging

1. Click the **iChat** menu, and then click **Preferences**.

2. Click **Accounts**.

3. Click **Bonjour**.

4. Select the **Enable Bonjour instant messaging** check box.

5. Click the **Close** button.

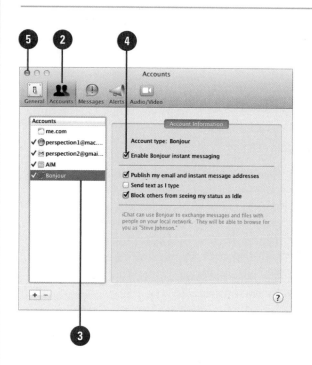

Did You Know?

You can send Bonjour message when you're done typing. Click the iChat menu, click Preferences, click Messages, clear the Send Text As I Type (Bonjour Only) check box, and then click the Close button.

You can send a SMS (short message service) text message to a mobile phone. Click the File menu, click Send SMS, click the pop-up, select the account from which you want to send the text message (you can't use Bonjour, Jabber, or Google Talk), type your buddy's cell phone number, and then click OK.

Start Bonjour Messaging

1. Click the **Window** menu, and then click **Bonjour List**.

 The Bonjour window opens, showing iChat local network users who are available for chatting.

2. Double-click the user to whom you want to send an instant message.

3. Type your message in the box at the bottom of the window.

4. Press Return, and then wait for a reply.

5. When you're done, click the **Close** button to end the session.

Did You Know?

You can use a keyboard shortcut to bring iChat to the front. Click the iChat menu, click Preferences, click Messages, select the Use A Keyboard Shortcut To Bring iChat To The Front check box, click the pop-up to select a shortcut, and then click the Close button.

You can quickly close other chats with a click. If you have multiple chats open at the same time, you can close all the other chats except the active one. Control-click the active chat, and then click Close Other Chats.

For Your Information

Sharing Your Screen with a Buddy

If you and your buddy are using Mac OS X, you can use iChat with any of the support account types to share your screens as if you were sitting in front of it. When you share your screen, your buddy has the same control over your computer as you do. During the screen sharing session, iChat starts an audio chat so you can talk about what your doing. To share your screen, select your buddy, click the Buddies menu, and then click Share My Screen or Ask To Share. You can switch between the two open desktops and copy files between your computers. When you're done, press Control+Esc to end the screen sharing session.

Changing the Appearance of a Chat

iChat makes it easy to customize the appearance of a chat to suit your own style and preference. You can modify the appearance of the balloons, or change a font style in a chat. The changes you make affect the format of your messages on your screen as well as messages on your buddies screen unless they have chosen to reformat incoming messages. When you reformat incoming messages, you override your chat buddy settings and display all incoming messages using your preferences. You can set your preferences and reformat settings in the Messages pane of iChat Preferences. You can also change the background of the chat window to a picture, which only appears on your computer.

Change the Appearance of a Chat

1. Click the **iChat** menu, and then click **Preferences**.

2. Click **Messages**.

3. Select or specify the various options you want to use:

 ◆ **My balloon color.** Click the pop-up, and then select a color.

 ◆ **My font color.** Click the pop-up, and then select a font color.

 ◆ **Set Font.** Click to select a font.

 ◆ **Reformat incoming messages.** Check to use your preferred settings, and then select a ballon and font color, and a font for the sender.

4. To highlight your name when its mentioned in a chat, select the **Watch for my name in incoming messages** check box.

5. Click the **Close** button.

Change the Chat Window Background

1. Click the **View** menu, and then click **Set Chat Background**.

2. Locate and select the background image file you want to use.

3. Click the image file you want to open.

4. Click **Open**.

Did You Know?

You can quickly remove a background from the chat window. Click the View menu, and then click Clear Background.

You can view a chat as text. Click the View menu, point to Messages, and then click Show As Text.

You can save an instant message. Click the File menu, click Save A Copy As, type a file name, select a location, and then click Save. To review a chat, click the File menu, click Open, select a transcript file, and then click Open.

You can save chats automatically. Click the iChat menu, click Preferences, click Messages, select the Save Chat Transcripts To check box, and then click the pop-up to select a folder location. To specify the number of messages to save, select the In new chat window, show check box, click the pop-up to select an option. Click the Close button.

Background image in Chat window

Getting Notification Alerts

When certain events, such as messages arrive or buddies log in, iChat can notify you with a sound, spoken message, or bounce of the iChat icon in the Dock. You can set alerts that apply to every buddy in the Alerts pane of iChat Preferences, or you can set specific notification alerts for each buddy in the Actions pane of the Show Info dialog.

Set Up Notification Alerts

1. Click the **iChat** menu, and then click **Preferences**.

2. Click **Alerts**.

3. Click the **Event** pop-up, and then select the type of event you want to be notified of.

4. Select or clear the **Play Sound** check box. If you select it, click the pop-up, select an occurrence, and then select or clear the Repeat check box if you want the alert to occur every time.

5. Select or clear the **Bounce icon in the Dock** check box. If you select the check box, select or clear the **Repeat** check box.

6. Select or clear the **Speak an announcement** check box, and then drag the slider to set the speech volume.

7. Select or clear the **Run AppleScript** check box. If you select it, choose the script you want.

8. Click the **Close** button.

Did You Know?

You can specify different alerts for each buddy. Select a buddy in your Buddy List, click the Buddies menu, click Show Info, click Alerts, select the options you want, and then click the Close button.

Getting Stared with FaceTime

FaceTime (**New!**) for Mac allows you make video calls to iPad 2, iPhone 4, iPod Touch (4th generation with iOS 4.1 or later), or another Mac. You can hear a voice and see a face without distracting window frame and controls in 720p HD clarity along with support for a widescreen 16:9 aspect ratio. All you need to get started is an Ethernet or Wi-Fi connection to the Internet, a camera and microphone, and an Apple ID and e-mail address, which you'll need to verify before first use. Just find the person you want to call in your contracts list or Address Book.

Get Started with FaceTime

1. Click the **FaceTime** icon in the Dock.

2. Enter your Apple ID and password, and then click **Sign In** or click **Create New Account** and follow the on-screen instructions.

 ◆ On first use, enter the e-mail address you want to use, and then click **Next**. Check your e-mail for a verification. It needs to be verified before you can use it with FaceTime.

3. Click the **FaceTime** menu, and then click **Preferences**.

4. Specify the FaceTime preference options you want:

 ◆ Turn On/Off FaceTime. Turns on or off FaceTime.

 ◆ Sign Out. Blocks all incoming calls. Click **Accounts**, and then click **Sign Out**.

 ◆ Location. Changes phone locations. Click **Accounts**, and then click **Change Location**.

 ◆ Email Address. Click to change or remove an email address.

 ◆ Add Another Email. Click to add another email account to FaceTime.

5. Click **Done**.

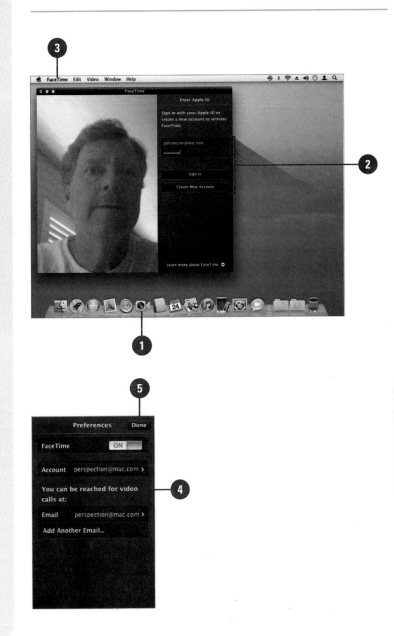

Making a Video Call with FaceTime

With FaceTime (**New!**) for Mac, video calls automatically adjust from landscape to portrait and back depending on the orientation or camera in use—front or rear—of the mobile device you're calling. However, if you prefer one over the other, you can set it in preferences. When you call an iPhone, you use a phone number. When you call an iPad, iPod touch or Mac, you use an e-mail address. When someone tries to reach you, the call rings through on every Mac or mobile device—iPad, iPhone, or iPod touch—you own even if FaceTime isn't running, unless you turn off FaceTime in preferences.

Video Calling with FaceTime

1. Click the **FaceTime** icon in the Dock and then sign in.

 ◆ To quickly return or re-initiate a call, Control-click the **FaceTime** icon in the Dock, select a call from the Recent Calls list, and then click **FaceTime**.

2. Select a contact from **All Contacts** or a group (click **Contacts**, and then click **Groups**). You can use the Search field to find a contact.

3. To place a call, click a phone number (iPhone) or click an e-mail address (iPad, iPod touch, or Mac). To end a call, click **End** or **Cancel**, or exit FaceTime.

4. To exit FaceTime (and still receive calls), click the **FaceTime** menu, and then click **Quit FaceTime**.

5. To receive a video call, click **Accept** in the call window. To block a call, click **Decline**.

6. To change orientation, click the **Video** menu, and then click **Use Portrait** or **Use Landscape**.

7. To turn FaceTime off (don't receive calls) or on, click the **FaceTime** menu, and then click **Turn FaceTime Off** or **Turn FaceTime On**.

 ◆ To pause a video call, click the **FaceTime** menu, and then click **Hide FaceTime**. To resume, click the **FaceTime** icon in Dock.

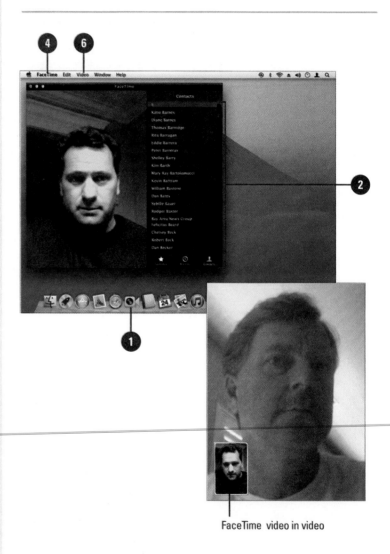

FaceTime video in video

Working with Music and Media

Introduction

Macs were born for multimedia, and even after more than 25 years, they're still considered a front runner when it comes to images, movies, and music. Mac OS X is bundled with several old friends, iTunes, and DVD and QuickTime Players, as well as some newer ones, Photo Booth.

The **iTunes** application is a software jukebox that comes with Mac OS X, yet it's also available on Microsoft Windows, so you can share music between Macintosh and Windows. iTunes allows you to sort through and organize your digital music collection, convert CD's into the digital format, and even burn your favorite music onto a CD. If that's not enough, iTunes come complete with a built-in link to the iTunes music store. So if you have an Internet connection, you're one click away from a music store that contains the latest songs, as well as billions (yes, I said billions) of songs from the past. And for those of you that like to listen to the radio while you work, iTunes comes equipped with its own Internet Radio.

If you have an iSight or other camera attached to your computer, you can use Photo Booth to capture photos just like you were sitting in a photo booth at a carnival. You can capture individual photos or create a short movie and add a backdrop or visual effects.

If your Mac includes an Apple Remote, you can use it to control iTunes, where you can access and play music and playlists, iPhoto slide shows, and videos and DVDs on your Mac or TV. You can also use the Apple Remote to deliver Keynote presentations and play music with the iPod Hi-Fi. The Apple Remote uses an infrared (IR) reception and works up to 30 feet within an unobstructed line of sight.

What You'll Do

Start and Set Up iTunes

View the iTunes Window

Set up iTunes to Automatically Play CDs

Get Music and Media from CDs and the iTunes Music Store

Use and Create Playlists

Add Media to a Playlist

Socialize with Ping

Subscribe and Play Podcasts

Use iPod or iPhone with iTunes

Listen to Internet Radio

Erase a CD or DVD

Burn CDs and Export to MP3 Players

Set iTunes Preferences

Capture Photos in Photo Booth

Record Movies in Photo Booth

Add Photo Booth Effects

Play and Browse DVD Movies

Customize the DVD Player

Play and Create QuickTime Movies

Explore iMovie, iDVD, and iPhoto

Starting and Setting Up iTunes

You can conveniently start iTunes from the Dock. Simply, click the iTunes icon in the Dock to start iTunes. The first time you start iTunes, the programs walks you through the process of setting up an Apple account (it's easy if you have a MobileMe account) and iTunes Store, which helps you discover new music and videos from your iTunes library. When you sign in to iTunes, you authorize your computer to play iTunes store purchases. When you download a media item, Apple lets you copy and play that item on up to five authorized machines (Mac or Windows). If you want to use a sixth computer, you need to deauthorize one and then authorize the other.

Start and Set Up iTunes

1. Click the **iTunes** icon in the Dock.

 ◆ You can also click the **Launchpad** icon in the Dock, and then click the **iTunes** icon.

2. If you started iTunes for the first time, follow the iTunes Setup Assistant step by step instructions to set up iTunes.

3. To use the iTunes Store, click the **Store** menu, click **Sign In** or **Create Account**, and then follow the account review or setup process as requested.

4. To download album artwork, click the **Advanced** menu, and then click **Get Album Artwork**.

5. To authorize or deauthorize a computer, click the **Store** menu, and then click **Authorize** or **Deauthorize**.

 ◆ To deauthorize a computer to play items from the Audible Web site, click the **Advanced** menu, and then click **Deauthorize Audible Account**.

 ◆ To deauthorize a computer you no longer own, you can deauthorize all your computers at once (only available once a year). Click the **Store** menu, and then click **View My Account**.

Create an account to iTunes Store

Viewing the iTunes Window

When you open iTunes, you're working in an organized window that gives you access to your movie and music collections, creates new Playlists, organizes your music, converts existing CD's into an iTunes collection, and burns selected media onto a CD or DVD (a writable CD or DVD drive is required). The same iTunes window that lets you listen and organize your music also lets you listen to Internet Radio and podcasts, or purchase music, movies, books, TV shows, and other media through the iTunes Music Store. In other words, once you open the iTunes application, everything you need to enhance your music experience, including listening to audio books, is right in front of your eyes.

Setting Up iTunes to Automatically Play CDs

When you open the iTunes application for the first time you'll be asked a few preference questions. For example, you are asked if you want iTunes to be the application your Mac uses for playing music files from the Internet, whether you want iTunes to ask permission every time it connects to the Internet, and whether you want the program to scan your home folder for all of your music. If you select not to have iTunes automatically scan your home drive for music files, you can always drag a folder into the iTunes window. It will automatically scan the folder for any music files, and then place them within the active Playlist.

Set Up iTunes to Automatically Play CDs

1. Click the **System Preferences** icon in the Dock, and then click the **CDs & DVDs** icon.

2. Click the **When you insert a music CD** pop-up, and then select **Open iTunes**.

3. Click the **Close** button to close the System Preferences window.

	CDs & DVDs	
When you insert a blank CD:	Ask what to do	
When you insert a music CD:	Open iTunes	
When you insert a picture CD:	Ignore	
When you insert a video DVD:	Open DVD Player	

Did You Know?

You can select another program to play music CDs. If you find an application better than iTunes at managing your record collection, you can always select Another Application from the CDs & DVDs pop-up menu.

Getting and Playing Music from CDs

If you have music on CD, you can quickly import it into iTunes. If you have System Preferences for CDs & DVDs set to automatically open CDs in iTunes, all you need to do is insert the CD and iTunes does the rest. The music on your CD is copied to your computer in your iTunes music library. Importing music can also be accomplished through the iTunes menu system, or it can be as simple as a drag and drop. After you download music from your CD, you can view and work with music displayed in a list, album list, as a grid (**New!**), or in Cover Flow, a 3D visual approach to flipping through your libraries. When you want to play a song, you can use the playback controls in the upper-left corner of the iTunes window or the ones in the full screen Cover Flow view.

Get Music from a CD and Play it in iTunes

1. Insert the CD into your drive.

2. If an alert message appears, asking for confirmation, click **Yes**.

 The music automatically downloads to your iTunes Music Library.

3. To view the music in different ways, click one of the view buttons: **List View**, **Album View**, **Grid View** (**New!**), and **Cover Flow View**.

 ◆ **Cover Flow.** Click the cover art Left and Right Arrows or drag the slider to view the music, or click the **Full Screen** button to view and playback music.

4. To play the music, select the tracks you want to play, and then use the playback controls.

Did You Know?

You can set CD import options in iTunes. Click the iTunes menu, click Preferences, click General, click Import Settings, select the options you want, and then click OK twice.

Song importing from a CD

Full Screen button

Getting Media from the iTunes Music Store

The iTunes music store is a dream come true for all of us that love music, but don't necessarily want to buy the whole album just to get our favorite song. The iTunes music store was not the first to make the purchase of songs or albums and other media easy, but they are considered the best at doing it. All you have to do to get started is sign in with an Apple ID and password, click the iTunes Store option, and that's it (assuming you have an Internet connection). You're ready to start hunting for the music, movies, TV shows, App Store programs, books, and podcasts you love. Once you download a media item, Apple lets you copy and play that item on authorized machines. When you move media to another computer, you are prompted to type in your Apple ID, which authorizes that computer to play that media.

Use the iTunes Music Store

① Click the **iTunes** icon in the Dock.

② Click **iTunes Store** in the Source pane.

③ Click on any of the various links to access that particular title.

④ Use the Search field and type a title, artist, or keyword to search, and then press Return.

⑤ Click an item to open it, if needed.

⑥ To navigate, click the **Back**, **Next**, **Home**, or category buttons below the toolbar. Click a button arrow to narrow down a category (**New!**).

Did You Know?

You can download songs for a buck.
My favorite part of iTunes is the ability to download selected songs from an album, without having to download an entire album. You can download any song for around a buck. In addition, the Music Store gives you the ability to download entire albums at a reduced rate over the individual songs.

7 To preview an item, double-click the item or click the **Preview** button; availability varies depending on the media item.

8 Click the buy/purchase, download, or subscribe button for the type of item you want; the button name varies depending on the item.

IMPORTANT *If you haven't set up your payment options (credit cards), Mac OS X prompts you to do so at this time.*

The media item is downloaded to your iTunes library. Click **Downloads** in the Source pane to display progress or pause, resume, or stop the process.

9 Quit iTunes.

Did You Know?

You can shrink the iTunes window. Click the Window menu, and then click Zoom. Click the Zoom command again to enlarge the window.

You can use the full window for iTunes Store. Click the View menu, and then click Use Full Window for iTunes Store (**New!**) to select it.

You can view different aspects of iTunes. Show Column Browser displays a three column view to make it easier to find items and navigate. Click the View menu, point to Column Browser, and then click Show Column Browser. Equalizer displays a dialog where you can adjust sound levels. Click the Window menu, and then click Equalizer. Visualizer displays a colorful light show. Click the View menu, and then click Show visualizer. Click the View menu, point to Visualizer, and then select an option.

Music **8**

8 Apps

Using and Creating Playlists

The iTunes application lets you add media from several different sources. For example, you might have some MP3 songs on your hard drive, and you want them stored within the iTunes application, or you have a music CD that you want converted into MP3 format. Whatever method you select, you'll first want to set up a Playlist to hold and organize your media. A **playlist** is a folder that holds media. For example, you could have a Playlist for all your Country & Western songs, one for your Rock & Roll; even one for audio books. iTunes comes with a set of playlists, or you can create your own. Playlists come in two flavors—Playlists and Smart Playlists. Playlists let you play the songs in the list again, play the songs in random order, or stop when the last song plays. Smart Playlists rebuild themselves according to the criteria you setup. For example, you might create a Smart Playlist that only plays the songs in the library you rate a 4-star or only Christmas songs.

Play and Create a Playlist in iTunes

1. Click the **iTunes** icon in the Dock.

2. To play all the songs in a Playlist, click the Playlist you want listen to, and then double-click the first song or click the **Play** button.

3. Click the **File** menu, and then click **New Playlist**.

4. Type a name for the Playlist, and then press Return.

5. To rename a playlist, click it once, click it again, type a new name, and then press Return.

6. Quit iTunes.

Did You Know?

You can drag a music folder from an open window into the Source pane. iTunes automatically creates a Playlist for the songs, and names the Playlist with the name of the dragged folder.

You can import your playlists. Click the File menu, point to Library, and then click Import. Only songs and videos in your iTunes are included in the Playlist.

Add a Smart Playlist to iTunes

1. Click the **iTunes** icon in the Dock.

2. Click the **File** menu, and then click **New Smart Playlist**.

3. Click the **Criteria** pop-up, and then select the main selection criteria.

4. Click the **Operator** pop-up, and then choose a selection method.

5. Type a word or phrase to search.

6. Click the **Add Criteria** (+) button to add an additional search option.

7. Select the **Limit To** check box and pop-up to limit the number of songs, time played, or max size.

8. Click the **Selected By** pop-up, and then select how to select songs.

9. Select the **Match only checked items** check box to limit selection to songs that are checked.

10. Select the **Live updating** check box to update the Smart Playlist as you add or subtract songs from the iTunes Library.

11. Click **OK**.

12. Name your Smart Playlist.

13. Quit iTunes.

See Also

See "Adding Media to Playlist" on page 324 for more information on creating a playlist using Genius.

Did You Know?

You can delete a playlist. *Select the playlist in the Source pane, click the Edit menu, and then click Delete.*

For Your Information

Understanding Copyright Laws

When you create Playlists you're working smart. Most iTunes users have hundreds, if not thousands of songs on their hard drives, and Playlists and Smart Playlists are the only way to help organize all those songs. A word of caution, make sure they are your songs. Piracy is a big problem in the music industry today, and it's not just what you take off the Internet. The iTunes application gives you the ability to create music tracks from most music CDs. That does not mean you can borrow all of your friend's music CDs and transfer them to your computer. Enjoy your music, but know the laws involving piracy, and copyright violation. Use your browser to search for the latest information about copyright laws in the U.S.

Adding Media to a Playlist

Whenever you add media to the iTunes application, it stores the media in a Library, and then creates a link to the selected Playlist. As a matter of fact, Playlists simply create links to the media in the iTunes Library. If you delete a Playlist or a media within a Playlist, it does not remove the song from the iTunes Library, only the link created in the Playlist is removed. If you want help from iTunes, you can create a Genius playlist, which sends music information about your libraries to iTunes Store, and creates a personalized playlist for you.

Add Media to a Playlist

① Click the **iTunes** icon in the Dock.

② Add media using any of the following options:

◆ Drag media from other libraries in iTunes to the Playlist.

◆ Click the **File** menu, and then click **Add To Library**. Locate the song or songs you want to add, and then click **Open**.

◆ Drag media files from an open folder to the Playlist in the iTunes window.

◆ Click the **Store** menu, and then click **Turn On Genius**. Follow the online steps to enable it. Select a song from a library, click the **Show/Hide iTunes Sidebar** button, and then click the **Start Genius** button. Click **Genius** in the Source pane to view the Genius playlist. When you're done, click the **Store** menu, and then click **Turn Off Genius**.

③ Quit iTunes.

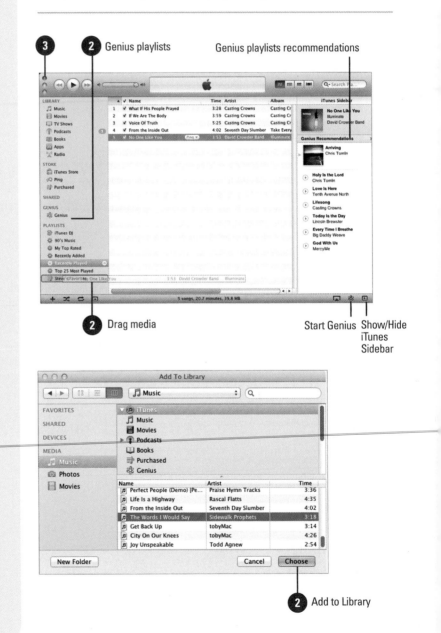

Genius playlists Genius playlists recommendations

Drag media Start Genius Show/Hide iTunes Sidebar

Add To Library

Add to Library

Socializing with Ping

Ping (**New!**) is a social network for music. With Ping, you can follow your favorite artists and friends to discover the music they're talking about, listening to, and downloading. You can see recent activity from artists in your library and anyone you follow from the iTunes Sidebar. You can also tell your follower's about the music you like and make recommendations in reviews. After you create a Ping profile, you can start using the free service.

Socialize with Ping

1. Click the **iTunes** icon in the Dock.

2. Click **Ping** in the Source pane.

3. On first use, click **Turn On Ping**, and then follow the on-screen steps as needed to create a profile.

4. To follow artists, click **Follow All** or **Follow** for a specific artist.

5. To invite friends to join you on Ping, click **Invite**, and then follow the on-screen steps to send e-mails.

 ◆ You can also click links to **Connect to Twitter** or **Import Contacts** from MobileMe, Hotmail, Yahoo! or AOL address book.

6. To review the people you're following, click **People** in the Ping sidebar, click the **People I Follow** tab, and then click a person.

 Review recent activity, and post comments as desired.

7. To stop following a person, click click **People** in the Ping sidebar, click the **People I Follow** tab, and then click **Stop Following**.

8. To post ping information on a track, select the track, click the **Ping** button, and then select an option.

9. Quit iTunes.

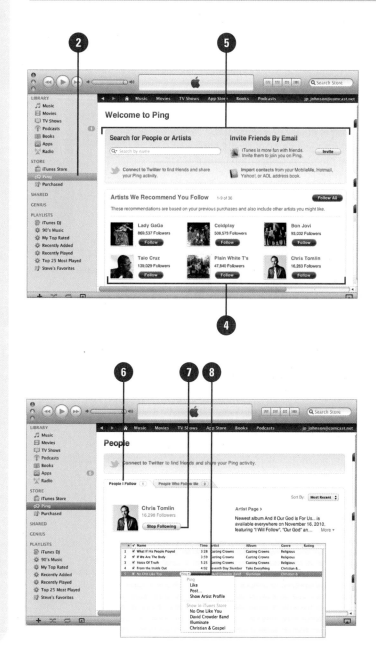

Subscribing and Playing Podcasts

Podcasts are radio and TV shows you can download from the Internet to your iTunes library. The iTunes Store provides free podcasts you can download at any time. If you like a podcast, you can subscribe to it and have it automatically downloaded as it becomes available. If you have an iPod, you can add podcasts to your player and play them on the go when you're not connected to the Internet.

Subscribe and Play Podcasts

1. Click the **iTunes** icon in the Dock.

2. Click **iTunes Store** in the Source pane.

3. Search for the podcast you want.

4. To subscribe to a podcast (only need to do once), display the podcast you want, click **Subscribe**, and then click **Subscribe** again if prompted.

 The podcast is downloaded to your iTunes library. Click **Downloads** in the Source pane to display progress or pause, resume, or stop the process.

5. Click **Podcasts** in the Source pane.

6. Click **Podcasts**, **Categories**, or **New** to display the podcasts you want, and then double-click the thumbnail (not "Play Selected").

7. Click the expand/collapse button (triangle) to expand the podcast listing in the iTunes window.

8. Click **Get All** to download all the podcasts or click **Get** to download an individual podcast.

9. To play a podcast, double-click the podcast. Point to the player to display playback controls and Close button to exit.

10. To unsubscribe to a podcast, select the podcast, and then click **Unsubscribe**.

11. Quit iTunes.

Using iPod or iPhone with iTunes

The iPod digital MP3 music/video player is so unique, it deserves a class all of its own. The iPod touch is the most successful digital music/video player ever created. Now you can also use the iPhone with iTunes. They're made for Macintosh and Windows computers, and it just so happens they work perfectly with the iTunes player. When you plug your iPod or iPhone cable into your computer, it automatically opens the iTunes application and synchronizes playlists, music, videos, podcasts, photos, contacts from your Address Book that you create on your iPod. The sync options have been reorganized and updated for ease of use (**New!**). The iTunes Store also includes games you can purchase and download. You can also manually make changes. It's a simple matter of deleting media you no longer want or dragging media into your iPod or iPhone.

Use iPod or iPhone with iTunes

1. Plug your iPod or iPhone into your computer (requires a FireWire or USB port). This also recharges your iPod or iPhone.

2. Click the iPod or iPhone device name in the Source pane.

3. Click the category tabs and set sync item options (**New!**), and then click **Sync** or **Apply**.

4. Click the expand/collapse button (triangle) to expand the device in the Source pane, and then select a library or Playlist.

5. To remove media, select an item in the iTunes window, and then press Delete.

6. To add media, drag a media item or Playlist from the iTunes window to the device in the Source pane.

7. Click the **Eject** button, to eject and remove the iPod.

 IMPORTANT *If you disconnect your iPod without performing an Eject, it could cause the iPod hard drive (and all your songs), to become corrupted.*

8. Quit iTunes.

Sync item options (**New!**)

Listening to Internet Radio

Listening to music is great, so is curling up with a cup of hot chocolate and your favorite audio book. However, sometimes you would just like to listen to a radio station. Maybe NPR (National Public Radio) is your thing, or possibly your looking for a radio station that just plays classical or jazz music. Whatever direction your tastes run, you are probably able to find it on the Internet radio, and iTunes makes the process of selecting and listening to a radio station as easy as turning on a traditional radio.

Listen to Internet Radio

1. Click the **iTunes** icon in the Dock.

2. Click **Radio** in the Source pane.

3. Select a group from the available options.

4. Click the expand button (triangle) to open the group.

5. Double-click on a station to begin the broadcast.

6. Use the **Play/Pause** button to turn the selected station on or off.

7. Use the **Previous** and **Next** buttons to move up and down through the radio station list.

8. Drag the volume slider in the upper left corner to adjust the volume.

9. Quit iTunes.

Did You Know?

You can add radio stations to the iTunes radio list. Click the Advanced menu, and then click Open Stream. Type in the station's Web address, and then click OK.

Erasing a CD or DVD

If you want to reuse a CD-RW or DVD-RW disc, you need to erase it first, which you can do with Disk Utility. Before you start, there is one thing you need to know. You can't erase a standard CD or DVD that was a previously recorded CD-R or DVD-R disc. During the process, you have the option to select Quick Erase. When you select Quick Erase setting, the contents on the CD or DVD gets overwritten when new information is placed over it. If you don't select Quick Erase setting, the contents is overwritten with zeros to completely erase the CD or DVD, which takes longer to finish.

Erase a CD or DVD

1. Click the **Launchpad** icon in the Dock, click the **Utilities** folder, and then click the **Disk Utility** icon.

2. Select the disc in the left column you want to erase.

3. Click the **Erase** tab.

4. Click the **Quickly** or **Completely** option.

5. Click **Erase**.

6. Click **Erase** to confirm you want to erase the CD.

7. Click the **Disk Utility** menu, and then click **Quit Disk Utility**.

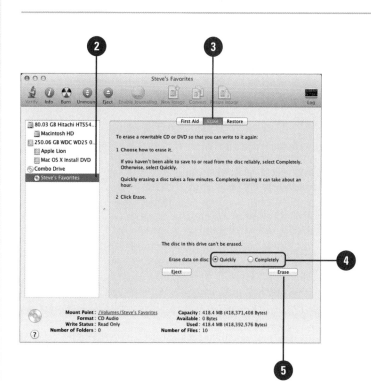

Burning CDs and Exporting to MP3 Players

While CD's are still around and popular, digital music players seem to be one of the "newer" technologies set to change how we listen to our tunes. iTunes gives us the option to use CDs and digital music players—we can burn our own customized music CDs or we can transfer the music files to any one of a number of digital music players. When you insert the CD, iTunes gives you the option of choosing the Playlist you want to use. If the playlist is too large to fit on a single CD or DVD, iTunes asks you for another disc. Digital music players, more commonly known as MP3 players, hold music files using the MP3 digital format. MP3 players can be thought of as a hard drive that holds music files, and then plays them back to you through a set of speakers or a headset. When you purchase your MP3 player, it comes with software designed to move music files from your computer hard drive to the drive located on the MP3 player. Some MP3 players, when connected to your computer, appear as an external hard drive.

Burn a Music CD

1. Click the **iTunes** icon in the Dock.

2. Create and select the Playlist you want to burn onto the CD.

 iTunes uses the name of the Playlist as the name of the CD.

3. Insert a blank CD into your drive, and then click **Ignore**, if prompted.

 IMPORTANT *You must have a writable CD or DVD drive.*

4. Click the **File** menu, and then click **Burn Playlist to Disc**.

5. Select a preferred speed, and disc format option, and then click **Burn**.

6. Quit iTunes.

Did You Know?

You can't burn more than 10 copies of your Playlist. If you do have a legitimate need for that 11th CD, all you need to do is change the sort order of the songs in the Playlist, and then you can burn 10 more.

Export to MP3 Players

1. Navigate to the iTunes music folder:

 Main Hard Drive/Home/Music/ iTunes/iTunes Media/Music.

2. Select a folder or a list of iTunes files that you want to move.

3. Drag the music files to the hard drive icon of your MP3 music player.

4. Click the **Eject** button in the Sidebar or control-click the MP3 player desktop icon, and then click **Eject**.

 IMPORTANT *Not all MP3 music players allow you to drag music files between your hard drive and the player icon. When this occurs you'll have to use the transfer software that came bundled with the player. Simply load the software and follow the onscreen instructions.*

Did You Know?

You can backup your iTunes library to a CD or DVD. Click the File menu, point to Library, click Back Up To Disc, select the options you want, insert a blank writable CD or DVD, and then click Back Up.

You can access the names of your songs on the Internet. Insert a music CD or DVD, click the Advanced menu, and then click Get Track Names. The iTunes application accesses the Gracenote music title repository, and then changes the dull Track1 and Track2, with the names of the song.

Setting iTunes Preferences

Like any application, iTunes gives you a Preferences panel that helps you adjust the software to fit your specific needs. The iTunes preferences give you precise control over how the program operates on your computer.

To set your preferences, or to review the defaults that have been set in iTunes, simply click the iTunes icon in the Dock. Click the iTunes menu, and then click Preferences. There you'll find almost every conceivable setting that is used in iTunes. For a summary view, we've shown you commonly used screens and what is contained on that Preference screen. After making any changes to the screens, simply click OK to change the setting or click Cancel to undo your change.

General: Controls text within the iTunes window.

Playback: Gives you options to play music and movies.

Sharing: Lets you share your music files with other users.

Advanced: Controls the Buffer, and helps manage and maintain the iTunes Music folder.

Capturing Photos in Photo Booth

If you have an iSight or other camera attached to your computer, you can use Photo Booth to capture photos just like you were sitting in a photo booth at a carnival. If you have a high-resolution FaceTime camera, Photo Booth can take high-resolution photos (**New!**). You can capture individual photos or create a short movie. In addition, you can include a backdrop or visual effects to your photo snapshots and movie recordings. Photo Booth provides a full-screen view with a theater look (**New!**). Photo Booth saves your photos as JPEG files and movies in a folder called Photo Booth, located in the Pictures folder in your Home folder. When you're done capturing photos, you can use them as a user account or iChat buddy picture, send them as an attachment in an e-mail, present them in a slide show or print them in a proof sheet.

Capture Photos in Photo Booth

1. Attach an Apple iSight or other video camera to your computer.

2. Click the **Photo Booth** icon in the Dock.

3. Click the **Take a still picture** button.

4. When you're ready to take a still picture, click the **Shutter** button.

 After a 3-second countdown, the screen flashes and Photo Booth takes a photo. The picture appears as a thumbnail in the bottom pane.

5. To preview a photo, select the thumbnail in the bottom pane.

6. To permanently delete a photo, select the thumbnail, and then click the **Delete** button in the bottom left corner of the thumbnail.

7. Click the **Shutter** button again to go back to live images.

8. To e-mail a photo or use a photo in a user account or buddy picture, use the buttons below the preview.

9. To present a slide show, click the **View** menu, click **Start Slideshow**, and then use the toolbar to navigate through the slide show.

Full Screen button

Full Screen view

Preview

Recording Movies in Photo Booth

In addition to capturing individual still photos, you can also record a movie in Photo Booth. You can create two types of movies, either a movie clip or a 4-up movie. A movie clip is a continuous recording of frames, while a 4-up movie is four snapshots taken very quickly to simulate a movie. The 4-up movies are saved as four JPEG files, while movie clips are saved as QuickTime MOV files. However, you can export the movie clip or 4-up movie as an animated GIF, which you can also use as an iChat buddy icon. If the movie is too long, you can pick the start and end frames to trim the edges (**New!**).

Record Videos in Photo Booth

1. Attach an Apple iSight or other video camera to your computer.

2. Click the **Photo Booth** icon in the Dock.

3. Click the **Take four quick pictures** or **Take a movie clip** button.

4. When you're ready, click the **Shutter** or **Record** button.

 For a 4-up movie, a 3-second countdown and a flash occurs for each photo. For a movie clip, the recording starts after a 3-second countdown.

5. When you're done recording a movie clip, click the **Stop** button.

6. To preview a movie, select the thumbnail, point to the bottom of the live image to display and then use the slider and **Pause/Play** button to view a movie clip.

7. To trim a movie (**New!**), select the thumbnail, point to the bottom of the live image to display, click **Trim**, drag end points, and then click **Close** or **Accept**.

8. To permanently delete a movie, select the thumbnail, and then click the **Delete** button in the left corner of the thumbnail.

9. Click the **Shutter** button again to go back to live images.

Play/Pause button

Drag end point to trim movie Close and Accept buttons

Adding Photo Booth Effects

Photo Booth includes backdrops and visual effects (**New!**) you can add to visuals to have some fun and create more interesting photo effect. A backdrop is a background that appears behind the camera image. You can use one of the backdrops provided by Photo Booth, such as New York, Paris, or Yosemite, to make it seem like your in an another place, or add and use one of your own. In addition to backdrops, Photo Booth also includes a set of visual effects, such as Comic Book, Sepia, X-Ray, and Light Tunnel, that you can use to create a fun and unique effect.

Add Photo Booth Effects

1. Attach an Apple iSight or other video camera to your computer.

2. Click the **Photo Booth** icon in the Dock.

3. Click the **Effects** button.

4. Click the Left and Right Arrows or swipe your trackpad or Magic Mouse (**New!**) to display more effects.

5. Select the backdrop or visual effect you want to use.

6. Point to the bottom of the live images. If a slide appears, drag it to adjust the visual effect level.

7. To remove an effect, select the **Normal** effect in the middle.

8. To add your own backdrop, drag it to a "Drag Backdrop Here" place holder.

9. When you're ready, select a picture button, and then click the **Shutter** button.

Backdrops

Visual effects

Swipe to display more effects

Did You Know?

You can export a movie as an animated GIF. Select a 4-up movie or movie clip in the bottom pane, click the File menu, click Export, type a name, specify a location, and then click Save.

Playing and Browsing DVD Movies

Okay, it's time to break out the popcorn and soda, because the DVD player in Sow Leopard is here. Using the DVD player, you can access a movie chapter by chapter, freeze the action, move forward and backward through the movie, and even play a movie in slow motion frame-by-frame. You can even watch your video in full screen mode while you work on another display. In addition, the DVD Player offers closed captioning. All that translates into a great viewing experience—sounds like a winner to me. If you have an Apple Remote, you don't even need to get up to control the DVD player.

Play and Browse DVD Movies with the DVD Player

1. Insert a DVD into the DVD drive of your computer to start the movie.

 ◆ You can also click the **Launchpad** icon in the Dock, and then click the **DVD Player** icon to start it.

2. Select from the following DVD Player options:

 ◆ Click the **Left**, **Right**, **Up**, **Down**, or **Return** buttons to navigate.

 ◆ Click the **Previous** or **Next Chapter** buttons to move between movie chapters.

 ◆ Click the **Play/Pause** or the **Stop** button to play/pause or stop the movie.

 ◆ Click the **Eject** button to stop the movie and eject the DVD.

 ◆ Click the **Title** or **Menu** buttons to view the movie title or menu.

 ◆ Drag the volume control to raise or lower the volume.

 ◆ Open the Options panel, and then select between Slow Motion, Step Frame, Return, Sub Title, Audio, or Angle.

3. At the top of the window, click the Video menu, and then select between the various viewing options.

4. To exit the movie without using the

Movie Player

Navigate | Volume Control | Slow Motion | Step Frame | Sub Title | Options panel | Audio

Previous; Hold to Fast Rewind | Stop | Return | Angle

Play & Pause | Next; Hold to Fast Forward

Customizing the DVD Player

In addition to the main DVD player controls, you can also customize your playback experience. With the new full-screen interface and Image Bar, you can quickly access playback controls, subtitles, and audio tracks, change the screen view and scale, and browse DVD content. You can also create video snippets from any DVD and set bookmarks, also known as key points, you can view again later.

Customize the DVD Player

1. Insert a DVD into the DVD drive of your computer to start the movie.

2. Select from the following Movie Player options:

 ◆ **Show/Hide Full Screen.** Press ⌘+F.

 ◆ **Image Bar.** Point to the bottom of the screen in Full Screen.

 ◆ **Create Video Clip.** Position the video, click the **Controls** menu, click **New Video Clip**, set the start and end frame, and then click **Save**.

 ◆ **Bookmark.** Position the video, click the **Controls** menu, click **New Bookmark**, enter a name, and then click **Add**.

 ◆ **View Bookmarks, Video Clips, and Chapters.** Click the **Window** menu, and then click **Bookmarks**, **Video Clips**, or **Chapters**.

 ◆ **Video Zoom or Color.** Click the **Window** menu, and then click **Video Zoom** or **Video Color**, select the **On** check box, and then adjust the levels.

 ◆ **Keyboard Shortcuts. Play**: Space bar, **Stop**: ⌘+. (period), **screen size**: ⌘+0 thru ⌘+3, **Switch to Finder**: Option+⌘+F.

3. To exit the movie without using the controller, press ⌘+Q.

Full Screen

Image bar Movie controls

Playing QuickTime Movies

QuickTime Player supports H.264 video decoding capabilities using the GPU (Graphics Processing Unit). QuickTime works with the MPEG4 format and other common formats, giving you access to movie clips. In addition, QuickTime delivers several performance enhancements, including ColorSync management, live resize, zero-configuration streaming at the best connection speed, surround sound in up to 24 channels, full screen playback, additional keyboard shortcuts to mirror Final Cut Pro, improved A/V controls, and closed captioning with up-to-date standards, and timecode or frame count display instead of movie time. QuickTime Player plays movies in a redesigned window with fade away playback controls and full-screen (**New!**) option. If you open a movie and it's upside down or sideways, you can rotate it (**New!**). If your movie contains chapter markers, QuickTime Player displays them in frame-based thumbnail images.

Play QuickTime Movies

1. Click the **Launchpad** icon in the Dock, and then click the **QuickTime Player** icon.

2. Click the **File** menu, and then click **Open** to load individual QuickTime (or other formatted) movies or click **Open URL** to load URLs.

 ◆ To open a recent movie, click the **File**, point to **Open Recent**, and then select a movie.

3. To rotate a movie (**New!**), click the **Edit** menu, and then click **Rotate Left**, **Rotate Right**, **Flip Horizontal**, or **Flip Vertical**.

4. Point to the movie to display movie controls (if necessary), drag the slider, and then click the movie controls to **Play/ Pause** and **Rewind** or **Forward** the movie.

 TIMESAVER *Press the Spacebar to play/pause a movie.*

5. To adjust the volume, drag the Volume slider.

6. Click the **View** menu, and then select from the available viewing options.

7. Quit QuickTime Player.

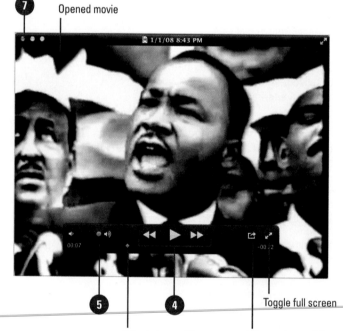

Opened movie

1/1/08 8:43 PM

Toggle full screen

Adjust play position

Trim movie or add it to iTunes, MobileMe, YouTube, Vimeo, Flickr, Facebook, or Mail

Customize QuickTime Playback

In the QuickTime Player, select from the following options:

◆ **Show/Hide Full Screen.** Press ⌘+F or click the **Full Screen** button (**New!**). Point to top of screen to display it in full screen.

◆ **Change Screen View.** Press ⌘+1 for Actual Size; press ⌘+3 for Fit to Screen; press ⌘+4 for Fill Screen; press ⌘+5 for Panoramic; press ⌘++ or ⌘+- for Increase Size or Decrease Size.

◆ **Show/Hide Chapters.** Click the **View** menu, and then click **Show Chapters**.

◆ **Closed Captioning.** Click the **View** menu, and then click **Show Closed Captioning**.

◆ **Show Movie Inspector.** Click the **Window** menu, and then click **Show Movie Inspector** to display movie information, and then click the **Close** button.

◆ **Show Export Progress.** Click the **Window** menu, and then click **Show Export Progress** to display progress information, and then click the **Close** button.

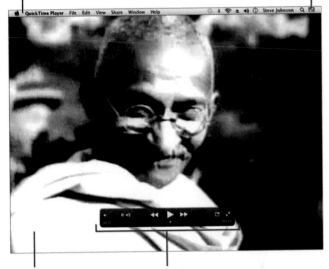

Point to top of screen to show menu bar Full Screen button

Full Screen view Movie controls

Show Movie Inspector

Did You Know?

You can listen to a movie in a different language. Click the View menu, point to Languages, and then select a language. If the languages are grayed out, the movie doesn't support it.

You can show movie subtitles while a movie plays. Click the View menu, point to Subtitles, and then select a language. If the languages are grayed out, the movie doesn't have subtitles.

Creating QuickTime Movies

QuickTime 10 provides powerful commands to record live video and audio directly from an iSight camera, FireWire camcorder, or microphone or capture all or part (**New!**) of your desktop screen with mouse clicks (**New!**) to disk. After you create or open a QuickTime movie, you can trim it shorter, or remove unwanted content, such as silence, or merge clips (**New!**) together. QuickTime also allows you to convert and share your media in iTunes, iPhone, iPod, or Apple TV, and publish your media to MobileMe, YouTube, Vimeo (**New!**), Flickr (**New!**), Facebook (**New!**), and Mail. You can also export your media in formats for iPod touch & iPhone 3Gs and audio only (**New!**) as well as for the web.

Create Movies, Audio, or Screens

1. Click the **Applications** folder in the Dock, and then click the **QuickTime Player** icon.

2. Click the **File** menu, and then click **New Movie Recording**, **New Audio Recording**, or **New Screen Recording**.

3. Click the **Down** arrow to select commands to adjust recording devices, quality, destination, and options, such as Show Mouse Clicks in Recording (**New!**).

4. Click the **Record** button.

 ◆ For a Screen Recording (**New!**), click to record full screen or drag to select a screen area, and then click **Start Recording**.

5. When you're done, click the **Stop** button.

 The media is automatically saved in the Movies folder.

5. To export the movie is another format, click the **File** menu, click **Export**, type a name, select a format and destination, and then click **Export**.

6. To export the movie to the Web, click the **File** menu, click **Export for Web**, type a name, select a destination and export format, and then click **Export**.

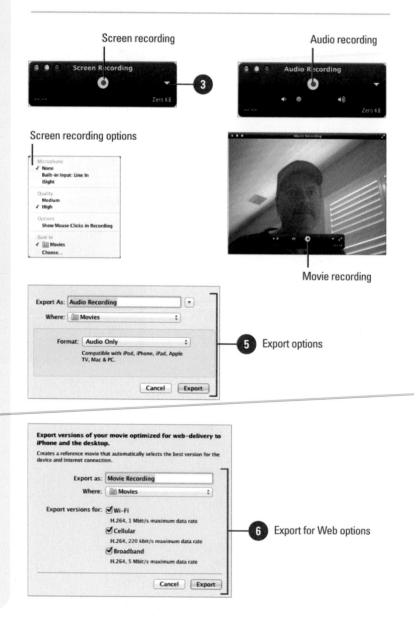

Screen recording

Audio recording

Screen recording options

Movie recording

5 Export options

6 Export for Web options

Edit QuickTime Movies

1. In the QuickTime Player, click the **File** menu, and then click **Open File**, select the movie you want to edit, and then click **Open**.

2. To merge multiple movies (**New!**), drag one movie from the original window to another movie window.

 Quicktime automatically scales or crops them as needed.

3. Click the **Edit** menu, click **Trim**, and then use any of the following:

 ◆ Drag play head as needed, and then drag the start and end of the trimming bar (yellow handles) to select the part of the movie you want to keep.

 ◆ Click the **Edit** menu, and then click **Select All Excluding Silence** to exclude the silent part of the movie.

4. Click **Trim**.

Red vertical line play head

Share QuickTime Movies

1. In the QuickTime Player, click the **File** menu, and then click **Open File**, select the movie you want to edit, and then click **Open**.

2. Click the **Share** menu, and then select a sharing option:

 ◆ **iTunes.** Compatible with iPod, iPhone, and Apple TV.

 ◆ **MobileMe Gallery.** Uploads to your MobileMe account.

 ◆ **YouTube, Vimeo, Flickr, or Facebook.** Uploads to your service account (**New!**) after sign in. Check account for movie upload size limits.

 ◆ **Mail.** Creates a movie attachment in Mail after selecting a movie size (**New!**).

iTunes options

MobileMe Galley options

YouTube options

Exploring iMovie, iDVD, and iPhoto

The **iPhoto** application lets you organize your images into user-defined folders, edit them, and even distribute them to your friends, by placing them on a CD or DVD, or directly over the Internet. iPhoto is part of the iLife suite of application, which is sold separately from Mac OS X.

When you open the iPhoto application, you're treated to the ultimate in organization and simplicity. For example, you own a digital camera, and you want to move the images from the camera to your computer. Most digital cameras come with their own proprietary programs that let you hook your camera up (USB or FireWire port), and then organize and manage your files. Fortunately, iPhoto does away with camera-specific programs. When you plug your camera in, iPhoto recognizes the device and lets you move the image files from the camera to iPhoto.

The **iMovie** application lets you create high-quality, professional movies. Using footage from your digital camcorder (MiniDV or Digital 8 format), you can edit and combine different movie files, create transitions between scenes, even capture live video, and then add an audio track (voice or music). iMovie is part of the iLife suite of application, which is sold separately from Mac OS X.

The iMovie application is simple to operate, yet powerful when it comes to creating professional movies, using footage from your digital movie camera, or any other digital multimedia files; including image stills and audio files.

The iMovie window is your working studio. Inside this one window, you have the ability to draw together all of the elements of your movie, and then arrange them by adding titles and transitions; you can even use special effects. For example, you could create a movie of a family members birthday, using a dozen movie clips, plus background music and narration. You can also add still images, create seamless fades between photos, and movies. It's all here inside the iMovie window.

The **iDVD** application comes bundled on all Macintosh computers that have a DVD burner. Using iDVD, you can create slideshows of pictures, or become a director and create your own DVD movies, using a digital camcorder. You even have iMovie to help you edit your home movies. iDVD is part of the iLife suite of application, which is sold separately from Mac OS X.

If you've ever wanted to test your skills at movie production, then the iDVD application is just what you've been waiting for all these years. There are all kinds of layout applications, such as applications for laying material out on paper (Adobe InDesign and Quark Xpress), and there are programs that layout Web pages (Adobe Dreamweaver). With that in mind, think of iDVD as a layout application for the creation of your Oscar-winning production. This gives you the ability to generate slideshows, videos, or a combination of both, along with menus, buttons (just like any other DVD), and then burn it onto a blank DVD that can be viewed by anyone that owns a DVD player.

The iDVD application is powerful, but just like any other layout program, it requires material to use for the layout. For example, when you open iDVD, you need access to video files, audio files, and graphics. The iDVD application doesn't create the materials that make up the DVD; it only organizes them. And, not all DVD players are created equal. Some DVD disks do not work in all the players on the market; especially older DVD players. For information on compatibility issues between DVD writers and DVD players, point your browser to: *http://www.dvdrhelp.com*.

Sharing Information in the Cloud

Introduction

iCloud is Apple's cloud service, which stores your music, photos, apps, calendars, and documents and wirelessly pushes them to all your devices, such as iPad, iPhone, iPod touch, and other Macs. iCloud integrates with your apps, so everything happens automatically. iCloud requires no syncing or management. iCloud is a free for iOS 5 and Mac OS X Lion users.

When you sign up for a free account, you get 5 GB of storage, which is plenty of space, considering that music, apps, books, and photos in Photo Stream don't count against your free storage. When you update your iPad, iPhone, or iPod touch to iOS5, apps—such as iTunes in the Cloud, Photo Stream, Documents in the Cloud, Apps, Books, and Backup, and Contacts, Calendar, and Mail—become integrated with iCloud. Files are redundantly stored on multiple devices across multiple storage facilities—powered by Heroku and Amazon's Simple Storage Service—preventing data corruption and loss.

If you have a MobileMe account, you'll want to transition to an iCloud account. MobileMe is an Apple subscription-based service that provides a centralized place on the Web to manage and synchronize e-mail, contacts, calendar, photo albums, and documents that you can access from a Mac, PC, iPhone, or iPod touch.

The core services provided by MobileMe have been rewritten to work with iCloud. MobileMe will no longer be available as a paid sync service. If you have an active MobileMe account as of June 6, 2011, your service has been extended through June 30, 2012, at no additional charge. After that date, the MobileMe service will no longer be available.

What You'll Do

Join the iCloud Community

Get Started with CloudApp

Work with CloudApp Raindrops

Set CloudApp Preferences

Use CloudApp on the Web

Change MobileMe Account Preferences

Manage MobileMe Mail

Create a MobileMe Address Book

Work with MobileMe Calendar

Creating a MobileMe Gallery

View and Share a MobileMe Gallery

Manage Files with iDisk

Set iDisk Preferences

Share Files with MobileMe iDisk

Joining the iCloud Community

iCloud (**New!**) is a cloud service that stores your content—music, photos, apps, contacts, calendars, e-mail, documents and more—and wirelessly pushes it to all your devices, such as your iPad, iPhone, iPod touch, Mac, and PC. iCloud requires no syncing or management. When you sign up for a free account, you get 5 GB of storage, which is plenty of space, considering that music, apps, books, and photos in Photo Stream don't count against your free storage. iCloud integrates on the Mac with the CloudApp (**New!**), which is available for download free from App Store. The CloudApp allows you to share images, links, music, videos and files using the CloudApp menu icon on the Finder menu bar and context menus (Control-click an item).

Get and View the CloudApp

1. Click the **App Store** icon in the Dock.

 ◆ You can also open your browser, and then go to *http://getcloudapp.com*, and then click the **Get it on the Mac App Store** button.

2. Perform a search in the Search field for *cloudapp*, and then click the link to preview it.

3. Click the **Free** button, and then click the **Install App** button.

4. Click the **CloudApp** icon on the Finder menu bar.

5. Click any of the following:

 ◆ **Open Web App.** Opens your browser and displays the iCloud login screen.

 ◆ **Getting Started with CloudApp.** Opens your browser and displays iCloud help information.

 ◆ **Autoupload Screenshots.** Select to automatically upload screenshot captures.

 ◆ **Preferences.** Opens CloudApp preferences. You can set upload options, sign out, or set Raindrop (plug-in) options

 ◆ **Quit.** Exits the CloudApp.

Sign In to the iCloud Community

1. Click the **Launchpad** icon in the Dock, and then click the **Cloud** icon.

 ◆ You can also open your browser, and then go to *http://getcloudapp.com*, and then click **Login**.

2. If you already have an account, click **Already have an account**, enter your e-mail address and password, and then click **Sign In**.

 Otherwise, continue with the following steps to create an account.

3. Enter your e-mail address and passwords.

4. Select the **I agree to the Terms of Service** check box.

5. Click **Register**, and then follow any additional online instructions.

6. To exit the CloudApp, click the **CloudApp** icon on the Finder menu bar, and then click **Quit**.

 The CloudApp menu icon is removed from the Finder menu bar.

Did You Know?

You can sign out and sign in using preferences. Click the CloudApp icon on the Finder menu bar, click Preferences, and then click Accounts. To sign out, click Sign Out. to sign in, enter your e-mail address and password, and then click Sign In.

Sign in to CloudApp

Start sharing files right now. Already have an account? Sign in.

Email: perspection@mac.com
Password: ••••••••
Forgot your password?

Don't have an account? Sign In

Welcome to CloudApp

Start sharing files right now. Don't have an account? Sign up for free. It only takes 30 seconds.

Email: perspection@mac.com
Password: ••••••••
Confirm Password: ••••••••
☑ I agree to the Terms of Service

Already have an account? Register

Open Web App...

🖼 Home Sense Logo.bmp ⓪
📄 Getting Started with CloudApp ②

✓ Autoupload Screenshots

Preferences...
Quit

Getting Started with CloudApp

CloudApp—available for download from the App Store—allows you to share images, links, music, videos and files. In addition to files, you can also share the address from your browser's address bar and selected text in a document. The CloudApp (**New!**) is available on the Finder menu bar and context menus (Control-click an item). It's pretty simple to use. Select a file or item, drag it to the CloudApp menu icon to drop it. When you hear a ding and see the icon turn blue, you know your drop to the iCloud is complete and ready to share with others. The CloudApp places a sharable link to the file on your Clipboard, which you can paste where you want, such as a document or e-mail message. CloudApp also puts your last few drops on the CloudApp menu, where you can see how many times a drop has been viewed or click to open it.

Share a File Using CloudApp

1. Sign in to iCloud.

2. Select the files or item you want to share on the cloud.

 ◆ You can also drop the address from your browser's address bar to share a bookmark as well as selected text from a document.

3. Drag the file or item and drop it on the **CloudApp** icon on the Finder menu bar or Control-click it, and then click **Upload with CloudApp**.

 TIMESAVER *Select a file or item, press* ⌘+C *to copy it, and then press Control+Option+C to drop it.*

 When you hear a ding and see the icon turn blue, the file is dropped to the cloud.

 A sharable link to the dropped file is copied to the Clipboard.

4. To use the link to the dropped file, place the insertion point where you want to paste the link, and then press ⌘+V.

 ◆ You can also Control-click, and then click **Paste**.

Upload with CloudApp command

Work with Recent Drops

1. Sign in to iCloud.

2. Click the **CloudApp** icon on the Finder menu bar.

3. Use any of the following:

 ◆ **Open the Drop.** click the drop.

 ◆ **Copy Drop's Link.** ⌘+click the drop.

 ◆ **Toggle Drop's Privacy.** Option+click the drop.

 ◆ **Delete Drop.** ⌘+Option+ click the drop.

Open Web App...

📁 Organized.rtfd.zip 0
🖼 Home Sense Logo.bmp 0
📑 Getting Started with CloudApp 2

✓ Autoupload Screenshots

Preferences...
Quit

For Your Information

Getting Automatic Drops

When you update your iPad, iPhone, or iPod touch to iOS5, your favorite apps—such as iTunes in the Cloud, Photo Stream, Documents in the Cloud, Apps, Books, and Backup, and Contacts, Calendar, and Mail (with a me.com account)—become integrated with iCloud. When you make purchases on iTunes or App Store, iCloud automatically can download the item to all your devices over Wi-Fi or network. iCloud stores your purchase history, so you can see what you have bought on any device. When you take photos, iCloud can automatically send it to the appropriate photo app on all your devices up to 1000 images.

Working with CloudApp Raindrops

CloudApp comes with a variety of plug-ins, called Raindrops (**New!**), that allow you to use iCloud services directly in your favorite apps, such as iPhoto, iTunes, Safari, and Photoshop. You can set Raindrop options in CloudApp preferences and trigger drop from apps to the cloud with the keyboard shortcut Control+Option+R. After you start a drop, the download progress becomes available on the CloudApp menu.

Work with CloudApp Raindrops

1 Click the **CloudApp** icon on the Finder menu bar, and then click **Preferences**.

2 Click **Raindrops**.

3 Select or clear the check boxes with the apps you want or don't want to enable.

4 Click the **Close** button.

5 Open the app in which you want to drop content with CloudApp.

6 Select the item you want to drop, and then press Control+Option+R.

When you hear a ding and see the icon turn blue, the file is dropped to the cloud.

7 Click the **CloudApp** icon on the Finder menu to display the dropped file along with download progress.

Upload progress

Setting CloudApp Preferences

CloudApp preferences allow you to set general, account, and raindrop options. You can access CloudApp preferences from the CloudApp icon on the Finder menu bar. You can set General preferences (**New!**) for when a drop is complete or when you login to your Mac. It also displays the keyboard shortcut (Control+Option+C) to drop items to the cloud from the Clipboard. If you want to sign out or sign in, you can use Account preferences. You can set Raindrop preferences to enable or disable drops to the cloud from within apps. It also displays the keyboard shortcut (Control+Option+R) to drop items from an app.

Set General CloudApp Preferences

1. Click the **CloudApp** menu icon, and then click **Preferences**.

2. Click **General**.

3. Select or clear any of the following check boxes:

 ◆ **Automatically copy link to clipboard.** Select to automatically copy a drop link to the clipboard when a drop is complete.

 ◆ **Play.** Select to play a specified sound when a drop is complete.

 ◆ **Show Growl notification.** Select to show a growl notification when a drop is complete.

 ◆ **Launch at login.** Select to start the CloudApp with you login to your Mac.

4. Click the **Close** button.

Using CloudApp on the Web

You can quickly open CloudApp on the Web from the CloudApp menu using the Open Web App command (**New!**). CloudApp on the Web allows you to view recent drops, change account information, and log out when you're done. The Drops section allows you to view recent drops as well as select files from your computer. The Account section allows you to update profile information, set privacy drop options, upgrade your account from Free to Pro plan (with enhanced features, such as custom sharing domains), or delete your account. The Log Out section allows you to quickly exit the CloudApp.

Change CloudApp Account Information

1. Click the **CloudApp** menu icon, and then click **Open Web App**.

2. If prompted, enter your e-mail address and password, and then click **Log In**.

3. Click **Account**.

4. Change any of the following options:

 ◆ **Settings.** Enter e-mail and password information to reset your account, and then click Update.

 ◆ **Privacy.** Select an option for a private or public drop link, and then click Update.

 ◆ **Custom Domains.** Specify a custom domain to share files; requires the upgraded fee based Pro plan.

 ◆ **Store.** Purchase the Pro plan.

5. To log out, click **Log Out**.

Use CloudApp on the Web

1. Click the **CloudApp** menu icon, and then click **Open Web App**.

2. If prompted, enter your e-mail address and password, and then click **Log In**.

3. Click **Drop**.

4. Click any of the categories under Library to display recent drops.

5. To change the view, click **Grid** or **List**.

6. To delete a file, select the check box next to it, and then click **Delete Selected**.

7. To upload a file from your computer, click the **File**, click the **Select a file on your computer** link, select the file, and then click **Choose**.

8. To log out, click **Log Out**.

Select file to upload to the cloud

Changing MobileMe Account Preferences

Once you're registered as a user, all of the advantages of the MobileMe site become instantly available; including the ability to read and send e-mail from your new mail account, manage contacts and a calendar, store and share your photos online, manage and backup files online, and synchronize MobileMe content across multiple computers and devices. You can access your MobileMe account settings from MobileMe preferences in System Preferences or online at the MobileMe Web site. When you login in to your online MobileMe account, you can set account preferences in the following areas: personal information, account options, billing info, password and storage settings, personal domain, security certificate, and Find My iPhone.

View MobileMe Account Preferences

1. Click the **System Preferences** icon in the Dock, and then click the **MobileMe** icon.

 ◆ If prompted, type your MobileMe member name and password, and then click **Sign In**.

2. Click **Account** tab.

 A quick summary of account details appears in MobileMe preferences. You can get more account details online.

3. Click **Account Details**.

4. Type your MobileMe member name and password, and then click **Log In**.

 MobileMe Account Settings Web page appears, displaying a summary of your account.

5. Click one of the category buttons in the left column to view your current settings.

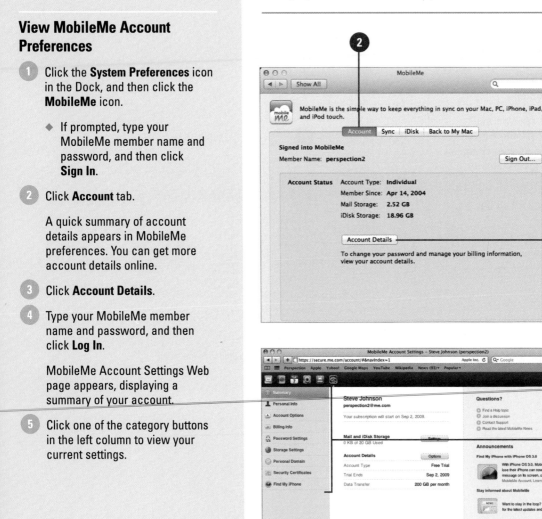

Change MobileMe Account Preferences

1 Open your browser, and sign onto your MobileMe account.

◆ You can access MobileMe log in at *www.mobileme.com*.

2 Click the **Account Settings** button.

3 Select from the following online MobileMe account options, and then change the options you want:

◆ **Summary Info.** Displays your account name and e-mail address, current disk usage, account details, help, and announcements.

◆ **Personal Info.** Sets account name and e-mail address, language and time, and update notifications.

◆ **Account Options.** Sets account subscription options.

◆ **Billing Info.** Accepts credit card information.

◆ **Password Settings.** Changes account password and sets security information.

◆ **Storage Settings.** Allocates online storage for iDisk and Mail.

◆ **Personal Domain.** Adds a Web domain so you can host a Web site using MobileMe.

◆ **Security Certificates.** Creates a certificate to keep your iChat information secure online.

◆ **Find My iPhone.** Helps you find your iPhone or iPod touch in case it gets lost.

4 Click **Save**, if needed.

MobileMe password settings

MobileMe storage settings

Managing MobileMe Mail

The MobileMe Mail service gives you a way to keep in touch with friends, family, and clients at home, or wherever you travel. And you don't even have to have your own computer. You can access, read, and save your e-mail using a Web browser on any computer, anywhere, through the *www.mobileme.com* Web site. After you setup or sign-in to a MobileMe account, you are now ready to receive and send e-mail to other MobileMe members, or to anyone with an Internet e-mail address. MobileMe Mail work in a similar way as Mac OS X Mail. MobileMe Mail also provides preferences, so you can customize the way it works.

Work with MobileMe Mail

① Open your browser and sign onto your MobileMe account.

◆ You can access MobileMe log in at *www.mobileme.com*.

② Click the **Mail** button.

③ Click the **Get New Mail** button to check for e-mail.

④ Click on an e-mail in your Inbox to open and read it in the preview pane below.

⑤ If you want, click the **Reply**, **Reply All** or **Forward** button to respond to an e-mail, and then click the **Send** button.

⑥ To put selected e-mail in the Trash folder, click the **Delete** button.

⑦ To create a new e-mail, click the **New Message** button to write an e-mail, and then click the **Send** button.

◆ Click the **Add Contacts** button to use contacts from the Address Book.

◆ Click the **Spelling** button to check spelling in the e-mail.

◆ If you're not finished with an e-mail, you can click the **Save Draft** button to store it in the Drafts folder for use later.

Send button Drafts button Spelling button Contacts button

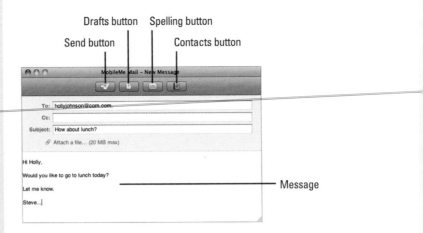

Message

Creating a MobileMe Address Book

Your MobileMe Address Book lets you store personal and business information on all your friends, relatives, and contacts, in one safe place. In truth, you might actually have two or three other places where this same information is stored, maybe Safari, the Address Book application that comes bundled with Mac OS X, or even your iPod. The MobileMe address book is used to maintain your mailing lists and e-mail contacts. However, before you despair of having to type in all those contacts again, Macintosh gives you a way to Sync all of the contacts and keep them up-to-date, no matter what application performed the changes.

Create a MobileMe Address Book

1. Open your browser and sign onto your MobileMe account.

 ◆ You can access MobileMe log in at *www.mobileme.com*.

2. Click the **Contacts** button.

3. To create a group for contacts, **New Group** button, type a name, and then press Return.

 ◆ To add a contact to a group, select the group and create a new contact or drag it to the group name.

4. To create a new contact, click **New Contact**, enter information, and then click **Save**.

5. To display contact information, click the contact name.

6. To modify the contact info, select the contact, click the **Edit Contact** button, and then click **Save**.

7. To remove a contact from the list, select the contact, click the **Delete Contact** button, and then click **Delete**.

8. To generate an e-mail for the selected contact, click the **Actions** button, and then click **Email Contact**.

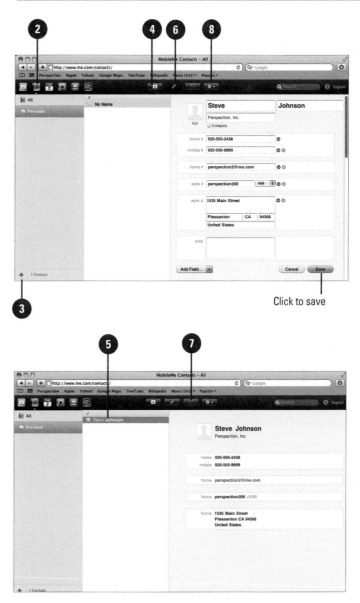

Click to save

Working with MobileMe Calendar

With MobileMe Calendar, you can keep track of all your activities, either work or personal. You can create separate calendars for different people, such as your family, or a team, or different types of activities. MobileMe Calendar gives you the ability to add new events or modify existing events directly in the Calendar window just like iCal. In fact, MobileMe Calendar works in a similar way as Mac OS X iCal. MobileMe Calendar also provides preferences, so you can customize the way it works.

Work with MobileMe Calendars

1. Open your browser and sign onto your MobileMe account.

 ◆ You can access MobileMe log in at *www.mobileme.com*.

2. Click the **Calendar** button.

3. To add a calendar or calendar group, click the **Add** (+) button, click **New Calendar** or **New Calendar Group**, type a name for the calendar, and then press Return.

4. Click a view button to find a date.

 ◆ Today. Click to display the current day.

 ◆ Day, Week, and Month. Click to display a day, week, or month at a glance. Use the Left or Right Arrows to move by the selected view.

 ◆ Mini-Month. Click a day or use the Left or Right Arrows. Click the **Show/Hide Mini-Month** button to show or hide the mini-month calendar.

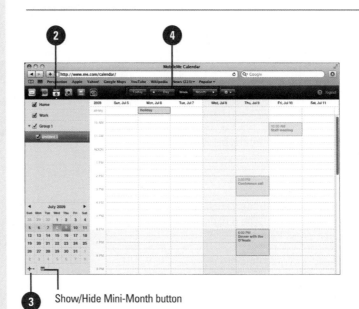

Show/Hide Mini-Month button

Did You Know?

You can delete a MobileMe calendar or event. In Calendar, select the calendar or event you want to delete, click the Actions button, and then click Delete.

Add or Edit MobileMe Calendar Events

1. Open your browser and sign onto your MobileMe account.

2. Click the **Calendar** button.

3. Click the calendar you want to add an event.

4. Click a view button to find the date to add.

5. Drag a time interval on the day you want to add an event.

6. Type a title for the event.

7. To adjust the time and day, drag the top or bottom edge of the event item, or drag the title to a new location.

8. To edit event details, double-click the event, make changes, and then click **OK**.

Change MobileMe Calendar Preferences

1. Open your browser and sign onto your MobileMe account.

2. Click the **Calendar** button.

3. Click the **Actions** button, and then click **Preferences**.

4. Select any of the following preference categories:

 ◆ **General.** Sets appearance and format options.

 ◆ **Advanced.** Sets options for time zone support and whether to hide or delete past events and to do items.

5. Click **Save**.

Creating a MobileMe Gallery

With MobileMe Gallery, you can create and manage an online gallery of photos and movies that you can share with other people from any computer, iPhone, iPod touch, or Apple TV. If you have iLife 08 or later or Aperture 2 or later on your Mac, you can create and publish photos to MobileMe. You can use .JPG, .PNG, or .GIF photo formats and the .MOV movie format in your gallery. However, you cannot directly use RAW images; you need to use Aperture 2 or later. When you share a gallery with MobileMe, you can set options to allow visitors to upload or download photos, add photos via e-mail, or see photo titles or the Gallery e-mail address.

Create a MobileMe Gallery

1. Open your browser and sign onto your MobileMe account.

 ◆ You can access MobileMe log in at *www.mobileme.com*.

2. Click the **Gallery** button.

3. To add a calendar, click the **Add** (+) button, type a name for the gallery, and then press Return.

4. Type a name for your album.

5. Select the check boxes you want to allow visitors to download photos, upload photos via the Web, or add photos via e-mail or iPhone.

6. Select the check boxes you want to show photo titles or the e-mail for uploading photos.

7. Select the Advanced options you want to hide the album or syncs with iPhoto or Aperture.

8. Click **Create**.

9. Click the **Upload** button, and then select the photos or video clips you want to add.

10. Click **Choose**, select the files that you want to add, and then click Select.

11. Click **Done**.

Modify a MobileMe Gallery

① Open your browser and sign onto your MobileMe account.

② Click the **Gallery** button.

③ Click **My Gallery**, if necessary to display the available albums.

④ Double-click the album you want to edit.

◆ To quickly view the images in the album, move your pointer in the album thumbnail in My Gallery.

⑤ Edit the album using any of the following:

◆ **Edit Item Title.** Click the title, edit the text, and then press Return.

◆ **Arrange Items.** Drag the items to another position.

◆ **Delete Items.** Select the items, and then click the **Delete** button.

◆ **Rotate Items.** Select the items, and then click the **Rotate Clockwise** button.

◆ **Settings.** Click the **Setting** button, change the options you want, and then click **Publish**.

Did You Know?

You can add photos from your iPhone to a gallery. In iPhone, setup a MobileMe account, select the photo you want in Camera or Photos, tap the Send Photo button, tap Send To MobileMe, tap the Gallery album to which you want to add a photo, type a title for the photo in the subject of the e-mail, and then tap the Send button.

Viewing and Sharing a MobileMe Gallery

You can view your MobileMe gallery using a browser on your computer, either Mac or PC, iPhone, iPod touch, or on Apple TV. When you view a MobileMe gallery, you can change view options to display it as a grid, mosaic, carousel, or slideshow; select color options to change the background; or drag the Zoom slider to change the view size. Depending on your gallery settings, you can allows visitors to download the entire gallery or an individual photos or movies, subscribe to the RSS gallery feed, upload photos or movies, upload the gallery by mobile phone or e-mail, or send an e-mail with a link to this gallery. A blue dot in an album indicates an album change.

View a MobileMe Gallery

1. Access a MobileMe gallery using any of the following methods:

 ◆ **Computer.** Open your browser (Mac or PC) and go to *http://gallery.me.com/member name*.

 ◆ **iPhone or iPod touch.** Open Safari, and then go to *http://gallery.me.com/member name*.

 ◆ **Apple TV.** Select **Photos** from the main menu, and then click **MobileMe**. Click **Add MobileMe Gallery**, and then type your MobileMe member name, and then select an album or movie to view it.

2. Click the album you want to view.

3. Use any of the following viewing options:

 ◆ **View.** Click **Grid**, **Mosaic**, or **Carousel** to view the album.

 ◆ **Color.** Click a color option to change the background.

 ◆ **Zoom.** Drag the **Zoom** slider to change the view percentage.

4. To view a slide show, click **Slideshow** to play a slide show, move your mouse to display playback controls, and then click buttons to pause, play, and exit full screen.

Share a MobileMe Gallery

1. Open your browser and go to *http://gallery.me.com/member name*.

2. Click the album you want to view.

3. Use any of the following options:

 ◆ **Download.** To download the entire gallery, deselect all items, click **Download**, click **Download**. To download a photo, click the photo, click the **Download** button.

 ◆ **Subscribe.** To open the feed for the selected album in your RSS feed reader, click **Subscribe**, and then click **OK**.

 ◆ **Upload.** To upload photos or movie, click **Upload**, type your name and address, type security characters, click **Choose Files**, select the files you want, and then click **Select**.

 ◆ **Send to Album.** To upload to the selected album by mobile phone or e-mail, send photos or movies to a Web address, click **Send to Album**, write down the Web address, and then click **OK**.

 ◆ **Tell a Friend.** To send an e-mail with a link to the selected album, click **Tell a Friend**, type your name, friend's e-mail address, and message, type security characters, and then click **Send**.

Did You Know?

You can add photos from your mobile phone to a gallery. Send an e-mail with a photo attached to your gallery address. (*http://gallery.me.com/your membername*).

Download gallery or file

Upload files

Subscribe to RSS feed

Tell a Friend via e-mail

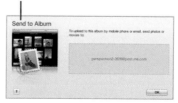
Send to Album

Managing Files with iDisk

Probably one of the coolest, and most-used features of a MobileMe account is iDisk. The iDisk service is like having up to 20 GB hard drive available to you anytime and anywhere you can plug into the Internet. The iDisk is perfect for performing off-site backups, or for storing large files for later use. For example, you could place large files in your iDisk (files that are too big to e-mail), and then download them when you get to your destination. Or if you have a high-speed Internet connection, you could simply use it as a secondary storage device. In addition, if you need more room, you can always upgrade and purchase more space. The good news is that once iDisk is open, you can treat it just like any other storage device on your computer. In fact, the Public folder located in your iDisk can be accessed by anyone owning a MobileMe account. This is the perfect place for placing a document that needs to be distributed to co-workers, or as a place to store photos for other MobileMe users to see.

Manage Files with iDisk

1. Click the **Go** menu, point to **iDisk**, and then click **My iDisk** (it is not necessary to be logged into your MobileMe account.)

2. If necessary, double-click on a folder to display its contents.

3. Drag items, files, or folders into any of the existing folders.

4. Click the **Close** button to close the iDisk window.

Did You Know?

You can't add folders to the iDisk window. If you try to drag a folder from your hard drive directly into the iDisk window, you'll be told that you don't have sufficient privileges; however, if you drop the folder inside of one of the pre-existing folders, the operation is successful.

You can check available iDisk storage space. In MobileMe, click the iDisk button, and then click the Info button (i) in the lower-left corner.

Display Files from MobileMe iDisk

1 Open your browser and sign on to your MobileMe account.

2 Click the **iDisk** button.

- ◆ You can access the iDisk Home folder at *http://idisk.me.com/membername*.

- ◆ You can access the iDisk Public folder at *http://public.me.com/membername*. If prompted, type *public* for the user name, and then type the password.

The MobileMe iDisk window opens, displaying a file hierarchy of the iDisk hard disk online.

3 Click the **Home** or **Public** folder, and then click folders to navigate to the location with the files you want to display from iDisk.

All the files you copied into the iDisk folders on your Mac now appear in MobileMe iDisk.

4 To create a new folder, select a folder location, click the **Actions** button, click **New Folder**, type a name, and then press Return.

5 To upload a file from your computer to iDisk (say from another computer), click the **Upload** button, click **Choose**, select the file, and then click **Select**.

6 To download a file or folder to the Downloads folder on your computer, select the file or folder, click the **Downloads** buttons, and then click **Download**.

Home folder

Access to Public folder

Public folder displayed on a PC in Windows

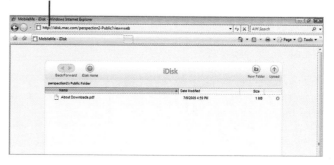

Setting iDisk Preferences

If you're not connected to the Internet, you can create a local copy of your iDisk on your computer, so you can make changes to it at any time. The next time you connect to the Internet, the local changes you made on your computer are synchronized with your iDisk online. If you need more iDisk space online, you can add more space for iDisk and MobileMe mail storage. You can find out current iDisk storage usage information on the iDisk tab in MobileMe Preferences. If you change the size of your iDisk storage, your local iDisk storage is automatically changed. If you are away from your computer, you can access your iDisk public folder online. The Web address is *http://public.me.com/membername*. The public folder is available to anyone who knows how to access it unless you add password protection, which you can set in the MobileMe Preferences.

Create a Local iDisk Copy

1. Click the **System Preferences** icon in the Dock, and then click the **MobileMe** icon.

2. Click the **iDisk** tab.

3. Click **Start**.

4. Click the **Update** pop-up, and then click **Automatically** or **Manually** to sync the content the next time you get online.

5. To stop the iDisk local sync, click **Stop**.

6. Click the **Close** button.

Did You Know?

You can access iDisk Public folder using Windows. For Windows 7 or Vista, create a mapped drive to the following address: *http://public.me.com/membername*. For Windows XP, download the iDisk Utility for Windows at *www.apple.com/mobileme*.

Change iDisk Public Folder Permissions

1 Click the **System Preferences** icon in the Dock, and then click the **MobileMe** icon.

2 Click the **iDisk** tab.

3 Select the **Allow others to write files in your public folder** check box or clear it to allow read only access.

If you selected the Read and Write option, it's important to set a password.

4 Select the **Password-protect your public folder** check box.

5 Type a password 6 to 8 characters, and then type it again to confirm it.

6 Click **OK**.

7 To change the password, click **Set Password**, type a new password, confirm it, and then click **OK**.

8 Click the **Close** button.

Did You Know?

You can connect to your iDisk public folder in MobileMe preferences. Click the System Preferences icon in the Dock, click the MobileMe icon, click the iDisk tab, and then click the link to your iDisk public folder.

Sharing Files with MobileMe iDisk

MobileMe iDisk makes it easy to share files with other people. You can share files by using the Public folder or the Share File command. The Public folder in MobileMe iDisk is available to anyone who knows how to access it unless you add password protection, which you can set in the MobileMe preferences. You can access a public folder at *http://public.me.com/ membername*. If prompted, type *public* for the user name, and then type the password. You can share a folder or file by simply copying it to your Public folder on your Mac or in MobileMe iDisk. If you want to share a file to a specific person, you can use the Share File command to send an access link to the file via e-mail.

Share Files from MobileMe iDisk Public Folder

1. Open your browser and sign on to your MobileMe account.

2. Click the **iDisk** button.

 ◆ You can access the iDisk Home folder at *http://idisk.me.com/ membername*.

3. To create a new folder, select a folder location in the Public folder, click the **Actions** button, click **New Folder**, type a name, and then press Return.

4. Drag folders or files to the Public folder on iDisk to copy them over.

5. To upload a file from your computer to iDisk, select the Public folder, click the **Upload** button, click **Choose**, select the file, and then click **Select**.

6. To rename a folder or file, click it, edit the name, and then press Return.

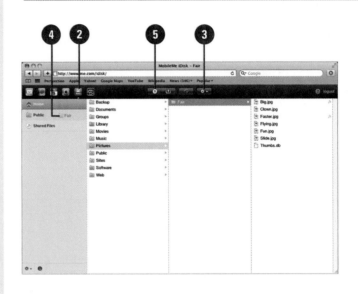

Did You Know?

You can compress files in MobileMe iDisk to save space. In MobileMe, select a folder or file, click the Actions menu, click Compress *folder* or *file name*.

For Your Information

Sharing Files from MobileMe iDisk via E-mail

If you want to share files using e-mail, you can use the Share File command to send them from MobileMe iDisk. Open your browser and sign on to your MobileMe account, click the iDisk button, click the Home or Public folder, and then click folders to navigate to display the files from iDisk you want to share. Select the file you want to share, and then click Share File. Type contact names or e-mail address, and a message. To add an expiration date, select the Link expires after X check box, click the pop-up, and then select a duration. To add a password, select the Password-protect file check box, and then type a password. When you're done, click Share.

Tracking and Synchronizing Information

Introduction

Computers can indeed be a blessing and a curse. On the one hand they give you instant access to mountains of information; on the other hand you're the one who has to organize and keep track of all that data. There are a lot of programs out there that claim to help you stay organized, using everything from day-planner software to relational databases. There's only one problem, you have to actually use those programs. That typically means learning new third party software, loading all your data and schedules, and then trying to keep it current, even if you move it to a different computer. This paragraph defined the problem; the next provides the solution.

When Apple introduced OS X, they touted it as a digital hub. The concept of a digital hub involves placing your daily schedules and contact data into the system one time. Then the hub would keep the data up-to-date and in sync with any other places and devices the same data is stored. With the release of Mac OS X, and applications like iCal, the folks at Apple achieved the dream of creating a true, easy-to-use digital hub in the cloud that can keep your information up-to-date on all your devices.

I have a graveyard of applications that promised to organize and make my life easier. However, the programs were difficult to manage, and they didn't move information easily between systems. In short, the promise was not the reality. When the latest version of Mac OS X was released, along with improved versions of its syncing and management programs, I was finally able to get control of the mountains of information that make up my daily life.

What You'll Do

View the iCal Window

Change Calendar Views

Create and Work with Calendars

Add and Edit Calendar Events

Publish and Subscribe to a Calendar

Work with Reminders

Print Calendars and Reminders

Set Up Synchronization

Reset Synchronization

Keep Track of Passwords with Keychain

Work with Keychains

Modify Keychains

Add Keychains

Viewing the iCal Window

iCal is the Mac version of a scheduling and time-management application. There are other programs out there that schedules and manages your time; however, iCal's native architecture (built by Apple), it's stability, and ability to transfer and sync information easily across multiple applications, makes it an easy choice for the busy executive, the harried designer/animator, or anyone who owns a Mac, and wants to keep track of what they're doing. iCal assists you by helping you automate repetitive events such as: Yoga every Friday at 8pm, the kids soccer practice, or that quarterly conference call with management. In addition, iCal notifies you of an event by using an alarm sound, pop-up note, or even e-mail. iCal uses a streamline new look user interface (**New!**) and full screen view (**New!**) with more room to make it easier to use. To access iCal, click the iCal icon in the Dock or open Launchpad, and then click the iCal icon.

Adding Calendar Accounts

If you use Google, Yahoo!, and Gmail, calendars, iCal can automatically set them up. Click the iCal menu, click Preferences, click Accounts, click the Add (+) button, enter your account e-mail address, and then click Create. iCal account assistance looks for any calendar accounts associated with the e-mail address. You can also add a calendar account for Exchange 2007 or later and CalDAV, however, you need to provide account details.

368

Changing Calendar Views

iCal provides different views for you to look at your calendar. You can view events by Day, Week, Month, and Year. The Day view (**New!**) provides a running list of your events on one side and a detailed schedule on the other, so you everything you need at a glance. Day view also includes a mini month so you can quickly switch between days. In addition to the traditional Week and Month views, you can also view 12 months at a time with Year view (**New!**). In Year view, iCal displays a map using colors to represent availability for each day (**New!**). If you need more room on the screen to view your calendar, you can switch to full screen view (**New!**).

Change Calendar Views

1 Click the **iCal** icon in the Dock.

2 To view the iCal window in full screen view, click the **Full Screen** button (**New!**).

◆ **Exit Full Screen**. Point to the top of the screen to display the menu bar, and then click the **Full Screen** button (**New!**).

3 Click a view button on the toolbar.

◆ **Day**. Displays a running list of events and schedule for the day (**New!**).

◆ **Week**. Displays a weekly schedule for each day of the week.

◆ **Month**. Displays a monthly schedule for each day of the month.

◆ **Year**. Displays a yearly view of availability for each day of the year (**New!**).

4 To display the current day, click **Today**.

◆ You can also click the Left and Right Arrow buttons to switch between days.

Day view

Year view

Creating and Working with Calendars

With iCal, you can keep track of all your activities, either work or personal. You can create separate calendars for different people, such as your family, or a team, or different types of activities. Separating your calendars makes it easy to focus on the information for a specific activity and share only that calendar with the people you want. You can also group related calendars together to make it easier to manage. iCal is not just a standard, one-size-fits-all calendar. As a matter of fact, you can customize the calendar to fit your particular needs. iCal gives you the ability to change how the calendar displays days, weeks, months, and years (**New!**). In addition, you can instruct iCal when to delete old events and even turn off alarms and time zone support.

Create and Work Calendars

1 Click the **iCal** icon in the Dock.

2 To add a calendar, click the **File** menu, point to **New Calendar**, select where you want to add the calendar, type a name for the calendar on the Calendar list, and then press Return.

3 Use the following buttons to navigate a calendar:

 ◆ Today. Click to display the current day.

 ◆ Day, Week, Month, and Year. Click to display a day, week, month, or year (**New!**). Use the Left or Right Arrows to move by the selected view.

4 Use the following to work with calendars:

 ◆ View Calendars. Click the **Calendars** button (**New!**).

 ◆ Rename. Click the **Calendar** button, click the calendar name, click it again, type a new name, and then press Return.

 ◆ Delete. Click the **Calendar** button, Control-click the calendar, and then click **Delete**.

 ◆ Color. Click the **Calendar** button, Control-click the calendar, click **Get Info**, change the color, and then click **OK**.

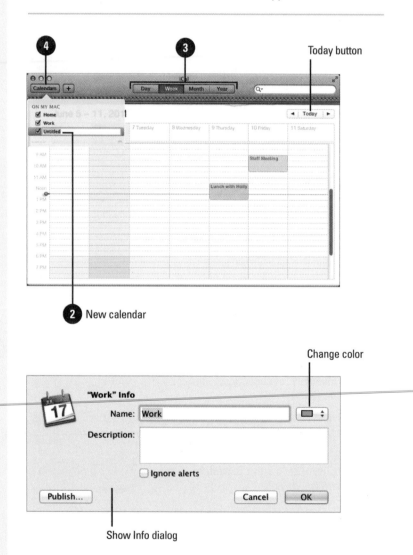

Today button

2 New calendar

Change color

Show Info dialog

Create a Calendar Group

① Click the **File** menu, and then click **New Calendar Group**.

TIMESAVER *Press Shift+⌘+N to create a calendar group.*

② Type a name for the group, and then press Return.

③ Drag existing calendars in the Calendar list into the group or click the **File** menu, point to **New Calendar**, and then select the new group to add to it.

④ To remove a calendar from the group, drag it out of the Calendar list.

Change iCal Preferences

① Click the **iCal** menu, and then click **Preferences**.

② Click **General**.

③ Select from the following iCal preferences:

◆ Day and Week Defaults. Use the pop-ups to specify defaults.

◆ Default Calendar. Use the pop-up to select a default calendar (**New!**).

◆ Show Time and Birthdays Calendar. Select to show time in month view and the birthdays calendar.

◆ Default Alarm. Select to add a default alarm to all new events and invitations.

④ Click **Advanced**, and then select to options you want to enable.

⑤ Click the **Close** button.

Adding and Editing Calendar Events

When you first create your iCal calendar, it represents where you are with your schedule at that moment in time. Unfortunately, things change and they can change often. Therefore, iCal gives you the ability to add new events or modify existing events directly in the Calendar window. You can also use Quick Add (**New!**) to enter an event using a regular language phrase like "Baseball at 1:00 on Saturday." iCal makes calendar modifications easy, and once complete, they can be transferred to other applications and devices. If you need detailed information for multiple events, you don't have to edit each one, you can use the Inspector window to display you what you need by simply clicking it.

Add or Edit Calendar Events

1. Click the **iCal** icon in the Dock.

2. To quickly add an event, click the **Quick Add** button (**New!**), type event information (a regular language phrase with name, time, and location), press Return, and then specify event details, and then click **Done**.

3. Click the **Calendars** button, and then click the calendar you want to add an event.

4. Click a view button to find the date to add.

5. Drag a time interval on the day you want to add an event.

6. Type a title for the event.

7. To adjust the time and day, use the following options:

 ◆ **Adjust Event Time.** Drag the top or bottom edge of the event.

 ◆ **Move Event Day.** Drag the title to a new location.

Did You Know?

You can quickly delete an iCal event.
In iCal, select the event you want to delete, and then press Delete.

For Your Information

Working with Attachments for an Event

If you have an attachment you want to include with an event, you can quickly attach it by dragging it to the event in the iCal window just like a drop box. When you send e-mail invitations to your attendees, the attachments go along with it. While you edit an event, you can also preview an attachment. Simply select it in the Edit dialog, and then press the Spacebar. Click the Close button to exit it. To delete an attachment, select it, and then press Delete.

Show or Edit Calendar Events Details

1. Click the **iCal** icon in the Dock.

2. To show event details, click the **Edit** menu, click **Show Inspector**, and then click an event.

3. Double-click the event you want to edit.

4. Click **Edit**.

5. Add the following event options:

 ◆ **Location.** Enter a location for the event.

 ◆ **All-day.** Check for all day event.

 ◆ **From/To.** Enter a From/To date.

 ◆ **Repeat.** Sets this to a repeating event.

 ◆ **Calendar.** Click to select the calendar this event is linked.

 ◆ **Alarm.** Lets you be notified before the event.

 ◆ **Attendees.** Adds attendees to the event list.

 ◆ **Attachments.** Adds file attachments to the event.

 ◆ **URL.** Click to add a URL address to the event.

 ◆ **Note.** Click to add any notes.

6. Click **Done**.

Did You Know?

You can export or import events. To export as a .ICS file, click the File menu, point to Export, click Export, type a name, specify a location, and then click Export. To import a .ICS file, click the File menu, click Import, select an import option, click Import, select the file, and then click Import.

Inspector window

Publishing and Subscribing to a Calendar

You can create a calendar that lists all of your appointments with detailed information and a To Do list that helps you keep track of everything from household chores to the research you need to do for next week's big funding conference. But what good is that information, if you're out of town, and you forgot to bring your trusty MacBook? By publishing your iCal calendar, you wouldn't have a problem. If you have a MobileMe account or a CalDAV workplace calendar server, publishing your calendar gives you access to that information anywhere there's a computer and an Internet connection. With CalDAV, you can also check the availability of people and resources. In addition, if someone else has published a calendar, you can gain access to it by subscribing. Not only does this give you access to your calendar, but any one that requires your scheduling information.

Publish a Calendar

1. Click the **iCal** icon in the Dock.

2. Click the **Calendars** button, and then select a calendar to publish.

3. Click the **Calendar** menu, and then click **Publish**.

4. Type a name for the calendar.

5. Click the **Publish on** pop-up, and then select a server location, such as MobileMe or CalDAV.

6. Select from the following options:
 - ◆ **Publish changes automatically**
 - ◆ **Publish titles and notes**
 - ◆ **Publish To Do items**
 - ◆ **Publish alarms**
 - ◆ **Publish attachments**

7. Click **Publish**.

8. Write down the URL as it appears. This is very important if you want to view your calendar or allow someone else to subscribe to it.

9. Click **Visit Page, Send Mail** or **OK** in the confirmation message.

10. To unpublish a calendar, select it, click the **Calendar** menu, click **Unpublish**, and then click **Unpublish**.

For Your Information

Backing Up or Importing Calendars

If you already have an electronic calendar, you can import it into iCal. To import all your calendars, click the File menu, point to Import, click Import, select the backup file, and then click Import. It's important to save a backup of your calendar for safe keeping. To backup all your calendars, click the File menu, point to Export, click iCal Archive, type a name, select a location, and then click Save.

Subscribe to a Calendar

1. Click the **iCal** icon in the Dock.

2. Click the **Calendar** menu, and then click **Subscribe**.

3. Type the URL full path name to the calendar with an ICS extension. You need to get the exact URL to the calendar from the person who published it.

4. Click **Subscribe**.

5. Select from the following options:

 ◆ **Name and Description**. Type a name and description for the calendar subscription.

 ◆ **Remove Alarms, Attachments, or Reminders.** Check to remove any of the items.

 ◆ **Auto-refresh**. Select to update the calendar, and then select how often the update occurs.

6. Click **OK**.

7. To unsubscribe to a calendar, click the **Calendars** button, Control-click the calendar you want to remove in the Calendar list, and then click **Delete**.

Did You Know?

You can quickly show the calendar on MobileMe Web site. Option-click a subscribed calendar, and then click Show Calendar on MobileMe.

You can check attendees' availability using CalDAV server. Select an event time, double-click the event, click Edit, and then type the names of the people you want to attend (select them if they pop up). To show availability, click Show Availability to open the Availability window. You can also use the Window menu.

Working with Reminders

Okay, you've created this awesome calendar that lists all of your appointments, plus things that you have to do (my wife calls this a honey do list). Not only does the iCal application let you create a Reminders list (**New!**), complete with every task on your list; it also helps you stay on schedule using audio or pop-up reminders. This is an easier solution than your wife tapping you on the shoulder, and asking you if you remembered to fix the screen on the back porch door.

Work with Reminders

1. Click the **iCal** icon in the Dock.

2. To create a new reminder, click the **File** menu, click **New Reminder**, type a name, and then click Return.

3. To show or hide reminders (**New!**), click the **View** menu, and then click **Show Reminders** or **Hide Reminders**.

4. When a reminder is completed, select the check box in the Reminders list.

5. To modify a reminder, double-click it, edit Priority, Due Date, Alert, Calendar, URL, or Note, and then click **Close**.

6. To delete a reminder, select it in the Reminders list, and the press Delete.

7. To change the sort order, click the **Sort Order** pop-up (**New!**), and then select an attribute.

 - To manually change the order, drag the reminder in the Reminders list.

8. To automatically hide or delete reminder, click the **iCal** menu, click **Preferences**, click **Advanced**, select or clear the hide and delete reminder options you want, and then click the **Close** button.

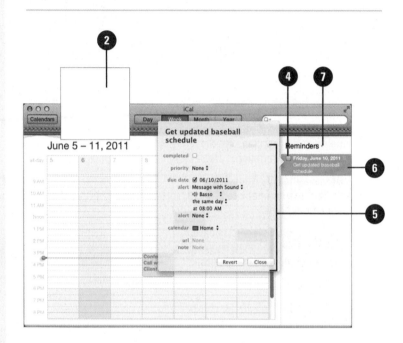

Advanced preferences

Printing Calendars and Reminders

Just like you can print documents and photographs, you can also print any of your calendars and reminders. iCal gives you the flexibility to specify the calendars you want to print and the related details you want to include, such as reminders with due dates, all-day events, mini-months (next and previous calendar months in the upper right corner of the page), and calendar keys (a print legend).

Print Calendars and Reminders

1. Click the **iCal** icon in the Dock.

2. Click the **File** menu, and then click **Print**.

3. Click the **View** pop-up, and then select the print layout you want.

4. Use the **Starts** and **Ends** pop-up to specify the date range you want.

5. Select the check boxes next to the calendars you want to print.

 If you select a calendar group, all the calendars are included.

6. Specify any other print options you want.

 ◆ **All-Day Events.** Includes all day events.

 ◆ **Reminders with Due Dates.** Includes reminders with due dates.

 ◆ **Mini-Months.** Includes the next and previous months.

 ◆ **Calendar Keys.** Includes a calendar legend.

 ◆ **Black and White.** Prints in black and white.

7. Click the **Text size** pop-up, and then select a text size for event headings.

8. Click **Continue**.

9. Select a printer and any print presets, and then click **Print**.

Setting Up Synchronization

If you've setup a MobileMe account, then you'll want to keep your off-site information up-to-date. You'll accomplish this by setting sync options on the MobileMe pane in System Preferences. You can specify exactly what you want updated, and even let your Macintosh perform automatic updates. You can sync any of the following items on your computer: Bookmarks, Calendars, Contacts, Dashboard Widgets, Dock Items, Keychains, Mail Accounts, Mail Rules, Signatures, and Smart Mailboxes, Notes, and System Preferences. When you synchronize the information on your computer with your MobileMe account online, you can access it from any Mac, which you can also synchronize.

Set Up MobileMe Synchronization

1. Click the **System Preferences** icon in the Dock, and then click the **MobileMe** icon.

2. Click the **Sync** tab.

3. Select or clear the **Synchronize with MobileMe** check box.

4. Click the **Synchronize with MobileMe** pop-up, and then select one of the following sync options:

 ◆ **Automatically.** Sync selected items when you make changes and connect to the Internet.

 ◆ **Every Hour, Day, or Week.** Sync selected items when you make changes at the specified interval.

 ◆ **Manually.** Sync selected items when you make changes and click **Sync Now**.

5. Select the check boxes next to the items you want to synchronize.

6. To use the MobileMe Sync menu in the menu bar, select the **Show status in menu bar** check box.

7. To manually sync the selected items, click **Sync Now**.

 ◆ Your can also select the **Sync Now** command on the MobileMe Sync menu.

8. Click the **Close** button.

Resetting Synchronization

If you're having problems synchronizing information or you're not sure whether you want to keep all the changes you have made, you can reset the information on your computer to match the information on your MobileMe account. You can select the information you want to reset, including bookmarks, calendars, contacts, dashboard widgets, dock items, keychains, Mail accounts and rules, notes, and system preferences. When you reset data, Mac OS X erases all the information on the destination device with the information on the source, so make sure this operation is what you want to do.

Reset MobileMe Synchronization

1. Click the **System Preferences** icon in the Dock, and then click the **MobileMe** icon.

2. Click the **Sync** tab.

3. Click **Advanced**.

4. Select the computer you want to reset sync information.

5. Click **Reset Sync Data**.

6. Click the **Replace** pop-up, and then click **All Sync Info** or select a specific item.

7. Select the Left or Right Arrow to specify the direction you want to replace. Left updates your Mac with MobileMe information and Right updates your MobileMe account with your Mac information.

8. Click **Replace**.

9. Click **OK** to confirm the replacement.

10. Click the **Close** button.

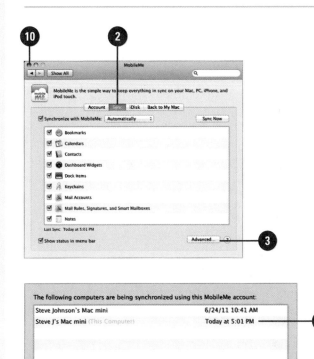

Keeping Track of Passwords with Keychain

The computer is a fantastic tool, however, the birth of the computer brought along another necessary evil, the creation of passwords. You have passwords for the Internet, FTP sites, login, and your MobileMe site. Passwords, passwords, and more passwords, they multiply like rabbits. Even cars and homes have password entrance systems (called keyless entry). The solution to the problem is to create keychains.

Apple's Keychain works in the background; every time you type your login password, you're typing in the master key, and Keychain responds by filling in all the passwords blanks from that point forward. Since Keychain functions in the background, it's invisible to most users. If Keychain were not available, every time you moved around the Internet, or accessed a hard drive, or almost any device, you would be required to type in the proper password.

If you need to make changes to individual keychains, you can use the Keychain Access utility application, which is located in the Utilities folder within the Applications folder. Click the Launchpad icon in the Dock, click the Utilities folder, and then click the Keychain Access icon.

Keychains and certificates

Categories

Passwords

Working with Keychains

When you open Keychain Access, you'll probably already have a list of keychains. If you don't see any keychains, you can use commands on the View menu to view and organize your keychains. With keychains in view, you can unlock and lock access to them, delete them, and add secure notes. If you receive a digital certificate from the Internet, you can add it to your keychain for easier access next time. A **digital certificate** validates users and Web sites on the Internet for credibility.

Work with Keychains

◆ **Show/Hide Keychains.** Click the **View** menu, and then click **Show Keychains** or **Hide Keychains**.

◆ **Unlock Keychain Access.** Select the keychain (such as login or System), click the **Lock** icon, type your password, and then click **OK**.

◆ **Lock Keychain Access.** Select the keychain (such as login or System), and then click the **Unlock** icon.

To change the password for Keychain access, click the **Edit** menu, and then click **Change Password for Keychain** *name*.

◆ **Delete Keychain Access.** Select the keychain (such as login or System), click the **File** menu, click **Delete Keychain** *name*, and then click **Delete References & Files** or **Delete References**.

◆ **Add a Secure Note.** Click the **File** menu, click **New Secure Note Item**, type a keychain name, type the note, and then click **Add**.

◆ **Change Default Keychain.** Select a new keychain, click the **File** menu, and then click **Make Keychain** *name* **Default**.

◆ **Remove a Keychain.** Select a keychain, press Delete, and then click **Delete**.

◆ **Add a Certificate to a Keychain.** Drag the certificate file onto the Keychain Access icon or double-click the certificate file, select a keychain, and then click **OK**.

Unlocked keychain Keychain description

Certificates Secure Notes

Modifying Keychains

The Keychain Access application gives you the ability to modify the elements within a keychain. For example, you could add an additional level of password protection, or insert a secure note. It would even be possible to delete or change the parameters of an existing element within the keychain. Since your Macintosh manages the keychain quite well in the background, it just depends on how much control you wish to exert over the Keychain already setup by your computer.

Modify Keychains

1. Click the **Launchpad** icon, click the **Utilities** folder, and then click the **Keychain Access** icon.

2. Click the **View** menu, click **Show Keychains**, and then select the keychain you want to manage.

3. Double-click a keychain password from the list.

4. Click the **Attributes** tab.

5. Select from the following options:

 ◆ **Name**. Type a new name for the keychain item.

 ◆ **Kind**. Type a new kind such as a MobileMe password or an Internet Connect.

 ◆ **Account**. Type a new account name for the keychain item.

 ◆ **Where**. Type a new location for the keychain item.

 ◆ **Comments**. Type any comments into the comments field.

6. Select or clear the **Show password** check box to show the password for this keychain item.

7. Click **Save Changes**.

8 Click the **Access Control** tab.

9 Select from the following options:

- ◆ **Allow all applications To access this item**. When selected, this item is not restricted.

- ◆ **Confirm before allowing access**. When selected, users have to click through to get to the item.

- ◆ **Ask for keychain password**. Select or clear the check box to require users to type the keychain password.

IMPORTANT *When you click the check box to show the keychain items password, you'll first be prompted for the keychain's master password.*

10 To add specific applications, click **Add** (+) button, and then select the applications.

11 To remove specific applications, click the application, and then click the **Remove** (-) button.

12 Click **Save Changes** to record your changes to the active keychain.

Adding Keychains

Although the Keychain application runs in the background, and is therefore invisible to most Mac users, you have the ability to add additional keychains to the current set. To do this you'll need detailed information on the keychain that you want to add, and an application to perform the addition. In your Utilities folder is a program called Keychain Access. This program allows you to add addition keychains to the existing set. For example, you might want a keychain to manage your computer (default keychain), and another keychain to manage and secure your business documents. Since the keychain application allows you to modify existing elements within a keychain, you could easily wind up locking yourself out of devices or Web sites. Caution is advised when accessing the Keychain Access application.

Add a Keychain and Password

1. Click the **Launchpad** icon, click the **Utilities** folder, and then click the **Keychain Access** icon.

2. Click the **File** menu, and then click **New Keychain**.

3. Type a keychain access name, and then select a save location.

4. Click **Create**.

5. Type a password for the keychain, verify it, and then click **OK**.

6. Click the **File** menu, and then click **New Password Item**.

7. Type the keychain name or URL for easy reference, an account name, and password.

 NOTE *Keychain passwords are case sensitive. Click the Show Typing check box to make sure your password is accurate.*

8. Click **Add**, type a password, and then click **OK**.

 IMPORTANT *Keychains store all of their information as encrypted data, and the password is part of the cipher that restores the information. If you forget your password, there is nothing you can do to restore the information.*

New Keychain

Save As: Private Data

Where: Keychains

Cancel Create...

③

④

Keychain Item Name:

www.apple.com

Enter a name for this keychain item. If you are adding an Internet password item, enter its URL (for example: http://www.apple.com)

Account Name:

Apple ID

Enter the account name associated with this keychain item.

Password:

••••••••••

Enter the password to be stored in the keychain.

Password Strength: Fair

☐ Show Typing

Cancel Add

⑦

⑧

Setting Up Accounts and Maintaining Security

15

Introduction

Mac OS X was designed from the ground up for sharing, and it really doesn't matter what you want to share. For example, you might want to set up a simple home-based network to share files between family members, or even hook your Macintosh into a major network using a combination of Windows, Unix, and Mac machines. In Chapter 16, "Managing Files Using a Network," you'll learn how to set up a functional network using a variety of methods; however in this chapter you'll learn how to create user accounts, manage those accounts, and even protect your information from being accessed by unauthorized individuals, using the File Vault application. In addition, Mac OS X lets multiple users log in and switch between accounts with the click of a button.

Correctly setting up user accounts is important to the security of your computer, so each account is assigned its own name, and individual password. Take care when setting up accounts that you don't give the user more privileges (access) than needed to perform their job. Also, when setting up accounts and passwords, make sure to be accurate in your typing of passwords. Passwords are case-sensitive, and if forgotten, data can be lost forever. When setting up accounts, you can have shared files that can be available for all users on your computer or network.

What You'll Do

Understand User Accounts

Activate the Login Window

Add a User Account

Delete a User Account

Set File Access Permissions

Set Account Access Privileges

Set Account Parental Controls

Specify Log In and Start Up Items

Set Fast User Switching

Set Security & Privacy Preferences

Restore Password Access

Protect Your Computer with FileVault

Manage Files with the Home Folder

Share Files with Other Users

Understanding User Accounts

When Macs were new, they didn't share very well; however, a lot has changed since then. OS X was designed for multi-users, and Lion has continued that tradition with the inclusion of easy user swapping and tighter file security. Think of a user account as a file drawer within a large file cabinet. A specific individual owns each file drawer, and they have access to that drawer through a unique key. That key gives them access to the contents of their drawer, and no other. Controlling the file cabinet is one person, who has a master key that gives her access to all of the file drawers; including her own. Individuals can do anything they please within their own drawer; including throwing away or adding files, but they can't access the other drawers. A User Account is a file drawer that holds all of the user's folders, files, applications; anything they select to add or subtract from their account.

The interesting thing is that on a Mac, the user account is more than just a file drawer; it's the whole user environment. Users create their own world—including desktop, fonts, and folders. For example, one user logs in and sees a background picture of her dog, while another user, logging in on the same computer, has a background of a beach in the Bahamas. In addition, users are assigned privileges that define where they can go, and what they can access. Let's say one user has access to the accounting system; including all the applications and files, and another user is locked out; all determined by the Administrator. The Administrator holds all the keys to all the accounts; they're the ones that set up the other user accounts and decide who can do what. If you're the owner of the computer, you're the Administrator. It's up to you to decide who does what on your computer.

Individual users

Folder contents

Users folder

Activating the Login Window

When you turn on your Macintosh for the first time, it's set up for instant access. You were asked during the initial setup to name your computer and assign a password. By default, the password protection system is not activated, so the next time you start up your Macintosh, you are granted access without having to select your account and type in your password. Before setting up User Accounts, it's a good idea to first activate password login, and then set up any additional accounts. When active, the login window appears every time you start up your computer and contains a list of all those with valid user accounts.

Activate the Login Window

1. Click the **System Preferences** icon in the Dock, and then click the **Users & Groups** icon.

2. If the screen is locked, click the **Lock** icon, type your password, and then click **OK**.

3. Click **Login Options**.

4. Click the **Automatic login** pop-up, and then select **Disabled** or a user.

 When you select a user, your computer automatically starts with this user account.

5. Click the **List of users** or **Name and password** options.

6. Select or clear the following settings to show options in the Login window:

 - **Show the Restart, Sleep, and Shut Down buttons.**
 - **Show Input Menu in login window.**
 - **Show password hints.**

7. Select or clear the **Use VoiceOver at login window** check box.

8. Select the **Show fast user switching menu as** check box if there is more than one user, and then use the pop-up to select a view.

9. Click the **Close** button.

Adding a User Account

Setting up user accounts involves careful consideration as to who is this person, and what they'll be able to access and do on the computer. Mac OS X makes the process of setting up accounts easy; but don't let the ease fool you into thinking it's unsecured. Mac OS X creates a tight wall of protection around each account. When you create a standard account, the security settings are set to their default values. Which means the account user has access to their own personal Home folder, and they are able to access applications on the hard drive. They don't have access to any other account, nor are they able to modify or delete any files or applications on the hard drive.

Add a User Account

1 Click the **System Preferences** icon in the Dock, and then click the **Users & Groups** icon.

2 Click the **Add** (+) button.

3 Click the **New Account** pop-up, and then select an account type.

4 Type a name for the new account, and then type a Short Name for the Account (used by the server).

IMPORTANT *The Short Name cannot contain any spaces and is case sensitive. System administrators in the corporate world typically come up with a naming convention so that all the users are set up in a consistent way. For example, Steve Johnson might be SteveJ to the server.*

5 Type and verify the password for the account.

6 Type a Hint for the password (optional).

7 Click **Create Account**.

8 Click the picture icon, and then select a picture for the account, or drag a picture file from a window or the desktop.

9 Click the **Close** button.

The Account has been added.

Deleting a User Account

Things change quickly in the computer world; an account for an employee that was valid a week ago is now invalid due to the employee quitting. Deleting user accounts is easy, and if planned correctly does not mean that the user's data and files are deleted. You can specify to hold all of the deleted account information in a temporary holding area; where it can be accessed for as long as necessary.

Delete a User Account

1. Click the **System Preferences** icon in the Dock, and then click the **Users & Groups** icon.

2. Select an account from the available users.

3. Click the **Delete** (-) button.

4. Select from the following options:

 - **Save the home folder in a disk image**. Click to save the home if you want the user back later.

 - **Do not change the home folder**. Click to deactivate the account and keep the home folder.

 - **Delete the home folder**. Permanently delete the home folder.

5. Click **OK**.

6. Type your password, and then click **OK** to delete the account.

7. Click the **Close** button.

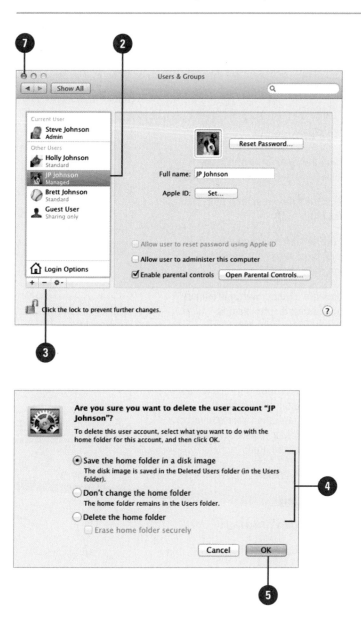

Setting File Access Permissions

As the Administrator, you have one additional area where you can control what users have access to is the File Info. The **File Info** window lets you, as the Administrator, decide who has access to which files and folders on your computer. For example, you could create a folder on the hard drive and give every user account access, or you could select one file within that folder and restrict access. In fact, you can give users the ability to read a file, but not modify, or let them read and modify the file. Since handling individual files would be a bit time consuming (computers typically hold thousands of files), your Macintosh helps out by assuming users do not have access to the hard drive's files and folders (it's up to you to give them access), and you can apply general access settings to all the files and folders nested within a folder (this saves you time).

Set File Permissions

1. Open the hard drive and then select a folder, application, or file.

2. Click the **File** menu, and then click **Get Info**.

3. If the screen is locked, click the **Lock** icon, type your password, and then click **OK**.

4. Click the expand button (triangle) for Sharing & Permissions.

5. If locked, click the **Lock** icon, enter password, and then click **OK** to unlock it.

6. Click the **Privilege** pop-ups to the right of system, admin, and everyone, and then select what type of access you want assigned to the selected item.

 ◆ **Read & Write**

 ◆ **Read Only**

 ◆ **Write Only (Drop Box)**

 ◆ **No Access**

7. Click the **Close** button.

Setting Account Access Privileges

Once you have set up a user account, it's up to you to decide exactly what that particular user can and cannot have access to. For example, you might create a user account for a graphic designer and give them access to all the design applications such as Adobe Photoshop and Illustrator; however, you don't want them messing around with the accounting programs, so you deny access to those specific applications. Once the access privileges are set for an account, they can be changed at a later date, but the Administrator is the only person authorized to change them.

Set Account Access Privileges

1. Click the **System Preferences** icon in the Dock, and then click the **Parental Controls** icon.

2. Select the account you want to modify.

3. Click **Enable Parental Controls**, if necessary.

4. Click the **Apps** tab (**New!**).

5. Select the **Only allow selected applications** check box, and then select the check boxes for the application you want this user to access.

6. Select or clear the **Allow User to Modify the Dock** check box to enable or not.

7. Click the **Others** tab (**New!**).

8. Select to restrict the user's ability to perform certain functions such as **Hide profanity in Dictionary**, **Limit printer administration**, **Limit CD and DVD burning**, or **Disable changing the password**.

9. Click the **Close** button.

See Also

See "Using Simple Finder" on page 92 for information on limiting the available items in the Finder. Great for kids!

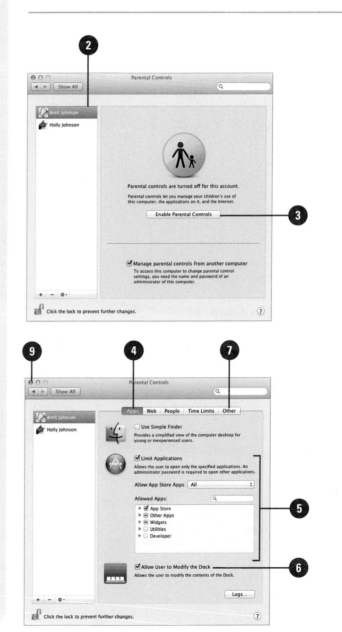

Setting Account Parental Controls

After you have set up a user account as the Administrator, you can enable and set parental controls. Parental Controls help you manage how your children use the computer. Parental Controls allows you to set limits on your children's Web access, Mail and iChat usage, the amount of time spent logged on the computer, and which games and programs they can use. You can set different settings for each user account on your computer, so you can adjust the level you want for each child. You can also review activity reports on a periodic basis to see what your children are doing on the computer.

Set Account Content Controls

1 Click the **System Preferences** icon in the Dock, and then click the **Parental Controls** icon.

2 Select the account you want to modify, and then click **Enable Parental Controls**, if necessary.

3 Click the **Web** tab.

4 Select one of the options:

◆ Allow unrestricted access to websites.

◆ Try to limit access to adult websites automatically. Click **Customize** to specify sites.

◆ Allow access to only these websites. Click the **Add** (+) and **Remove** (-) buttons to add and delete items from the allowable Web site list.

5 Click the **Other** tab.

6 Select or clear the **Hide profanity in Dictionary** check box.

7 Click the **Close** button.

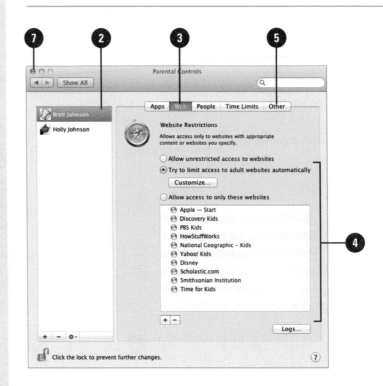

Did You Know?

You can view user account log activity. In Parental Controls Preferences, click the Apps tab, click Logs, use the pop-ups to show activity and group the results, select a log collection and log, and then click Open.

Set Mail and iChat Controls

1. Click the **System Preferences** icon in the Dock, and then click the **Parental Controls** icon.

2. Select the account you want to modify, and then click **Enable Parental Controls**, if necessary.

3. Click the **People** tab.

4. Select or clear the **Limit Mail** and **Limit iChat** check boxes.

5. Click the **Add** (+) and **Remove** (-) buttons to add and delete addresses from the allowable list.

6. Select the **Send permission requests to** check box, and then type an e-mail address.

7. Click the **Close** button.

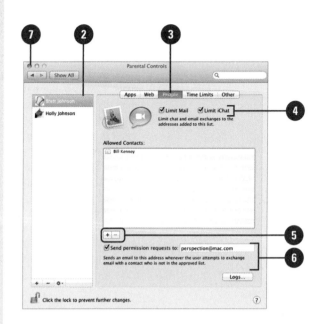

Set Time Limits

1. Click the **System Preferences** icon in the Dock, and then click the **Parental Controls** icon.

2. Select the account you want to modify, and then click **Enable Parental Controls**, if necessary.

3. Click the **Time Limits** tab.

4. Specify options for the following time limits:

 ◆ **Weekday time limits.**

 ◆ **Weekend time limits.**

 ◆ **Bedtime.**

5. Click the **Close** button.

Specifying Log In and Start Up Items

When you first turn on your computer, it begins by access the operating system and performing a standard start up. A normal start up involves performing a system check, and then if login is activated, opening the login window and requiring you to select your account and type in your password. At that point, Mac OS X opens your desktop and it's off to work. However, there is a way that you can alter the start up procedure, by specifying Start Up, and/or Log In items. **Start Up items** are applications or scripts that you decide to launch every time your computer is turned on. **Log In items** are specified by individual users, and launch whenever their account is accessed. For example, you might have a Start Up item (a script) that accesses the company network. In addition, you have a Log In item (a file) that launches your personal day planner, when you log in. The network script launches each time the computer is turned on, but the day planner only launches when you log in to your account. The individuals who own accounts on your computer set up log in items. In fact, log in items are one of the few things the Administrator cannot do—the user must set them up.

Work with Log In Items

1. Click the **System Preferences** icon in the Dock, and then click the **Users & Groups** icon.

2. Select your account (Administrator only).

3. Click the **Login Items** tab.

4. Click the **Add** (+) button to locate a particular application or file you want opened every time you log in.

5. If necessary, click the **Remove** (-) button to remove an item from the startup list.

6. Select the **Hide** check box to open the application or file but hide it until you're ready to work.

7. Click the **Close** button.

 TIMESAVER *To see a list of all hidden applications or files, press ⌘+Tab. You'll see a list of all open applications. Continue to press A, and then press Tab to move through and select any hidden application.*

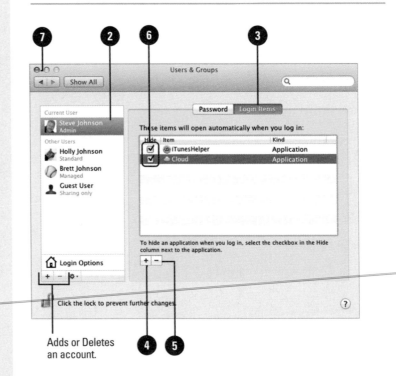

Adds or Deletes an account.

Work with Start Up Items

1. Double-click the **System** folder to open it.

2. Open the Startup Items folder.

3. Add items to the folder by dragging and dropping.

4. Remove items by dragging them out of the folder.

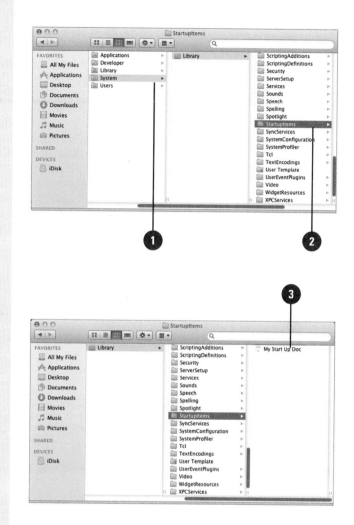

Did You Know?

If you don't want to drop an application into the Startup Items folder, create an alias of the application (or file), and place the alias into the folder. That way, you still have access to the original item, and if you no longer want the item in the Startup Items folder, all you have to do is move it to the trash.

You can create Startup commands. Since Start Up items load every time your computer is running; it's a great way to perform routine maintenance and security. For example, you can create a script that instructs the system to perform hard drive diagnostics every seven days. Since the items are placed within the Startup Items folder, it doesn't matter who logs into the computer; the functions load and perform as instructed.

See Also

See "Creating Aliases" on page 88 for information on how to create and use an alias.

Setting Fast User Switching

One of the advantages to having multiple users and owning Mac OS X, is the ability to quickly switch between users. For example, one of your users wants to quickly check her e-mail. Before Leopard, you would have to close out all your files, log out, and then let her log in, but not any more. Mac OS X allows more than one user access to your computer, and lets you switch back and forth on the fly without closing anything. Think of a large box, and each side of the box represents a user account, along with their personalized desktop, specific folders and applications. To access a new account you simply rotate the box to display another face. That's exactly how it looks when you switch users using Fast User Switching. As you watch, the screen rotates to another face on the box displaying another user, and your account is still active. When she's finished checking her e-mail, all you have to do is switch back. It's that simple, and on systems with multiple users, this one feature can save you a lot of wasted time.

Enable Fast User Switching

1. Click the **System Preferences** icon in the Dock, and then click the **Users & Groups** icon.

2. If the screen is locked, click the **Lock** icon, type your password, and then click **OK**.

3. Click the **Login Options** button.

4. Select the **Show fast user switching menu as** check box.

5. Click the pop-up, and then select a user view option: **Name**, **Short name**, or **Icon**.

6. Click the **Close** button.

See Also

See "Switching Users" on page 22 for information on switching between different users.

Setting Security & Privacy Preferences

The Security & Privacy pane in System Preferences allows you to set options that prevent others from using your computer, such as requiring a password to unlock and change system preferences or wake your computer from sleep or screen saver, logging you out automatically if you're inactive for a certain amount of time, and disabling automatic login all together. The Privacy tab (**New!**) in the Security & Privacy pane provides a central location for enabling and disabling location services and Apple's diagnostic and usage data collection. You can manage which apps and websites can access your location information from local Wi-Fi networks. When an app requests your location, an icon appears in the menu bar.

Set Security & Privacy Options

1. Click the **System Preferences** icon in the Dock, and then click the **Security & Privacy** icon.

2. Click the **General** tab.

3. Select or clear the check boxes related to all user accounts:

 - **Require password after sleep or screen save begin.** Select a delay interval.

 - **Disable automatic login.**

 - **Require an administrator password to access system preferences with lock icons.**

 - **Log out after _X_ minutes of inactivity.**

 - **Show a message when the screen is locked** (**New!**).

 - **Automatically update safe downloads list** (**New!**).

 - **Disable remote control infrared receiver.**

4. Click the **Privacy** tab (**New!**).

5. Select or clear the **Send diagnostic & usage data to Apple** check box.

6. Select or clear the **Enable Location Services** check box, and then select or clear check boxes for each app.

7. Click the **Close** button.

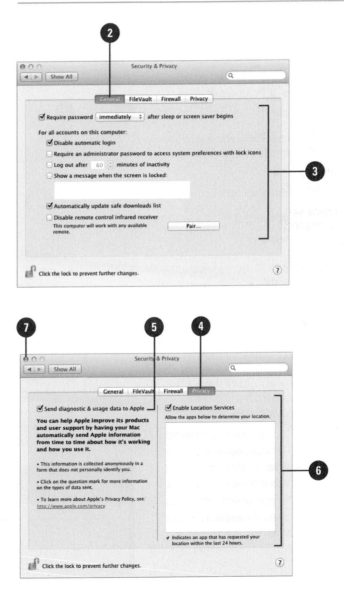

Restoring Password Access

System Administrators are the ones that control the computer; they're the ones that set up other user accounts, and they are the ones, that tell you what you can and cannot access on that particular computer. The System Administrator knows all... sees all. However, what if the System Administrator forgets their password? Well first of all, don't tell anyone and don't worry, because you have two possible ways to get back to work. If you forget your login password with FileVault disabled, you can use an Apple ID associated with your account to reset your login password (**New!**). You can set the Apple ID association in Users & Groups preferences. If you forget your login password with FileVault enabled, you can use the recovery key produced when you turned it on. In the login screen, click the account, click the Question Mark (?) (**New!**) in the password field, and then click the Arrow (FileVault off) or Reset it using your Recovery Key link (FileVault on). If you know the administrator password and want to change account passwords, you can use the Password tab in Users & Groups preferences to make the change.

Set and Restore a Password Using your Apple ID

1. Click the **System Preferences** icon in the Dock, and then click the **Users & Groups** icon.

2. Select the administrator account.

3. Click the **Password** tab.

4. Click **Set**.

5. Enter your Apple ID and password, and then click **OK**.

 ◆ If you don't have an Apple ID, you can click **Create Apple ID** to get one.

6. Click the **Close** button.

7. In the login window, click the account, click the Question Mark (?) in the password field, and click the following:

 ◆ FileVault off. Click **Reset it using your Apple ID**, enter an Apple ID and password, and then click **Reset Password**.

 ◆ FileVault on. Click **Reset it using your Recovery Key**, and then enter your recover key.

Reset Password for Specific Users

1. Click the **System Preferences** icon in the Dock, and then click the **Users & Groups** icon.

2. Select the administrator account or any other account.

3. Click the **Password** tab.

4. Click **Change Password**.

5. Enter your old and new password, password hint, and then click **Change Password**.

6. Click the **Close** button.

Did You Know?

The Installer includes several utilities. Restart your computer, hold down ⌘+R during start up to open installer utilities. The utilities include Restore From Time Machine Backup, Reinstall Mac OS X, Get Help Online, and Disk Utility. On the Utilities menu, you also have access to Firmware Password Utility, Network Utility, and Terminal.

For Your Information

Resetting the Master Password

Your operating system has an Administrator password, and a Master password. If you know the master password, you have no problems whatsoever. However, if you set up a master password, turned on FileVault, and then forgot your Master password... well, not even Mac OS X can help you out of that situation, you're data is lost forever. It is therefore recommended that you create a Master password, and use FileVault to secure your sensitive documents. To reset the Master password, click the System Preferences icon in the Dock, click the Users & Groups icon, select the administrator account, click the Actions button, click Change Master Password, enter a password (current, new, and verify) and a hint, and then click OK. You use the Master password in the login window. In the login window, click the administrator account, click the Question Mark (?) in the password field, click Reset it using your Master Password, and then enter your password.

Protecting Your Computer with FileVault

FileVault 2 gives you security over your sensitive files and applications. FileVault 2 gives you the ability to encrypt all the files on a hard disk (**New!**)—including external USB and FireWire drives (**New!**)—using password encryption (your log in password). It's so strong, that if you forget your password and don't know the password, no one is able to open the files—they are lost forever. It's theorized that breaking the FileVault 2 encryption with XTS-AES 128 data security would take a password-guessing program over 100 trillion years to figure it out. Therefore, if you decide to use FileVault, please don't forget your password, known as a recovery key. To help you keep it safe, you can send it to Apple, where you can call them with security information to get it (**New!**),. After you set FileVault, the security encryption and decryption happens on the fly (**New!**), so you don't have to worry about doing anything; simply use your files normally. If someone else tries to access them, FileVault keeps them out.

Protect Your Computer with FileVault

1. Click the **System Preferences** icon in the Dock, and then click the **Security & Privacy** icon.

 IMPORTANT *Encrypting the entire contents of your hard drive requires the System Administrator.*

2. Click the **FileVault** tab.

3. Click **Turn On FileVault** (all other uses must be logged off).

4. If necessary, click **Enable User**, and enter the password for each user, and then click **Continue**.

5. Write down the recovery key and place it in a safe place, and then click **Continue**.

6. Select an option to store or not store the key with Apple, and then click **Continue**.

7. Click **Restart** to begin the encryption process.

 You can check the progress of the encryption in the FileVault tab in Security & Privacy preferences.

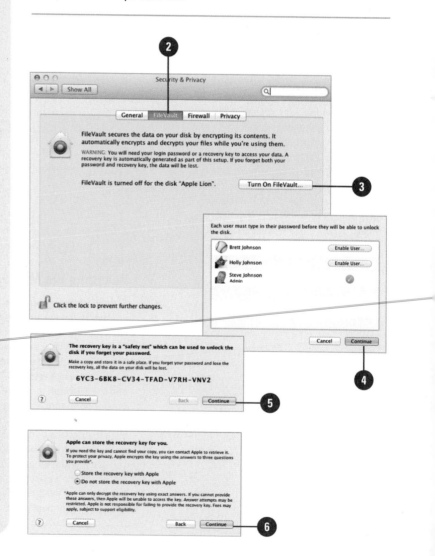

Managing Files with the Home Folder

In a further attempt to organize, as well as secure your computer, each user account is assigned a Home folder. The **Home folder** is where all your account stuff is stored. That means all of your files, images; anything that you've created within your personal account, is stored in this folder. When users sign on to their accounts, they have the ability to add or delete files to their Home folder; however, they cannot access the Home folder of any other user, and they cannot add folders or delete files from any place else but their own Home folder. This gives you a tremendous degree of control over users, and prevents them from accidentally (or purposely) deleting or reading sensitive data. For example, users cannot create folders on the main hard drive, nor can they delete applications from the Applications folder. The other areas of the computer are effectively locked out.

Users folder Home folder

Home folder Folders in Home Home folder
folder documents

Sharing Files with Other Users

When you set up a user account, that person has access to the files in his Home folder. Depending on the level of access, he can open applications, possibly read or access information on the hard drive, but he won't have access to any sensitive areas, or anyone else's Home folder. What if you want to give a file to another co-worker, but you can't drop it into their folder, and the co-worker can't access your Home folder. That's where Macintosh comes to the rescue with shared folders.

When you open your Home folder you'll see a folder named Public. The Public folder contains a nested folder named Drop Box. The **Drop Box folder** is a place where anyone can drop items for you to use. As another user, I can place things into your Drop Box, and you can place things in my Drop Box, but I can't see what's in your Drop Box, nor can I change any items. In other words, files check in but they don't check out.

Finally, there is a **Shared folder**, located in the Users folder. The Shared folder is the only folder (other than your own Home folder) where you have full access to the files it contains.

Public folder Drop Box folder

Universal Shared folder

Managing Files Using a Network

Introduction

Networks are interesting systems. Not too many years ago, a network was defined as two or more computers, connected together by physical cables or telephone lines. They were slow, and they went down (crashed) as much as they were up. The word, network, could bring fear to the hearts of even the stoutest computer system managers. Today, networks are rock solid and reliable. The Web can be defined as one huge network of interconnected computers around the world.

Networks connect more than computers; they work with PDA's, cell phones, televisions, and even wristwatches. And no longer do networks require physical cables. If your computer is equipped with a wireless port, you can connect to the Internet and surf the Web or even check your e-mail, from most major airports and hotel lobbies, without plugging your computer into anything.

In addition, the speed of today's networks allows us to move massive amounts of information, and even conduct real-time video-conferences. Macintosh computers were born to network, even when networking was a difficult proposition, the minds at Apple were working hard to make it fast, easy, and secure; and with the release of Mac OS X Lion, the ability to set up a local network, or one that stretches around the world, is becoming easier and easier.

Using built-in systems, you can even configure a wireless network—using Wi-Fi or Bluetooth (wireless technologies). You can share files and information with other computers with ease and even set up protection (firewalls) to guard against unauthorized access or potential viruses. It's all made possible with a Macintosh, and the Lion operating system.

What You'll Do

Use Network Sharing Services

Set Up File Sharing

Share an Internet Connection

Configure an Internet Firewall

Set Up a Local Area Network

Set Up a Network Connection

Set Up for Different Network Connections

Set Up a Bluetooth Wireless Network

Move Items with Bluetooth

Set Bluetooth Preferences

Browse the Network with the Finder

Connect to Another Computer

Share Files Wirelessly with AirDrop

Control a Computer with Screen Sharing

Set Up Mac and Windows to Share Files

Connect from a Windows 7, Vista, or XP Computer

Connect to a Network Over the Internet

Explore Additional Utility Applications

Using Network Sharing Services

Sharing Services are a collection of options that allow you to define what your computer shares with other computers over a network. For example, if you want to use your computer as a Web server, you would select the Web Sharing service, or by selecting the Printer Sharing service, you can share the printers on your computer with anyone else on the network. When you share files on a network, you need to tell other users your computer's Internet Protocol (IP) address or name. If your computer goes to sleep, you can continue to share its files with other computers and devices. If you're on a local network, you can use the .local hostname as an alternative to a network address. You can find and change your computer name in Sharing Preferences. To prevent accidental changes to your settings, click the Lock button, located in the bottom-left corner of the Sharing window. The next time you try to make changes, you'll be prompted for your Administrator's password.

Use Network Sharing Services

1. Click the **System Preferences** icon in the Dock, and then click the **Sharing** icon.

 Your computer's name appears at the top of the Sharing pane. The network location for this computer appears below the name.

2. To change your computer's name, modify the text in the Computer Name field.

3. Select or clear the check box next to any of the following network services to activate or disable it:

 ◆ **DVD or CD Sharing**. Select to allow other users to access this computer's DVD or CD.

 ◆ **Screen Sharing**. Select to allow other users to access and control your computer.

 ◆ **File Sharing**. Select to allow other users to access this computer's Public folders.

 ◆ **Printer Sharing**. Select to allow other users to share this computer's printers.

Click to prevent accidental changes to your settings.

- ◆ **Scanner Sharing**. Select to allow users to access this computer's scanner.

- ◆ **Web Sharing**. Select to allow users access to the Web pages, located in the Sites folders.

- ◆ **Remote Login**. Select to allow others to login to this computer.

- ◆ **Remote Management**. Select to allow users access to this computer through the Apple Remote Desktop application.

- ◆ **Remote Apple Events**. Select to allow users to send Apple Events to this computer (optional password protection).

- ◆ **Xgrid Sharing**. Select to allow Windows users access to the computer's Public folders.

- ◆ **Internet Sharing**. Select to allow users access to the Internet through your connection.

- ◆ **Bluetooth Sharing**. Select to allow users access to connected Bluetooth wireless devices.

④ Select or specify the options you want for the selected network service; options vary depending on the service.

⑤ Click the **Close** button.

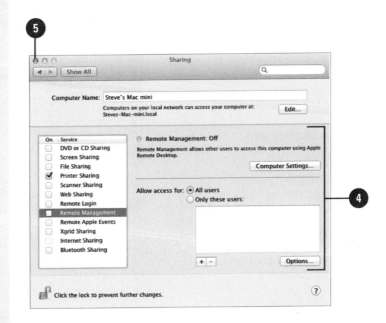

Did You Know?

You can change your computer's local name. Click the Edit button to change the name of your local computer. The local computer name is the name that displays with all the other computer names in a network listing.

Setting Up File Sharing

Whenever you set up a network, regardless of the type, you'll have to configure your computer to communicate with the network. Macintosh computers are big on security, and they won't let your computer talk to any other computer unless you give the other computers permission. Permission involves setting up file sharing options, and then creating accounts with specific user names, passwords, and permissions.

Set Up File Sharing and Permissions

1. Click the **System Preferences** icon in the Dock, and then click the **Sharing** icon.

2. Select the **File Sharing** check box.

3. Select the shared folder you want to set permissions.

 ◆ To add a shared folder to the list, click the **Add** (+) button, select the folder, and then click **Add**.

4. Select the user you want to change permissions.

 ◆ To add a user to the list, click the **Add** (+) button, select a user from your Address Book, and then click **Add**.

5. Use the pop-ups to the right of the user name to set any of the following permissions:

 ◆ **Read & Write.**

 ◆ **Read Only.**

 ◆ **Write Only (Drop Box).**

 ◆ **No Access.**

6. Click the **Close** button.

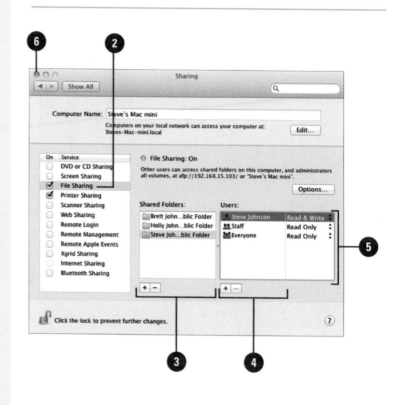

For Your Information

Creating Privileges for Users and Groups

You can decide who gets to go where and do what. There are four levels of access—Read & Write (allows user to access and change the file), Read Only (allows user to access the file, but not make changes), Write Only (Drop Box), and No Access. The levels are pretty self-explanatory; however, if you give someone Read & Write privileges, you're giving them full control over the file. For example, someone could open a text document and basically erase the contents of the letter or completely rewrite it.

Set Advanced File Sharing Options

1 Click the **System Preferences** icon in the Dock, and then click the **Sharing** icon.

2 Select the **File Sharing** service; the option doesn't have to be turned on (checked).

3 Click **Options**.

4 Select from the following options:

- **Share files and folders using AFP.** Select to share files with Mac computers using AFP (Apple Filing Protocol).

- **Share files and folders using FTP.** Select to share files with an FTP (File Transfer Protocol) site.

- **Share files and folders using SMB.** Select to share files with Microsoft Windows computers. Select the user accounts you want to use, and type a password upon request.

5 Click **Done**.

6 Click the **Close** button.

Sharing an Internet Connection

If you have an always-on Internet connection, such as a cable modem or DSL, you can share that connection with all the other people in your network in two ways: purchase a router and gate everyone into the connection, or use the built-in Internet Sharing (it's free). The one requirement is that Internet Sharing must be activated on the Macintosh that's connected to the Internet.

Share an Internet Connection

1 Click the **System Preferences** icon in the Dock, and then click the **Sharing** icon.

2 Select **Internet Sharing**.

3 Click the **Share Your Connection From** pop-up, and then select the method used for sharing.

4 Check Ports that other computers are using.

5 Select the **Internet Sharing** check box.

6 Click **Start**.

IMPORTANT *If the Internet computer is shut down or in Sleep mode, the other network users won't be able to access the Internet.*

7 Click the **Close** button.

Are you sure you want to turn on Internet sharing?

If your computer is connected to a network, turning on Internet sharing may affect the network settings of other computers and disrupt the network. Contact your system administrator before turning on Internet sharing.

Start Cancel

Configuring an Internet Firewall

If you're using a broadband Internet connection (always on), it's possible that a hacker could gain entrance to your system without your knowledge, and do some extensive damage or make off with your secret recipe for beef paprikash. Fortunately, Mac OS X comes equipped with Firewall protection. A **Firewall** is a gatekeeper that in essence, stands guard over your computer; keeping it safe from all attackers. If vandals try to gain entrance to your computer, the Firewall attempts to shut them out. While no Firewall provides perfect protection from all Internet attacks, you can probably sleep soundly, knowing you probably have one of the most sophisticated protection systems on the market today.

Configure an Internet Firewall

1. Click the **System Preferences** icon in the Dock, and then click the **Security & Privacy** icon.

2. Click the **Firewall** tab.

3. Click **Start** to enable firewall settings or click **Stop** to disable it.

4. To set specific firewall settings, click **Advanced**, set the options you want, and then click **OK**.

 ◆ **Block all incoming connections.** Select to block all incoming connections.

 ◆ Click the **Add** (+) and **Remove** (-) button to modify the applications list of allowable incoming connections.

 ◆ **Automatically allow signed software to receive incoming connections.** Select to allow an incoming connection for certified signed software.

 ◆ **Enable stealth mode.** Select to provide no response from uninvited traffic.

5. Click the **Close** button.

Advanced firewall options

Setting Up a Local Area Network

Almost any Macintosh computer comes out of the box network ready. Setting up a Local Area Network or LAN, is fairly straightforward. **Local Area Networks** are a group of local computers hooked together. For example, you could create a LAN for the computers in your office or create a LAN for your home computers. Macintosh even allows you to connect with Windows computers without having to purchase additional software. In fact, all of the software you'll need to create and maintain a LAN is built into Macintosh OS X. All you have to do is buy a couple of cables, connect two or more computers together, and you're ready to network. Let's complicate the situation and say that you're going to hook up more than two computers.

In that case, you'll need an Ethernet cable for each computer and an Ethernet hub. A **hub** is a device that lets you connect multiple computers together. Every Macintosh sold comes with an Ethernet port. To set up a LAN, draw out the layout for the network to determine where the computers are and the distance between each unit. Purchase the cables (make sure they're long enough), and the Ethernet hub (you can purchase Ethernet supplies at almost any electronic store). Plug one end of the Ethernet cables into each of the computers, and the other end into the hub (make sure you plug the hub into an electrical outlet). Once the network is established, you'll need to set up the individual computers for file sharing and to recognize the LAN.

Local Area Network

Hub device

Setting Up a Network Connection

With Mac OS X, you can connect to other computers, local and wide area networks and to the Internet. You can can connect to other computers or networks using an Ethernet, FireWire, or Wi-Fi connection. If you are connecting to the Internet, you can connect with a DSL or cable modem, an Wi-Fi wireless connection, or a telephone modem. After you set up the physical network hardware, you can use the Network pane in System Preferences to setup a network connection. To make the process easy, you can use the Network Setup Assistant to walk you through the steps. If you're having problems with a network, you can also use the Network Setup Assistant to help you fix the problem.

Set Up a Network

1. Click the **System Preferences** icon in the Dock, and then click the **Network** icon.

2. Click **Assist Me**.

3. Click **Assistant**.

 ◆ Diagnostics. If you're having problems with a network connection, click **Diagnostics**, and the follow the instructions.

4. Type a location name, such as Home or Work, and then click **Continue**.

5. Click the option with the network connection you want to make.

6. Click **Continue**.

7. Enter network specific information for the selected network, and then click **Continue**; the requested information varies depending on the selected network.

8. Click **Done**.

See Also

See "Setting Up an Ethernet Connection" on page 221 or "Setting Up a Wireless Connection" on page 222 for information on manually setting up networks.

Click for diagnostics

Setting Up for Different Network Connections

If you connect to networks and the Internet in different ways, you can save network connects to suit your needs. For example, you connect to your network at home with a wireless Wi-Fi connection and your network at the office with an Ethernet connection. You can save different network configurations for different purposes, so you can optimize your network connections. When you have multiple network connections, Mac OS X tries to connect in the order provided in Network Preferences. You can change the network connection order and save the network connection as a new location, so you only need to do this once. The default location, Automatic, provides setting for each of your computer's network services, including Ethernet, Wi-Fi, or a dial-up modem.

Set Up or Modify Different Networks Connections

1. Click the **System Preferences** icon in the Dock, and then click the **Network** icon.

2. Use the following methods to work with your connections:

 ◆ **Edit a Location.** Click the Location pop-up, and then select the location you want to modify.

 ◆ **Create a Location.** Click the **Location** pop-up, click **Edit Location**, click the **Add** (+) button, type a name, and then click **Done**.

 ◆ **Remove, Rename or Duplicate.** Use the Edit Location dialog to delete, rename or duplicate a network location.

3. To change the connection priority, click the **Actions** button, click **Set Service Order**, drag the network service icons to the positions you want, and then click **OK**.

4. To remove a network connection, click the **Remove** (-) button.

5. To revert your changes, click the **Revert**.

6. Click the **Close** button.

Edit Location

Set Service Order

Setting Up a Bluetooth Wireless Network

Macintosh computers have several methods for creating networks. There are standard networks using Ethernet cables, and hubs; there are wireless networks; and then there are Bluetooth networks. **Bluetooth** technology is not so much a network, as it is a simple wireless technology that lets you transmit files and data to any other Bluetooth equipped device. For example, you could use Bluetooth to sync to your Bluetooth PDA, or even use your Address Book, and Bluetooth to automatically dial your Bluetooth cell phone. If you really want to throw away the cables, Apple makes a Bluetooth enabled keyboard and mouse. Bluetooth uses radio signals to communicate with any other Bluetooth device, up to a maximum range of thirty feet. Think of it this way, any Bluetooth device can communicate with any other Bluetooth device, if they are both turned on and within thirty feet of each other. And setup is a breeze with the Bluetooth Setup Assistant.

Set Up a Bluetooth Wireless Network

① Click the **System Preferences** icon in the Dock, and then click the **Network** icon.

② Select Bluetooth in the list.

◆ If Bluetooth is not available, click the **Add** (+) button, select Bluetooth DUN as the network, and then click **Create**.

③ Turn on the Bluetooth device and place it within 30 feet of your computer.

④ Click **Set Up Bluetooth Device**.

The Bluetooth Setup Assistant appears.

⑤ Click **Continue**, and the step through the assistant specifying the device type and passkey to pair the device and the computer.

The Bluetooth Preferences dialog appears.

⑥ To delete a pairing, select it, and then click the **Delete** (-) button.

⑦ Click the **Close** button.

Moving Items with Bluetooth

Once you've set up your Bluetooth devices, it's a simple matter to transfer files to the Bluetooth device. For example, you have a PDA device and you want to move a text file from your computer to the device. The process of moving a file from your computer to your Bluetooth device is the same; however, since each Bluetooth device is different, the process of moving a file from the device to your computer is different for each device. Consult your owner's manual for information on how to move information to your computer, from the Bluetooth device.

Move Items with Bluetooth

1. Turn on the device and place it within 30 feet of your computer.

2. Click the **Launchpad** icon in the Dock, click the **Utilities** folder, and then click the **Bluetooth File Exchange** icon.

3. Select the file you want to send.

4. Click **Send**.

5. Select the Bluetooth device from the available list.

6. Click **Send**.

7. Click the **Close** button.

Setting Bluetooth Preferences

After you set up a Bluetooth wireless network on your computer, you can use System Preferences to control how to send and receive files between your computer and other Bluetooth devices. You can use the Settings tab to make your Mac discoverable by other Bluetooth devices and specify whether you want to require a password. The File Exchange tab allows you to indicate what happens when someone sends you a document: accept it, refuse it, or ask what to do. Finally, the Devices tab lets you set up the use of other Bluetooth devices; use pairing to set passwords for security purposes.

Set Bluetooth Preferences

1. Click the **System Preferences** icon in the Dock, and then click the **Bluetooth** icon.

2. Select or clear the check boxes you want:

 ◆ **Bluetooth Power.**

 ◆ **Discoverable.**

3. To set the following advanced options, click **Advanced**, and the click **OK**.

 ◆ **Open Bluetooth Setup Assistant at startup if no keyboard is detected.**

 ◆ **Open Bluetooth Setup Assistant at startup if no mouse or trackpad is detected.**

 ◆ **Allow Bluetooth devices to wake this computer.**

 ◆ **Reject incoming audio requests.**

4. To use the Bluetooth Status menu, select the **Show Bluetooth Status in the menu bar** check box.

5. Click the **Close** button.

Advanced options

Browsing the Network with the Finder

The Finder serves as a focused network browser application. From the Go menu, you can access the Network window, which displays all the computers available on your network. If you're not sure what is available, this is the place to browse the network. You can also access a network from the Sidebar, which displays all shared computers. After you display a networked computer, you can use all the find tools available on your Mac to locate files. For example, you're looking for a file with a specific name. You've used the Finder application, and checked on your machine, but can't seem to find it. The other option is that it's on your co-workers computer. The good news is that with the Finder application, not only can you search your computer; you can search any other computer on the network.

Browse All Networks with the Finder

1. In Finder, click the **Go** menu, and then click **Network**.

2. Double-click a network computer to browse its contents.

Browse a Specific Network with the Finder

1. Open a Finder window.

2. Click the Shared triangle to display available networks, if necessary.

3. Select the network you want to view.

4. Double-click a folder to browse its contents.

Search for Files in a Network

1. Login to another computer on the network.

2. Open the Finder window.

3. Select the network in which you want to search in the Sidebar under Shared.

4. In the Search field, type the search criteria.

5. In the Search bar, select the network name.

Access Networks from the Finder Sidebar

1. Click the **Finder** menu, and then click **Preferences**.

2. Click **Sidebar**.

3. Select the check boxes under Shared that you want to display:

 ◆ **Back to My Mac**

 ◆ **Connected Servers**

 ◆ **Bonjour Computers**

4. Click the **Close** button.

Connecting to Another Computer

Once you've connected several computers together into a network, and configured your computer for file sharing, the next step is to begin communicating. In order to communicate with another computer, you'll need access to a user account. Typically a user account defines you with a specific name, password, and permissions. Once you log into the other computer, you'll be able to access the areas (permissions) granted to you by the Systems Administrator.

Connect to Another Computer

1. Turn on all the computers.

2. Click the **Go** menu, and then click **Connect To Server**.

3. Connect using one of the following methods:

 ◆ Click **Browse**, and then double-click on one of the available server icons.

 ◆ Type the computer's Server Address, and then click **Connect**.

 ◆ **Windows (SMB/CIFS).**
 Example:
 smb://DNSname/sharename;
 smb://IPaddress/sharename

 ◆ **Macintosh (AFP).** Example:
 afp://ComputerName.Compa nyName.com

 ◆ **FTP.** Example:
 ftp://user@DNSname;
 ftp://DNSname;
 ftp://user:password@ DNSname

 ◆ **NFS.** Example:
 nfs://DNSname/pathname

 ◆ Click the **Recent Servers** button, and then select a server address from the list of available options.

4. Type your Name and Password.

5. Click **Connect**.

Type Server Address | Recent Servers

Enter your name and password for the server "admin".

Connect as: ◯ Guest
 ⦿ Registered User

Name: stevejohnson

Password: ••••••••

☑ Remember this password in my keychain

Cancel | Connect

⑥ Select the area of the other computer you want to access.

⑦ Click **OK**.

> **IMPORTANT** *The other computer now functions and acts as a hard drive on your computer.*

⑧ Click the network computer icon in the Sidebar to display its contents.

⑨ Work with your computer; drag files from your computer to the networked computer or vice versa.

Did You Know?

You can identify the IP (Internet Protocol) address of your computer. Click the Apple menu, and then click System Preferences. Click Network, and then select the network connection in the list. The current IP address is displayed next to the network connection when available.

Click to connect as a different user

Connecting to Your Mac Using a MobileMe Account

With MobileMe, you can use Back to My Mac to access your computer and other services, such as file sharing and screen sharing, from another computer on the Internet. Before you can use it, you need to start it on the computer you want to access and all the other computers you want to use to access it. You can start Back to My Mac in the MobileMe pane in System Preferences. If you want to use file and screen sharing, you need to enable them using the Sharing pane in System Preferences. With Sidebar, you can view and access a shared Mac on your network and control it with permission of the owner.

Start or Stop Back to My Mac

1 Click the **System Preferences** icon in the Dock, and then click the **MobileMe** icon.

2 Click the **Back to My Mac** tab.

3 Click **Turn On Back to My Mac** or **Turn Off Back to My Mac**.

4 To setup file sharing options, click **Open Sharing Preferences**.

5 Click the **Close** button.

Did You Know?

You can display shared devices in the Sidebar. Click the Finder menu, click Preferences, click Shared, select the Back To My Mac check box, and then click the Close button.

Access Your Mac with Back to My Mac

1 Open a Finder window.

2 Click your Mac computer in the Sidebar under Shared.

The files on your Mac computer appears in the Finder window.

3 Work with your computer as you normally do; drag files from your computer to the networked computer or vice versa.

Back to My Mac connection

Sharing Files Wirelessly with AirDrop

AirDrop (**New!**) allows you to quickly send files wirelessly to anyone around you. AirDrop doesn't require any setup, passwords, or preferences to change. It's as simple as dragging and dropping. AirDrop automatically for people nearby within about 30 feet of you who are using AirDrop. Simply, click the AirDrop icon in the Sidebar of a Finder window. AirDrop displays nearby users with their contact pictures and computer names in the AirDrop window. To share a file with someone, simply drag it to that person's picture in the AirDrop window. Once the person accepts the file, it's transferred directly to their Downloads folder. AirDrop creates a firewall between you and the person you are sharing a file with as a safety precaution to prevent anyone from accessing your computer. AirDrop uses TLS encryption for secure transfers. When you're done, simply close the Finder window or click outside AirDrop, which also makes your Mac no longer visible to others. AirDrop uses Wi-Fi to transfer files, so you need to make sure it's enabled in Network preferences.

Share Files with AirDrop

1. In a Finder window, lick **AirDrop** in the Sidebar.

 The people nearby your computer appear in the AirDrop window.

2. Open another Finder window with the files you want to send.

3. Drag the file you want to send to the person's picture.

4. Click **Send**.

 ◆ On the other person's computer, click **Save and Open**, **Decline**, or **Save**. Upon acceptance, the file is downloaded to their the Downloads folder.

5. To cancel an incoming transfer, open the Downloads stack in the Dock, and then click the **Close** button (x) in the icon.

Drag file to contact icon in AirDrop

Did You Know?

You can use Spotlight with AirDrop. From the Spotlight menu, you can drag items to AirDrop (**New!**).

Controlling a Computer with Screen Sharing

You can share your computer with other users. In fact, you can let other users display your screen on their monitor in full screen view (**New!**) and control your computer as if they were sitting in front of it. If a friend needs assistance, you can use screen sharing to take control and provide online help. You can control a Mac with any user account without interrupting someone using another user account (**New!**). You can use an Apple ID to access another computer with Lion; simply add their Apple ID to the list of authorized users and they can log in with their credentials. While you control another computer, you can observe only (**New!**) or have full access to everything on the machine. The Sharing toolbar (**New!**) is available with a variety of tools, such as screen resolution, Clipboard access and screen capture. Before you can use screen sharing, you need to enable the option in Sharing Preferences.

Set Permissions for Screen Sharing

① Click the **System Preferences** icon in the Dock, and then click the **Sharing** icon.

② Select the **Screen Sharing** check box.

TROUBLE? *If Remote Management is already selected, you don't need to select Screen Sharing. Remote Management includes screen sharing.*

③ Select from the following screen sharing options:

◆ **All users**. Select to allow all users to access and control your computer.

◆ **Only these users**. Select to allow specific users access to access and control your computer. Click the **Add** (+) button and then select the users you want from your Address Book.

④ To set access options, click **Computer Settings**, select the check box settings you want for access permission, and then click **OK**.

⑤ Click the **Close** button.

Computer settings

Share Computer's Screen

1 Enable screen sharing on the computer you want to share in Sharing Preferences.

2 Click the Mac computer in the Sidebar under Shared.

3 Click **Share Screen**.

4 Select a sharing option, and specify your username and password as needed.

◆ **By asking for permission.** Asks permission from the current user to share their screen.

◆ **As a registered user.** Connects using a login name and password; if the remote computer is set to the *Only these users* option, the login name needs to be in the list.

◆ **Using an Apple ID.** Uses an authorized Apple ID in Users & Groups preferences to share their screen.

5 Click **Connect**.

The screen for the other computer appears in the sharing viewer.

6 Use your Mac computer as if you were in front of it.

◆ Show/Hide toolbar. Click the **View** menu, and then click **Show Toolbar** or **Hide Toolbar**.

◆ **Switch between Control and Observe mode.** Click toggle button on toolbar.

◆ **Capture screen to file.** Click button on toolbar.

◆ Preferences. Click the **Screen Sharing** menu, and then click **Preferences**.

7 When you're done, click **Connection** menu, and then click **Close**.

Full Screen button

Shared screen

Screen Sharing app icon

Setting Up Mac and Windows to Share Files

Before you can share files between Macintosh and Windows computers, you need to set up file sharing options. When you enable file sharing on a Mac computer to share files with Windows users, Mac OS X uses the Samba server software to provide SMB/CIFS file services. Now Windows users can connect to a Mac computer using normal network services. After you share a folder on a Windows computer, you can share files with Mac users. You may need to disable the Internet Connection Firewall or make sure the TCP port 445 is open. To connect to the Windows computer, users need the network address, workgroup name, and the user name and password for the shared folder.

Set Up a Mac to Share Files with Windows

1. Click the **System Preferences** icon in the Dock, and then click the **Sharing** icon.

2. Select the **File Sharing** check box.

3. Click **Options**.

4. Select the **Share files and folders using SMB** check box.

5. Select the check boxes to enable a user account for sharing.

6. Type a password, and then click **OK**.

7. Click **Done**.

8. Provide the address of your computer displayed in the Sharing pane to Windows users you want to share your computer.

9. Click the **Close** button.

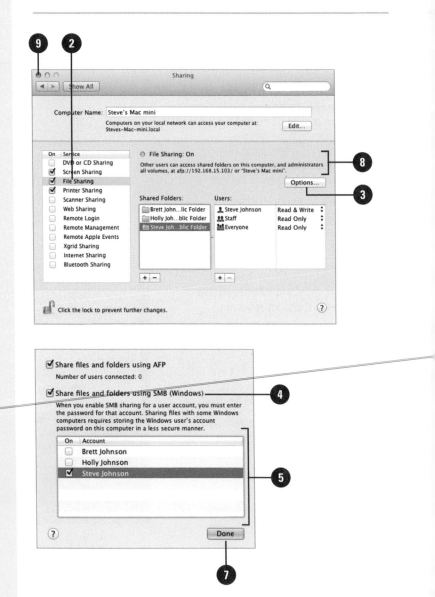

Connecting from a Windows 7 or Vista Computer

After you enable File Sharing in the Sharing Services area of the System Preferences, Windows computers can connect to your computer. Most networks consist of multiple types of computers and operating systems. For Windows 7 or Vista, the Network window lets you view the entire network, including servers, domains, and workgroups. For a Windows 7 or Vista computer on your immediate network, you can browse the network to access the Macintosh computer.

Connect from a Windows 7 or Vista Computer on a Local Network

1. Display the Networks connected to your computer.

 ◆ **Windows 7.** Click the **Start** button, click **Computer**, and then click **Network** in the Navigation pane.

 ◆ **Windows Vista.** Click the **Start** button, and then click **Network**.

 TROUBLE? *For those using different versions of Windows, consult the online help system for specific instructions.*

2. Double-click the Mac Computer icon to display the shared files, folders, and devices on the computer. If necessary, type a user name and password for the Mac account.

3. Double-click a Mac drive or shared folder.

4. When you're done, click the **Close** button.

Windows 7

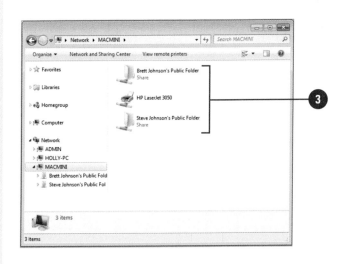

Connecting from a Windows XP Computer

After you enable File Sharing in the Sharing Services area of the System Preferences, Windows computers can connect to your computer. Most networks consist of multiple types of computers and operating systems. For Windows XP, My Network Places lets you view the entire network or just your part of the network to give you access to the servers, domains, and workgroups on the network. For a Windows XP computer on your immediate network, you can browse the network to access the Macintosh computer. If the Windows XP computer is outside your immediate network, you need to add a network place using the Macintosh computer address displayed in the Sharing pane when you enabled Windows Sharing.

Connect from a Windows XP Computer on a Local Network

1. Click the **Start** button, and then click **My Network Places**.

 TROUBLE? *For those using different versions of Windows, consult the online help system for specific instructions.*

2. In the Network Tasks area, click **View Workgroup Computers**.

3. If the computers are not in the same workgroup, click **Microsoft Windows Network**, and then double-click **Workgroup**.

4. Double-click the Mac Computer icon to display the shared files, folders, and devices on the computer. If necessary, type a user name and password for the Mac account.

5. When you're done, click the **Close** button.

Connect from a Windows XP Computer Outside Your Network

1. Click the **Start** button, and then click **My Network Places**.

2. In the Network Tasks area, click **Add A Network Place**, and then click **Next**.

3. Click **Choose Another Network Location**, and then click **Next**.

4. Type the network address of your Macintosh computer. You can find the address in the Sharing pane under Services. Be sure to type it exactly as shown.

5. Click **Next** to continue.

 TROUBLE? *If the addresses are not working, click View Some Examples for help.*

6. Type a name for the network place or use the suggested one, and then click **Next**.

7. To open the network, select the **Open This Network Place When I Click Finish** check box.

8. Click **Finish**.

See Also

See "Using Network Sharing Services" on page 404 for information on enabling Windows sharing and find the network address of your Macintosh computer.

Shortcut to a network

Connecting to a Network Over the Internet

You can create a VPN (Virtual Private Network) connection to securely connect your computer to a network over the Internet. The computer you want to connect to must support a VPN and Internet connection. Before you create a connection, you need to have the server or IP address of the VPN computer. The first time you setup a VPN, you need to select a VPN protocol, either L2TP Over IPSec or PPTP. Use L2TP (Layer Two Tunneling Protocol) over IPSec (Internet Protocol Security), where security is a concern between your computer and Windows XP, or use PPTP (Point-to-Point Tunneling Protocol) where security issues are not as much a problem, but where backward compatibility with older systems is a concern. You can use the Show VPN Status menu to easily connect and disconnect from the VPN, and show connection information. If you want a create a private connection within your physical network, you can create a VLAN (Virtual Local Area Network).

Create a VPN Connection

1. Click the **System Preferences** icon in the Dock, and then click the **Network** icon.

2. Click the **Add** (+) button.

3. Click the **Interface** pop-up, and then click **VPN**.

4. Click the **VPN Type** pop-up, and then click **L2TP Over IPSec** or **PPTP**.

5. Type a name for the connection.

6. Click **Create**.

7. Type the Server Address and Account Name.

8. Click **Authentication Settings** to specify a password or other credentials.

9. To display the modem menu for easy connection access, select the **Show VPN Status In Menu Bar** check box.

10. Click **Connect** to start a VPN connection.

11. When you're done, click the **Close** button, and then save the configuration, if necessary.

Create a VLAN Connection

1. Click the **System Preferences** icon in the Dock, and then click the **Network** icon.

2. Click the **Actions** button, and then click **Manage Virtual Interfaces**.

3. Click the **Add** (+) button, and then click **New VLAN**.

4. Type a name for the VLAN connection.

5. Click the **Interface** pop-up, and then click a network connection.

6. Click **Create**.

7. Click **Done**.

8. Specify any settings provided for the network, such as IP Address, Subnet Mask, and Router, and DNS Servers.

 ◆ If you want assistance, click **Assist Me**, and then follow the instructions.

9. When you're done, click the **Close** button, and then save the configuration, if necessary.

See Also

See "Setting Up an Ethernet Connection" on page 221 for information on setting up a LAN connection.

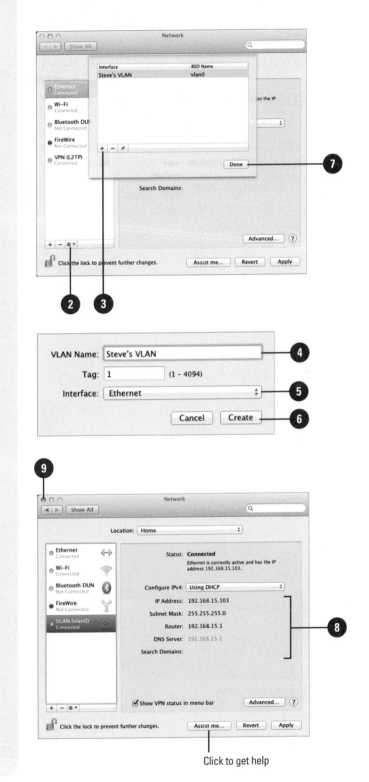

Click to get help

Exploring Additional Utility Applications

The Utilities folder, located within the Applications folder, is host to several dozen applications and utilities that help you manage the daily activities with running your Macintosh computer system, internet and wireless connections, and troubleshooting. It's possible that you might go your entire life and never access some of the more obscure utilities located in this folder; however you should explore the available options, because some of them are useful.

Ping, Finger, and Whois. Info displays your IP (Internet Protocol) address and other network information. NetStat displays technical information about your network. Ping allows you to test an Internet connection. Finger allows you to find out about an e-mail address, while Whois allows you to find out about a domain. When you're experiencing problems with your service, it's possible that a service technician may ask you some of this information.

Network Utility

The Network Utility holds information on Web sites, and offers the ability to perform standard Internet services such as: Info, NetStat,

AirPort Utility

The AirPort Utility lets you monitor the connections within an existing AirPort/Wi-Fi network. In addition, you can use the utility to manually setup new connections.

Info NetStat

Ping Whois

Maintaining Your Computer

Introduction

Once you've bought your Macintosh computer, installed the operating system and all your applications, it's important to be able to keep all that software up-to-date; especially the operating system software. With the consistent updates that Apple is making to the operating system, Mac OS X helps you keep all the software up-to-date with the click of a button.

In addition, loss of data can be a tragic occurrence, so Mac OS X lets you archive or copy data from your computer to an external disk (just remember to keep your backups off-site). It also helps you monitor activities on your system, see who is currently using your computer, and how much processing power each program is using. This gives you the ability to fine-tune your system for maximum performance. If your system seems to be slowing down, or you're experiencing more crashes than usual (a rare occurrence on a Mac), you can use programs to optimize and repair day-to-day problems, and keep your system in tiptop shape.

Remember that maintaining your computer requires more on your part than the launching of a couple of programs. The Macintosh computer comes with several internal fans that help keep the inner workings cool; however, those fans also pull in dust. You should open your computer and vacuum out the interior about once a year, and dust the exterior surface about once a month. In addition, make sure the computer has enough room around it for air to circulate. Finally, make sure all the cables you have strung from the computer to all your peripherals are out of harms way, and in good condition. In past years, attempting to maintain your computer system was a challenge; however, today it's easy to keep things running smoothly.

What You'll Do

Download and Install Software

Automate Software Updates

Open Compressed Files

Compress and Uncompress Files and Folders

Use Application Services

Understand Disk File Systems

Format and Copy a Disk

Fix Disk Problems

Optimize a Disk

Start Your Computer From a Mac OS Disk

Migrate Information Between Macs

Monitor System Activities

View System Messages with the Console

View System Information

Force a Restart

Downloading and Installing Software

Let's face it, a computer without software is simply a very expensive boat anchor. On the other hand, software without a computer is useless. Once you install your software, it's important to keep up with all the updates, patches, and fixes. Mac OS X comes bundled with literally dozens of software packages—everything from disk repair utilities to image-capture applications. In addition, hackers are causing problems and Apple stays on top of them with updates to the operating system, which you can download from the Internet. After you download a software package, you can re-use the package file (.pkg) to install it on another Mac without re-downloading.

Download and Install Software

1. Click the **Apple** menu, and then click **Software Update**.

 A screen appears with a status bar checking for software updates.

 IMPORTANT *Performing software updates requires an Internet connection.*

2. Click **Show Details**, if necessary.

3. Check the software updates you want to load (if available).

4. Select an update, to read more information about that specific product.

5. Click the **Install Items** button.

6. Type your Administrator name and password.

7. Click **OK**.

 Mac OS X begins installing the software. Follow any onscreen instructions, and then close it

Software updates available

Toggles to Hide Details

Button name will differ based on the number of items selected to be installed.

Did You Know?

You can uninstall software using the Trash icon. There's no uninstall program for Mac OS X. So, to uninstall an application, drag its folder from the Applications folder to the Trash icon in the Dock.

Automating Software Updates

Trying to keep up with all your software updates use to be a hassle, but not any more. Not only does Mac OS X let you quickly download all your operating system software updates; it lets you automate the process. When you automate software updates, you select a specific time interval between checks. For example, you could instruct Mac OS X to check for available updates every month. You can even download important updates in the background, so it doesn't interrupt your workflow. With the ability not only to update your software, but also to automate the entire process, there is no longer any excuse for not having up-to-date software.

Automate Software Updates

① Click the **System Preferences** icon in the Dock, and then click the **Software Update** icon.

② Click the **Scheduled Check** tab.

③ Select the **Check For Updates** check box.

④ Click the **Updates** pop-up, and then select how often you want to check for updates.

⑤ Select the **Download important updates automatically** check box to download updates without interrupting your workflow.

⑥ Click **Check Now** to check for any current updates.

⑦ To check all the updates you've currently installed, click the **Installed Updates** tab.

⑧ A list of updated files appears.

You can scroll through the updates to view any changes to your system.

⑨ Click the **Close** button.

Opening Compressed Files

Not all compressed file formats are self-extracting. For those files you'll need a program capable of uncompressing (extracting) the files. Stuffit Expander is a universal utility that helps you open up all those pesky compressed files that other users and companies send you. The latest version (Stuffit 2009 v13), opens almost any compressed format including: .sit, .sea, .hqx, and, .bin. In addition, Stuffit can open files compressed using WinZip (Windows compression utility), and the UNIX formats: .tar, .gzip, and .bzip. For example, you receive a WinZip file from your parents showing pictures of their trip to Hawaii or you download the latest software patch for your word-processing program, and it came in the .hqz format. With Stuffit Expander, you're only seconds away from viewing those pictures and updating that word processor.

Open Compressed Files with Stuffit Expander

1. Open the **Applications** folder, and then open the **Utilities** folder or the **Stuffit** folder to locate the Stuffit Expander.

2. Select a compressed file.

3. Drag and drop the file over the **Stuffit Expander** icon.

4. Stuffit Expander uncompresses the file, and places it in the same location as the compressed file.

Did You Know?

The .dmg file format is self-extracting.
A very popular format for OS X is the .dmg (disk image) format. When you double-click a .dmg file, it extracts the contents and creates a disk icon, which you can access and use just like any other Macintosh disk.

Mounted drive

Compressing and Uncompressing Files and Folders

You can compress files and folder in special files that compress the contents to decrease the size of the files they contain. Compressed folders are useful for reducing the file size of one or more large files, thus freeing disk space and reducing the time it takes to transfer files to another computer over the Internet or network. A compressed file is denoted by a ZIP icon. You can compress one or more files in a compressed file by using the Compress command on the File menu. When a file is compressed, a copy is used in the compression, and the original remains intact. You can uncompress, or extract, a file from the compressed folder by double-clicking the compressed file icon. The compressed files and folder are uncompressed into a folder called Archive.

Compress and Uncompress Files and Folders

❶ Select a file, group of files, or a folder.

❷ Click the **File** menu, and then click **Compress.**

Archive creates a zipped file with the same name as the original item.

❸ To restore an archived zip, double-click its icon.

IMPORTANT *Remember that a back up of your data is your insurance of recovery after a disk crash or other catastrophic system failure. Always keep your backups offsite, or in a protected location, such as a fireproof safe. As tragic as a fire would be, the damage would be compounded if your backups were also destroyed.*

See Also

See "Opening Compressed Files" on page 434 for information on opening compressed files with Stuffit Expander.

Uncompressed files ❸ Compressed file

Using Application Services

Application Services are a Mac OS X feature that lets you efficiently use content from one application to another application. Services are available on the Application menu in an application, such as TextEdit or Finder, based on the situation or in a shortcut (context) menu. For example, you could use the Services option to send selected text information in an e-mail, or make a sticky note in TextEdit. You can individually disable or enable each service in the Keyboard preferences. With Automator, you can now build your own services, making a repetitive task simple to use.

Use Application Services

1. Open an application.

2. Click the **Application** menu, and then point to **Services**.

3. Select from the available commands in the Services application you want.

Change Services Preferences

1. Click the **System Preferences** icon in the Dock, and then click the **Keyboard** icon.

2. Click the **Keyboard Shortcuts** tab.

3. Click **Services** in the left column.

4. Select or clear the check boxes next to the services you do or don't want under the task type, such as Text, Internet, or Pictures.

5. Click the **Close** button.

Understanding Disk File Systems

When you work on a computer, you're utilizing applications that are stored on the computer's hard drive. As you work, you're accessing and writing files back to the hard drive. For example, you open MS Word, create a document, and then save it using the name: MyLetter.doc.

Mac OS X stores files and programs on your hard drive using a system of tracks and sectors; similar to a pie cut into equal triangular pieces. In addition, Mac OS X divides the hard drive into logical file systems, which can help you organize your files and projects.

When you open your hard drive, you'll see that Mac OS X has created several folders to organize your creative efforts. There's a folder for applications, and a folder for the System files—there's even a folder that contains all the users for the particular computer, and another for your documents.

Typically, when you load an application for the first time, you're asked to hold the application within the Applications folder. This gives Mac OS X the ability to control the program, and even helps you when it comes time to check for updates. As you use your computer, you'll probably begin adding folders for your various projects. It's important that you create a disk file system that's well organized. Well organized file systems help you locate and retrieve files quicker and, if properly created, help you to move them from machine to machine. For example, you create a project folder for a major video project: everything that pertains to that project (video, audio, files, text, graphics), are all organized into folders within that one folder. When it come times to publish, move, or archive that information, all your files are conveniently organized in one location.

Tracks

Sectors

Organized contents with folders

File folder

Formatting and Copying a Disk

Computers are wonderful devices; however, it's the information they hold that makes them important. Not only is that information important on your computer, it might also be something you want to send to someone else or archive. In order to send or archive, you'll first need a disk. When you format a disk, you're actually telling the operating system to scrub the disk of all information, and prepare it for use. Make sure you backup any important data before performing the formatting operation. When using the Disk Utility to copy, Mac OS X creates a mirror copy of the original. This differs from dragging and dropping a file onto a disk icon. When you drag and drop, the OS places the new files in whatever space is available. However, when you use Disk Utility, it places the files in exactly the same tracks and sectors as the original.

Format a Disk

1. Click the **Launchpad** icon in the Dock, click the **Utilities** folder, and then click the **Disk Utility** icon.

2. Select the volume (disk) you want to format (you cannot format the startup drive).

3. Click the **Erase** tab.

4. Click the **Volume Format** pop-up, and then select from the following options:

 ◆ **Mac OS Extended (Journaled).** Uses the same HFS Plus filing system as Mac OS Extended, and keeps a journal of your activities. Journaling makes for shortened startup times, and helps in the event of a crash.

 ◆ **Mac OS Extended.** Formats the disk using HFS Plus filing system (helps to compress files and maximize file space).

 ◆ **UNIX File System.** Formats a disk for use on a UNIX system.

 ◆ **MS-DOS File System.** If available, formats a disk for use on a Windows (MS-DOS) system.

5. Type a Name for the formatted disk.

6. Click **Erase**.

Warning message

Volume or disk statistics

Copy a Disk

① Click the **Launchpad** icon in the Dock, click the **Utilities** folder, and then click the **Disk Utility** icon.

② Click the **Restore** tab.

③ Drag a disk image into the Source input box (the disk to copy).

④ Drag a disk image from the Disk Volume column into the Destination input box (the disk to copy onto).

⑤ Click **Restore**.

Did You Know?

You can copy information from a disk over the Internet. Type the URL of the disk you want to restore from into the Source input box.

You can create a new disk image. Select a disk or folder icon in the Disk Volume column, and then click the New Image button.

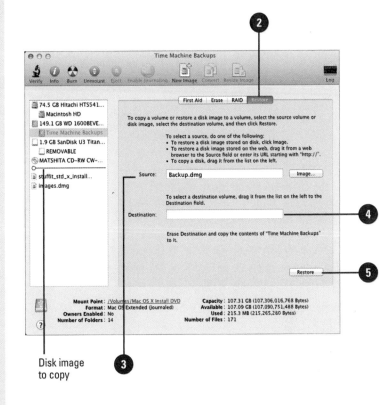

Disk image to copy

Fixing Disk Problems

It's not unusual for a hard drive to experience problems. When problems occur on the main hard drive, it can produce lock ups and slower performance. Apple helps to solve this problem by letting you perform disk repairs to any drives with the exception of the start up drive. For example, you could use disk repair to fix problems on a damaged JAZZ drive, or a secondary hard drive. Apple's Disk Utility locates and fixes problems with catalog and storage files. When information in these areas is damaged, it can cause trouble opening files and slowing down performance.

Fix Disk Problems

1. Click the **Launchpad** icon in the Dock, click the **Utilities** folder, and then click the **Disk Utility** icon.

2. Click the **First Aid** tab.

3. Select a non-startup volume (you cannot repair the startup drive).

4. Click **Repair Disk**.

 IMPORTANT *You cannot repair the Startup volume. To perform a Repair Disk on the Startup volume, you'll have to reboot from a different disk.*

5. Repeat steps 3 and 4 until all your disks have been repaired.

 TIMESAVER *Applications such as Norton Utilities and Tech Tools can help to further enhance and optimize your hard drives, by performing a defrag, or by performing error checks to files not available with the Apple Disk Utility.*

Optimizing a Disk

Your computer uses a storage device to hold applications and data. Typically this would be the main hard drive. Not only is the storage of that information important, but timely retrieval is also an important consideration. Every computer user wants their system to run as efficiently as possible. Faster computers should perform operations such as: opening applications, saving files, and performing normal operations faster than older computers. However, you may notice that after a while your computer doesn't seem to be operating as fast as it did previously—files that took a few seconds to open now take a minute. The problem lies in the optimization of the hard drive, and Mac OS X gives you several ways to optimize your hard drive. Benchmark tests reveal that keeping your hard drive in tiptop shape, actually makes the drive perform eight to ten percent faster. That means programs operate faster, opening and working on graphic files is faster; everything is faster. Time spent in optimizing your hard drive is time well spent.

Optimize a Disk

① Click the **Launchpad** icon in the Dock, click the **Utilities** folder, and then click the **Disk Utility** icon.

② Click the **First Aid** tab.

③ Select the Startup volume from the available options.

④ Click **Repair Disk Permissions** (available only for volumes with Mac OS X installed).

> **IMPORTANT** *Disk Permissions are required by the operating system, and can become damaged. When they are damaged, normal operations become slower.*

Starting Your Computer From a Mac OS Disk

If you want to use a previous version of Mac OS X, you need to install it on a different disk or partition disk. When you want to use the previous version of Mac OS X, you can use the Startup Disk pane in System Preferences to set Mac OS X version as your startup disk. When you restart your computer, Mac OS X version starts. If you want to switch back to Mac OS X Lion, you need to use the Startup Disk pane in System Preferences to reset the startup disk.

Restart to a Mac OS X Disk

1. Click the **System Preferences** icon in the Dock, and then click the **Startup Disk** icon.

2. Click the Mac OS X icon system folder you want to use as the startup disk.

 An alert message appears, asking for confirmation.

3. Click **Restart**, and then click Restart again as confirmation.

 TIMESAVER *Hold down the Option key while you restart your computer, select a startup disk, and then click Restart.*

Migrating Information Between Macs

Instead of trying to re-create Mac settings manually from an old computer on a new Mac computer, you can use the Migration Assistant. With two connected computers, you can use the Migration Assistant to transfer important files and Mac settings from one computer to another. You can transfer information to a Mac from another Mac or PC (**New!**) on the same network, a backup disk, or another startup disk, or you can transfer information from a Mac to another Mac on the same network. The Migration Assistant can transfer user accounts, applications, network and computer settings, files, and volumes. For a PC (**New!**), you can transfer documents, contacts, calendars, e-mail accounts, and photos. Before you can use the Migration Assistant, you need the administrator user name and password to gain access.

Use the Migration Assistant

1. Click the **Launchpad** icon in the Dock, click the **Utilities** folder, and then click the **Migration Assistant** icon.

2. Select the migration method you want to use:

 ◆ **From another Mac, PC, Time Machine backup, or other disk.** Transfers information to this Mac from another Mac, PC (**New!**), Time Machine backup, or other disk.

 ◆ **To another mac.** Restores information tp another mac on the same network.

3. Click **Continue**.

4. Enter the administrator name and password, and then click **OK**.

5. Follow the on-screen instructions for your migration option, which includes selecting the information you want to transfer; steps vary depending on your migration method.

6. Click **Continue** as prompted.

7. When the process is complete, click **Quit**.

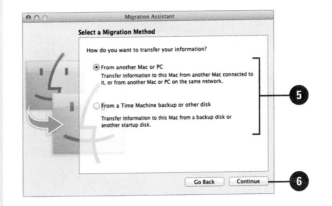

Monitoring System Activities

Mac OS X lets you view exactly how much processor power the various files and applications you have open are using, by utilizing the Activity Monitor. The Activity Monitor is a highly accurate tool that gives you up-to-date information on the various operations currently being used on your computer. It gives you the ability to view the process on a live graph, and even to halt various processes. In addition, if you own a multi-processor Mac, you'll see a separate graph for each processor to let you know how well the operating system is dividing the load.

Monitor System Activities

1. Click the **Launchpad** icon in the Dock, click the **Utilities** folder, and then click the **Activity Monitor** icon.

2. Select a process from the available options.

3. To view more information, click the **Inspect** button.

4. To save the current process list, click the **File** menu, and then click **Save**.

5. To force a quit of the selected process, click the **Quit Process** button.

6. To search for a specific process, enter a search string in the Filter field.

CPU statistics

System Memory statistics

7. To view selected processes, click the **Process** pop-up.

8. Select from the following monitoring tabs:

 ◆ **CPU.** Select to view a graph of the process currently active.

 ◆ **System Memory.** Select to view the current distribution of system memory.

 ◆ **Disk Activity.** Select to view information on the current disk activities.

 ◆ **Disk Usage.** Select to view disk usage on the selected disk (click the Disk pop-up to select a disk).

 ◆ **Network.** Select to view the current activity across the network.

9. Click the **Close** button.

Disk Activity statistics

Disk Usage statistics

Network statistics

Viewing System Messages with the Console

The Console utility is a viewer that displays all the text-based messages sent between the Macintosh operating system, and all open applications. While this utility may seem a bit much for the average Macintosh user, it's of great value to programmers, or would-be programmers, because it gives you information on how the operating system communicates with OS X applications.

View System Messages with the Console

1. Click the **Launchpad** icon in the Dock, click the **Utilities** folder, and then click the **Console** icon.

2. Click **Show Log Lists**, and then select from the available Console logs.

3. To erase the current log, click **Clear Display**.

4. To reload the active log, click **Reload**.

5. To add a day/date stamp to the log, click **Insert Marker**.

6. To look for a specific function, type a search value into the Filter field.

7. To add or subtract buttons from the Console toolbar, click the **View** menu, and then click **Customize Toolbar**. Drag the item to add or subtract.

8. To change the font used in displaying Console messages, click the **Font** menu, and then click **Show Fonts**.

9. If necessary, make any changes to the Font family and size.

10. Click the **Close** button.

11. Click **Done**.

Viewing System Information

The System Information gives you an exact record of what applications you have installed on your computer; along with information on the installed hardware, system extensions, and current network. It's a great place to go, if you're curious about what you've got. For example, the System Information not only gives you information on your installed applications, it also tells what version (including patches) you've got, and the last time you updated it. The System Information also gives you detailed information on your processor; its speed, and any external devices, such as your hard drives and scanners.

View System Information

1. Click the **Launchpad** icon in the Dock, click the **Utilities** folder, and then click the **System Information** icon.

2. Select an item from the Contents column.

3. View information on the selected item in the Info window.

4. Click the **View** menu, and then select from **Short Report**, **Standard Report** (default), or **Extended Report**.

5. Click the **File** menu, and then click **Save Print** or **Export** the current report.

6. Click the **Close** button.

Selected application

Did You Know?

You can use System Information to check if you have a CD or DVD record-able drive on your computer. Launch System Information from the Utilities folder, click the triangle to expand the Hardware category, click the ATA (internal), USB, FireWire, or SCSI category, and then look for CD-R, DVD-R, CD-RW, or DVD-RW. Any of these means you can burn a CD or DVD. If it says simply CD or DVD, then you can't.

Forcing a Restart

When OS X was first unveiled to the Apple community, many users sat back and waited to see how this new operating system would fit into the Mac world, and over the years, it has won over even its harshest critics. With its ability to process information ultra fast, and its UNIX base, it has become the system of choice for the discriminating Mac user. Apple OS X is the first "true" multi-processing operating system to appear in the Mac market. When you open a program, the UNIX-based operating system runs the application within a protected area of the CPU memory. When a second program is opened, it gets its own CPU working areas. What that means to you is that a program crash no longer means restarting your computer. All you have to do is force the program to quit. In the event of a system lockup, you can even instruct the operating system to force a restart.

Force a Restart

1. Click the **Apple** menu, and then click **Force Quit**.

2. Click **Finder**.

3. Click **Relaunch** to conduct a mini restart of the operating system.

 TIMESAVER *If your system is so locked up that you can't access the Force Quit command, just hold down the* ⌘*+Control+Power keys to force your computer to restart.*

4. Follow any onscreen instructions for restarting.

Did You Know?

When you perform a mini restart, you're just relaunching the Finder. Any other programs that were open remain open.

Managing Hardware

Introduction

Computer systems are composed of more than just a computer (that's why they're called systems). A computer houses a hard drive, and is connected to a keyboard, mouse, trackpad and video display. All of these hardware devices are required to operate your computer. For most users that's just the start, you'll probably have one or more printers, a scanner; maybe even a second monitor. Then of course, there are digital cameras, fax machines... you get the idea.

Computers are made up of a group of hardware devices, and like a conductor at a symphony, Mac OS X helps you work with those devices, by making the installation, management, and removal easy. In addition, Mac OS X can help you manage color between devices, help you install MIDI (audio) devices, and even make Internet communications easy. If the worst of the worst problems occur (a system crash), there are steps you can perform to bring your computer system back on line, and you don't even have to be a techie.

What You'll Do

Install Hardware Devices

Remove Hardware Devices

View Hardware Settings

Change Keyboard Settings

Change Mouse Settings

Change Trackpad Settings

Change Monitor Display Settings

Measure Display Colors with the Digital Color Meter

Select Colors with the Color Picker

Match Colors to Devices with ColorSync

Configure Audio MIDI Devices

Prevent Hardware Problems

Installing Hardware Devices

Years ago, hardware installation required all kinds of techniques and special skills. A hardware device such as a printer, could take hours to set up. There were all kinds of cabling problems, and even after it was installed, there were numerous settings to complete before you could use the device. Today, many devices are plug-and-play. You can now go out to your local computer store, pick up a FireWire hard drive, plug it in to your computer, and immediately begin using it. The same is true for many other devices, such as card readers and digital cameras. Even if the device requires the installation of a driver (printers and scanners usually do), a double-click on the install application and answering a few simple questions is typically all that's needed.

Install Hardware Devices

1. Insert the install CD or DVD into your computer (assuming the device is not plug-and-play) or navigate to the installer on your computer or network.

2. Launch the installation application.

 TROUBLE? *Some installations require the device be plugged into your computer. Make sure the device is plugged in, and if necessary, powered on.*

3. Follow the instructions for installing the device (some devices may require a reboot of the system).

4. When the installation is finished, follow the on-screen instructions to end the process.

Did You Know?

You can run a hardware test. Disconnect all external devices except keyboard, mouse, display and speakers. Restart your computer and hold down D during startup. At the Apple Hardware Test chooser screen, select a language, press Return, and then follow the on-screen instructions, which varies depending on the hardware.

Removing Hardware Devices

Installing hardware can be relatively easy: you insert the installation CD or DVD and follow the onscreen instructions. However, when you remove a hardware device, the software that ran the device is still on your computer. It's important to remove any software that is no longer needed for two reasons: it takes up space on your hard drive, and it could cause problems in the future with the installation of other hardware devices.

Remove Hardware Devices

1. Startup your computer.

2. Use the third-party software's installer CD or DVD to remove the recently installed software.

 IMPORTANT *If you do not have the original CD or DVD, check the manufacturer's Web site. Most have an uninstall program that you can download for free.*

3. If you are uncertain about which software was installed last, perform the following steps:

 ◆ Open the Startup Items folder, located in the Library folder, and temporarily remove one or more items.

 ◆ Perform a restart and see if the problem goes away.

4. If the problem still exists, perform the additional steps:

 ◆ Open the Extensions folder pr hardware device, such as Printers, folder located in the Library folder.

 ◆ View files by Date Modified.

 ◆ Temporarily move into a folder any relevant, recently modified, third-party .kext files, and then restart the computer.

 ◆ Add back the moved .kept files one at a time and restart, until the problem reoccurs.

5. Click the **Close** button.

Startup items

Printer items

Viewing Hardware Settings

Most hardware devices have settings that control how the device operates. For example, all ink-jet printers have settings that control the type of paper used, how the inks are applied to the paper and, if your printer has more than a single paper tray, which tray is used for the current printing process. Mac OS X uses the System Preferences panel to display all of the available hardware settings for the major components of the operating system. In addition, when you install specific hardware devices such as a third-party mouse or video-control board, you'll see an icon for controlling the device in the System Preferences.

View Hardware Settings

1 Click **System Preferences** icon in the Dock.

The Hardware section holds the icons to the standard hardware devices for Mac OS X.

2 Click an icon to view or modify the hardware settings of the selected device.

3 When you're finished viewing or modifying the settings, select the following options:

◆ **About.** Provides information on the manufacturer of the device; including the hardware version and Web site (if any).

◆ **Help.** Gives you access to the Help dialog for the selected device.

◆ **Revert.** Puts the settings back to their previous selections.

◆ **Apply Now.** Applies the changes to the settings.

◆ **Close.** Closes the pop-up.

Hardware section

Changing Keyboard Settings

Your keyboard is another one of those wonderful devices that help us communicate with a computer. Keyboards have what is called a **tactile feel** (the way the keys bounce back when they're pressed). Although you can't control the tactile feel of a keyboard, you can control how the keyboard's repeat functions work through System Preferences. Keyboard shortcuts allow you to quickly perform a task by pressing keys on your keyboard. You can change or disable many global keyboard shortcuts, the same shortcuts in all applications, to avoid conflicts or customize to suit your own work preferences.

Change Keyboard Settings

1. Click **System Preferences** icon in the Dock, and then click the **Keyboard** icon.

2. Click the **Keyboard** tab.

3. Drag the **Key Repeat Rate** slider to adjust the speed at which a repeating key is typed.

4. Drag the **Delay Until Repeat** slider to adjust the length of time you have to hold down a key before it begins repeating.

5. Click the **Close** button.

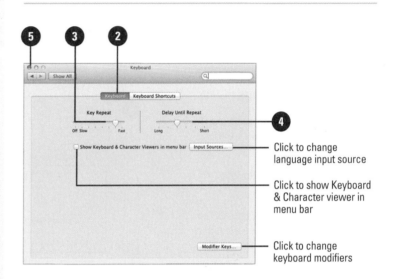

Click to change language input source

Click to show Keyboard & Character viewer in menu bar

Click to change keyboard modifiers

Customize Keyboard Shortcuts

1. Click **System Preferences** icon in the Dock, and then click the **Keyboard** icon.

2. Click the **Keyboard Shortcuts** tab.

3. Click the category with the shortcuts you want to customize.

4. To disable a shortcut, clear the check box next to the description.

5. To change a key combination, click the characters, hold down the new shortcut key combination you want.

6. Click the **Close** button, and then restart any application that uses it.

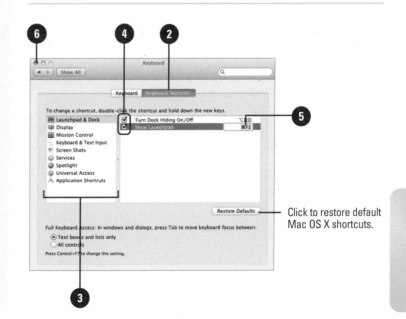

Click to restore default Mac OS X shortcuts.

Changing Mouse Settings

When you use any computer, a mouse is an important part of the computing experience. Computers communicate with the user through a series of Graphical User Interfaces or a G.U.I. (pronounced Gooey). The user communicates with the computer through several devices, such as: a touch screen, a keyboard, a drawing tablet and a mouse. Using a mouse requires a bit of hand-to-eye coordination: You see something on the screen (a button perhaps), and you move the mouse pointer over the object and click. Apple understands the importance of the mouse, and gives you ways to control its movement and sensitivity through preferences located in System Preferences. If you have a Magic mouse, you can set options for gestures (**New!**); see Trackpad preferences on the next page for similar option related information. If you have a Bluetooth wireless mouse, you can set it up a new device, check battery levels, and select other Bluetooth-related options.

Change Mouse Settings

① Click **System Preferences** icon in the Dock, and then click the **Mouse** icon.

② Drag to adjust the following options:

- ◆ **Tracking Speed.** Controls the speed of the mouse as you drag across your mouse pad.

- ◆ **Scrolling Speed.** Controls the scrolling speed of the mouse.

- ◆ **Double-Click Speed.** Controls the speed at which you must double-click your mouse.

③ To use the scroll wheel on your mouse, select the **Zoom using scroll wheel while holding** check box, click the pop-up, and then select a shortcut key. To set additional zoom options, click **Options**.

④ To set Bluetooth wireless options, click **Set Up Bluetooth Mouse**, and then follow the on-screen instructions.

⑤ Click the **Close** button.

Changing Trackpad Settings

If you're using a Mac notebook with a Multi-Touch trackpad, you can use a variety of gestures to move around and get work done on your Mac. In Trackpad preferences (**New!**) in System preferences you can set options in three categories—Point & Click, Scroll & Zoom, and More Gestures—to enable the gestures that you want to use. You can set options to enable swipe between pages and full-screen apes, as well as access Mission Control, Launchpad, and the desktop.

Change Trackpad Settings

1. Click **System Preferences** icon in the Dock, and then click the **Trackpad** icon.

2. Click the following tabs to adjust trackpad options:

 - **Point & Click.** Select options related to pointing and clicking.

 - **Scroll & Zoom.** Select options related to scrolling and zooming.

 - **More Gestures.** Select options related to launching and working with apes.

3. For individual options, click the Down arrow or drag a slider to select a specific setting.

4. To set Bluetooth wireless options, click **Set Up Bluetooth Mouse**, and then follow the on-screen instructions.

5. Click the **Close** button.

Did You Know?

You can set scroll direction preference. When you scroll or swipe in Lion (**New!**), content moves in the same direction as your finger. If you want to restore the previous operating system scroll behavior, simple clear the Scroll with finger direction check box in Mouse or Trackpad preferences.

Point & Click options

More Gestures tab

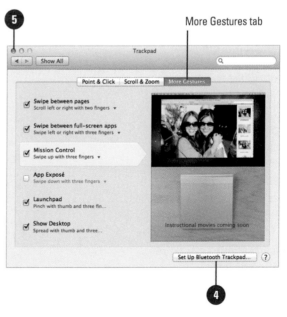

Changing Monitor Display Settings

Your monitor is the main interface between you and your computer. A monitor displays all your programs and mouse movements. Without a monitor, you would in fact be attempting to operate your computer with your eyes closed. Apple, in a effort to give you the best possible view of its wonderful operating system interface, gives you the ability to modify how your monitor displays data, through options located in System Preferences.

Change Monitor Display Settings

① Click **System Preferences** icon in the Dock, and then click the **Displays** icon.

② Click the **Display** tab.

③ Select from the following options, which vary depending on the display:

◆ **Resolutions.** Select a display resolution from the options.

◆ **Colors.** Click the pop-up, and then select the number of colors to display.

◆ **Refresh Rate.** Click the pop-up to set a refresh rate.

◆ **Detect Displays.** Searches for any additional displays attached to the computer.

◆ **Show Displays In Menu Bar.** Check to display the Displays icon on the Apple menu bar.

◆ **Number Of Recent Modes.** Click the pop-up, and then select how many recent modes to display.

◆ **Brightness.** Changes the brightness of the monitor (a Mac laptop feature).

◆ **Automatically Adjust Brightness As Ambient Light Changes.** Automatically adjusts the brightness of the monitor to compensate for external lights (a Mac laptop feature).

④ Click the **Color** tab.

⑤ Select from the following color options:

◆ **Show Profiles For This Display Only.** Check to display profiles for the current monitor.

◆ **Open Profile.** Click to open a profile.

◆ **Delete Profile.** Click to delete a profile.

◆ **Calibrate.** Click to calibrate the color of the monitor.

⑥ Click the **Close** button.

Display Calibrator Assistant

For Your Information

Smoothing Fonts On-Screen

If the fonts on your screen look fuzzy, you can set a screen option to smooth the fonts appearance. Click the System Preferences icon in the Dock, click the General icon, click the Font Smoothing Style pop-up, and then select the best option for your monitor. Automatic is best for the main display, while Standard works the best for an old style CRT monitor. If you have a flat panel display, Medium is the best option. When text smoothing, also known as antialiasing, is enabled, smaller fonts can be harder to read. If you need to use small fonts in your documents, set the font size you want before text smoothing kicks in. When you're done, click the Close button.

Measuring Display Colors with the Digital Color Meter

Have you ever wondered what the exact color value of an item on your monitor would be if measured using RGB (red, green, and blue) values? Or how about the hexadecimal value of a color (useful if you design Web pages)? Color is an important part of any designer's life, and the Digital Color meter lets you accurately sample colors from your monitor. Since the cursor determines the sampled color, you'll need to learn a few shortcut keys to lock the color information.

Measure Display Colors with the Digital Color Meter

1. Click the **Applications** folder in the Dock, click the **Utilities** folder, and then click the **Digital Color Meter** icon.

2. Click the **Color** pop-up, and then select a color space to measure.

3. Drag the **Aperture Size** slider left or right, to decrease or increase the area used for the taking of a screen shot.

4. Move the mouse over the monitor to measure the color directly underneath the cursor.

5. To lock the aperture's location horizontally, press ⌘+X. To unlock it, press ⌘+X again.

6. To lock the aperture's location vertically, press ⌘+Y. To unlock it, press ⌘+Y again.

7. To show/hide the mouse location in the preview, press ⌘+L.

Selecting Colors with the Color Picker

The world of color on a computer is a very subjective place to live. For example, you might be using a new Macintosh Studio Display, and someone else might be using a Sony LCD monitor. What this means to you is, a color displayed on your hardware device (monitor) might look slightly different on another computer using a different monitor. In addition, it's possible that two people, owning the same monitor, may have them adjusted differently. While creating consistent color output is a difficult thing, Mac OS X gives you a stable color picking system, which helps to stabilize colors systems. The Macintosh Color Picker is accessed through an application, such as TextEdit, MS Word or Photoshop, or any application that lets you select colors.

Select Colors with the Color Picker

1. Open an application, such as MS Word or TextEdit.

2. Display the Colors window.

 ◆ In MS Word, select a button, such as text color, and then click **More Colors**.

 ◆ In TextEdit, click the **Format** menu, point to **Font**, and then click **Show Colors**.

3. Click a palette, and then select a color from the available color profiles:

 ◆ **Color Wheel.** Drag the scroll bar vertically to adjust the brightness, and then click inside the ball, to select a color.

 ◆ **Color Slider.** Select a color mixing method from the pop-up, and then drag the sliders to select a color.

 ◆ **Color Palettes.** Select a pre-designed color palette from the pop-up, and then select the color from the available list.

 ◆ **Image Palettes.** Displays a spectrum of colors. Click in the spectrum to select a color.

 ◆ **Crayons.** Select a color from the available crayons.

4. Click the **Close** button.

TextEdit

Color Wheel Color Palettes

Crayons

Matching Colors to Devices with ColorSync

The ColorSync utility gives the designer the ability to match up colors between devices, and to check on and repair the device color profiles present on the computer. As you might have figured out by now, computer monitors are not the best at maintaining color accuracy; especially between monitor and print. The ColorSync utility strives to maintain a color standard between devices, by acting as a translator between different devices. The original scanned image, your monitor, and the output printing device are all examples of where color needs to be synced, and it is achieved though the ColorSync utility.

Match Colors to Devices with ColorSync

① Click the **Applications** folder in the Dock, click the **Utilities** folder, and then click the **ColorSync Utility** icon.

② Click **Profile First Aid**.

③ Click **Verify** (to view) or **Repair** (to fix) the color profiles installed on your computer.

④ Click **Profiles**.

⑤ View a gamut grid of the color profiles installed for your computer (click the user option to view color profiles created by you).

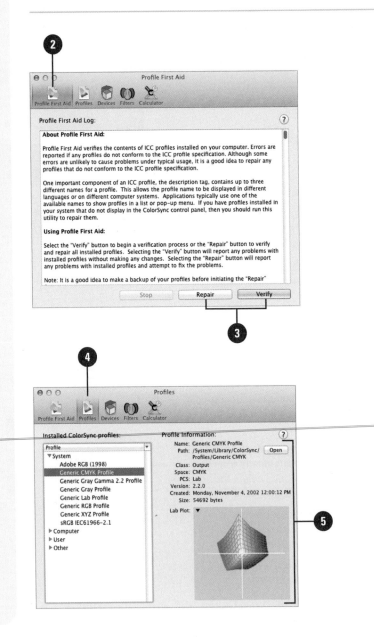

6. To select and assign color profiles to all installed devices, click **Devices**.

7. To view information on the currently installed filters, click **Filters**.

8. Click **Add** (+) or **Remove** (-) button to add a new filter, or delete the selected filter.

9. Click the **Down Arrow** icon, point to any of the following commands, and then select the option you want:

 ◆ **Duplicate Filter.**

 ◆ **Add Color Management Component.**

 ◆ **Add Image Effects Component.**

 ◆ **Add PDF Retouch Component.**

 ◆ **Add Domain Information.**

 ◆ **Add Comments.**

 IMPORTANT *The ColorSync Utility gives you the ability to view and change the color profiles used by different devices. This is an area where you don't want to experiment. Have a good understanding of color theory, before attempting to change any of the ColorSync settings.*

10. Click the **Close** button.

Configuring Audio MIDI Devices

Macintosh computers were born to work with music, and as the years advanced they got better and better. The Audio MIDI (Musical Instrument Digital Interface) Setup utility is designed to help you setup all your input and output sound equipment, such as microphones, speakers, and multichannel audio interfaces, either built-in or external. In most cases, the default settings work the best. However, if you do work a lot with audio, Apple has made the process of adding, monitoring, and adjusting external devices, such as electronic keyboards and speakers, a snap. If you have multiple audio devices, you can combine them together, known as aggregating devices, to add capacity. For example, if you have an two 6 channel audio devices, you can combine them to work as a single 12 channel audio device.

Configure Audio MIDI Devices

1. Click the **Applications** folder in the Dock, click the **Utilities** folder, and then click the **Audio MIDI Setup** icon.

2. To create an aggregate device, click the **Add** (+) button.

 ◆ To remove an aggregate device, select it, and then click the **Remove** (-) button.

3. Select the audio device you want to configure.

4. To use the selected device for sound input or sound output, or to play system sounds, click the **Actions** button, and then select an option.

5. If you're using an audio device that sends its own timing messages, click the **Clock source** pop-up, and then select an option.

6. Click the **Input** or **Output** tab, if available.

7. If you have multiple sources and prefer a different source option, click the **Source** pop-up, and then select an option.

 The Mac automatically selects the appropriate source option for you.

8 Based on your audio device, click the **Sample Rate** and **Bit Depth** pop-ups (under Format), and then select an appropriate setting.

9 To set the volume for each channel, drag the **Volume** sliders.

10 To configure surround sound (multichannel) speakers, click **Configure Speakers**, select the options you want, click **Apply**, and then click **Done**.

- ◆ Select **Stereo** or **Multichannel** device type, and then select a surround sound version for multichannel.

- ◆ Select the device channel for each speaker.

- ◆ To test the speaker connection, click a speaker to play a sound.

11 Click the **Close** button.

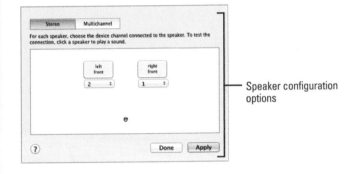

Speaker configuration options

Preventing Hardware Problems

Whenever you add hardware devices to your computer, the possibility exists that a problem will occur. Problems can fall into several categories: The device doesn't work, the device doesn't work the way you expect, or the computer refuses to boot. Apple's built-in management systems make hardware problems a rare event. However, a few careful steps on your part can help to make problems almost non-existent.

Check for hardware device compatibility

Not all hardware devices are compatible with your particular version of Macintosh. For example, you could purchase a video driver board, which works fine in a G4 model, but won't function in a G5 or later. Make sure the user's manual lists your model of Macintosh.

Check for software compatibility

Many hardware devices require installation software to operate. Even though OS X has been in the market for a couple of years, there are still hardware devices with accompanying installation software that is not compatible with the OS X operating system. In addition, the operating system changed the rules on computer architecture; therefore, make sure the software is not just OS X compatible, but is also Lion compatible.

Check the Internet

Software changes (almost on a weekly basis), when you purchase a piece of hardware, that box may have been sitting on the shelf for months. Make sure you access the device's Internet site, and determine if you have the latest version of the software.

Plan for the future

If you haven't purchased an Intel-based Mac (yet), you probably will in the future. Be advised that some of your hardware devices may not work with the new architecture. When you purchase new hardware, check the manufacturer's Web site, and see if they plan on supporting future Macintosh computers.

When the worst happens

Sometimes you install a hardware device, and your Macintosh refuses to startup. Many times it's because you just installed a new hardware device. Unfortunately, when you disconnect the device your Mac still won't startup. The reason is because the software that runs the device is still installed. When this happens you can attempt a fix by performing a "Safe" boot.

First, you'll need to power down your computer. After your computer has shut off, go ahead and press the power button. After you hear the startup tone, immediately press and hold the Shift key. You'll release the Shift key when you see the gray Apple and progress indicator (looks like a spinning gear).

The Safe Mode takes awhile to boot (several minutes). That's because Safe Mode performs a system check before starting. Then, you'll use the hardware device's installation DVD to remove the installed hardware. After that is done, restart your computer the normal way (without holding the Shift key).

If removing the device software does not solve the problem, your glitch may be caused by something more serious. You can attempt a reinstall of the Mac OS X operating system, but before doing that, go online and check out the Apple Web site and search for help on your problem. When there is no solution but to start over, or get a new device, you'll need to remove the hardware device and the software that controls it.

Working with Mac OS X Along with Windows

Introduction

If you have an Intel-based Mac computer, you can install and run Microsoft Windows XP (Service Pack 2 or later), Windows Vista, or Windows 7 on your computer. All you need is Boot Camp Assistant, related drivers, and your Microsoft Windows installation disc.

The Boot Camp Assistant helps you set up a Windows partition on your computer's hard drive and then start the Windows operating system installation. After you complete the initial installation, you need to install Boot Camp drivers to complete the installation and start your Mac in either Windows or Mac OS X. The Boot Camp drivers, available on your Mac OS X Lion installation disc, allow you to use your Apple keyboard to emulate a standard PC keyboard, an Apple Remote (if your computer is equipped with one) to control iTunes and Windows Media, Bluetooth wireless devices, an iSight camera, and Wi-Fi wireless network connectivity, and change brightness and contrast controls for built-in displays. After you finish the Windows installation and Boot Camp driver update, you can use Windows on your Mac.

If you no longer want to run Microsoft Windows on your Mac computer, you can remove it using Boot Camp Assistant. When you remove Windows, the Boot Camp Assistant removes the Windows software and restores your hard disk back to a single partition.

What You'll Do

Prepare a Mac for Windows

Install Windows on a Mac

Start Up with Mac OS X or Windows

Use Windows on a Mac

Remove Windows

Preparing a Mac for Windows

Before you can install Microsoft Windows XP (Service Pack 2 or later), Windows Vista, or Windows 7 on your Mac, you need to meet the minimum hardware requirement for your Mac, create a partition on your hard disk for the Windows software, and have a single-full Windows (32-bit version) installation disc. You can use the About This Mac command on the Apple menu to check your hardware configuration and Boot Camp Assistant to create a partition for the Windows software. Before you install Windows on your Mac computer, it's critical to make a back up of the important files on your computer; better safe than sorry.

Prepare a Mac for Windows

1. Before you can install and set up Windows on your Mac, your computer needs to meet the following minimum requirements:

 ◆ An Intel-based Mac computer.

 ◆ A USB keyboard and mouse, or a built-in keyboard and touch pad.

 ◆ Mac OS X version 10.7 or later; the lastest version of the Mac OS X is recommended.

 ◆ At least 10 GB of free space on the installation disk.

 ◆ Internal disk with a single partition, formatted as a Mac OS X Extended (Journaled) volume.

 ◆ 2 GB or more of RAM when running Windows 7 or Vista on a Mac computer.

 ◆ A licensed copy of Windows XP Home Edition or Professional, Windows Vista, or Windows 7.

2. Click the **Launchpad** icon in the Dock, click the **Utilities** folder, and then click the **Boot Camp Assistant** icon.

About This Mac computer information

Utilities folder

3. Read the Introduction screen, and then click **Print Installation & Setup Guide** to have this important document handy during your Windows installation, and then click **Continue**.

4. Select an option to download Windows Support software for this Mac, and then click **Continue**.

5. If your computer has more than one internal disk, select the disk you want to use, select the partition option you want, and then click **Continue**.

6. Use the default size (recommended), or specify the size you want. Either, drag the divider to set the size of the partition or click **Divide Equally** or **Use 32 GB**.

 The partition must be at least 5 GB and leave at least 5 GB of free space on the Mac OS X partition.

 IMPORTANT *A partition larger than 32 GB cannot be formatted as a FAT volume.*

7. Click **Partition**, and then wait for the completion of the partition.

8. Click **Quit and Install Later** to perform the Windows install at another time, or go to the next page and follow the instructions to start the installation.

Have a Problem?

Having Trouble Partitioning a Disk

If you have a problem creating a partition, you may need to update your system software and the firmware on your computer. Firmware is software embedded in hardware components. Boot Camp requires Mac OS X 10.4.6 or later and the latest firmware. To update your system software, click the Apple menu, and then click Software Update. To update your firmware, go to the Apple Downloads Web site at *www.apple.com/support/downloads*, search for firmware updates for your computer and follow the instructions.

Installing Windows on a Mac

After you create a partition on your Mac computer for the Windows software, you can start the Microsoft Windows XP (Service Pack 2 or later), Windows Vista, or Windows 7 installation on your Mac with a single-full Windows (32-bit version) installation disc. During the Windows installation, you need to reformat the new Windows partition, so you can boot (startup) from Windows. You can reformat the Windows partition with the NTFS (XP, Vista, or 7) or FAT (XP only) format. NTFS provides reliability and security, while FAT provides compatibility, which allows you to read and write file on the Windows partition from Mac OS X. After you complete the Windows installation, you need to update Boot Camp drivers on your Mac computer, which are available on your Mac OS X Lion installation disc, to install Mac-specific drivers for graphics, networking, audio, Wi-Fi wireless connectivity, Bluetooth, iSight camera, Apple keyboards, Apple Remote, and brightness control for built-in displays.

Install Windows on a Mac

1. Create a partition on your Mac computer for the Windows software; see "Preparing a Mac for Windows Software" on page 466 for specific details.

 IMPORTANT *To install Windows using Boot Camp, you must be logged in as an administrator.*

2. If you quit Boot Camp Assistant without installing Windows, click the **Launchpad** icon in the Dock, click the **Utilities** folder, click the **Boot Camp Assistant** icon, and then click the **Start the Windows installer** option.

3. Click **Continue**.

4. Insert your Windows installation disc, and then click **Start Installation**.

 IMPORTANT *Do not install an earlier version of Windows XP and try to update it.*

5 Follow the Windows installation instructions until you need to decide where to install Windows.

◆ **Windows XP.** Select **C:Partition3 <BOOTCAMP> [FAT32]**, and then select an NTFS or FAT format partition option.

◆ **Windows 7 or Vista.** Click **Disk 0 Partition 3 BOOTCAMP**, click **Drive option (advanced)**, click **Format**, and then click **OK**.

6 Finish the Windows installation, and then eject the Windows Installation disc.

7 Insert your Mac OS X Lion installation disc.

◆ If the installer doesn't automatically start, double-click the setup.exe file on the disc to start installing drivers.

8 Follow the on-screen instructions. Don't click Cancel in any of the dialog boxes; click **Continue**. Click **Finish**, and then click **Yes** to restart.

9 After your computer restarts, follow the instructions in the Found New Hardware Wizard to update your software drivers (Windows XP only).

Did You Know?

You can upgrade Windows XP to Windows 7 or Vista. Restart your Mac using Windows, insert your Windows 7 or Vista installation or upgrade disc, follow the on-screen instructions, insert the Mac OS X Lion disc, and then follow the on-screen instructions as needed to update the drivers.

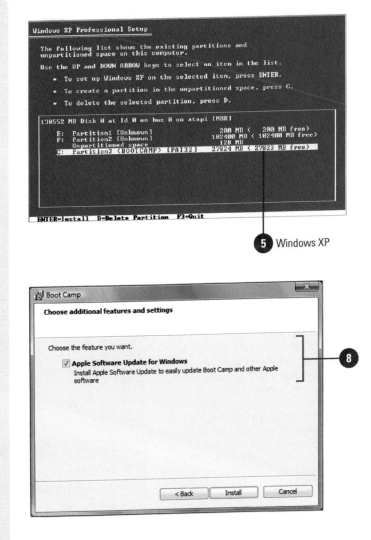

5 Windows XP

Starting Up with Mac OS X or Windows

After you install Microsoft Windows and Boot Camp drivers, you can start up your Mac computer in either Mac OS X or Windows. You can set the default operating system you want to use on a regular basis using Startup Disk preferences on the Mac or the Boot Camp Control Panel on Windows, and then use quick controls to directly restart your computer in the other operating system or select an operating system while starting your Mac computer.

Set the Startup Disk for Mac OS X or Windows

1. Start up using either of the following:

 ◆ **In the Mac OS X.** Click the **Apple** menu, click **System Preferences**, and then click **Startup Disk**.

 ◆ **In Windows.** Click the **Start** button on the taskbar, click the **Boot Camp** icon in the notification area on the taskbar, and then click **Boot Camp Control Panel**. Click **Continue** to access the system utility.

2. Select the startup disk with the operating system you want to use by default.

3. To start up that operating system now, click **Restart**.

4. Click the **Close** button (Mac) or **OK** (Win).

Mac OS X

Windows

470

Start Up with Mac OS X or Windows

◆ **Select an OS when you startup.** As your computer starts up, hold down the Option key until disk icons appear, select the startup disk with the operating system you want, and then click the arrow below the icon.

◆ **Restart to Mac from Windows.** In Windows, click the **Boot Camp** icon in the notification area, click **Restart in Mac OS X**, and then click **OK**.

◆ **Restart to Windows from Mac.** In Mac OS X, click the **Apple** menu, click **Restart**, click **Restart**, hold down the Option key until disk icons appear, select Windows, and then click the arrow below the icon.

Select an OS when you start up

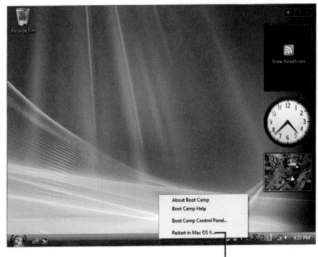

Restart to Mac from Windows

Using Windows on a Mac

After you finish the Windows installation and Boot Camp driver update, you can use Windows on your Mac. The Boot Camp drivers allow you to use your Apple keyboard to emulate a standard PC keyboard, use function keys, eject discs using the Eject key on the keyboard, change the volume using the Volume Down or Up keys, right-click using an Apple Magic Mouse or trackpad, use an Apple Remote (if your computer is equipped with one) to control iTunes and Windows Media, use Bluetooth wireless devices, attach and use an iSight camera, and connect to a wireless network using Wi-Fi. In addition, you can work with files between your Mac OS X and Windows disks. Due to HFS+ support, you can now access files (read-only) on your Mac from Windows for review or save with a different name to make changes.

Use Windows on a Mac

◆ **Disable remote control.** In Windows, click the **Boot Camp** icon in the notification area, and then click **Boot Camp Control Panel**, click the **Remote** tab, select the **Disable remote control infrared receiver** check box, and then click **OK**.

◆ **Pair or Unpair a remote control.** A Mac computer can only use one remote at a time. Use a remote, you need to pair it with the computer. Hold the remote close to the computer (3 to 4 inches) and point the remote at the front, press and hold down Menu and Next buttons on the remote for 5 seconds until a chain link symbol appears.

If you want to change remotes, you need to unpair the current one first. In Windows, click the **Boot Camp** icon in the notification area, and then click **Boot Camp Control Panel**, click the **Remote** tab, click **Unpair**, and then click **OK**.

◆ **Restart after a power failure.** In Windows, click the **Boot Camp** icon in the notification area, and then click **Boot Camp Control Panel**, click the **Power** tab, select the **Restart automatically after a power failure** check box, and then click **OK**.

Remote control options

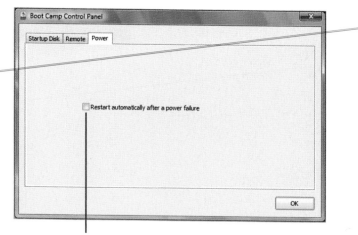

Restart after a power failure

- **Use a Bluetooth Device.** In order to use a Bluetooth wireless device with Windows, you need to pair the device with your computer.

 In Windows, open the Bluetooth Devices control panel, click the **Devices** tab, click **Add**, and then follow the wizard instructions.

 Use the following numeric passkeys: Wireless Magic Mouse, enter four zeros: *0000*. Apple Wireless keyboard, enter six to sixteen digits.

- **Copy Files Between Mac OS X and Windows.** If you installed Windows XP on a partition formatted with FAT, you can open and save files on your Windows disk, or copy files between your Mac OS X disk and Windows disk.

 If you installed Windows XP, Vista, or 7 on a partition formatted with NTFS, you can open files on your Windows disk from Mac OS X, or copy files from Windows to Mac OS X. However, you cannot copy or save any files to the protected Windows disk.

 IMPORTANT *Windows files need extensions (for example, .doc) to identify the file type. Most programs come in both Mac and Windows versions, so there should be no problem there. If it's a Mac only file type, you may need to convert it for Windows use.*

- **Use the Apple Keyboard with Windows.** Refer to the table for specific keyboard commands you can use on your Apple keyboard to emulate a standard PC keyboard.

 You can also use the Eject key and Volume Down and Up keys on the Apple keyboard to perform commands not available on the standard PC keyboard.

File on Mac disk

Windows Disk Mac disk

Files on Windows disk

Apple Keyboard with Windows

PC Key Command	Apple External	Built-in Mac
Control+Alt+Delete	Control-Option-Delete	Control-Option-Delete
Alt	Option	Option
AltGr	Control-Option	Control-Option
Backspace	Delete	Delete
Delete	Delete	Fn-Delete
Enter	Return	Return
Enter (num keypad)	Enter	Enter
Insert	Help	Fn-Enter
Num lock	Clear	Fn-F6
Pause/Break	F16	Fn-Esc
Print Screen	F14	Fn-F11
Print active window	Option-F14	Option-Fn-F11
Scroll/Lock	F15	Fn-F12

Removing Windows

If you no longer want to run Microsoft Windows on your Mac computer, you can remove it using Boot Camp Assistant. When you remove Windows, the Boot Camp Assistant removes the Windows software and restores your hard disk back to a single partition. All the information on the Windows partition is erased, so it's critical to make a back up of the important files on your computer before you start the removal process.

Remove Windows from a Computer with a Single Internal Disk

1. Start your Mac computer in Mac OS X.

2. Click the **Launchpad** icon in the Dock, click the **Utilities** folder, and then click the **Boot Camp Assistant** icon.

3. Click **Continue**.

4. Click the **Create or remove a Windows partition** option.

5. Click **Continue**.

6. Enter your name and password, and then click **OK**.

7. Click **Restore**.

8. When you're done, click **Quit**.

Did You Know?

You can use Disk Utility to remove Windows on a single-volume disk. Click the Launchpad icon in the Dock, click the Utilities folder, and then click the Disk Utility icon to erase the disk and reformat it as a Mac OS X volume.

Remove Windows from a Computer with Multiple Internal Disks

① Start your Mac computer in Mac OS X.

② Click the **Launchpad** icon in the Dock, click the **Utilities** folder, and then click the **Boot Camp Assistant** icon.

③ Click **Continue**.

④ Click the **Create or remove a Windows partition** option.

⑤ Click **Continue**.

⑥ Select the disk with the Windows software.

⑦ Click the **Restore to a single Mac OS partition** option.

⑧ Click **Continue**.

⑨ Enter your name and password, and then click **OK**.

⑩ Click **Restore**.

⑪ When you're done, click **Quit**.

Backing Up Everything with Time Machine

Introduction

Backing up your files is an important part of protecting and maintaining your computer. If you accidentally deleted a file or lose files due to a computer problem, you can recover them with a backup.

Time Machine is a Mac OS X application that allows you to back up everything on your computer on a regular basis without any additional work on your part after the initial set up. The first time you use Time Machine, it backs up everything on your computer, including system files, applications, accounts, preferences, music, photos, movies, and documents. As you work and make changes on your computer, Time Machine backs up only the things that have changed.

Time Machine works best when you dedicate and use the same disk for you backups. You can use an internal or external disk as the back up disk. You can keep your backups secure by backing up to an external USB or FireWire drive encrypted with FileVault 2. When you attach an external disk to your Mac computer, Time Machine asks if you want to use the device for backups and automatically sets everything up for you.

Backups are organized and store by date. You can browse and recover individual files, folders, or your entire computer. You can also burn backup CDs and DVDs, copy files onto another disk, or use your iDisk if you have a MobileMe account.

What You'll Do

Set Up Time Machine for Backups

Perform a Backup

Exclude Items from a Backup

Work with a Backup

Recover Backed Up Items

Recover an Entire Computer System

Create a Disk Image to Backup Files

Burn a CD or DVD from a Disk Image

Restore a Disk Image

Back Up Files onto a CD or DVD

Setting Up Time Machine for Backups

Time Machine works best when you dedicate and use the same disk for your backups. You can use an internal (except for your startup disk) or external disk (such as a FireWire or USB disk) with encryption using FileVault 2 (**New!**) as the back up disk. If you have partitioned a disk, you can use the partition as a back up disk too. The disk you use must be in the Mac OS Extended (Journaled) format, and must have Access Control Lists (ACLs) enabled. When you attach an external disk to your Mac computer, Time Machine asks if you want to use the device for backups and automatically sets everything up for you. The first time you start Time Machine, the program backs up everything on your computer. This may take a while, so it would good to start the initial set up and use for a time when your computer is idle, such as a late evening or weekend, so it can work overnight. However, if you use Time Capsule (a wireless hard drive designed to work with Time Machine), it's about 50 percent faster. As you work and make changes on your computer, Time Machine backs up only the things that have changed.

Set Up Time Machine Preferences

1. Click **System Preferences** icon in the Dock, and then click the **Time Machine** icon.

2. To show a status menu, select the **Show Time Machine status in the menu bar** check box.

3. Slide the switch to **ON**.

4. Click **Select Backup Disk**.

5. Click one of the available disks you can use for backups. If you have Time Capsule, select **Set Up Other Time Capsule**, and then open the AirPort Utility to set it up.

6. To encrypt the disk, select the **encrypt backup disk** check box.

7. Click **Use for Backup**.

 ◆ If you encrypt, enter the password information, and then click **Encrypt Disk**.

8. If your disk needs to be erased before you can use it with Time Machine, click **Erase** or **Choose Another Disk**.

9. Click the **Close** button.

478

Performing a Backup

Time Machine keeps track of everything on your Mac computer. The first time you start Time Machine, the program backs up everything on your computer. As you work and make changes on your computer, Time Machine backs up only the things that have changed. If you want to manually perform a backup, you can Control-click the Time Machine icon in the Dock or click the Time Machine Status menu to access the Back Up Now command.

Start a Manual Back Up

① Control-click the **Time Machine** icon in the Dock or click the **Time Machine Status** menu.

② Click **Back Up Now**.

Time Machine status information appears in the Time Machine Status menu.

③ To stop the backup, Control-click the **Time Machine** icon in the Dock or click the **Time Machine Status** menu, and then click **Stop Backing Up**.

◆ You can also click the **Stop** button (X) in the Time Machine preferences window.

Did You Know?

You can backup files to your iDisk. If you have an iDisk, you can't use it with Time Machine. Instead, you can use the Backup utility to copy files to your iDisk; check the MobileMe Web site at *www.apple.com/mobileme/*.

You can back up all the Macs in your wireless network. If you have a hard disk connected to your AirPort Extreme Base Station or Time Capsule, you can use Time Machine to back up all your Macs wirelessly. All you need to do is select your AirPort Disk or Time Capsule as the backup disk for each computer connected to the wireless network.

Time Machine Status menu

Latest Backup: Today, 12:10 AM

Back Up Now
Enter Time Machine

Open Time Machine Preferences...

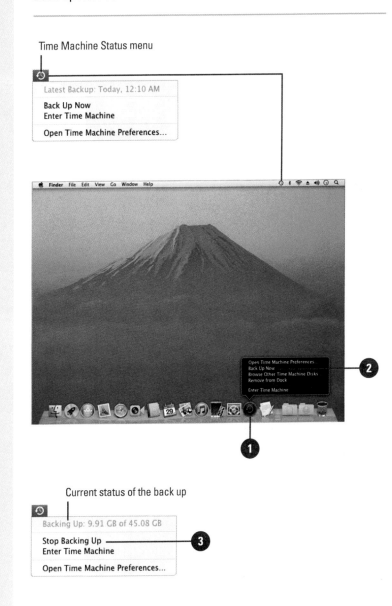

Current status of the back up

Backing Up: 9.91 GB of 45.08 GB

Stop Backing Up ──── ③
Enter Time Machine

Open Time Machine Preferences...

Excluding Items from a Backup

If you already have copies of files, such as third-party programs (Microsoft Office, Adobe Creative Suite, etc.), on CD, DVD, or in another location, you can exclude them from regular backups to save space on your backup disk. Time Machine assumes you want to back everything up unless you specifically add it to the nonbackup list, which you can modify using Time Machine preferences.

Exclude Items from a Backup

1. Click **System Preferences** icon in the Dock, and then click the **Time Machine** icon.

2. Click **Options**.

 A list appears with the available disks you can use for backups with Time Machine.

3. Click **Add** (+), and then select the items you don't want to be backed up, and then click **Exclude**.

 ◆ If you select the System folder, an alert appears, asking you for confirmation.

 The backup disk is automatically included in the list.

4. To remove an item from the list, select the items you want to be backed up, and then click **Remove** (-).

5. Select or clear the **Notify after old backups are deleted** check box.

6. Select or clear the **Lock documents after last edit** check box (**New!**). Select a duration from the pop-up menu.

7. Click **Done**.

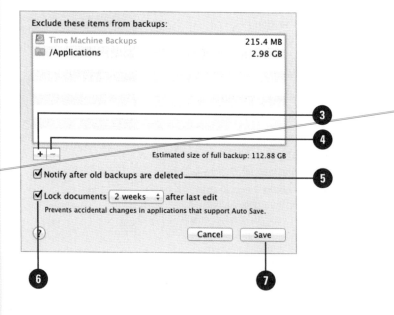

Working with a Backup

If a backup is interrupted for some reason, such as a network connection problem, detached external disk, or power outage, Time Machine tries to automatically resume the backup when the problem is corrected. If Time Machine doesn't automatically resume, you can manually restart it. If you want to pause a backup, you can also manually stop it by using the Time Machine Status menu or by using the Time Machine icon in the Dock. The Time Machine Status menu icon rotates as the takes place. If a problem occurs, the icons changes to an alert symbol. Also, the first item on the menu displays status information about the current or last back up.

Work with a Backup

◆ **Pause/stop a backup.** Click the **Time Machine Status** menu, and then click **Stop Backing Up**.

◆ **Resume/start a backup.** Click the **Time Machine Status** menu, and then click **Back Up Now**.

◆ **Run out of space.** As the backup disk fills up, Time Machine deletes older backups to make room for new ones. If you run out of space, you can attach a new backup disk to complete the process.

◆ **Local snapshots.** When you're away from your Time Capsule or backup drive, Time Machine keeps a spare "local snapshot" copy of the files you create, modify, or delete right on your portable Mac (**New!**); not on desktops. If you accidentally delete a file while on the road, you can recover it from a local copy. To stop taking local snapshots, turn the Time Machine off in preferences.

◆ **Combined timeline.** When you connect your Mac to your Time Capsule or backup drive, Time Machine automatically displays everything you did while not connected with your existing backups, so it looks like you never left (**New!**).

Time Machine Status menu

Latest Backup: Today, 12:10 AM

Back Up Now
Enter Time Machine

Open Time Machine Preferences...

 Finder File Edit View Go Window Help

Open Time Machine Preferences...
Back Up Now
Browse Other Time Machine Disks...
Remove from Dock

Enter Time Machine

Resume/ start a backup

Current status of the back up

Icon changes to indicate a problem

Backing Up: 9.91 GB of 45.08 GB

Stop Backing Up
Enter Time Machine

Open Time Machine Preferences...

Latest Backup: Failed...

Back Up Now
Enter Time Machine

Open Time Machine Preferences...

Pause/stop a backup

Click to find out the problem

Recovering Backed Up Items

If you've been using Time Machine to back up your computer, and you lose or accidentally delete a file or folder, you can use Time Machine or Time Machine along with Spotlight to recover it. You can even recover older versions of files that you have changed. Spotlight makes it easy to perform a search for the backup file or folder you want to recover, and Time Machine allows you to recover it. The recovered item is restored to its original location on your computer. Time Machine may ask if you want to overwrite one or more folders so it can restore an item to its original location. If you encrypted the backup disk with FileVault 2 in Time Machine, you need to provide the password to restore the data (**New!**).

Recover Items Using Time Machine and Spotlight

1. Open a Finder window.

2. Type a search word or phrase in the Search box from the item you want to recover.

3. Click the **Time Machine** icon in the Dock.

4. Use the arrows and the timeline to browse through the Time Machine backups. Your search is performed in every window.

5. Narrow down your search to find the item you want to restore, and then select it.

6. Click **Restore**.

 The window appears on the desktop along with a Copy dialog box.

7. Click **Keep Original** to keep the original file instead of the backup, **Keep Both** to keep the original and the backup, or **Replace** to replace the original with the backup.

Timeline

Click to exit Time Machine

Selected backup to restore

Recover Items Using Time Machine

① Open the window or location (desktop or e-mail Inbox) where the recovered item will appear.

② Click the **Time Machine** icon in the Dock.

③ Use the arrows and the timeline to browse through the Time Machine backups. Your search is performed in every window.

④ When you find the item you want to restore, select it.

⑤ Click **Restore**.

The window appears on the desktop along with a Copy dialog box.

⑥ Click **Keep Original** to keep the original file instead of the backup, **Keep Both** to keep the original and the backup, or **Replace** to replace the original with the backup.

Click to exit Time Machine

Selected backup

Recovering an Entire Computer System

If your entire computer system or startup disk becomes corrupt or damaged, you can recover it using Time Machine. If you're experiencing problems after you install a Mac OS X software update, you can use Time Machine to revert back to a previous version of the Mac OS to fix the problem. Remember, any additional changes you've made to your computer after installing the Mac OS X software update will be removed, so you need to make copies of those changes on another disk. To perform a recovery, you don't need a Mac OS X Installation disc to start the process; all you need to do is hold down ⌘+R (**New!**) during a bootup; it's always available.

Recover an Entire System Using Time Machine

1. Connect your Time Machine backup disk to your computer, if necessary.

2. Click the **Apple** menu, click **Restart**, and then click **Restart**.

3. During bootup, hold down ⌘+R.

 The built-in Mac OS X Utilities program starts.

4. In the installer, click **Restore From Time Machine Backup**.

5. Click **Continue**.

6. In the Restore Your System screen, click **Continue**.

7. Select the Time Machine backup volume you want to use.

8. Click **Continue**.

 ◆ If network drive, click **Connect to Remote Disk**, enter name and password, and then click **Connect**.

9. Select the Time Machine backup you want to restore.

10. Click **Continue**.

11. Select the restore destination volume.

12. Click **Restore**.

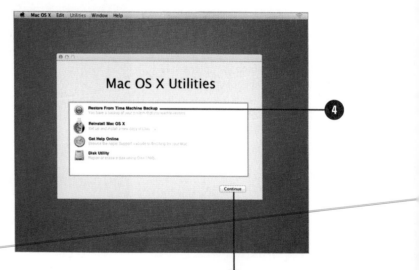

Revert Back to a Previous Version of Mac OS X

1. Connect your Time Machine backup disk to your computer, if necessary.

2. Click the **Apple** menu, click **Restart**, and then click **Restart**.

3. During bootup, hold down ⌘+R.

 The built-in Mac OS X Utilities program starts.

4. In the installer, click **Restore From Time Machine Backup**.

5. Click **Continue**.

6. In the Restore Your System screen, click **Continue**.

7. Select the Time Machine backup volume you want to use.

8. Click **Continue**.

 ◆ If network drive, click **Connect to Remote Disk**, enter name and password, and then click **Connect**.

9. Select the most recent Time Machine backup to restore your computer to the state it was before you installed an update.

10. Click **Continue**.

11. Select the restore destination volume.

12. Click **Restore**.

Creating a Disk Image to Backup Files

If you can't fit all the files and folders you want to backup onto a single CD or DVD, you can use the Disk Utility to create a compressed disk image of the files and folders. A **disk image** is a file that contains other files and folders you can mount on your desktop like a hard disk or CD or DVD disc. You can create a disk image with an existing disk, volume, CD or DVD, or folder, or create a blank one, and then drag files to it. After you create a disk image (.dmg extension), you can burn it on a CD or DVD, copy it to another Mac or network, or e-mail it to another Mac user. Creating a disk image of your Mac OS X installation disc is a useful way to make a backup copy of your Mac OS X installation for added protection.

Create a Disk Image to Backup Files and Folders

1. Click the **Launchpad** icon in the Dock, click the **Utilities** folder, and then click the **Disk Utility** icon.

2. Click the **File** menu, point to **New**, and then click **Disk Image from Folder** or **Disk Image from *<disk name>***.

3. If you want to create a disk image from a folder, select it.

4. Click **Image**.

5. Type the name you want for the disk image, and then specify the location where you want to save it.

6. Click the **Image Format** pop-up, and then click **compressed** to create a smaller disk image or **read-only** to create a faster disk to create and open.

7. To require a password to open the disk image, click the **Encryption** pop-up, and then select the option you want.

8. Click **Save**. If you required a password, enter it twice, and then click **OK**.

9. To restore a disk image, select the disk image, click the **Images** menu, and then click **Scan Image for Restore**.

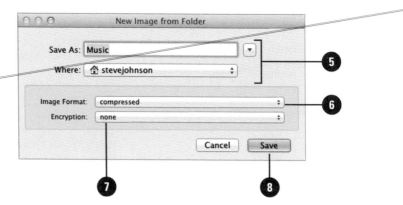

Create a Blank Disk Image as a Backup

1. Click the **Launchpad** icon in the Dock, click the **Utilities** folder, and then click the **Disk Utility** icon.

2. Click the **File** menu, point to **New**, and then click **Blank Disk Image**.

3. Type a name for the disk image, and then specify the location where you want to save it.

4. Select from the following options:

 ◆ Enter a name or use the default.

 ◆ Click the **Size** pop-up, and then select the size you want.

 ◆ Select the **Format** pop-up, and then select **Mac OS Extended (Journaled)** for Mac computers or **MS-DOS (FAT)** for Windows or Mac computers.

 ◆ To require a password to open the disk image, click the **Encryption** pop-up, and then select the option you want.

 ◆ Click the **Partitions** pop-up, and then select the partition scheme that matches the type you want to create.

 ◆ Click the **Image Format** pop-up, and then click **read/write disk image**.

5. Click **Create**.

6. If you required a password, enter it twice, and then click **OK**.

 The blank new disk image mounts on your desktop.

7. Drag the files and folders you want to include in the disk image onto the mounted disk on your desktop.

For Your Information

Recording or Duplicating a Data CD or DVD

You can use Disk Utility to quickly create a CD or DVD from data on your computer or make a copy of a CD or DVD that contains information. Once you create a disk image, you can make multiple copies from the same disk image. If you select the Leave Disc Appendable option during the process, you can create a **multisession CD** or **DVD**; you burn data on a CD-R or DVD-R now, and then add to it later until there is no more room, just like a CD-RW or DVD-RW. You can use the CD or DVD to transfer files from one computer to another, backup data for safekeeping, or restore the files on a disk.

Burning a CD or DVD from a Disk Image

After you create a disk image, you can burn it on a CD or DVD, which makes it easy to make a backup copy of important files, move files to another computer, or share files with other Mac users. This is also a useful way to make a backup of your Mac OS X installation DVD from a disk image of the installation DVD disc. After you select the disk image you want to burn to a CD or DVD in Disk Utility, you can select the Burn options you want before the actual burn takes place.

Burn a CD or DVD from a Disk Image

1. Click the **Launchpad** icon in the Dock, click the **Utilities** folder, and then click the **Disk Utility** icon.

2. Click the **Burn** button on the toolbar.

3. Navigate to and select the disk image you want to burn.

4. Click **Burn**.

5. Click the **Down Arrow** button to show advanced burn options.

6. Select the Burn Options and After Burning settings you want.

7. Insert a writable CD or DVD disc into your read/writable drive.

8. Click **Burn**.

 A status bar appears, indicating the current progress of the burn.

9. Click **OK**.

Restoring a Disk Image

After you create a disk image, you can use Disk Utility to restore it to a disk. This is useful when you want to re-create all the contents of the disk image to a disk. Disk Utility allows you to select the source and destination for the restored files. You can even erase the destination before the restoration occurs. If you only want to restore only a few files, you can access the content of the mounted disk image on your desktop like any other hard disk and copy it to another location.

Restore a Disk Image to a Disk

1. Click the **Launchpad** icon in the Dock, click the **Utilities** folder, and then click the **Disk Utility** icon.

2. Select the disk in the list at the left.

3. Click the **Restore** tab.

4. Drag the disk image to the Source field or click **Image**, and then select the disk image.

5. Drag the destination disk you want to the Destination field.

6. Click **Restore**, and then click **Restore** again to confirm the restoration.

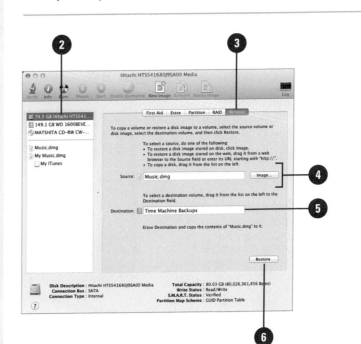

Did You Know?

You can get information about your disk. Click the Launchpad icon in the Dock, click the Utilities folder, click the Disk Utility icon, select the disk or volume in the list at the left, click the Info button. When you're done, click the Close button twice.

Backing Up Files onto a CD or DVD

If you can write (burn) files to a CD or DVD, you can create and use a burn folder to backup important files. Burn folders are useful for regularly backing up a set of files or for burning multiple copies of a folder. You can create a burn folder from the Finder. The files and folders you drag into the burn folder are ready to be written to a CD or DVD. The Finder creates aliases to the items in the burn folder. The original items are not moved. When you burn the files to a CD or DVD, the original files are burned to the disc.

Copy Files onto a CD or DVD from the Finder

① Click the desktop background or open the window where you want to create and use a burn folder.

② Click the **File** menu, and then click **New Burn Folder**.

③ Type a name for the burn folder.

④ Drag the items you want to burn to a disc into the burn folder.

The Finder creates aliases to the items in the burn folder. The original items are not moved.

⑤ Open the burn folder to burn a CD or DVD.

⑥ Click **Burn**.

TIMESAVER *If the burn folder is in the sidebar of the Finder window, click the burn icon next to the burn folder name.*

⑦ Insert a writable CD or DVD disc into your read/writable drive.

The original files and any folders are burned to the disc.

◆ If the Finder can't find an original file, it asks you to cancel the burn or continue without the file.

⑧ Type a name for the CD or DVD, and then select a burn speed.

⑨ Click **Burn**.

Automating Your Work

Introduction

Automator is a program that lets you automate the things you frequently like to do on your Mac. You don't need to be a programmer to create automations. With Automator, all you need to do is assemble a series of **actions** into a workflow to complete a task. Each action performs an individual step, such as opening a file, creating an event in iCal, or importing photos in Image Capture. You can create your own actions or use one of the many pre-built ones available in Automator library.

When you start Automator, a dialog box appears asking you to choose from a group of templates, also known as starting points, that help you create the first part of your workflow. There are several templates you can use to help you get started: Workflow, Application, Service, Folder Action, Print Plugin, iCal Alarm, and Image Capture Plugin. After you choose a template, you see an untitled workflow with a blank workflow action in the Workflow pane you can fill in. You create a workflow by dragging additional actions or variables into the Workflow pane, arranging them into the order you want from top to bottom, and specifying the settings you want for each action or variable.

When you have more than one action in a workflow, Automator frequently passes information from one action to another starting from the top. When you run a workflow, each action receives information from the previous action (input) and passes information to the following action (output). If an action needs to receive a certain type of information, it needs to be placed in the workflow following an action that outputs that type of information.

In addition to Automator, you can also use AppleScript, an English-like scripting language, to run prebuilt or custom-made scripts to automate actions performed by the computer. AppleScript lets you write your own mini applications to help with repetitive tasks.

What You'll Do

Introduce Automator

View the Automator Window

Get Started with Automator

Open an Existing Workflow

Open an Example Workflow

Work with an Example Workflow

Add Actions to a Workflow

Add Variables to an Action

Record an Action

Work with Workflows

Run and Stop a Workflow

Save a Workflow

Use a Workflow as a Plug-in

Understand AppleScript Basics

Use Ready-Made AppleScripts

Write and Record AppleScripts

Use AppleScript with Automator

Introducing Automator

Anyone can create a workflow in Automator. All it requires is the Automator application available in the Applications folder, and a little knowledge about the process.

When you start Automator, a dialog box appears asking you to choose from a group of templates that help you create the first part of your workflow. There are several templates you can use to help you get started: Workflow, Application, Service, Folder Action, Print Plugin, iCal Alarm, and Image Capture Plugin. If you already have an existing workflow, you can open it from the dialog box.

After you choose a template, you see an untitled workflow with a blank workflow action (except for Custom) in the Workflow pane you can fill in. You create a workflow by displaying Actions or Variables in the Library pane, selecting the name of the application or category you want to use from the Library list, specifying what you want it to do with it in the Action or Variable list, and dragging it into the Workflow pane to assemble the steps you want to automate.

Automator Window

The Automator window consists of different parts, including Toolbar buttons, Library pane, Library list, Action or Variable list, Search box, Description view, and Workflow pane.

Toolbar buttons

The top part of the Automator window displays a toolbar with buttons you can use to make it easier to work with Automator. On the left side of the toolbar, Automator provides two default buttons: Hide/Show Library and Media. The Hide/Show Library button) hides or shows the Library pane, while the Media but-

ton makes it easy to add media to your workflows. On the right-side of the toolbar, Automator provides three default buttons, known as Workflow control buttons: Record, Stop, and Run. The Record button creates a workflow by recording of your mouse movements, while the Stop and Run buttons stop and play back the current workflow. These are not the only toolbar buttons available in Automator. You can use the Customize Toolbar command on the View menu to add and remove the buttons you want and change the button size and display.

Library pane

The left side of the Automator window is the Library pane, which displays the available actions and variables you can use to create Automator workflows.

Action list

When you click the Actions button at the top of the Library pane, a Library list and Action list appear. The Library list displays every program, including some OS utilities, on your Mac that you can use to create Automator workflows. When you select a program, the Action list changes to show the actions related to the program. Mac OS X provides improved and new actions, for Preview, the Internet, RSS, and the Finder. At the bottom of the Library list, you can use Smart Groups, including Most Relevant, Most Used, and Recently Added, or create your own to make it easier to displays the actions you want to use.

Variable list

When you click the Variables button at the top of the Library pane, a Library list and Variable

list appear. The Library list displays OS utilities categories on your Mac that you can use to create Automator workflows. When you select a program, the Variable list changes to show the available variables you can use to store values and create more flexible workflows.

Search box

The Search box at the top of the Library pane is similar to the one you find in other parts of Mac OS X. In Automator, the Search box makes it easier to find the actions or variables you want to use. Before you start a search, select a category from the Library list. As you type in the Search box, Automator displays the actions or variables that match your criteria from the selected category. If you want to search through more than one category, you can press ⌘ to select the ones you want. If you want to search all the categories, click Library at the top of the Library list. The results of your search appear in the Action or Variable list in order of relevance to your search criteria. When you're done, you can click the small gray X button in the Search box to return to the complete list of actions.

Description view

The Description view at the bottom of the Library pane displays a description of the selected action or variable. The description provides information about what the action or variable does, what requirements it needs to get started, what kind of data it needs as input, what options are available, and what kind of action it performs as a result. If you need more room to display the Action or Variable list, you can click the Show Or Hide The Description View button at the bottom of the Library pane.

Workflow pane

The Workflow pane is where you place the actions and variables you want to use to create a workflow. The Workflow pane displays and tracks a flow of information from one action or variable to the next creating the results you want. In the Workflow pane, you can change the order of items, set item specific settings and options, display item descriptions, and show the results for specific ones.

Workflow log

The Show Or Hide The Workflow Log button at the bottom of the Workflow pane shows or hides the workflow log, which allows you to track what your workflow is doing.

Workflow variable list

The Show Or Hide The Workflow Variable List button at the bottom of the Workflow pane shows or hides the workflow variable list, which allows you to track the current values for the variables you use in your workflow.

More to come

Developers are always creating new actions for you to use. Check out the Apple Web site at *www.apple.com/downloads/macosx/automator* for more information and details, or visit *www.automatorworld.com/category/actions*. After you download them to your computer, you can use the Import Actions command on the File menu to add them to your Library list in Automator. Writing your own actions is out of the scope of this book. For details, see the Apple Developer Web site at *www.apple.com/macosx/features/automator*.

Viewing the Automator Window

Search box

Toolbar

Action and
Variable lists

Workflow
pane

Description
view

Library pane

Workflow log

Getting Started with Automator

When you start Automator, a dialog box appears asking you to choose from a group of templates, also known as starting points, that help you create the first part of your workflow. You can use any of the following templates to help you get started: Workflow, Application, Service, Folder Action, Print Plugin, iCal Alarm, and Image Capture Plugin. After you choose a template, you see an untitled workflow with an action in the Workflow pane you can fill in.

Get Started with Automator

1. Click the **Launchpad** icon in the Dock, and then click the **Automator** icon.

 Automator opens, displaying the Templates dialog.

2. Click a template icon:

 ◆ **Workflow.** Use to creates a workflow document.

 ◆ **Application.** Use to create an executable workflow application.

 ◆ **Service.** Use to create a service for use in another application or the Finder; a plug-in workflow.

 ◆ **Folder Actions.** Use to perform batch folder operations, such as opening or adding files; a plug-in workflow.

 ◆ **Print Plugin.** Use to run a workflow when you print a file. An item appears on the PDF menu in the Print dialog box; a plug-in workflow.

 ◆ **iCal Alarm.** Use to open iCal and create a new event; a plug-in workflow.

 ◆ **Image Capture Plugin.** Use to import photos from a camera or scanner with Image Capture; a plug-in workflow.

3. Click **Choose**. If prompted, select your content, and then click **Add**.

 ◆ Click **Close** to exit the dialog without taking any action.

Description of selected template

For Your Information

Starting a Workflow with a Set of Files

If you wanted to create a new workflow with a specific set of files, you can use the shortcut menu in the Finder to quickly get started. In Finder, select the files you want to use in the new workflow. Control-click the selected files, point to Automator, and then click Create Workflow. Automator opens with a new workflow and the selected files are in the first action.

Opening an Existing Workflow

After you save a workflow as a Workflow (.workflow) or Application (.app) file, you can open either one at any time to modify or run it. You can open a workflow by using the standard Open dialog box in Automator. You can access the Open dialog box from the New dialog box when you start Automator from the Finder or from the Open command on the File menu in Automator.

Open an Existing Workflow

1. Use one of the following methods:

 ◆ **In Finder.** Click the **Launchpad** icon in the Dock, click the **Automator** icon, and then click **Open an Existing Workflow**.

 ◆ **In Automator.** Click the **File** menu, and then click **Open**.

 TIMESAVER *Press* ⌘+O *to open the Open dialog.*

2. Click the **Type** pop-up, and then select **All** or a workflow type.

3. Select the place from which you want to open the file.

 TIMESAVER *Click the Where pop-up to select from a list of recent places you already visited.*

4. Click the document you want to open.

5. Click **Open**.

6. To close a workflow, click the **File** menu, and then click **Close**.

Did You Know?

You can open a workflow file directly. In Finder, double-click the workflow file icon (.workflow) you want to open.

You can create a new workflow. Click the File menu, and then click New. The templates dialog box appears or a blank custom workflow appears.

Opening an Example Workflow

Automator comes with four example workflows you can open to see what a completed one looks like. The examples show you how to a workflow can display movie trailers in Safari, import photos from a Photo Album posted on your MobileMe site into iPhoto, and process images with the Quartz composition filter. The process images workflow may not be a real useful workflow at first glance. However, it's a good example of batch processing.

Open an Example Workflow

1 Start Automator, click the **Workflow** icon, and then click **Choose** to open Automator with a blank workflow.

2 Click the **Help** menu, and then click **Open Examples Folder**.

The Workflows folder opens, displaying four example workflows.

◆ **Display Trailers in Safari.** Displays movie trailers from *www.apple.com* in Safari.

◆ **Import MobileMe Photo Album into iPhoto.** Imports photos from a Photo Album posted on your MobileMe site into iPhoto.

◆ **Process Images.** Batch process images with the Quartz composition filter.

3 Double-click the workflow file you want to open.

The workflow file opens, displaying actions in the Workflow pane.

4 To close a workflow, click the **File** menu, and then click **Close**.

Working with an Example Workflow

The best way to learn how to create a workflow is to go through an example. Automator comes with three example workflows you can open to see what a completed one looks like. The process images workflow is a good example of batch processing images. The example processes images with the Quartz composition filter. However, you can easily change the workflow to modify the image size or convert it to another format.

Work with an Example Workflow

1 Start Automator, click the **Workflow** icon, and then click **Choose** to open Automator with a blank workflow.

2 Click the **Help** menu, and then click **Open Example Folder**.

3 Double-click the **Process Images .workflow** icon.

4 Examine the following actions in the Workflow pane:

◆ **Ask for Confirmation.** Displays a dialog box with information you provide for the user's benefit. You can change the button names and click the Robot icon to change it.

◆ **Get Specified Finder Items.** Lets you specify the files you want to process. You can use the Add or Remove buttons or drag files directly from the Finder.

◆ **Copy Finder Items.** Makes copies of the files to protect the originals.

◆ **Apply Quartz Composition Filter to Image Files.** Applies the filter to the selected image files.

◆ **Open Images in Preview.** Opens the specified image file in Preview.

5 To execute the workflow, click the **Run** button on the toolbar.

For Your Information

Controlling Input and Output

You can control the input and output within a workflow. Some actions allow you to choose whether you want to receive results from a previous action. If so, select this check box (names vary depending on action). If available, select the Use Results from Previous Action option from the pop-up menu on the action in the Workflow pane. When you start a workflow from the shortcut menu in Finder (see "Using a Workflow as Plug-ins" on page 506), any items you select are passed into the workflow as input. If you don't want this to happen, you can set the first action to ignore input. Control-click the title bar for the first action, and then click Ignore Input.

Modify an Example Workflow

1 Start Automator, click the **Workflow** icon, and then click **Choose** to open Automator with a blank workflow.

2 Click the **Help** menu, and then click **Open Example Folder**.

3 Double-click the **Process Images .workflow** icon.

4 Instead of working from a specified folder, let's have the Finder ask you where to get the image files.

◆ **Get Specified Finder Items.** Click the **Delete** button (X) on the Get Specified Finder Items title bar, click **Files & Folders** in the Library list, and then drag the **Ask for Finder Items** action to the same place as the deleted action.

5 Instead of applying the Quartz filter, let's change the image type.

◆ **Change Type of Images.** Click the **Delete** button (X) on the Apply Quartz Composition Filter to Image Files title bar, click **Photos** in the Library list, and then drag the **Change Type of Images** action to the same place as the deleted action.

6 Click the **File** menu, click **Save As**, specify a new name, and then click **Save**.

7 To execute the workflow, click the **Run** button on the toolbar.

Ask for Finder Items action

Adding Actions to a Workflow

You can add one or more actions to create the workflow you want. Automator includes actions (**New!**) that can turn text into images, turn text documents into ePub books, display and retrieve web content, and enable encoding for video and audio files. Many text-based actions support RTF (Rich Text Format) (**New!**). When you have more than one action in a workflow, Automator frequently passes information from one action to another starting from the top. When you run a workflow, each action receives information from the previous action (input) and passes information to the following action (output). Data detector text input objects—such as URLs, addresses, and phone numbers—have the option to pass full text selection or only found text (**New!**). If an action needs to receive a certain type of information, it needs to be placed in the workflow following an action that outputs that type of information. The type of input an action needs appears in the title bar. If the input and output don't match or it's not being received from the previous action, the information appears in red to indicate a problem.

Add Actions to a Workflow

1. Start Automator and use a template or open the workflow you want.

2. Click the **Actions** button in the Library pane.

3. Click the category or application from the Library list to display the actions you want.

4. Drag the action you want to the Workflow pane.

5. Enter information and specify the settings you want for the action; the information and settings vary depending on the action.

6. To show and set additional options, click the **Options** button, and then specify the ones you want to set. To hide the options, click the **Options** button again.

 ◆ To allow a user to select action settings, select the **Show Action When Run** check box.

 The availability of the Options button varies depending on the action.

Adding Variables to an Action

A variable stores a value that you can use in a workflow. For example, you can use variables to get the current time or today's date, unique text and data, or even a script. You can add variables directly to a workflow or to a compatible editable field or pop-up of an action. If you need a variable, yet you're not ready to use it, you can declare it in the Variables log for later use. In some cases, you can declare or create a a variable directly in an action.

Add Variables to an Action

1. Start Automator and use a template or open the workflow you want to add variables to an action.

2. Click the **Variables** button in the Library pane.

3. Click the category from the Library list to display the actions you want.

4. Use any of the following methods to add a variable to an action:

 ◆ **Add to Workflow.** Drag variable into the Workflow pane. The "Get Value of Variable" action appears.

 ◆ **Add to Action.** Drag variable into an editable field or pop-up menu of an action. The variable is added to the Variables log.

 ◆ **Declare in Log.** Drag the variable to the Variables log. You can declare it without using it immediately.

5. Enter information and specify the settings you want for the variable; the information and settings vary depending on the variable.

6. To show and set additional options, click the **Options** button, and then specify the ones you want to set. To hide the options, click the **Options** button again.

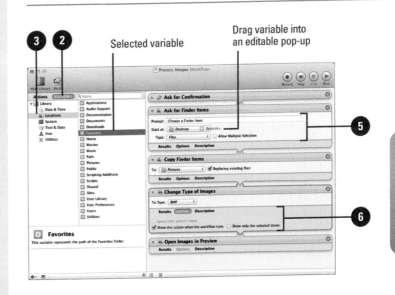

Selected variable

Drag variable into an editable pop-up

Recording an Action

If you can't find a pre-built action that meets your needs, you can record your own. Automator records your keyboard and mouse event to create a custom action, known as the "Watch Me Do" action. After you record the "Watch Me Do" action, you can adjust the playback speed and timeout settings, as well as delete any events you don't want. Before you can record an action, you need to select the "Enable access for assistive devices" check box in the Universal Access preferences.

Record an Action

1. Set up your environment the way you expect it to be before you start to record.

2. Start Automator and create or open the workflow you want to add a recorded action.

 ◆ If a dialog appears, click the **Open Universal Access** button, select the **Enable access for assistive device** check box, and then click the **Close** button.

3. Click the **Record** button on the toolbar.

 The Automator Recording message appears with the Stop button.

4. Perform the steps you want to record, and then click the **Stop** button.

5. To test your recording, click the **Run** button on the toolbar.

6. Adjust the settings you want for the recorded action.

 ◆ Delete Event. Select the event, and then type Delete.

 ◆ Rearrange Event. Drag an event to change the order.

 ◆ Adjust Timeout. Click the Timeout up and down arrows.

 ◆ Adjust Speed. Drag the **Playback speed** slider.

Working with Workflows

After you add actions to your workflow, you can work with them to create the results you want. In the Workflow pane you can arrange actions in a different order; remember the input and output needs to match. If you need the same action in another place, you can copy and paste it. If you don't always need an action, you can disable it for now and then enable later. If you want to add media to a workflow, you can use the Media browser. If you can't locate a certain action, you can use the Search box to try and find it. If you still can't find it, you can import actions developed by others.

Work with Workflows

◆ **Collapse/Expand.** Click the triangle to the left of the action title.

◆ **Arrange.** Drag the action title bar in the Workflow pane to a new place.

◆ **Copy.** Select the action in the Workflow pane, click the **Edit** menu, click **Copy**, click in the workflow where you want to insert the action, click the **Edit** menu, and then click **Paste**.

◆ **Disable.** Control-click the action title bar, then click **Disable**.

◆ **Enable.** Control-click the action title bar, then click **Enable**.

◆ **Delete.** Click the **Delete** button (X) on the title bar of the action in the Workflow pane.

◆ **Browse Media.** Click the **Media** button on the toolbar. Displays the media browser where you can select and use audio, photos, and movies.

◆ **Import.** Click the **File** menu, click **Import Actions**, navigate to and select the actions you want, and then click **Import**.

◆ **Find.** Enter a word or phrase in the Search box, and then press Return. To clear the search, click the **Delete** button (X) in the Search box.

◆ **View Log.** Click the **View** menu, and then click **Show Log**. You can also use the View Results action in a workflow.

Find Collapse/Expand Enable/Disable

View log of variables or events

Browse Media

Running and Stopping a Workflow

When you finishing creating a workflow, it's important to test (run) it to make sure it works the way you want it to. When you run a workflow (all at once with the Run button or one step at a time with the Step button), Automator executes each action from top to bottom, displaying status messages at the bottom of the window. As each action completes, a green checkmark appears in the bottom left-corner of the action indicating the action worked correctly. If a problem occurred, such as the input and output not matching, a red x appears.

Run and Stop a Workflow

1 Start Automator and create or open the workflow you want to run.

2 To view the values stored in variables as a debugging tool, click the **Show or hide the workflow log** button to display the log.

3 Click the **Run** button on the toolbar to play the entire workflow or click the **Step** button to play the workflow one step at a time.

Automator executes each action from top to bottom, displaying status messages at the bottom of the window.

TIMESAVER *Click the View menu, and then click Show Log to view all the status messages.*

4 If a dialog box appears, requesting information or files, fulfill the request.

As each action completes, a green checkmark appears in the bottom left-corner of the action indicating the action worked correctly. If a problem occurred, such as the input and output not matching, a red x appears.

5 To stop the workflow, click the **Stop** button on the toolbar.

6 To show the results of a specific action, click the **Results** button at the bottom of the action. To hide the results, click the **Results** button again.

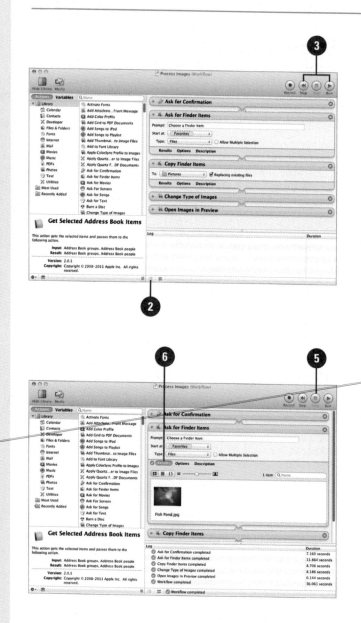

Saving a Workflow

As you work on a workflow, Automator automatically saves it with Auto Save (**New!**). If the workflow is Untitled, you can give it a name. Automator periodically saves your workflow, however you can save a version (**New!**) or create a duplicate (**New!**) at any time. With the Duplicate To command (**New!**) on the File menu, you can resave a workflow to a different template type. When you use the Workflow or Application templates, you can save a workflow as a .workflow) or .app file. A Workflow file is one you open, modify, and run in Automator. An Application file is one you can double-click on your Mac, drag it to the Dock, and assign a keyboard shortcut to make it easier to launch.

Save a Workflow

1. Start Automator and create (Workflow or Application) or open the workflow you want to save.

2. Click the **File** menu, and then click **Save** (for new Untitled workflows) or **Save a Version** (for existing named workflows).

3. For new Untitled, type the name you want for the workflow file.

4. Click the **Where** pop-up, and then select the location where you want to save the file.

5. Click the **File Format** pop-up, and then click **Workflow** or **Application**.

6. Click **Save**.

Did You Know?

You can revert to the previously saved workflow. Click the File menu, click Revert, and then click Revert.

You can customize the toolbar. Click the View menu, click Customize Toolbar, drag toolbar items to the toolbar, specify display options as text, icons, or both, and to use the small size or not, and then click Done.

You can print a workflow. Click the File menu, click Print, select the print options you want, and then click Print.

Using a Workflow as Plug-ins

When you create a workflow with the template type Folder Actions, Print Plugin, iCal Alarm, or Image Capture Plugin, Automator saves it as a plug-in type. Saving your workflows as a plug-in allows you to automate tasks in different places and situations on your Mac. For example, you can run a workflow from the Finder's shortcut menu, an event in iCal, the import feature in Image Capture, or a print dialog box.

Use a Workflow as a Plug-in

1. Start Automator and create or open the workflow with the following type:

 ◆ **Service.** Use to create a service for use in another application or the Finder.

 ◆ **Folder Actions.** Use to perform batch folder operations, such as opening or adding files.

 ◆ **Print Plugin.** Use to run a workflow when you print a file. An item appears on the PDF menu in the Print dialog box.

 ◆ **iCal Alarm.** Use to open iCal and create a new event named after plug-in.

 ◆ **Image Capture Plugin.** Use to import photos from a camera or scanner with Image Capture.

2. Click the **File** menu, and then click **Save As**.

3. Type the name you want for the plug-in.

4. Click **Save**.

Did You Know?

You can create self-installing actions and services. (**New!**) As with Safari plug-ins, Automator actions and services can be installed from the desktop by double-clicking their icons and approving the permission dialog.

Understanding AppleScript Basics

The AppleScript language is your way of communicating with your operating system; instructing it to perform specific tasks. Who wants to do the same tasks over and over again... no one. For example, adding the .jpg extension to 150 graphic files that have to move to a system that requires extensions. There is an easier way to perform repetitive tasks, and that's with AppleScript. **AppleScript** is an English-like scripting language that is used to write script files, and those files automate actions performed by the computer (like adding an extension 150 times).

ActionScripting is more than a language that repeats recorded actions; AppleScript can make decisions based on user-interaction or by analyzing data, documents, or situations. And with Mac OS X and the AppleScript Studio, you can create powerful Mac OS X applications with the Aqua look-and-feel written entirely in AppleScript. AppleScript is an automation language that helps us get through the mundane tasks of working on a computer and that's more than worth the time and effort spent in learning AppleScript.

AppleScript provides shortcuts for complex tasks such as naming files, resetting preferences, or connecting to the Internet, and the AppleScript Studio comes bundled with dozens of pre-written scripts that can immediately help you with your daily computer tasks. In addition, the automated workflow gives consistency, and speed to any Macintosh project. Since more can be accomplished in the same amount of time, you become more efficient—all through the power of AppleScript. To create your own AppleScripts, open the AppleScript editor, and type the script using precise language limitations.

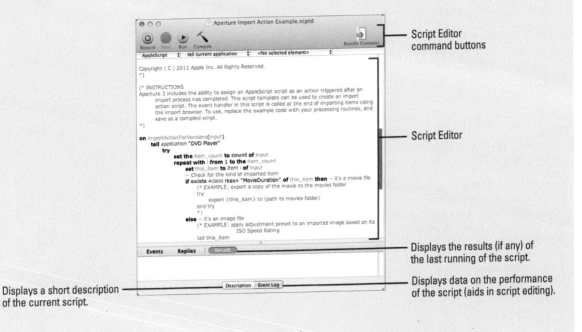

Script Editor command buttons

Script Editor

Displays the results (if any) of the last running of the script.

Displays data on the performance of the script (aids in script editing).

Displays a short description of the current script.

Using Ready-Made AppleScripts

You can use AppleScript right away, by working with AppleScripts created by the friendly folks at Apple. To gain access to the ready-made scripts, open the Applications folder, select the AppleScript folder, and then select Example Scripts, or do it the easy way by activating the built-in Script menu. When you activate (display) the Script menu, the Script icon appears on the right side of the menu bar and is available in the Finder and whenever you open an application. For example, you can click the Scripts icon, point to Printing Scripts, and then click Convert To PDF.

Display the Script menu and Enable Script Helpers

1 Click the **Launchpad** icon in the Dock, click the **Utilities** folder, and then click the **AppleScript Editor** icon.

2 Click the **AppleScript Editor** menu, and then click **Preferences**.

3 Click **General**.

4 Select the **Show Script menu in menu bar** check box.

5 Select or clear the **Show Computer scripts** check box to show or hide library scripts.

6 Click the **top** or **bottom** option to specify where to show application scripts on the menu.

7 Click **Editing**.

8 Select the **Use Script Assistant** check box to enable the assistant, which tries to complete portions of scripts as you type.

9 Select the **Show "tell" application pop-up menu** check box to enable it, which helps create scripts to be run in applications, such as Mail rule scripts.

10 Click the **Close** button.

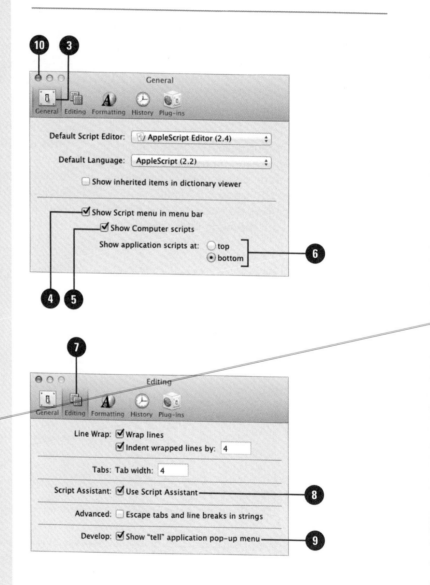

Use Ready-Made AppleScripts

1. On the right side of the menu bar, click the **Scripts** icon.

2. Point to a script category, if necessary.

3. Select a script option. Some of the useful scripts include:

 ◆ **Add to File Names** and **Add to Folder Names**. Add text to the beginning or end of every file or folder in the active Finder window.

 ◆ **Replace Text in Item Names**. Replaces text in file and folder names.

 ◆ **Trim File Names** and **Trim Folder Names**. Removes file extensions or text from the beginning or end of every file or folder in the active Finder window.

Open Example Scripts Folder

1. On the right side of the menu bar, click the **Scripts** icon.

2. Point to **Open Scripts Folder**, and then click one of the Scripts Folder (Finder, User, or Computer).

3. Double-click the example folder you want, if necessary.

4. Double-click the script you want to execute.

Did You Know?

You can add your scripts to the Scripts menu. Open the Example Scripts folder in the AppleScripts folder, create a folder with the name you want on the Scripts menu, and then drag your script into the folder. The script name appears on the Scripts menu.

Writing and Recording AppleScripts

Anyone can write AppleScripts. All it requires is the Script Editor application available with Mac OS X, and knowledge of the AppleScript language. The AppleScript editor lets you type script directly into the editor window, or you can click the Record button, and then perform some Mac operation, as the editor records each step as you work. There are many places where you can go to increase your AppleScript understanding; however, point your browser to *http://www.apple.com/applescript/*, and then click the Resources link to access current resources dealing the creative techniques for AppleScript.

Write and Record AppleScripts

1. Click the **Launchpad** icon in the Dock, click the **Utilities** folder, and then click the **AppleScript Editor** icon.

2. Type the Script directly into the Script Editor window.

 ◆ Start New. Click the **File** menu, and then click **New**.

 ◆ Start New with a Template. Click the **File** menu, point to **New** from **Template**, point to category (Aperture, Droplets, iChat, or Mail), and then select then select a template (**New!**).

3. To record within the active script, click the **Record** button.

4. Click the **Run** button to run the active script.

5. Click the **Stop** button to stop the running of the active script.

6. Click the **Compile** button to create a version of the active script.

7. Click the **File** menu, and then click **Save**, or **Save As** to save the script using a unique name and location.

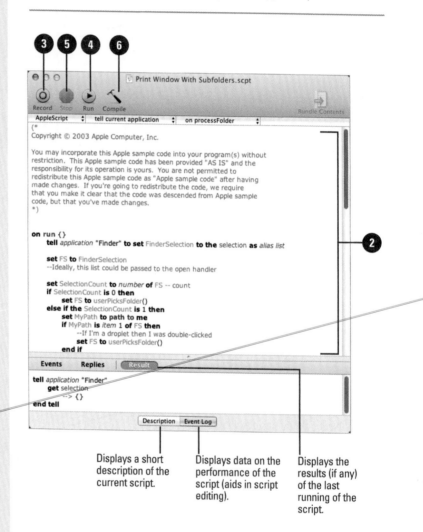

Displays a short description of the current script.

Displays data on the performance of the script (aids in script editing).

Displays the results (if any) of the last running of the script.

Open and Modify a Script from the Scripts Menu

1. On the right side of the menu bar, click the **Scripts** icon.

2. Point to a script category, if necessary.

3. Option-click the script you want to open.

 The Script Editor opens, displaying the selected script.

4. Modify the script as you want.

 ◆ **Use the Script Assistant.** As you type, it looks for possible matches. You'll see the suggestion in gray. Press Esc to accept it. Press Option+Esc to see a list of suggestions. Enable in Editing preferences.

 ◆ **Use the "tell" application pop-up menu. (New!)** It create scripts to be run within specific applications, such as a Mail rule script. The menu appears in the Navigation Bar above the script, next to the language selection pop-up. Enable in Editing preferences.

5. Click the **Run** button to run the active script.

6. Click the **Stop** button to stop the running of the active script.

7. Click the **Compile** button to create a version of the active script.

8. Click the **File** menu, and then click **Save As** to save the script using a unique name and location.

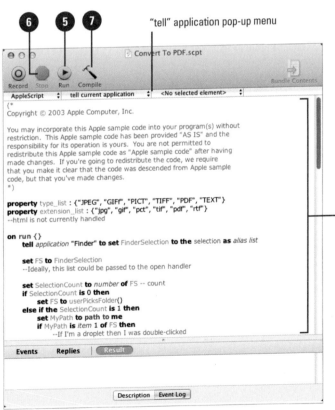

"tell" application pop-up menu

Using AppleScript with Automator

You can add an AppleScript script to a workflow. Simply, drag the Run AppleScript action into your workflow, and then enter your script into the small script editor within the action. Automator is a scriptable application. You can use AppleScript in the Script Editor to develop and execute workflows. To help you write the scripts, you can view the Automator's AppleScript dictionary. Open the Utilities folder window, open another window with the Applications window. Drag the Automator icon (located in the Applications folder) onto the Script Editor icon (located in the Utilities folder).

Use AppleScript with Automator

1. Start Automator and use a template or open the workflow you want.

2. Click the **Actions** button in the Library pane.

3. Click the **Utilities** category from the Library list.

4. Drag the **Run AppleScript** action you want to the Workflow pane.

5. Type the script you want in the action.

6. To run the script, click the **Run** button in the action below the title bar.

7. To compile the script, click the **Compile** button to create a version of the active script.

8. To run the workflow, click the **Run** button on the toolbar.

Appendix: Installing Mac OS X Lion

A

Introduction

If you're upgrading to Mac OS X Lion from a previous version of Mac OS X, this appendix describes how to prepare and install Mac OS X Lion. The temptation is to download the Installation app from the Mac App Store and start the installation, but you can avoid problems by making sure your computer is ready for Mac OS X Lion. Before you install Lion, you need to check your computer hardware and software and make several setup decisions that relate to your computer. When you're ready to start the installation, the Mac OS X Lion Setup Assistant walks you through the process.

What You'll Do

Prepare to Install Mac OS X Lion

Determine the Current Mac OS Version

Get Mac Information

Get Mac OS X Lion from the App Store

Install Mac OS X Lion

Reinstall Mac OS X Lion

Preparing to Install Mac OS X Lion

The Apple Installer guides you through many of the choices you need to make, but there are some decisions and actions you need to make before you start the installation. In order to run Mac OS X, you'll need at least 2 GB of physical RAM, and at least 4 GB of available space on your hard disk for the installation. And your Mac needs to be one of the models that can run Mac OS X with Mac OS X 10.6.6 or later and the Mac App Store installed. If you have Mac OS X 10.5 Leopard, you'll need to upgrade to Snow Leopard 10.6 first, and then update it to 10.6.6.

Confirm that your hardware can run Mac OS X Lion Version 10.7

Mac OS X Lion Version 10.7 requires a Macintosh with an Intel Core 2 Duo, Core i3, Core i7, or Xeon processor, a DVD drive, at least 2 GB MB of physical RAM and a built-in display or a display connected to an Apple-supplied video card supported by your computer.

Verify you have enough hard drive space.

While the amount of disk space required depends on your computer and the way you are installing Mac OS X, you are recommended to have at least 5 GB of available space on your hard drive, or 8 GB of disk space if you install developer tools.

Update computer firmware.

You may need to update your computer's firmware. You can check the Apple Software Updates web site at *www.apple.com/support/downloads* to see if your computer needs it.

Check out third party hardware compatibility

Third Party Hardware. Mac OS X Version 10.7 Lion includes out-of-the-box functionality for many hardware devices. Mac OS X will automatically configure itself to support most hardware. However, some devices may need additional driver support from the manufacturer. Please check with the manufacturer of your product to see if Mac OS X Version 10.7 compatible drivers are available.

Third Party Hardware Specifics. If you have a third-party SCSI card or video card attached to your computer and the installer or Mac OS indicates there are problems, try removing the cards or adding a terminator or disk drive to the SCSI card.

Reinstall Mac OS X Lion

If you have problems with your installation and want to reinstall the Mac OS X Lion software to correct it, you can do it without the installation discs. Hold down ⌘+R during a restart bootup. To erase a disk first, click Disk Utility, and then click Continue. To reinstall Lion, click Reinstall Mac OS X, click Continue, and then follow the onscreen installation instructions.

Uninstall Mac OS X Lion

Unfortunately, there isn't any clean way, like an uninstall application, to uninstall Mac OS X10.7. The only real way is to backup your Home folder, Applications folder, Library folder, and anything else you want to save, and then erase the hard drive and install the operating system you want to use.

Determining the Current Mac OS Version

If you're not sure what version of the Mac operating system you've currently installed on your computer, you can use the About This Mac command or the Startup Disk utility to find out. The About This Mac command on the Apple menu displays the currently installed version and provides access to Software Update to upgrade it and More Info about the hardware with the System Information application. If you have multiple versions installed on different drives, you can use the Startup Disk Utility to quickly find out what is installed. You can access the Startup Disk utility from System Preferences in the Dock.

Check About This Mac for Mac OS X Version

1. Click the **Apple** menu.

2. Click **About This Mac**.

 The OS version appears in the window.

3. Click the **Close** button.

3

Mac OS version

Check Startup Disk Utility for Mac OS X Version

1. Click the **System Preferences** in the Dock.

2. Click the **Startup Disk** icon.

 The OS version for the connected hard drives appear in the pane.

3. Click the **Close** button.

3

Mac OS versions

Getting Mac Information

With the About This Mac Command (**New!**), you can get quick and easy access to information about your Mac. The About This Mac dialog provides a centralized place to view information on your Mac's displays, storage, and memory. In addition, you can get access to support information, such Apple's Help Center, Mac OS X Support, User Manuals, Specifications, and hardware support, and service information, such as service and repair coverage and status.

Get Mac Information

1. Click the **Apple** menu, and then click **About This Mac**.

2. Click **More Info**.

 The OS version appears in the window.

3. Click the tab with the information you want to view.

 ◆ **Overview.** Displays processor, memory, graphics, serial number and software version information.

 ◆ **Displays.** Displays display information, and access to user manual and Display preferences.

 ◆ **Storage.** Displays disc information and access to Disk Utility.

 ◆ **Memory.** Displays memory usage and upgrade instructions.

 ◆ **Support.** Provides access to Apple support and documentation.

 ◆ **Service.** Provides access to service and repair information for your Mac.

4. Click the **Close** button.

Overview tab

Memory tab

Support tab

Getting Mac OS X Lion from the App Store

If your Mac can run Lion—a computer with an Intel Core 2 Duo, Core i3, Core i7, or Xeon processor—and you have installed the latest version of Snow Leopard 10.6.6 or later, you can buy and download Lion from the App Store (**New!**). After you download the software, you can run the installer to complete the process. You can install it on all your authorized Mac computers (**New!**).

Getting Mac OS X Lion from the App Store

1. Click the **App Store** icon in the Dock.

2. Click **Sign In** in Quick Links, enter your Apple ID and password, and then click **Sign In**.

3. If needed, search for Mac OS X Lion in the Search field.

4. Click the Mac OS X Lion preview, icon or name, and then click **Buy App** and **Install App**.

5. If prompted, enter an administrator's name and password, and click **Done** to download and install.

6. To get download and install status, click the **Purchases** button on the toolbar, or click the **Launchpad** icon in the Dock, and then view the app's icon and progress bar.

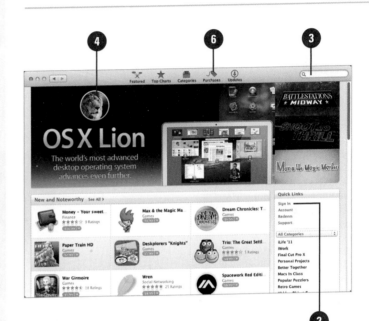

Installing Mac OS X Lion

There are several different kinds of installation: clean (new or erased disk), upgrade from Mac OS 10.0 through 10.6, reinstall Mac OS 10.7, or restore Mac OS 10.7 using Time Machine. The Mac OS X Setup Assistant guides you step-by-step through the process of installing Mac OS X Lion no matter what the installation type. You insert the installation disc, and then follow the on-screen instructions (read the instructions, select options, and then click Continue) to complete the process. As you go through the process, you can click the Back button at any time to change option in previous screens. The installation process takes about 30 to 45 minutes if all goes well, which is faster than previous versions.

Install Mac OS X Lion

① Download the Mac OS X Lion installation software from the Mac Apps Store to your Mac hard drive.

See page 517, "Getting Mac OS X Lion from the App Store" for specific details.

② Double-click the **Mac OS X** Lion installer icon, and then click **Continue**.

③ If you want, read the license agreement, and then click **Agree**, and then click **Agree** again to continue.

④ In the Select Destination screen, select the disk or partition to install Mac OS X (click **Show All Disks** as needed).

⑤ Click **Install**.

Please wait while Mac OS X prepares your computer for installation, restarts your computer, and starts to install files.

⑥ Step through the Setup Assistant and click **Continue** as you go (click **Back** to change options):

◆ Welcome. Read the material.

◆ Language and Keyboard. Select a language.

- ◆ **Transfer Information.** Select an option.
- ◆ **Apple ID.** Enter your Apple ID and password.
- ◆ **Create Your Account.** Enter your account information.
- ◆ **Select a Picture for This Account.** Take a snapshot or select a picture.
- ◆ **Select time Zone.** Take a snapshot or select a picture.
- ◆ **Registration Information.** Enter your individual information.

7 Upon completion, click **Start Using Lion**.

Did You Know?

You can use Recovery HD to help with installation problems. Mac OS X Lion provides Recovery HD, which takes the place of an installation DVD by providing recovery tools such as Disk Utility. to access the Recovery HD, shutdown the computer and hold ⌘+R while booting (**New!**).

You can use other languages. Mac OS X Lion is available in Arabic, Czech, Turkish, and Hungarian (**New!**).

For Your Information

Erasing and Partitioning a Hard Disk

During the Mac OS X install, you can erase the hard disk you plan to install Lion and install a clean version with the factory settings. Click the Apple menu, click Restart, and then click Restart. During bootup, hold down ⌘+R. In Mac OS X Utilities, click Disk Utility, click Continue, select a hard drive, and then click the Erase tab. Click the Format pop-up menu, select Mac OS Extended (Journaled), type a name for the disk, and then click Erase. In addition, you can partition your hard disk into several volumes before you install Mac OS X. When you partition a disk into volumes, the entire disk is erases, so it's important to back up your files first. In Disk Utility, click Partition. When you partition the disk, you need to select a disk format. The typical choice in most cases is Mac OS Extended (Journaled). Upon completion, quit Disk Utility, and then follow the remaining on-screen instructions to complete the install.

Reinstalling Mac OS X Lion

OS X Lion includes a built-in restore partition, allowing you to repair or reinstall OS X without the need for installation discs (**New!**). OS X can be re-installed on your Mac from Recovery HD mode (**New!**). Recovery HD mode includes access to Time Machine (**New!**) for backup restores and the Safari web browser, so you can check your e-mail or browse the Apple Support site (**New!**). In order to access Recovery HD mode, shutdown the computer and hold ⌘+R while booting.

Reinstalling Mac OS X Lion

1. Click the **Apple** menu, click **Restart**, and then click **Restart**.

2. During bootup, hold down ⌘+R.

 The built-in Mac OS X Utilities program starts.

3. Select an option for the Start Up window:

 ◆ **Restore From Time Machine Backup.** Re-install OS X from a Time Machine backup. You need to previously backed up your entire computer.

 ◆ **Reinstall Mac OS X.** Re-install a clean version of the OS X.

 ◆ **Get Help Online.** Access the Web for online help. You need an Internet connection on your computer or click the Wi-Fi menu (upper right corner).

 ◆ **Disk Utility.** Start the Disk Utility program for erase disk options.

4. Click **Continue**.

5. Follow the on-screen instructions to re-install Mac OS X; steps vary depending on the re-install option.

Did You Know?

You can access other utilities. In Mac OS X Utilities, you can access the Firmware Password Utility, Network Utility, and Terminal app from the Utilities menu.

New! Features

Mac OS X Lion

Mac OS X Lion means superior results faster, with new features and enhancements that help you build Web sites and Internet applications. It provides a combination of visual layout tools, application development features, and code editing support, enabling developers and designers at every skill level to create visually appealing, standards-based sites and applications quickly and easily.

Only New Features

If you're already familiar with Mac OS X Snow Leopard, you can access and download Mac OS X Lion New Features to help make your transition to the new version simple and smooth. The Mac OS X Lion New Features—including a more detailed list of new features—as well as other Mac OS X Snow Leopard to Mac OS X Lion transition helpers are available on the Web at *www.perspection.com.*

What's New

If you're searching for what's new in Mac OS X Lion, just look for the icon: **New!**. The new icon appears in the table of contents and throughout this book so you can quickly and easily identify a new or improved feature in Mac OS X Lion. The following is a brief description of each new feature and it's location in this book.

Accessibility

◆ **VoiceOver (p. 118, 120, 123)** You can create groups of preferences for specific uses and assign VoiceOver commands to single keys. It also offers an improved drag-and-drop experience for blind and seeing impaired users. The VoiceOver Utility includes a search field to help you find specific features.

Address Book

◆ **New Look and Full Screen (p. 140-145)** Browse your contacts in a new look screen without the clutter of a sidebar or status bar in Full Screen view. See your buddy's availability while in Address Book and make FaceTime calling.

◆ **Yahoo! Support (p. 141, 144-145)** When you add or update a Yahoo! account to Address Book, your Yahoo! contacts appear.

◆ **Social Network Profiles (p. 142-143)** Address Book lets you quickly access the social network profiles for your contacts, including Facebook.

AirDrop

◆ **Wireless File Sharing (p. 421)** AirDrop uses drag-and-drop file sharing to send files wirelessly to anyone around you. No setup, configuration or network required. AirDrop uses Peer-to-Peer Wi-Fi between participating Macs.

App Store

◆ **Lion Available (p. 517)** You can buy and download Lion from the App Store. You can download and install it on all your authorized Macs.

◆ **App Updates (p. 128-129)** When an update is available for an app, the App Store makes efficient use of bandwidth, delivering only updated data.

Auto Save

◆ **Auto Save (p. 152)** Apps developed with Auto Save can automatically save changes to your document as you work.

◆ **Revert, Duplicate, or Lock (p. 152)** Apps with Auto Save let you easily undo recent changes with Revert. Duplicate creates a copy of a document and places it next to the original. You can lock a document at any time to prevent changes.

FaceTime

◆ **FaceTime (p. 313-314)** FaceTime for Mac lets you make video calls to other Intel-based Mac computers, iPad 2, iPhone 4, or the latest iPod touch.

◆ **Video Calls and Full Screen (p. 313-314)** A Full Screen view puts FaceTime video calls in their own space. When someone calls you, FaceTime rings through on all your Macs. Video calls also automatically adjust to screen orientation.

FileVault

◆ **FileVault (p. 398-400)** FileVault 2 encrypts the entire drive—either internal or external USB and FireWire—live on your Mac, so you can continue to work as it encrypts. FileVault 2 uses XTS-AES 128 encryption to secure the data.

Finder

◆ **Resize Windows from any Edge (p. 15)** You can resize a window from any side.

◆ **Resume (p. 24)** Apps resume when launched and the system resumes on restart unless you choose a clean start.

◆ **All My Files (p. 28-29)** All My Files gathers all your files—no matter where they're located—and displays them in an organized view.

◆ **Sort Files (p. 32-33)** A button in the Finder toolbar that lets you sort files by category. Sort files by kind, application, date modified, date added, or size.

◆ **Group as Folder (p. 42-43)** Instantly create a folder from selected files by using the "New Folder with Selection" command.

◆ **Merge Folders (p. 45)** When you try to combine two folders with the same name, the Finder offers to merge them into a single folder.

◆ **Keep Both Files (p. 45)** When you attempt to add a file or folder to a folder that contains the same name, the Finder offers to keep both files or merge folders.

◆ **Search Suggestions (p. 66-67)** As you type in the search field, the Finder dynamically suggests relevant matches based on the contents of your Mac.

Full-Screen Apps

◆ **Full-Screen Apps (p. 135)** Lion includes built-in support for full-screen apps. Full-Screen Apps have a Full Screen button in the window title bar. When an app is in Full Screen view, the menu bar is hidden.

iCal

◆ **New Look and Full Screen (p. 368-369)** A new look gives you more room to browse and edit your events and view your calendar in Full Screen view.

◆ **Day View (p. 369)** Day view makes it easy to stay on top of a busy day.

◆ **Year View (p. 369)** Year view lets you see 12 months at a time, displaying a heat map using colors to represent availability for each day.

◆ **Quick Add (p. 372)** Simply enter a regular-language phrase like "Mary's Birthday at 8 p.m." or "Lunch with John" and let iCal add the event for you.

iChat

◆ **Yahoo! Messenger (p. 290-291)** Use iChat to stay in touch with your Yahoo! buddies. Sign in with your Yahoo! ID.

◆ **Unified Buddy List and Status (p. 294, 296, 298)** iChat brings your buddies together in one buddy list no matter what service they use. Share a single availability and status message with all your buddies no matter what service.

◆ **Movable Tabs (p. 300)** Movable tabs let you organize your chats by dragging and dropping.

Install and Restore Utilities

◆ **Built-in Lion (p. 520)** Lion includes a built-in restore partition, allowing you to repair or reinstall OS X without the need of installation discs.

Launchpad

◆ **Launchpad (p. 132-133)** Launchpad is a full-screen home for all the apps on your Mac. It creates full-screen pages to accommodate your apps and adds new pages as you add more apps.

Mail

◆ **Formatting Bar (p. 269)** The Formatting bar provides easy access to editing capabilities for creating lists, customizing fonts, and changing paragraphs.

◆ **Layout (p. 271)** A new layout for Mail takes advantage of the widescreen display as well as provides a Full Screen view, so you can read and send email.

◆ **Favorites Bar (p. 271)** The Favorites bar provides a horizontal layout of your favorite mail folders and their unread accounts to give you one-click access.

◆ **Inline Controls (p. 272)** Messages include convenient inline controls that make it easy to reply to, forward, or delete a message.

◆ **Conversations (p. 278-279)** Mail automatically groups related messages in conversations. You can find all the messages related to the one you're reading.

◆ **Search Suggestions and Attachments (p. 283)** Mail suggests the most relevant matches for your search term based on the contents of your email. Find attachments fast by searching for an attachment using its filename or its content.

Mission Control

◆ **Exposé (p. 20-21, 90-91)** Exposé in Mission Control groups windows of the same app. Click to bring the window you want forward.

◆ **Spaces (p. 20-21, 90-91)** You can add and remove desktop spaces in Mission Control. Each desktop space can have its own desktop picture.

Multi-Touch Gestures

◆ **Gestures (p. 6)** Lion includes new animations, such as rubber-band scrolling, zooming, and swiping.

Photo Booth

◆ **Full-Screen and New Look (p. 333)** Photo Booth delivers a full-screen view with a new look that makes you feel as if you're in an actual photo booth.

◆ **Trim Video Clips (p. 334)** Create video clips with the new trim feature. Photo Booth displays the frames; all you need to do is pick the start and end frames.

◆ **Effects (p. 335)** Have even more fun with the built-in camera on your Mac with nine new effects that use facial tracking technology.

Preview

◆ **Full-Screen (p. 150-151)** Preview takes your document to Full Screen view.

◆ **Smart Magnify (p. 150-151)** The Smart Magnify tool makes it a snap to focus on a specific part of a PDF or image without zooming the entire document.

◆ **Search Results (p. 150-151)** With the Sidebar, you can read the text, learn the number of matches per page, and see a thumbnail of the page.

◆ **Add Signatures (p. 150-151)** You can add your signature to PDF documents.

◆ **Auto Save and Versions (p. 150-151)** Preview supports Auto Save, automatically saving the changes to images and PDFs. Browse previous versions of PDFs and images and revert to an earlier version if you need to.

Privacy

◆ **Preferences (p. 397)** Security preferences include a Privacy pane for enabling and disabling location services and diagnostic and usage data collection. When an app requests your location, an icon appears in the menu bar.

QuickTime Player

◆ **Full-Screen (p. 338)** Display your QuickTime video in Full Screen view.

◆ **Rotate Clips (p. 338)** If a video is upside down or sideways, you can rotate it.

◆ **Export Audio Only (p. 340-341)** The Export Audio Only feature produces an AAC audio track that's perfect for listening on the go or posting audio-only files.

◆ **Merge Clips (p. 340-341)** You can combine multiple clips into a single movie.

◆ **Capture a Screen Region (p. 340-341)** You can record part of the screen, such as a specific window. Screen capture lets you show mouse or trackpad clicks, highlighting the pointer each time you click an object on the screen.

◆ **Sharing Options (p. 340-341)** Share your video directly to Vimeo, Flickr, Facebook, iMovie, and Mail.

Safari

◆ **Full-Screen (p. 226-227)** Display Safari and web sites in Full Screen view.

◆ **Reading List and Reader (p. 226, 232-233)** Reading List lets you save web pages to read later.

◆ **Private AutoFill (p. 242-243)** Safari lets you fill out forms quickly while keeping your personal information private.

◆ **Downloads List (p. 250-251)** When you download files, an arrow button appears to show you the progress of your download. You can drag downloaded files from the Downloads list to your desktop for easy organization.

◆ **Find Option (p. 244-245)** When you use Find, you can choose to search for text that either contains or starts with the text you type in the search field.

◆ **Custom Content in Extensions (p. 252-253)** Safari allows extensions to show custom HTML content from the extension's toolbar.

◆ **View or Remove Website Data (p. 254)** You can see a list of all the web sites that have stored data on your computer, which you can also clear.

Screen Sharing

◆ **Full Screen (p. 422-423)** Display screen-sharing in Full Screen view.

◆ **Per-user Screen Sharing (p. 422-423)** You can remotely log in to a Mac with any user account on that computer and control it.

◆ **Observe Only Mode (p. 422-423)** The Observe Only mode lets you watch a remote computer without controlling the mouse or trackpad movements.

◆ **Screen Sharing Toolbar (p. 422-423)** Screen sharing includes a toolbar with useful tools, such as screen resolution, Clipboard access, and screen capture.

Spotlight

◆ **Drag and Drop (p. 56, 421)** You can drag items from the Spotlight menu, which makes it quick and convenient to send a document via email or AirDrop.

◆ **Quick Look Results (p. 56)** The Spotlight menu shows Quick Look previews for search results.

◆ **Search Web (p. 56)** When you choose Search Web from the Spotlight menu, Safari opens and displays search results using your default search engine.

◆ **Search Wikipedia (p. 56)** When you choose Search Wikipedia from the Spotlight menu, the Dictionary app opens and displays the Wikipedia entry for the term.

System

◆ **Quick Look Types (p. 38)** Quick Look includes more content types, including web page links in email, addresses as Google maps, Address Book contacts, and Spotlight results.

◆ **Lookup (p. 175)** Double-tap with three fingers to select a word in any OS X app and Lion looks up information from the dictionary and thesaurus, and the web with related Wikipedia entries. Results are displayed inline under the word.

◆ **Windows Migration (p. 443)** You can migrate all the information from your PC to your Mac; Lion automatically transfers your documents, contacts, calendars, email accounts, and photos stored in Picasa to the right place on your Mac.

System Preferences

◆ **Turn App Indicator Lights Off (p. 18, 86)** You can give your Dock a clean look with no indicator lights by turning them off in Dock preferences.

◆ **Overlay Scroll Bars (p. 98)** The overlay scroll bars appear when you need them and fade away when you don't.

◆ **Interact with iTunes Artwork in Screen Saver (p. 101)** Turn your screen saver into a jukebox. Just click an album to play the songs while in the screen saver.

◆ **Online Accounts (p. 258)** The Mail, Contacts, and Calendars pane in System Preferences gives you a central location to set up and manage all your accounts, including Microsoft Exchange, Gmail, Yahoo!, and AOL.

◆ **Magic Mouse and Trackpad Preferences (p. 454-455)** Mouse and Trackpad preferences allow you to customize the gestures for your input device.

Text and TextEdit

◆ **Character Picker (p. 164)** Hold down a letter and a dialog appears listing all alternative and accented characters; click a character to select it.

◆ **Auto-Correction (p. 171)** Auto-correction displays suggested spellings below the word.

◆ **Quick Look For Attachments (p. 174-175, 192-193)** Use Quick Look to preview web addresses and images in TextEdit.

◆ **Formatting Bar (p. 178)** TextEdit includes a streamlined formatting bar that provides convenient access to fonts, colors, lists, and other editing capabilities.

◆ **Inline Find (p. 176-177)** When you search for text in a document, TextEdit highlights all the occurrences in yellow for easy identification.

◆ **Auto Save and Versions Support (p. 152)** TextEdit automatically saves all the changes you make to a document. You can browse previous versions of a document and revert to an earlier version.

Time Machine

◆ **Local Snapshots (p. 481)** Time Machine keeps a spare copy of the files you create, modify, or delete right on your Mac.

◆ **Encrypted Backups (p. 478)** Keep your Time Machine backups secure by backing up to an external USB or FireWire drive encrypted with FileVault 2.

Versions

◆ **Automatic Versions (p. 152)** Each time you open a document, Lion automatically saves the current version. It also saves a new version every hour while you work, building a history of the document as you go.

◆ **Manual Versions (p. 152)** You can manually create a version of a document at any time by choosing "Save a Version" from the File menu.

◆ **Browse Versions (p. 152)** Using an interface similar to Time Machine, you can browse the version history of a document to see how it looked at any time.

◆ **Restore Previous Versions (p. 152)** To go back to a previous version, just replace the current version with the earlier one.

◆ **Delete Versions (p. 152)** You can delete an old version of a document. In the Versions browser, click the arrow in the title bar, and choose Delete This Version.

Index

i

A

Abstract Background, 100
Access Control Lists (ACLs), 478
accounts. *See also* Mail
 iChat accounts, creating, 290-291
Acrobat Reader. *See also* PDF files
 downloading, 209
actions. *See* Automator
ActionScripting, 507
activating/deactivating
 fonts, 155
 login window, 387
 windows, 12-13
activities preferences, setting, 122-123
Activity Monitor, 444-445
Address Book, 127, 131.
 archiving data, 141
 Bluetooth with, 412
 creating, 140-141
 Dashboard displaying, 158-159
 Directory for sharing information, 145
 editing contact information, 142-143
 faxes, addressing, 214
 iChat buddies from, 296
 images, adding, 142
 iPhoto pictures from, 142
 managing contacts, 144
 MobileMe Address Book, 355
 pictures to contacts, adding, 142
 printing from, 143
 Safari Bookmarks bar, adding to, 238-239
 sending e-mail from, 266-267
 sharing, 144-145
 Smart Addresses, using, 266
 Spotlight searches, keywords for, 57
 subscribing to, 145
 vCards, 141, 144-145

Administrator, 386
 file permissions, setting, 390
 master password, restoring, 398-399
 Safari preferences, setting, 253
 in Simple Finder, 92
Adobe Acrobat. *See also* PDF files
 downloading, 209
AIM, iChat with, 289, 291
 with Address Book, 142-143
AirDrop
 sending files wirelessly, 421
AirPort. *See also* Wi-Fi
 Admin Utility, 430
 configuring connection, 218
 desktop icon, 5
 iChat with, 308
 with Mac for Windows, 465, 472
 making Internet connection with, 224
 multiple connections with, 219
 network port configuration for, 223
 printers, sharing, 202-203
 setting up, 222
AirPort Extreme Base Station, 481
alerts
 changing sounds, 112
 forms, sending nonsecure, 243
 iChat notification alerts, 312
 speaking voice for, 116
Alex
 default speaking voice, setting, 116
 interface options, setting, 117
 for VoiceOver, 120
aliases, 75, 395
 creating, 88-89
alignment
 of document text, 178
 of e-mail message text, 269
 of tables, 185

All My Files, 28-29
AND operator, searching with, 57
animated GIFs
 creating, 297
 movies as animated GIFs, exporting, 335
anti-aliasing, 98-99
Anywhere mode, 168
AOL and iChat, 217, 289-290
 setting up accounts, 258
appearance (general) options, changing, 98-99
Apple
 sending diagnostic & usage data to, 397
Apple Account number for iTunes Music Store, 320
Apple Background, 100
Apple Developer Connection Web site, 162
Apple Events, sharing, 405
Apple Hardware Test, 450
Apple ID
 password, changing, 398-399
Apple Magic Mouse, 6, 33, 132
 Dashboard preferences, changing, 157
 with Mac for Windows, 472
Apple Remote, 465.
 iPod Hi-Fi, 315
 with Mac for Windows, 465, 472
AppleScripts, 131
 with Automator, 512
 basics of, 507
 displaying Script menu, 508
 example Scripts folder, opening, 509
 opening from Scripts menu, 511
 ready-make AppleScripts, using, 508-509
 recording, 510
 Script Assistant, 508, 510-511
 templates, starting new, 510
 writing, 510
AppleTalk printers, installing, 198-199
applications, 1, 127. See also aliases; third-party applications
 different program, opening documents with, 29
 full-screen, using, 135
 icons, 10
 Info window, information in, 50-51
 installing third-party applications, 129a
 launching, 132

 list of, 131
 nonresponding, quitting, 138
 opening, 134
 quitting, 138
 showing/hiding, 136
 Spotlight searches, keywords for, 57
 switching between, 136-137
 System Information, viewing system information with, 447
Application Services, using, 436
Applications folder, 26-27
App Store, 131
 Apple Push Notification, 128
 buy and download apps, 128-129
 install apps, 128-129
 using with Launchpad, 132
archiving. See also backing up
 Address Book data, 141
 Create Archive command, 435
 e-mail, 281
ARPANET (Advanced Research Projects Agency Network), 217
Arrange By button and menu, 32
arrows in dialogs, 9
Assist Me, help with, 407
attachments
 deleting from e-mail, 277
 iCal calendar event attachments, working with, 372
 with instant messages, 303
 in replies to e-mail, 275
 saving files, 277
 sending files as, 276
 Spotlight results as, 63
 viewing, 276-277
audio chats. See iChat
audio MIDI devices, configuring, 462-463
authentication preferences for Bluetooth, 415
AutoFill for Safari forms, 242
Automator, 131, 491
 Action list, 492, 494
 actions, 491
 adding, 500
 recording actions, 502
 variables to action, adding, 501
 AppleScripts with, 512
 Description view, 493, 494

example workflow
 modifying, 499
 opening, 497
 working with, 498
existing workflow, opening, 496
input and output, controlling, 499
introduction to, 492-493
Library pane, 492, 494
modifying example workflow, 499
plug-ins with, 499, 506
printing workflow, 505
recording actions, 502
running and saving workflows, 504-505
Search box, 493, 494
starting, 495
stopping workflow, 504
toolbars, 492, 494
 customizing, 505
Variable list, 492-493, 494
variables to action, adding, 501
Watch Me Do action, 502
window, parts of, 492-494
Workflow log and panes, 493, 494
Workflow variable list, 493, 494
working with workflows, 503
autosaving TextEdit preferences, 194
Auto Save, 152
 duplicating document, 152
 locking/unlocking documents, 152
 reverting to last saved, 152
 using with
 Automator, 505
 Preview, 150-151
 TextEdit, 190-191

B

Back button on toolbar, 17
backdrops in Photo Booth, 335
backgrounds
 desktop backgrounds, selecting, 100
 in e-mail message text, 269
 iChat window background, changing, 311
backing up, 477. See also archiving; disk
 image; Time Machine
 on CDs or DVDs, 490
 compressed files and folders, 435
 e-mail, 281

formatting, backups prior to, 438
iCal calendar, 373
to iDisk, 479
iTunes library, 331
MobileMe, backing up files, 362-363
Back to My Mac, accessing computer with, 420
baseline for characters, changing, 182
BBEdit, 436
BinHex format, 251
birthday calendars, 371
 Address Book, 142-143
blocking
 e-mail, 284-285
 iChat buddies, 302
 pop-up windows, 255
Bluetooth.
 Application Services with, 436
 desktop icon, 5
 with Mac for Windows, 465, 472-473
 making Internet connection with, 224
 moving items with, 414
 Passkey with, 413
 preferences, setting, 415
 printers, installing, 199
 setting up network, 412-413
 sharing, 405
boldfacing
 document text, 178
 e-mail message text, 269
 fonts, 155
Bonjour, 289
 list of Web sites, viewing, 238
 printers
 installing, 198-199
 sharing, 202-203
 problems with, 308
 saving chats, 311
 starting messaging, 309
 turning on, 308
bookmarks. See also Safari
 with DVD Player, 337
Bookmarks Library. See Safari
Boolean operators with Spotlight search, 57
Boot Camp Assistant, 110, 465. See also
 Mac for Windows
 installing Windows on Mac, 468-469
 preparing Mac for Windows, 466-467

Boot Camp Assistant *(continued)*
 removing Windows with, 474-475
 upgrading from beta, 467
BOOTP (boot protocol), 221
borders for table cells, 185
bouncing e-mail, 284-285
Braille, VoiceOver supporting, 120, 123
brightness on monitor, changing, 456
broadband connection. *See* cable modems
browsers. *See* Web browsers
buddies. *See* iChat
bulleted lists, 184
 in e-mail message text, 269
burning. *See* CDs; DVDs
Business, Dashboard displaying, 158-159
.bzip files, opening, 434

C

cable modems, 218
 Ethernet with, 221
 firewalls for, 409
 sharing connection, 408
cache
 for e-mail, 260
 Safari cache, emptying, 236
calculations. *See also* Calculator
Calculator, 131
 conversions, performing, 146-147
 Dashboard displaying, 158-159
 working with, 146
CalDAV
 setting up accounts, 258
 workplace calendar server, 374-375
CardDAV
 Address Book, 144-145
 setting up accounts, 258
calendars. *See* iCal
cards. *See also* vCards
case-sensitivity
 for finding/replacing text, 176
 of passwords, 3
CD-ROMs, 27
CD-Rs, 27
CD-RWs, 27, 52
CDs. *See also* iTunes
 adding/removing files/folders from, 53
 backing up files on, burning, 490

 creating, 53
 disk image, burning from, 488
 erasing, 329
 music CDs, burning, 330
 preparing to burn, 52
 Sidebar, burning disk with, 16
 start settings, changing, 111
 System Information, viewing information with, 447
 uneven CDs, loading, 27
Cellos voice, 116
cell phones.
 Bluetooth preferences, setting, 415
 iPhones with iTunes, 327
cells in tables, 184-185
center-alignment
 of document text, 178
 of tables, 184
change of address notification, 140
characters
 baseline, changing, 182
 for file names, 42
 spacing, changing, 182
 special characters, inserting, 188
check boxes in dialogs, 9
check marks in menus, 7
Chess, 127, 139
children. *See* parental controls
Chinese handwriting, 169
cleaning up
 files and folders set by clean up, 33
 Icons view, items in, 32-33
clicking with mouse, 6
Clipboard
 document text on, 166-167
 Web page text, copying, 249
Close button for windows, 12
closed captioning in QuickTime Player, 339
closing
 dialog options, 9
 documents, 191
 windows, 12-13
CloudApp. *See also* iCloud
 CloudApp menu, 344-345
 drops, working with, 347
 introduction, 343
 joining, sign in, 344-345
 preferences, 349

raindrops, 348
sharing files, 346-347
sign out, 345
uploading, picture, 189
Web App, using, 350-351
collating print output, 206
color labels
 for files and folders, 40-41
 for Find window searches, 67
 names, changing, 41
Color Picker, selecting with, 459
colors. *See also* ColorSync
 Color Picker, selecting with, 459
 Digital Color meter, using, 458
 for document text, 178
 with DVD Player, 337
 for e-mail message text, 269
 for fonts, 155
 highlight colors, changing, 98
 for iChat chats, 310
 for instant message text, 300-301
 monitor options, 456
 palettes, selecting, 459-460
 printer speed and, 196
 printing, matching for, 207
 for quoted text, 274
 of Sticky Notes, 153
ColorSync
 for fax documents, 215
 matching colors to device with, 460-461
 for printed documents, 207
columns. *See also* List view; tables
 windows, headings for, 12
Columns view, 30
 customizing window views, 80-81
 keyboard options in, 37
 Preview column, 37
 viewing folders in, 37
Comic Book effect, 335
commands, 7. *See also* specific commands
 Startup commands, 395, 399
 VoiceOver commands, 124-125
comments
 Info window options, 51
 in Keychain, 382
compatibility of hardware devices, 464

compressing/uncompressing
 attachments, files for, 276
 compressed files, 435
 downloaded applications, 129a
 files and folders, 33
 restoring compressed files, 435
 Safari, disk images in, 251
 Stuffit Expander, opening compressed
 files with, 33, 129a, 434
computers. *See also* networks
 Find window searching, 66
 iTunes, authorizing/deauthorizing, 316
 local name, changing, 405
 maintaining, 431
 several computers, connecting, 418-419
 stand-alone computers, starting on, 2
Console utility, viewing system messages
 with, 446
contacts. *See* Address Book
contents, Find window searches by, 67
contextual menus, 8
conversions with Calculator, performing,
 146-147
cookies, 254
 deleting, 256
cool genie effect, 87
copies for printing, 206
Copy command, 44
copying. *See also* drag-and-drop
 Automator workflows, 503
 documents, text in, 167
 with Exposé, 45
 files and folders, 44-45
 Find window files, 69
 formatting, 187
 hard disk, 439
 icons, 10-11
 ruler, 179
 Sidebar, copying folders with, 16
 Web page text, 249
 Windows and Mac OS X, files between,
 472-473
copyrights
 documents, inserting in symbol in, 188
 iTunes and, 323
 spacing for symbol, 182
 Web page text, copying, 249
Corel WordPerfect Page Setup, 204-205

Cover Flow, 30
 customizing window views, 80-81
 iTunes, working with music in, 319
 viewing files in, 36
cover pages, creating, 207, 211
CPU activity, viewing, 445
Create Archive command, 435
credit cards
 for iTunes Music Store, 319-320
CSS, 162
currency conversions, calculating, 146-147
Customize Toolbar dialog, 82-83
customizing
 Automator toolbars, 505
 Dock, 86-87
 DVD Player, 337
 Exposé, 90
 fonts, 155
 keyboard shortcuts, 453
 QuickTime Player, 338-339
 RSS feeds, 240
 Safari window, 226
 Sidebar, 84-85
 Spaces, 91
 views, 30
 widgets, 161
Cut command, 44

D

Dashboard, 131
 deleting widgets, 160-161
 full-screen app, using, 135
 installing widgets, 160
 preferences, changing, 157
 pre-installed widgets, using, 158-159
 showing/hiding widgets on, 158
 Web Clip widget, creating, 162
 working with, 156
Dashcode, 162
data detector, 171
dates and times
 announcing, 103
 files and folders arranged by, 33
 international options, changing, 104-105
 menu bar clock, using, 103
 setting, 102-103
 showing, 103
 Spotlight searches, keywords for, 57
 time zones, setting, 102
 World Clock, displaying, 158-159
deleting. *See also* Dock; iChat; Mail; Safari
 Address Book contacts, 142-143
 aliases, 88
 attachments from e-mail, 277
 Automator workflows, 503
 Dashboard widgets, 161
 documents, text in, 166
 downloaded file, 251
 e-mail, 280-281
 files and folders, 48
 hardware devices, 464
 iCal events, 372
 Keychain names, 381
 List view, columns in, 35
 printers, 198-199
 print queue, job from, 210
 recently used documents, 165
 Safari History list entries, 236
 securely deleting files and folders, 49
 stacks from Dock, 19
 third-party preferences, 95
 toolbar icons, 83
 user accounts, 389
Description view on Automator, 493, 494
design themes, 5
desktop. *See also* icons
 backgrounds, selecting, 100
 introduction to, 4-5
 screen, 2
Desktop folder, 28-29
desktop printers, using, 207
Development menu, Safari, 253
Devices section, Sidebar, 16
DHCP (Dynamic Host Configuration
 Protocol), 221
dialogs
 closing options, 9
 language options, setting, 104-105
 navigating in, 9
dial-up connections, 220
Dictionary, 131, 163. *See also* spell and
 grammar checking
 adding words to, 172
 AppleScript dictionary, Automator, 512
 Dashboard displaying, 158-159

looking up words with, 174
parental controls, setting, 175
preferences, setting, 174-175
recent searches, viewing, 175
Digital 8 camcorders with iMovie, 342
digital cameras. *See* Image Capture; iPhoto
digital certificates with Keychain, 381
Digital Color meter, 458
digital hub, cloud, 367
Digital Video (DV) camcorders, 291
Directory, 131
Address Book information, sharing, 145
disabled persons. *See* Universal Access
disk file system, 437
activities, monitoring, 444-445
Console, viewing system messages with, 446-447
copying disk, 439
formatting disks, 438
optimizing disk, 441
problems, fixing, 440
System Information, viewing system information with, 447
disk image
blank disk image as backup, 487
burning CD/DVD from, 488
creating, 486-487
restoring to disk, 489
disks. *See also* disk file system; hard drive
ejecting disks, 54
mounting disks, 54
opening/viewing, 26-27
Disk Utility, 52. *See also* backing up; disk file system
copying disk, 439
formatting disks, 438
restoring disk images with, 489
Windows, removing, 474-475
.dmg file format, 434
DNS (Domain Name Server), 218
for modems, 220
Dock, 5. *See also* showing/hiding
aliases on, 88-89
applications, launching, 132-133
customizing, 86-87
deleting
items, 87
stacks, 19

Launchpad, using, 132-133
moving items from, 87
showing/hiding, 86
hidden Dock, displaying, 18
stacks, 19
Simple Finder, 92
stacks, 19
documents, 163. *See also* attachments; Dictionary; faxing; HTML
bulleted lists, adding, 184
character spacing, changing, 182
closing, 191
copying text, 167
corrections in, 170
creating, 164
deleting text, 166
different program, opening with, 29
editing text, 166-167
existing documents, opening, 165
file formats for, 164
files, adding, 189
finding/replacing text in, 176-177
formatting
copying/pasting, 187
text, 178
grammar-checking, 172-173
handwritten text, inserting, 168-169
hyphenation, setting, 181
icons, 10
images, adding, 189
inserting text, 166
line spacing, changing, 183
lists, adding, 184
Microsoft Word file, saving as, 164, 190
movies, adding, 189
moving text, 167
numbered lists, adding, 184
opening, 28-29
page breaks, inserting and deleting, 183
Page Setup options for, 204
paragraph indents, setting, 181
paragraph tabs, setting, 180
PDF files, saving as, 209
Plain Text files, saving as, 190-191
previewing printed documents, 208
protecting, 190
read-only files, saving documents, 190
recent documents, opening, 165

documents *(continued)*
- RTF file, saving document as, 164, 190
- rulers, using, 179
- selecting text in, 166
- spacing
 - character spacing, changing, 182
 - line spacing, changing, 183
- speaking text in, 175
- special characters, inserting, 188
- spell-checking, 172-173
- styles, applying, 186-187
- tables, adding, 184-185
- text wrap, changing, 181
- typing errors, correcting, 170
- undoing/redoing actions in, 170
- viewing, 28-29
- Web page, opening, 228-229

Documents folder, 28-29
dots per inch (dpi), 196
double-clicking with mouse, 6
downloading. *See also* iTunes; Safari
- Acrobat Reader, 209
- deleting downloaded file, 251
- disk images, 251
- iChat versions, 291
- installing downloaded applications, 129a
- MobileMe services backup, 362
- printer drivers, 197
- software, 432
- stopping downloading of file, 251
- widgets, 156

Downloads folder, 28-29
Downloads window
- clearing settings, 256
- working with files in, 250-251

dpi (dots per inch), 196
drag-and-drop
- document text, moving/copying, 167
- files and folders, copying/moving, 45
dragging
- aliases, 89
- with mouse, 6
drivers for printers, 197
Drop Box folder in Home folder, 47, 402
DSL (digital subscriber line), 218
- Ethernet with, 221
- sharing connection, 408

DVD Player, 131, 315
- browsing movies with, 328
- customizing, 337
- key points, creating, 337
- playing movies with, 328
DVD-R and DVD-RWs, 27, 52
DVDs, 27. *See also* iDVD
- adding/removing files/folders from, 53
- backing up files on, 490
- creating, 53
- disk image, burning from, 488
- erasing, 329
- preparing to burn, 52
- start settings, changing, 111
- System Information, viewing information with, 447
- uneven DVDs, loading, 27

E

editing
- Address Book contact information, 142-143
- color labels, 40
- documents, text in, 166
- keychains, 382-383
- Smart folders, 70-71
Edit menu Undo/Redo commands, 43
editing movies, 340-341
ejecting disks, 16, 54
- desktop icon, 5
ellipses (...)
- full text, showing, 34
- in menus, 7
e-mail. *See also* Mail
- MobileMe mail, 354
embedding movies and images, 189
emoticons in instant messages, 300-301
empty Trash warning, turning on/off, 49, 79
encryption
- FireVault using, 400
- Recovery key, password, 398-399
- Keychain data, 384
entry fields in dialogs, 9
EPS (Encapsulated PostScript) files, 150
erasing CDs/DVDs, 329
Esc key, 9
ESPN, Dashboard displaying, 158-159

Ethernet. *See also* AirPort
 configuring connection, 218
 for LANs, 410
 networks, 218
 setting up connection, 221
Eudora mail, importing, 259
example workflow. *See* Automator
exporting. *See* importing/exporting
Exposé. *See also* Mission Control
 copying items with, 45
 customizing, 90
 Dashboard preferences, changing, 157
 moving and copying files with, 45
 using with Mission Control, 20-21
 space with, 21
extensions, Safari, 252
external disks, 27

F

Facebook
 Address Book, 142-143
 QuickTime, 340-341
 Safari extension, 252-253
FaceTime, 131
 Address Book, 142-143
 preferences, 313
 starting, 313
 using with Preview, 150-151
 video call with iPad, iPod touch or
 Mac, 313-314
Fast User Switching, enabling, 396
favorites
 folder, 29
 style favorites, applying, 186-187
faxing, 195
 Address Book, addressing faxes from,
 214
 automatically receiving faxes, 216
 cover pages, creating, 207, 211
 receiving faxes, 216
 scheduling faxes, 215
 sending fax documents, 214-215
 sleep mode, turning off, 216
 status of fax, checking, 215
Feedback window for speech recognition,
 114-115
file extensions

different program, opening documents
 with, 29
 for document files, 164
 Find window searching, 66
 renaming files, effect of, 43
 showing/hiding, 79
File Info window, 390
file management, 25
file permissions
 for copying and moving files, 45
 setting, 390
files, 1. *See also* aliases; Exposé; file
 permissions; Home folder; iDisk;
 naming/renaming
 arranging files, options for, 33
 Bluetooth, moving with, 414
 colors, organization by, 40
 Columns view, working in, 37
 compressing, 33
 copying, 44-45
 Cover Flow, viewing with, 36
 deleting, 48
 documents, adding to, 189
 e-mail as file, saving, 282
 Icons view, viewing in, 32-33
 Info window, information in, 50-51
 instant messages, sending with, 303
 kind
 arrangement of files by, 33
 Find window search for files by, 67
 List view, working in, 34-35
 moving, 44-45
 Network Sharing Services, 404, 406-407
 Quick Look, viewing in, 38
 recently used files, opening, 134
 restoring deleted files, 48-49
 sorting by column, 35
 Stationery Pad, 50-51
FileVault
 computer, protecting, 400
 passwords with, 400
 Recovery key, password, 398-399
 turning on/off, 400
File Transfers manager in iChat, 303
filters. *See also* Quartz Filters
 Spotlight results, filtering, 60
 viewing information on, 461
Final Cut Pro, 338-339

Finder, 1. *See also* CDs; DVDs; Finder
 Preferences; indexing
 Application Services with, 436
 Automator workflow from, 506
 Help menu, 72
 icons view, customizing, 80
 introduction to, 4-5
 mouse pointer in, 6
 networks, browsing, 416-417
 Simple Finder, 92
 Spotlight results in, 63
 toolbar, customizing, 82-83
 undoing actions in, 43
 window opening, customizing, 78
Finder Preferences, 26, 75
 Advanced preferences pane, 76
 description of, 76
 file extensions, showing/hiding, 79
 General preferences pane, 76
 icons on desktop, specifying, 77
 Label preferences pane, 76
 Sidebar preferences pane, 76
 spring-loaded folders, turning on/off, 46
finding/replacing
 documents, text in, 176-177
 Wrap Around option, 176-177
Find window
 files, searching for, 66-67
 hard to find information, searching
 for, 68
 naming/renaming
 files, 69
 searches by name, 67
 results, working with, 69
Finger service, 430
firewalls, 219
 configuring, 409
 printers, sharing, 202-203
FireWire, 54
 FireVault protecting, 400
flash drives, 27
Flickr, Quicktime, 340-341
Flight tracker, Dashboard display, 158-159
folders, 25. *See also* aliases; Exposé; iDisk;
 naming/renaming; Smart folders;
 spring-loaded folders
 arranging folders, options for, 33
 Automator workflow from, 506

bookmarks folder, creating, 238
 colors, organization by, 40
folders
 Columns view, working in, 37
 compressing, 33
 copying, 44-45
 creating, 42
 deleting, 48
 icons, 10
 Icons view, viewing in, 32-33
 Info window, information in, 50-51
 kind
 arrangement of files by, 33
 Find window search for files by, 67
 List view, working in, 34-35
 moving, 44-45
 Quick Look, viewing in, 38
 Recent Folders list, 39
 restoring deleted folders, 48-49
 Safari bookmarks, creating folder, 238
 sorting by column, 35
 Spotlight searches, keywords for, 57
 types of, 26-27
Font Book, 127, 131
 activating/deactivating fonts, 155
 managing fonts with, 154
fonts
 defined, 178
 for document text, 178
 for e-mail message text, 269
 for iChat chats, 310
 for instant message text, 300-301
 locating, 155
 on-screen smoothing, 457
 Safari font preferences, setting, 253
 size, 178
 smoothing styles, changing, 98-99
 Spotlight searches, keywords for, 57
 TextEdit preferences, setting, 194
forcing a restart, 448
foreign languages. *See* languages
formatting. *See also* documents
 copying/pasting, 187
 disks, 438
 e-mail message text, 269
 instant message text, 300-301
 international options, changing, 104-105

TextEdit preferences, setting, 194
forms, filling out, 242-243
Forward button on toolbar, 17
forwarding e-mail, 274-275
frames, 225
 printing Web page frame, 246
full-screen
 apps, using, 135
 interface with DVD Player, 337
 Safari, using, 226, 227

G

general preferences, changing, 98-99
gestures for ink
 Ink Pad recognizing, 169
 turning on/off, 126
gestures for trackpad, 6
Get Info button, 69
Get Info dialog box, 63
G5 architecture, 464
Gmail calendar account, 368
Go menu, 39
Google
 Address Book from, 142-143
 Application Services with, 436
 clearing search settings, 256
 Dashboard displaying, 158-159
 iCal calendar account, 368
 iChat, Google Talk with, 289, 290
 Search box, 244-245
 setting up accounts, 258
Gmail
 setting up accounts, 258, 260-261
Grab, 436
 screen shots, capturing, 149
Gracenote music title repository, 331
grammar checking. See spell and grammar
 checking
graphics. See also images
 Quartz Extreme enhanced graphics, 100
 RTFD files for, 164
grid settings, overriding, 33
grouping/ungrouping
 iCal, creating calendar groups, 370-371
 iChat buddy groups, managing, 298-299
 Spotlight results, 62

GUI (graphic user interface), 1, 454
.gzip files, 251
 opening, 434

H

hackers, firewalls and, 409
handwriting
 documents, inserting handwritten text
 in, 168-169
 Chinese, in, 169
 ink preferences, setting, 126
hard drive, 27. See also disk file system
 Find window searching, 66
 FireVault protecting, 400
 Info window, information in, 50-51
 optimizing, 441
 Recovery key, password, 398-399
 System Information, viewing informa-
 tion with, 447
 Web page, opening, 228-229
hard to find information, searching for, 68
hardware, 449
 Apple Hardware Test, 450
 ColorSync, matching colors to device
 with, 460-461
 compatibility, checking for, 464
 installing devices, 450
 for Mac for Windows, 466
 preferences, 94
 viewing, 452
 problems, preventing, 464
 removing devices, 451
 Safe boot, performing, 464
 settings, viewing, 452
hearing impaired users, preferences, 118
help
 Assist Me, help with, 407
 browsing for, 72-73
 for iChat, 72, 292
 for Internet connection, 219
 searching for, 72-73
 with Spotlight, 74
 VoiceOver help, 121
hexadecimal color values, 458
highlight colors, 98
History list. See Safari

Home folder, 28-29, 388
 desktop, opening from, 29
 Drop Box folder, 47, 402
 Find window searching, 66
 managing files with, 401
 Public folder, 28-29, 47, 402
 Shared folder, 47, 402
Home page. *See* Safari
hot spots, VoiceOver, 121, 124
HTML (Hypertext Markup Language)
 Dashcode, 162
 documents in, 164
 links to HTML files, adding, 193
 opening HTML documents, 192
 plain HTML code files, creating, 192-193
 TextEdit, creating HTML documents
 with, 192-193
 Web page code, viewing, 248
HTTP (Hyper-Text Transfer Protocol), 229
hubs for LANs, 410
hyperlinks. *See* links
hyphenation, setting, 181

iBook sleeping options, 109
iCal, 131.
 adding calendar accounts, 368
 adding calendar events, 372
 attachments for event, working with, 372
 Automator workflow from, 506
 backing up calendar, 373
 creating calendars with, 370-371
 Dashboard displaying, 158-159
 deleting events, 372
 details of event, editing, 373
 editing calendar events, 372-373
 full-screen app, using, 135, 368-369
 groups in calendar, creating, 370-371
 importing/exporting events, 372
 preferences, changing, 371
 printing calendar and Reminder lists, 377
 publishing calendar, 374
 reminders
 creating, 376
 printing, 377
 restoring calendar, 373
 shared calendars, finding, 374

Spotlight searches, keywords for, 57
 subscribing to calendar, 374-375
 view, changing, 369
 viewing window, 368
iChat, 127, 131, 289, 343. *See also* Bonjour
 accounts, creating, 258, 290-291
 adding buddies, 296
 with AirPort, 308
 alerts, setting, 312
 animated GIF, creating, 297
 appearance of chat, changing, 310
 Application Services with, 436
 audio chats, 304
 enhancing, 306
 automatically reopening chats, 311
 away messages, 294
 backdrops, adding, 306
 background of window, changing, 311
 bandwidth speed for video chats,
 changing, 304-305
 blocking buddies, 302
 collecting chats in single window, 301
 custom status messages, creating, 294
 deleting
 buddies, 296
 groups of buddies, 299
 downloading versions of, 291
 e-mail, responding to, 274
 emoticons, inserting, 300-301
 files with message, sending, 303
 formatting message text, 300-301
 full-screen app, using, 135
 groups of buddies, managing, 298-299
 help in, 72, 292
 links with messages, sending, 303
 notification alerts, 312
 parental controls for, 392-393
 passwords for, 291
 performance and quality specs, 305
 Photo Booth
 effects, adding, 306
 video clips in, 334
 pictures
 of buddies, 297
 theater presentations, 306-307
 of video chats, 305
 receiving instant messages, 300
 recording video chats, 307

renaming buddy groups, 299
searching for buddies, 298-299
sending instant messages, 300
sharing screens, 309
signing in and out, starting, 292
status, changing, 294
Status menu, using, 294-295
Tab bar, 300-301
text, viewing chat as, 311
theater presentations, hosting, 306-307
turning on/off
 groups, use of, 298
 Status menu, 295
video chats, 304
 backdrops, adding, 306
 bandwidth speed, changing, 304-305
 enhancing, 306
 installing hardware for, 291
 monitoring, 305
 Photo Book effects, adding, 306
 pictures of, 305
 recording, 307
 theater presentations, 306-307
viewing window, 293
view of buddy list, changing, 299
iCloud. *See also* CloudApp
CloudApp menu, 344-345
introduction, 343
joining, sign in, 344-345
sign out, 345
icons. *See also* Trash
copying, 10-11
customizing views of, 80-81
deselecting, 10-11
on desktop, 4
disk icons, displaying, 27
Finder Preferences for displaying, 77
moving, 10-11
selecting, 10
Sidebar, removing icon from, 16
for Spotlight, 55
Icons view, 30
arranging items in, 32-33
customizing window views, 80-81
spring-loaded folders, opening, 46
iDisk, 16, 343
backing up files to, 479

displaying files from, 363
managing files with, 362
passwords, changing, 365
preferences, setting, 364-365
Public folder, 363, 366
 permissions, changing, 366
sharing, 366
iDVD, 52
exploring, 342
iListen, 116
Image Bar with DVD Player, 337
Image Capture, 131
Automator workflow from, 506
working with, 148
images. *See also* attachments
Address Book, adding images to, 142
documents, adding to, 189
iChat buddy picture, changing, 297
previewing, 150-151
Safari, saving Web page images in, 249
Spotlight searches, keywords for, 57
IMAP (Internet Messages Access Protocol), 261
mailboxes for, 279
iMovie, 342
Import Bookmarks command, 237
Import Image command, 436
importing/exporting. *See also* iTunes
Address Book contacts, importing, 141
 from Yahoo! Address Book, 141
animated GIF, exporting movie as, 335
Automator workflows, 503
iCal events, 372
iTunes, music from CDs to, 319
mailboxes to Mail, 259
MP3 players, exporting music to, 330
QuickTime, exporting movies, 340-341
Inbox. *See* Mail
indents
documents, 181
for e-mail message text, 269
indexing, 55
Info window options, 51
search, files for, 67
Info window
file information on, 50-51
options, setting, 51

infrared (IR) technology, 223, 315
ink-jet printers, 196
Ink Pad, 168
ink preferences, setting, 126
installing. *See also* uninstalling
 Dashboard widgets, 160
 hardware devices, 450
 printers, 198
 software, 432
 third-party applications, 129a
 Windows on Mac, 468-469
instant messages, 289. *See also* Bonjour; iChat
 SMS (short message service) text, 308
Intel-based Mac computers. *See* Mac for Windows
inter-line spacing, 183
international options, changing, 104-105
Internet, 217. *See also* AirPort; downloading; firewalls; wireless connections
 Assist Me button, 219
 connecting to, 218-219
 hardware problems, checking on, 464
 history of, 217
 modems, setting up, 220
 multiple connections, 219, 223
 parental controls for, 392-393
 searching, 244-245
 security, 219
 sharing connections, 219, 405, 408
 songs, finding names of, 331
 status menus for connecting to, 224
Internet Explorer, 217
Internet Radio, 315
 iTunes window settings, 317
 listening to, 328
iPhones with iTunes, 327
iPhoto, 52.
Automator example workflow for, 497
 description of, 342
 e-mail, adding photos to, 268
IP (Internet Protocol). *See also* printers
 identifying address, 419
 for ISPs (Internet service providers), 218
 Sharing Service requiring, 404
iPad
 synching with Address Book, 144-145

iPhone
 syncing with Address Book, 144-145
iPhoto
 getting pictures for Address Book, 142
 getting pictures for iChat, 297
iPod touch
 Automator example workflow for, 497
 disks, 27
 synching with Address Book, 144-145
 with iTunes, 315, 327
 unmounting, 54
iSight, 127, 291. *See also* Photo Booth
 with Mac for Windows, 465, 472
 using with Preview, 150-151
ISPs (Internet service providers), 218
 attachments and, 276
 Safari preferences, setting, 253
italicizing
 document text, 178
 e-mail message text, 269
 fonts, 155
iTunes, 52, 131, 315.
 Address Book, 144-145
 aspects of iTunes, viewing, 321
 automatically playing CDs with, 318
 backing up library, 331
 Boot Camp Assistant and, 465
 copyright laws and, 323
 Dashboard displaying, 158-159
 downloading
 from CDs, 319
 from iTunes Music Store, 320-321
 Genius playlist, 324
 iMix, creating, 323
 importing/exporting
 CDs, music from, 319
 MP3 players, exporting music to, 330
 playlists, 322, 324
 iPhones with, 327
 iPods with, 327
 with Mac for Windows, 472
 minimizing window, 321
 multiple libraries, creating, 319
 Ping, 325
 playing music from CDs, 319
 playlists
 burning music CDs from, 330

creating, importing/exporting, 322-324
media, adding, 324
Smart Playlists, building, 322-323
podcasts, listening to, 326
preferences, setting, 332
radio list, adding stations to, 328
setting up, 316
Smart Playlists, building, 322-323
starting, 316
viewing window, 317
volume control for, 112
iTunes Mini Store, 316
iTunes Music Store, 317
iMix, creating, 323
using, 320-321
iWork, in Preview, 150-151

J

Jabber and iChat, 289, 290
Java, Safari enabling, 254
JavaScript
Dashcode, 162
Safari, enabling in, 254
joining iCloud community, 343, 344-345
Junior voice, 116
junk e-mail, 284-285
justification
of document text, 178
of tables, 185

K

kerning, changing, 182
keyboards
Calculator, using with, 146
changing settings, 453
international options, changing, 104-105
with Mac for Windows, 465, 472-473
Universal Access options, 118-119
VoiceOver help, 124
keyboard shortcuts, 7
applications, switching between, 137
customizing, 453
with DVD Player, 337
for Exposé, 90
Spotlight, setting for, 64-65
turning on, 9
with VoiceOver, 124

Keyboard Viewer, 104-105
Keychain
access controls, setting, 383
adding keychains, 384
description of, 380
modifying, saving keychains, 382-383
working with, 381
keywords
for Find window searches, 67
for Internet searches, 244
for Spotlight searches, 57
kilometer to miles conversions, 146-147

L

labels. *See also* color labels
Address Book labels, 140, 143
files and folders arranged by, 33
landscape orientation printing, 205, 206
languages
dictionary sources, 174
in documents, 165
Info window options, 51
international options, changing, 104-105
LANs (local area networks). *See also* AirPort
Ethernet connection for, 221
iChat with, 308
setting up, 410
with Sharing Service, 404
Windows Vista computers, connecting
from, 425
Windows XP computers, connecting
from, 426-427
laser printers, 196
Launchpad
adding or removing apps, 132
using folders, 132-133
using with App Store, 128-129
layout
for fax documents, 215
for printing, 207
LDAP (Lightweight Directory Access
Protocol)
Address Book, 144-145
setting up accounts, 258
left-alignment
of document text, 178
of tables, 184
left indent marker, 181

libraries. *See* iTunes
Library folder, 26-29
Library pane on Automator window, 492
Light Tunnel effect, 335
line height/spacing, changing, 183
links
 e-mail message, sending links in, 276
 to HTML code files, 193
 instant messages, sending with, 303
lists. *See* bulleted lists; numbered lists
List view, 30
 color labels, sorting files and folders, 40
 customizing window views, 80-81
 rearranging, widening columns in, 35
 showing/hiding folders in, 34
 sorting files and folders in, 35-36
 spring-loaded folders, opening, 46
local disk, 27
location services, 397
locking/unlocking preferences, 97
logging in, 1
 items, specifying, 394
 with Network Sharing Services, 405
logging out, 23
Login window, 2
 actions from, 3
 activating, 387
 bypassing, 3
lowering characters, 182
LTP Over IPsec protocol, 428

M

MacBinary format, 251
MacBook OS X DVD, keeping, 399
Mac Finder. *See* Finder
Mac for Windows, 465. *See also* Boot Camp Assistant
 installing Windows on Mac, 468-469
 Migration Assistant
 between Mac and PC, 443
 multiple internal disks, removing
 Windows from computer with, 474
 preparing, 466-467
 removing Windows, 474-475
 starting after installation of, 470-471
 using Windows on Mac, 472-473

Mac OS X, 478
 applications, list of, 131
 CD, restoring passwords with, 399
 Migration Assistant, 443
 OS X DVD, keeping, 399
 restarting with, 110
 Time Machine for reverting to previous
 version, 484-485
 Server account, creating, 258
 Windows files, copying, 472-473
Magic Mouse. *See* Apple Magic Mouse
Magic Trackpad, 6, 33, 132
Mail, 131, 257. *See also* Address Book;
 attachments
 accounts
 adding, 261
 advanced options, setting, 263
 managing, 262-263
 setting up, 259, 260
 addressing e-mail, 266-267
 advanced account options, setting, 263
 Application Services with, 436
 archiving e-mail, 281
 authentication of, 263
 backing up e-mail, 281
 BCc address field, 265
 blocking e-mail, 284-285
 bouncing e-mail, 284-285
 Cc field, 266
 composing e-mail, 265
 conversation, organized by, 278-279
 data detectors, managing information
 with, 268
 dates and times, setting, 102
 deleting, 280-281
 options, changing, 281
 diverting incoming e-mail to mailboxes,
 285
 draft e-mail, saving, 282
 Exchange, Microsoft, support, 258,
 260-261
 Favorites bar, 271
 file, saving e-mail as, 282
 flagging, color-coded, 283-284
 formatting message text, 269
 forwarding e-mail, 274-275
 full-screen app, using, 135, 271
 grammar-checking e-mail, 265

importing mailboxes and e-mail, 259
incoming e-mail, setting rules for, 286
instant message, replying to e-mail with, 274
junk e-mail options, 284-285
links in e-mail message, sending, 276
mailboxes
 for backing up e-mail, 281
 diverting incoming e-mail to, 285
 new mailbox, creating, 278
 organizing e-mail in, 279
 Smart Mailbox, creating, 287
 standard mailboxes, 278
Message List view, changing, 271, 273
new e-mail, checking for, 272
new mailbox, creating, 278
notes
 creating, 267
 searching for, 283
offline viewing, keeping copies for, 263
opening e-mail, 272-273
Out of Office message, creating, 286
parental controls for, 392-393
passwords for, 259, 263
photographs, adding, 268
preferences for addressing, 266-267
previous recipients list, sending e-mail with, 266-267
printing e-mail, 281
priority to mail, adding, 265
quoted text in, 274
reading and receiving e-mail, 272-273
recovering deleted e-mail, 280
redirecting e-mail, 274-275
replying to, 274
resending messages, 285
RSS feeds, subscribing to, 288
rules, creating, 286
saving e-mail, 282
searching e-mail for text, 283
sending e-mail, 265
servers, 260-261
 removing mail from, 263
signatures, creating, 270
Smart Addresses, using, 266
Smart Mailbox, creating, 287
sorting messages, 279
speaking voice, adding, 268

spell-checking e-mail, 265
Spotlight searches, keywords for, 57
starting, 259
stationery, adding, 268
threads, sorting e-mail by, 279
to-do tasks
 searching for, 283
 tracking, 267
Trash mailbox, 278
window, viewing, 264
maintaining computer, 431
master password, restoring, 398-399
maximizing/minimizing
 changing options, 98
 Dock, 86
 iTunes window, minimizing, 321
 slowing minimization, 87
me card, Address Book, 141
media
 iTunes playlists, adding to, 322, 324
Media browser for Automator workflows, 503
memory
 calculation results, saving, 147
 Info window options, 51
 system memory, viewing, 445
menu bar, 5
 Bluetooth placed on, 413
 clock, using, 103
 Displays icon on, 456
 rearranging status icons on, 8
 status of fax, showing, 215, 216
menus
 contextual menus, 8
 language options, setting, 104-105
 pull-down menus, 8
 working with, 7
metadata, 55
 specific metadata, searching for, 68
 Spotlight, finding information with, 56
microphones with iChat, 304
Microsoft. *See also* Mac for Windows; Microsoft Word; Windows 7 or Vista; Windows XP
 Excel, Address Book for faxes with, 214
 Exchange 2007, 2010 or later
 Address book, 144-145
 calendar, 368

Microsoft *(continued)*
 Mail, Contacts & Calendar, 258
 Mail server, 258, 260-261
 Internet Explorer, 217, 225
 Office documents, in Preview, 150-151
 Outlook/Outlook Express, importing
 e-mail to, 259
Microsoft Word
 Address Book for faxes with, 214
 documents as files, 164, 190
 formatting text in documents, 178
 opening documents in, 29
 Page Setup options, 204-205
MIDI
 devices, configuring, 462-463
Migration Assistant
 between Mac and PC, 443
MiniDV camcorders with iMovie, 342
Minimize button for windows, 12, 15
mini restarts, 448
Mission Control, 131
 copying items with, 45
 customizing, 90-91
 customizing with Dashboard, 157
 moving and copying files with, 45
 using 20-21
MobileMe, 343. *See also* iDisk
 accessing account, 352
 Address Book, 144-145, 355
 backing up files with, 362-363
 calendar, adding, 356
 events, 357
 preferences, 357
 connecting to computer with, 420
 e-mail, managing, 354
 gallery, 358-361
 creating and modifying, 358-359
 viewing and sharing, 360-361
 iDisk, sharing, 366
 joining MobileMe community, 352
 Mail services, 354
 preferences for account, changing,
 352-353
 setting up accounts, 258, 260-261
 signing on to, 352
MobileMe synchronization
 resetting, 379
 setting up, 378

modems, 218. *See also* cable modems
 configuring connection, 218
 setting up connection, 220
monitors. *See also* colors
 display settings, changing, 456-457
 fonts on screen, smoothing, 457
mounting disks, 54
mouse. *See also* Apple Magic Mouse
 changing settings, 454
 pointer, 6
 Universal Access options, 118-119
 windows, resizing, 15
 working with, 6
Mouse Keys, 118-119
movies. *See* videos
Movies folder, 28-29
moving. *See also* drag-and-drop; navigating
 Address Book contacts, 142
 Bluetooth, items with, 414
 Dock items, 87
 documents, text in, 167
 with Exposé, 45
 files and folders, 44-45
 icons, 10-11
 Mailboxes on screen, 279
 Safari, bookmarks in, 237
 Sidebar, moving folders with, 16
 spaces, window between, 21
 windows, 14
MP3 players, exporting music to, 330-331
MR (Memory Recall) button, 147
multi-function devices, 196
Multi-Touch gestures, 6, 33, 132
music, 315. *See also* CDs; iTunes; MIDI
 finding names of songs, 331
 Spotlight searches, keywords for, 57
Music folder, 28-29
muting sounds, 112
me card, Address Book, 141

N

naming/renaming. *See also* Find window;
 Keychain
 color label names, changing, 41
 files and folders, 42-43
 arranging by names, 33
 iChat buddy groups, 299

Info window options, 51
Mailboxes, 279
Safari Bookmarks Library collection, 239
user accounts, short name for, 388
Nature Background, 100
navigating
in dialogs, 9
with VoiceOver, 121, 122
Web pages, 228-229
nesting tables, 185
Netscape Navigator, 217, 225
Mail, importing e-mail to, 259
NetStat, 430
network disks, 27
Info window, information in, 50-51
Network Preferences pane, connecting to
Internet with, 224
network printers, 202-203
accessing shared printers, 202-203
installing, 198
networks, 403. *See also* AirPort; Bluetooth;
LANs (local area networks); network
printers; Network Sharing Service
activity, viewing, 445
Bonjour messaging on, 289
Finder, browsing with, 416-417
other computers, connecting to, 418-419
port configuration, 223
privileges for users and groups, creat-
ing, 406
searching for files on, 417
several computers, connecting to, 418
Sidebar, accessing from, 417
System Information, viewing system
information with, 447
utilities, 430
VPN (Virtual Private Network), VLAN
(Virtual Local Network), connecting
with, 428-429
Windows, sharing Mac files with, 424
Network Sharing Service, 404-405
file sharing, setting up, 406-407
Internet Sharing, 408
Network Utility, 430
New dialog box, 496
no access for network users, 406
nonresponding applications, quitting, 138

notes. *See also* Mail; Sticky Notes
Keychain, adding secure notes with, 381
NOT operator, searching with, 57
NPR, listening to, 328
NSFNET, 217
NTFS, reformatting with, 468
NTSC format with iMovie, 342
numbered lists, 184
in e-mail message text, 269
numbering
international options, changing, 104-105
recent items, changing numbering of,
98-99
NumPad Commander, 121, 123

O

Open dialog box in Automator, 496
opening
applications, 132-133, 134
Dashboard, 156
disks, 26-27
documents, 28-29
Info window options, 51
recent applications and documents, 39
recently used applications, 134
Scripts menu, scripts from, 511
windows, 12-13
operating system, 1
optimizing hard drive, 441
Option buttons in dialogs, 9
orientation for printing, 205, 206
OR operator, searching with, 57
outlining
document text, 178
fonts, 155
Out of Office message, creating, 286

P

page breaks, inserting and deleting, 183
Page Setup
individual defaults, setting up, 205
for printers, 200
printing and range options, 204-206
for text wrap, 181
pages per minute (ppm), 196
PAL format with iMovie, 342

Palm OS devices. *See* PDAs (personal data assistants)

panes. *See also* specific panes
 working with, 7

paper feed for printing, 207

paper handling for fax documents, 215

paper size for printing, 200, 204, 206

paragraphs
 indent markers, 181
 spacing, 183

parental controls
 for Dictionary, 175
 logging activity with, 392
 time limits, setting, 393
 for user accounts, 391, 392-393

partitioning disks, 467

passwords. *See also* Keychain
 with FireVault, 400
 hints, adding, 388
 for iChat, 291
 iDisk passwords, changing, 365
 for Internet connections, 218
 for logging out, 23
 from login window, 387
 for MobileMe account, 352-353
 for Mail, 259, 263
 password, changing, Apple ID, 398-399
 Recovery key, FileVault, 398-399
 on shared computers, 3
 in Simple Finder, 92
 tips on creating, 398

Paste command, 44

pasting
 Automator workflows, 503
 formatting, 187
 ruler, 179

path bar
 for windows, 12

PDAs.
Bluetooth with, 412
 networks with, 403

PDF files
 Auto Save, in Preview, 150-151
 documents as PDF files, saving, 209
 downloading Acrobat Reader, 209
 previewing, 150-151
 Safari, viewing in, 247

Saving in, TextEdit, 190
 signatures, adding, in Preview, 150-151
 Spotlight searches, keywords for, 57
 working with, 151

pen cursors, 126

People, Dashboard displaying, 158-159

permissions. *See also* file permissions
 for screen sharing, 422

phones. *See* cell phones

Photo Album, Automator example for, 497

Photo Booth, 131, 315. *See also* iChat
 animated GIF, creating, 297
 capturing photos in, 333
 effects, adding, 335
 proof sheets, 333
 videos
 effects, 306
 recording, 334

Photo Browser, 268

photographs.
 e-mail, inserting in, 268
 iChat buddy picture, changing, 297

Photoshop Preview, opening files in, 150

pictures. *See* images

Pictures folder, 28-29

Ping service, 325, 430

Pipe Organ voice, 116

Places section, Sidebar, 16

Plain Text Encoding pop-up, 165

Plain Text files
 documents as Plain Text files, saving, 191
 TextEdit preferences, setting, 194

playlists. *See* iTunes

plug-and-play devices, 450

plug-ins
 Automator with, 499, 506
 compatible plug-ins, checking, 255
 Safari, enabling in, 254

podcasts.
 listening to, 326

pointing with mouse, 6

POP (Post Office Protocol), 261

pop-up menus, 8
 in dialogs, 9
 on toolbar, 17

pop-up windows, blocking, 255

portrait orientation printing, 205, 206

PostScript files, 201
 PDF file, converting to, 150
PowerBook/MacBook
 sleeping options, 109
 wireless connections, 222
power failure restart options, 108-109
power strips, 450
ppm (pages per minute), 196
PPoE (Point to Point Protocol over
 Ethernet), 221
 making connection with, 224
PPTP protocol, 428
preferences. *See also* Finder Preferences;
 hardware; iChat; Safari; System
 Preferences
 Bluetooth preferences, setting, 415
 Dictionary preferences, setting, 174-175
 Dock preferences, setting, 86-87
 iCal preferences, changing, 371
 iDisk preferences, setting, 364-365
 iTunes preferences, setting, 332
 Language & Text, 104-107
 MobileMe account preferences, chang-
 ing, 352-353
 Mail, addressing, 266-267
 Sidebar preferences, changing, 84-85
 Spotlight preferences, customizing, 64
 TextEdit preferences, setting, 194
 for Time Machine, 478
 VoiceOver preferences, setting, 122-123
presentation keyword for Spotlight, 57
Preview, 131, 150-151
Preview column, Columns view, 37
Preview File Open command, 150
previewing
 dialogs, area in, 9
 Info window options, 51
 printed documents, 208
 print image, 206
Print command, 206-207
printer drivers, 197
printers. *See also* Bonjour; network printers
 adding or removing, 198-199
 default settings, setting, 200
 description of, 196
 desktop printers, using, 207

IP (Internet Protocol)
 for installing printers, 199
 for sharing printers, 202-203
 manually adding, 198-199
 Network Sharing Services, 404
 PostScript Printer Desc. (PPD) files, 201
 sharing, 202-203, 404
 Sharing Service, 404
 specific settings, setting, 201
Printer Setup Utility, printer drivers in, 197
Printers folder, displaying printers in, 207
Print & Scan preferences, 200-201
printing, 195
 from Address Book, 143
 Automator workflow, 505
 basic print options, setting, 206-207
 cover pages, creating, 207, 211
 e-mail messages, 281
 help topics, 73
 iCal calendar and Reminder lists, 377
 Page Setup options, 204-205
 previewing printed documents, 208
 queues, managing, 207, 210
 reverse order printing, 207
 saving print options, 215
 to shared printers, 203
 two print jobs with two printers, 205
 Web pages, 246
Print Queue utility, 207
privacy preference in Spotlight, 64-65
Private Browsing, 228
privileges for users and groups, 406
proof sheets in Photo Booth, 333
protocols, 261
proxies, 218
Public folder. *See also* iDisk
 in Home folder, 28-29, 47, 402
publishing iCal calendar, 374
pull-down menus, 8
Push button in dialogs, 9

Q

Quartz Extreme enhanced graphics, 100
Quartz Filters
 Automator example workflow for, 497
 for printed documents, 207

Quick Erase setting, 329
Quick Look
 attachments, viewing, 276-277
 toolbar button, 17
 viewing files with, 38
QuickTime movies, 334
 iMovie, 342
 streaming options, 338-339
 in theater presentations, 307
QuickTime Player, 131, 315
 creating and editing movies, 340-341
 full-screen, 338-339
 playing movies, 338-339
 publish to MobileMe, YouTube, Vimeo,
 Flickr, Facebook, and Mail, 340-341
 quitting applications, 138
 rotate movies, 338-339
 sharing movies, 340-341
quoting text in e-mail, 274

R

radio. See also Internet Radio
 podcasts, listening to, 326
raising characters, 182
read and write permissions
 for moving/copying files, 45
 for network users, 406
 in Shared folder, 47
read-only permissions
 documents as read-only files, 190
 for moving/copying files, 45
 for network users, 406
 in Public folder, 47
Reading button, Safari, 226
 using, 232-233
Reading List, Safari, 226
 using, 232-233
Recent Folders list, 39
recently used items
 applications, opening, 134
 documents, opening, 165
 numbering, changing, 98-99
recording
 AppleScripts, 510
 Automator actions, 502
 video chats, 307

recovering. See restoring
Recovery key, FileVault, 398-399
Redo command, 43
redoing. See undoing/redoing
refresh rate, setting, 456
registration symbol, inserting, 188
reloading Web pages, 228-229
Reminders lists. See also Mail
 iCal, creating with, 376
removable disks, 27
 Info window, information in, 50-51
Rendezvous Web sites, adding, 238
replacing. See finding/replacing
resizing. See size/resizing
resolution
 monitor resolution, setting, 456
 of printers, 196
restarting, 24
 forcing a restart, 448
 from Login window, 3
 with Mac OS X, 110, 442
 power failure restart options, 108-109
 in Target Disk Mode, 110
 Time Machine backup for, 481
restoring
 calendar with iCal, 373
 compressed files and folders, 436
 deleted files and folders, 48-49
 disk image, 489
 e-mail, 280
 master password, restoring, 398-399
Return key, 9
reverse order
 fax documents, sending, 215
 printing pages in, 207
RGB (Red, Green, Blue) colors, 458
right-alignment
 of document text, 178
 of tables, 184
right indent marker, 181
routers, 218, 408
RSS feeds. See also Safari
 customizing, 240
 Mail, subscribing in, 288
 widgets and, 156
RTFD files, documents as, 164
RTF files

documents as, 164, 190
formatting text in, 178
rulers, showing/hiding, 179

S

Safari, 131
 Address Book to Bookmarks bar, adding,
 238-239
 advanced preferences, setting, 253
 alerts for nonsecure forms, 243
 appearance (general) preferences,
 setting, 253
 AutoFill preferences, setting, 242
 bookmarks, 226
 creating and deleting pages, 237-239
 folder, creating, 238
 organizing, 239
 for RSS feeds, 240-241
 Spotlight searches, keywords for, 57
 synching on multiple computers, 239
 tabs, opening with, 230-231
 Bookmarks Library, 237
 deleting bookmarks in, 238-239
 organizing bookmarks in, 239
 renaming collection, 239
 cache, emptying, 236
 compressing/uncompressing disk
 images, 251
 cookies, preferences regarding, 254
 copying text from Web page, 249
 customizing window, 226
 default browser, selecting, 256
 deleting
 bookmarks, 238-239
 History list entries, 236
 different window, opening page in, 231
 disk images, downloading, 251
 downloading
 files, downloading, 250-251
 Home page, 252
 Downloads window, working with files
 in, 250-251
 encoding preferences, setting, 253
 extensions, 252
 font preference, setting, 253
 forms, filling out, 242-243
 full-screen app, using, 135
 general preferences, setting, 252

grammar-checking in, 243
help information in, 72
History list
 clearing settings, 256
 preferences, setting, 252
 viewing, 236
Home page
 changing, 235
 going to, 228-229
 preferences, setting, 252
HTML code, viewing, 248
navigating in, 228-229
nonworking Web pages, 255
opening Web pages in, 228
PDF files, viewing, 247
pictures from Web page, saving, 249
pop-up windows, blocking, 255
preferences
 advanced preferences, 253
 general preferences, 252-253
 security& privacy preferences,
 setting, 254
printing Web pages, 246
reloading pages, 228-229
resetting settings for, 256
RSS feeds
 bookmarking, 240-241
 customizing, 240
saving
 information in Web page, 248-249
 text of Web page, 248
security
 pop-up windows, blocking, 255
 preferences, setting, 254
security & privacy preferences, setting,
 254
size of text, changing, 231
SnapBack page, 245
spell-checking in, 243
starting application, 226
style sheet preferences, 253
synching bookmarks on computers, 239
tabs
 opening Web page with, 230-231
 setting browsing options for, 230
Top Sites, 234
viewing window, 227
Web Clip widgets, creating, 162

Safe boot, performing, 464
Save As dialog box, 190
saving. *See also* Safari
 attachments, files in, 277
 Automator workflow, 505
 Bonjour chats, 309
 e-mail, 282
 Keychain, changes in, 383
 print options, 215
 Smart folders, copy of, 71
 Web page information, 248-249
scanning
 documents, 212-213
 images, 212-213
scanner information, viewing, 447
scheduling. *See also* iCal
 fax documents, 215
 faxes, 215
screen savers, setting up, 101
screen sharing
 permissions, setting, 422
 using, 423
screen shots, capturing, 149, 340-341
Script Editor, 510
 Application Services with, 436
Script menus. *See also* AppleScripts
 adding scripts to, 509
 Automator workflow from, 506
 displaying, 508
 opening scripts from, 511
scroll bars
 changing action of, 98
 options, changing, 98
search boxes
 in Automator, 493, 494
 on toolbar, 17
 for windows, 12
search engines, 244-245
Search For section, 16
 Smart folders, using, 70-71
searching. *See also* Dictionary;
 finding/replacing; Find window;
 Spotlight
 Automator workflows, 503
 e-mail for text, 283
 for hard to find information, 68
 for help, 72-73
 Internet, 244-245

 metadata searches, 68
 network, files on, 417
 with VoiceOver, 121
secret folder hierarchy menu, 39
security. *See also* Keychain; passwords;
 Safari
 Internet security, 219
 for logging out, 23
 for switching between users, 22-23
 security & privacy preferences, setting,
 397
selecting
 documents, text in, 166
 icons, 10
Sepia effect, 335
servers. *See also* Mail
 Find window searching, 66
 Mac OS X Server account, 258
 Web Sharing service, 404
Shared folder in Home folder, 47, 402
Shared section, Sidebar, 16
sharing. *See also* network printers; Network
 Sharing Service; screen sharing
 Address Book, 140, 144-145
 buddies, screens with, 309
 Home folder, sharing files in, 402
 iCal calendars, 374
 iChat screens, 309
 Internet connections, 219
 Network Sharing Services, 404-405
 printers, 202-203, 404
 starting on shared computer, 2-3
 widgets, 156
 Windows, Mac files with, 424
 Windows Vista computers, connecting
 from, 425
Sharing Preferences, 404
shortcuts. *See* aliases; keyboard shortcuts
Show All command on Spotlight menu, 58
showing/hiding. *See also* Dock
 applications, 136
 Dashboard, widgets on, 158
 with Exposé, 20
 file extensions, 79
 List view, folders in, 34
 Mailbox list, 279
 rulers, 179
 Sidebar and toolbars, 16-17, 84

Show Inspector, 50
Show Modem Status menu, 220
Show View Options command, 32
shutting down, 24
 from Login window, 3
 options, setting, 108-109
Sidebar
 customizing, 84-85
 networks, accessing, 417
 preferences, changing, 84-85
 shared devices, displaying, 420
 showing/hiding, 16, 17, 84
 Smart folders, using, 70-71
 using, 16
 for windows, 12
sight impaired users, preferences, 118-119
signatures to e-mail, 270
 adding, in Preview, 150-151
Simple Finder, 92
size/resizing. *See also* compressing/uncompressing
 files and folders arranged by size, 33
 Find window searches by size, 67
 font size, 178
 help text, 73
 Web page text, 231
 windows, 12, 14-15
Ski Report, Dashboard displaying, 158-159
sleep mode, 24
 faxes, turning off to receive, 216
 from Login window, 3
 setting sleep options, 108-109
slider in dialogs, 9
slideshows for Spotlight results, 63
Slow Keys, 118-119
Smart folders
 changing search criteria for, 71
 creating and editing, 70-71
 saving copy of, 71
 Sidebar, using in, 70-71
Smart Mailbox, creating, 287
Smart Magnify tool, Preview, 150-151
Smart Playlists, building, 322-323
smart searches with VoiceOver, 121
SMB/CIFS
 file services, 424
 sharing printers with, 202-203
smileys in instant messages, 300-301

smoothing fonts on screen, 457
SMS (short message service) text, sending, 308
SMTP (Simple Mail Transfer Protocol), 261
SnapBack page, 245
Snap to Grid setting, 33
software. *See also* hardware
 automating updates, 433
 compatibility, checking for, 464
 downloading, 432
 installing, 432
 removing hardware device software, 464
 uninstalling, 48, 432
Solid Colors Background, 100
sorting
 by color labels, 40-41
 e-mail messages, 279
 Find window file results, 69
 List view, files and folders in, 34-35
 Spotlight results, 62
 widgets, 161
sounds. *See also* alerts; VoiceOver
 changing sound effects, 112
 dates and times, announcing, 103
 input options, setting, 113
 MIDI devices, configuring, 462-463
 output options, setting, 113
 Spotlight searches, keywords for, 57
Spacebar with spring-loaded folders, 46
Spaces. *See also* Mission Control
 customizing, 90-91
 Dashboard preferences, changing, 157
 grouping windows into, 21
spacing
 character spacing, changing, 182
 line spacing, changing, 183
Speakable Commands window, 114
speaking voice. *See also* Alex; VoiceOver
 document text, speaking, 175
 for e-mail, 268
 interface options, setting, 117
speech recognition, 114-115. *See also* Alex
 with Address Book, 140, 143
 Application Services with, 436
 enabling, 115
 for Sticky Notes, 153
 using, 115

speed of printers, 196
spell and grammar checking, 163
 adding words to dictionary, 172
 for documents, 172-173
 e-mail, 265
 in Safari, 243
 in Spotlight, 59
Spotlight, 55
 backed-up items, recovering, 482-483
 canceling search, 57
 desktop icon, 5
 e-mail, searching for, 283
 filtering results, 60
 finding information with, 56-57
 grouping results, 62
 help with, 74
 keyboard shortcuts, setting, 64-65
 keywords for searches, 57
 metadata, finding information with, 57
 preferences, setting, 64-65
 privacy preferences, setting, 64-65
 sorting results, 62
 viewing results in window, 58-59
 windows, working with, 58-59
 working with results, 63
Spotlight Search box, 74
spring-loaded folders
 customizing, 78
 using, 46
stacks on Dock, 19
starting. *See also* restarting
 Automator, 495
 Bonjour messaging, 309
 CDs, changing start settings for, 111
 DVDs, changing start settings for, 111
 with Fast Startup Switch, 442
 iChat, 292
 iTunes, 316
 Mac for Windows, 470-471
 Mac OS 9 disk, starting from, 442
 power failure restart options, 108-109
 Safe boot, performing, 464
 specifying startup items, 394-395
 stand-alone computer, 2
Startup commands, 395, 399
startup disk, 26-27
 selecting, 110

Startup Disk Control Panel, 110
stationery for e-mail, 268
Stationery Pad in Info window, 50-51
status bar
 in Safari, 226
 for windows, 12
status menus
 in iChat, 294-295
 Internet, connecting to, 224
Sticky Keys, 118-119
Sticky Notes, 131
 Application Services with, 436
 creating, 153
 Dashboard displaying, 158-159
Stocks, Dashboard displaying, 158-159
Stuffit Expander, 33, 129a, 434
styles
 deleting style favorites, 186-187
 documents, applying to, 186-187
 favorite styles, applying, 186-187
 for fonts, 155
 Safari style sheets, 253
 toolbar styles, changing, 83
submenus, 8
subnet masks, 218
subscribing
 to Address Book, 145
 to iCal calendar, 374-375
 to podcasts, 326
 to RSS feeds, 288
subscript characters, 182
summary
 of Application Services, 436
 of printer options, 207
superscript characters, 182
surge protectors, 450
switching
 between applications, 136-137
 between Dock applications, 18
 Fast User Switching, enabling, 396
 between help libraries, 72
 between users, 22-23
 between windows, 14
symbols. *See also* copyrights; trademarks
 registration symbol, inserting, 188
synchronization. *See also* MobileMe,
 Yahoo!, iPhone, iPad, iPod touch syn-
 chronization

of Address Book, 140

Safari bookmarks on multiple computers, 239

System Administrator. *See* Administrator

System folder, 26-27

System Preferences, 93. *See also* hardware; monitors; QuickTime movies; VoiceOver

Bluetooth preferences, setting, 415

dates and times, setting, 102-103

description of, 94-95

desktop backgrounds, changing, 100

general preferences, changing, 98-99

ink preferences, setting, 126

international options, changing, 104-105

Internet preferences, list of, 94-95

keyboard settings, changing, 453

language & text options, 171, 172

locking/unlocking, 97

mouse settings, changing, 454

network preferences, list of, 94-95

overall preferences, list of, 95

personal preferences, list of, 94

Print & Scan preferences, 200-201, 202-203

screen savers, setting up, 101

Security & Privacy pane, 397

sleeping options, setting, 108-109

sounds, controlling, 112-115

speaking voice, setting, 116-117

speech recognition options, 114-115

Spotlight searches, keywords for, 57

Startup disk, selecting, 110

Universal Access preferences, 118-119

viewing, 96

System Information, viewing system information with, 447

system recovery with Time Machine, 484

T

tab bars in Safari, 226

tables

cells, 184-185

documents, adding to, 184-185

merging cells in, 185

nesting tables, 185

tabs. *See also* Safari

in dialogs, 9

paragraph tabs, setting, 180

tab stops, setting, 180

tactile feel of keyboard, 453

Take Video Snapshot button, 142

.tar files, opening, 434

Target Disk Mode, restarting computer, 110

TCP/IP, 422

for modems, 220

telephones. *See* cell phones

television podcasts, listening to, 326

text. *See also* documents; Mail

encoding, selecting, 226

iChat chat as text, viewing, 311

in Safari, 226

substitution, preferences, 106-107

TextEdit, 29, 131, 163. *See also* documents

Application Services with, 436

automatic opening documents in, 79

Page Setup options, 204-205

preferences, setting, 194

speaking text in, 175

for Web design, 192-193

text substitution, 106-107, 171

text wrap

changing, 181

TextEdit preferences, setting, 194

theater presentations, hosting, 306-307

thesaurus, 174

third-party applications. *See also* software

installing, 129a

System Preferences, 95

threads, sorting e-mail by, 279

Time Capsule, 478, 481

Time Machine, 131, 477

entire computer system, recovering, 484

excluding items from backup, 480

preferences, setting up, 478

previous version of Mac OS X, reverting to, 484-485

recovering backed-up items, 482-483

restarting backup, 481

setting up, 478

starting manual back up, 479

system, recovering, 484-485

working with backup, 481

time management. *See* iCal

times. *See* dates and times

time zones, setting, 102

title bars
 aliases, creating, 89
 for windows, 12
toolbars. *See also* Automator
 adding icons to, 83
 customizing, 82-83
 deleting icons from, 83
 Finder toolbar, customizing, 82-83
 parts of, 17
 rearranging icons on, 83
 in Safari, 226
 showing/hiding, 16, 17
 styles for, 83
 for windows, 12
 working with, 7
trackpad, 6
trademark symbols
 documents, inserting in, 188
Translation, Dashboard displaying, 158-159
Trash, 10
 empty Trash warning, turning on/off, 49, 79
 files and folders in, 48
 securely deleting files and folders, 49
 software, uninstalling, 48, 432
 uninstalling software with, 48, 432
transfer information
 between Mac and PC, 443
troubleshooting
 Bonjour problems, 308
 disk problems, 440
 hardware problems, 464
 Safe boot, performing, 464
turning on/off. *See also* iChat
 Bonjour, 308
 Dock hiding, 18
 empty Trash warning, 49, 79
 FireVault, 400
 gestures, 126
 keyboard shortcuts, 9
 spring-loaded folders, 46
Twitter, connect with Ping, 325
 Safari extension, 252-253

U

underlining
 document text, 178

e-mail message text, 269
 fonts, 155
Undo command, 43
undoing/redoing
 Address Book mistakes, 143
 documents, actions in, 170
 file deletions, 49
 in Finder, 43
 ink recognizing, 126
Unicode for languages, 165
uninstalling
 hardware, 451
 software, 48, 432
Unit Converter, Dashboard display, 158-159
Universal Access, 118-119. *See also* VoiceOver
 Automator actions and, 502
UNIX compressed files, opening, 434
unmounting networks, 54
updating
 automating software updates, 433
 from Boot Camp beta, 467
 widgets, 157
up/down arrows in dialogs, 9
URLs (Uniform Resource Locators), 228
 Application Services with, 436
 home page, typing address for, 235
USB
 FireVault protecting, 400
user accounts, 386
 access privileges, setting, 391
 adding, 388
 deleting, 389
 Fast User Switching, enabling, 396
 file permissions, setting, 390
 parental controls, setting, 391, 392-393
 short name for, 388
user & groups preferences, 94-95. *See* accounts and user accounts.
user names for Internet connections, 218
Users folder, 26-29
Utilities folder, 489

V

Variable list on Automator window, 492-493, 494
vCards, 141, 144-145

in attachments, 276

 e-mail, including with, 270

verbosity preferences, setting, 122

video cameras, 291

videos. *See also* DVD Player; iChat; Photo Booth; QuickTime movies; QuickTime Player

 animated GIF, exporting movie as, 335

 Dashboard displaying, 158-159

 documents, adding to, 189

 iMovie, 342

 Spotlight searches, keywords for, 57

View buttons on toolbar, 17

views and viewing. *See also* specific views

 changing window views, 30-31

 customizing views, 30

 disks, viewing, 26-27

 documents, viewing, 28-29

 hardware settings, 452

 iCal window, 368

 iTunes window, 317

 System Preferences, 96

Vimeo, QuickTime, 340-341

Virtual Network Computing (VNC), 422

visible files, searching for, 67

VoiceOver, 118

 Braille, support for, 120, 123

 commands, using, 124-125

 description of, 120-121

 hot spots, 121, 124

 keys for, 121

 preferences, setting, 122-123

 searches and utility, 121

VO keys, 121

volume. *See* sounds

Volume desktop icon, 5

VPN (Virtual Private Network), 428

VLAN (Virtual Local Area Network), 429

W

Wacom for handwriting recognition, 168

waking up options, setting, 108-109

Watch Me Do action, 502

Weather, Dashboard displaying, 158-159

Web addresses. *See* URLs (Uniform Resource Locators)

Web browsers, 225. *See also* Safari

 default browser, selecting, 256

 history of, 217

 Mail, starting, 259

Web Clips widget, creating, 162

Web pages. *See also* HomePage; RSS feeds; Safari

 copying text from, 249

 different window, opening page in, 231

 Image Capture, building with, 148

 navigating, 228-229

 nonworking Web pages, 255

 printing, 246

 reloading, 228-229

 saving, 248

 searching within, 244-245

 size of text, changing, 231

Web sites, 225. *See also* HomePage; Web pages

 for printer driver downloads, 197

Whois service, 430

widgets, 156. *See also* Dashboard

Wikipedia, 174

windows, 1

 activating, 12-13

 Columns view opening new windows, 37

 Exposé, using, 20

 Finder Preferences for customizing, 78

 mouse, resizing with, 15

 opening/closing, moving, 12-14

 sizing/resizing, 12, 14-15

 spaces, grouping windows into, 21

 switching between, 14

 TextEdit preferences, setting, 194

 views, changing, 30-31

Windows Media

 Boot Camp Assistant and, 465

 with Mac for Windows, 472

Windows 7 or Vista. *See also* Mac for Windows

 LANs, connecting to, 425

 upgrading Windows XP to, 468

Windows XP. *See also* Mac for Windows

 LANs, connecting to, 426-427

 outside network, connecting, 426-427

 upgrading to Windows Vista, 468

WinZip, opening files compressed by, 434

wireless connections, 218. *See also* AirPort; Bluetooth
 infrared technology, 223
WordPerfect Page Setup options, 204-205
workflow. *See* Automator
World Clock, displaying, 158-159
write-only permissions for net users, 406
WYSIWYG, 208

X

X-Ray effect, 335

Y

Yahoo! Address Book,
 importing and syncing, 141
 creating an account, 144-145, 258
Yahoo! calendar account, 258, 368
Yahoo! instant message account, 290-291
YouTube, QuickTime, 340-341

Z

Zoom button, 12, 15
zooming in/out
 with DVD Player, 337
 in Preview, 151